A RED ROSE IN THE DARK

SELF-CONSTITUTION THROUGH THE POETIC LANGUAGE OF ZELDA, AMICHAI, KOSMAN, AND ADAF

EMUNOT: JEWISH PHILOSOPHY AND KABBALAH

SERIES EDITOR
Dov Schwartz (Bar-Ilan University, Ramat Gan)

EDITORIAL BOARD
Ada Rapoport Albert (University College, London)
Gad Freudenthal (CNRS, Paris)
Gideon Freudenthal (Tel Aviv University, Ramat Aviv)
Moshe Idel (Hebrew University, Jerusalem)
Raphael Jospe (Bar-Ilan University, Ramat Gan)
Ephraim Kanarfogel (Yeshiva University, New York)
Menachem Kellner (Haifa University, Haifa)
Daniel Lasker (Ben-Gurion University, Beer Sheva)

ACADEMIC STUDIES PRESS

A RED ROSE IN THE DARK

SELF-CONSTITUTION THROUGH THE POETIC LANGUAGE OF ZELDA, AMICHAI, KOSMAN, AND ADAF

DORIT LEMBERGER

TRANSLATED BY EDWARD LEVIN

Boston
2016

Library of Congress Cataloging-in-Publication Data:
A catalog record for this book is available
from the Library of Congress.

ISBN 978-1-61811-493-8 (hardback)

ISBN 978-1-61811-494-5 (electronic)

Cover design by Ivan Grave.

On the cover: "Heroic Roses," by Paul Klee, 1938.

Book design by Kryon Publishing,
kryonpublishing.com

Academic Studies Press

28 Montfern Avenue

Brighton, MA 02135, USA

press@academicstudiespress.com

www.academicstudiespress.com

Contents

Preface

> Two pictures of a rose in the dark. One is quite black; for the rose is not visible. In the other, it is painted in full detail and surrounded by black. Is one of them right, the other wrong? Don't we talk of a white rose in the dark and of a red rose in the dark? And don't we nevertheless say that they can't be distinguished in the dark?[1]

Ludwig Wittgenstein developed a methodology for linguistic investigation in the twentieth century that significantly fashioned the conception of language. This methodology is not limited to the philosophy of language, and relates to many additional disciplines, such as psychoanalysis, art, and literary scholarship. The importance of his researches for the philosophical conceptualization of mental processes in general, and specifically those of self-constitution, is widely recognized. *A Red Rose in the Dark* seeks, for the first time, to apply Wittgensteinian

1 Ludwig Wittgenstein, *Philosophical Investigations*, 4th ed., ed. P. M. S. Hacker and J. Schulte, trans. G. E. M. Anscombe, P. M. S. Hacker, and J. Schulte (Chichester: Wiley-Blackwell, 2009), para. 515.

methodology to the research of four important corpora in contemporary Hebrew literature. It will examine the process of self-constitution in these corpora, using Wittgenstein's universal insights. This interpretation offers an alternative perspective for sociohistorical study and highlights grammatical structures as reflecting mental processes, when historical and ethnic aspects are shunted aside.

A Red Rose in the Dark examines how poetic language facilitates distinguishing between different types of roses in the dark. The poet, like the philosopher in the above passage, selects words from everyday language and combines them with a light yet precise touch: sketching experiences that evade us in the everyday usage of language. Some of these experiences cannot be perceived empirically, and can be fashioned only by imagination. The genre of lyrical poetry is based on the act of imagination, since it focuses on self-reflection. It therefore invites the readers to such an experience, one that is likely to expand and enrich their selfhood, through "similarities and dissimilarities that are meant to throw light on features of our language."[2]

How can the poet's unique language be identified? How does a poetic corpus become a meaningful language-game in a certain cultural context? How does poetic identity come about, and how can its limits be delineated? These questions will be examined from an interpretive viewpoint influenced by Wittgenstein's insights—first and foremost, the following two arguments:

> *Essence* is expressed in grammar.[3]
> Grammar tells what kind of object anything is. (Theology as grammar.)[4]

Wittgenstein made a decisive and formative contribution to understanding the ways in which we fashion our selfhood in language, in various contexts. This constitution lends itself to a comparative

2 Wittgenstein, *Philosophical Investigations*, para. 130.
3 Wittgenstein, *Philosophical Investigations*, para. 371.
4 Wittgenstein, *Philosophical Investigations*, para. 373.

examination of examples.[5] This is not a random sampling, and must be preceded by the selection of a certain order for the exploration of these phenomena. This is only one of many possible orders, but is necessary so that there will be sense to our examination. Focusing on language, however, will not resolve all the interpretive issues; at times, the reverse will be the case. Language so bewitches our understanding that we can be trapped in confusions, such as between an object and what denotes it, for example: between inner processes that are generated in the first person and those generated between individuals and that can be described in the second and third persons, and more.[6]

The book will explore self-constitution in the poetry of four twentieth-century Hebrew poets whose contribution to and importance for Hebrew literature needs no elaboration: Zelda, Yehuda Amichai, Admiel Kosman, and Shimon Adaf. My personal taste undoubtedly influenced the choice of poets, but in a manner that conducts a dialogue with cultural and universal characteristics. At a time when the place of poetry in Hebrew literature is in retreat, it is important, and fascinating, to examine how the genre of lyric poetry constitutes self, corresponding to the questions of identity that trouble its composer. The interpretive direction in the book is meant to provide accessibility to these corpora by focusing on self-constitution, based on the assumption of its relevance for many individuals, especially in the postmodern age. I will attempt to show how poetry enriches the possibilities of identity in a way that, on the one hand, blazes new paths to emotion and rational consciousness, and, on the other, arouses the criticism and

5 "Our clear and simple language-games are not preliminary studies for a future regimentation of language [. . .] Rather, the language-games stand there as *objects of comparison* which, through similarities and dissimilarities, are meant to throw light on features of our language. For we can avoid unfairness or vacuity in our assertions only by presenting the model as what it is, as an object of comparison—as a sort of yardstick; not as a preconception to which reality *must* correspond. [. . .] We want to establish an order in our knowledge of the use of language: an order for a particular purpose, one out of many possible orders, not *the* order. For this purpose we shall again and again *emphasize* distinctions which our ordinary forms of language easily make us overlook" (Wittgenstein, *Philosophical Investigations*, para. 130–32).

6 "Philosophy is a struggle against the bewitchment of our understanding by the resources of our language" (Wittgenstein, *Philosophical Investigations*, para. 109).

self-determination of the reader on various questions of life that always remain unanswered.

The questions I raised will be examined in three tracks, namely, the three ways of grammatical activity: poetic grammar, dialogic grammar, and mystical grammar. These are three "orders" that were formulated following Wittgenstein's argument that grammar acts in all the ways needed by humans.[7] The familiar ways use the rules of syntax, logic, or empiricism, but truth be told, the rules of a language-game can be constituted in independent, creative, consensual, or controversial fashion. The objects of experience will likely function as grammatical rules that constitute expressions of pain, longing, or any other inner expression that becomes manifest in language and is common to those speaking the language-game in which this expression is constituted. At times lyrical poetry exposes various tensions by its focus on the speaker's gaze, which often confronts the world.

Why poetry and not prose? Each of these poets also wrote in additional genres: Zelda wrote "impressions," and attested to how natural she felt when she wrote prose and drama; Amichai wrote prose and drama; Kosman has authored many academic research works; and Shimon Adaf has written seven prose books and a wealth of essays of various sorts. I focus on poetry because of the relevance of the language-game of poetry for examining self-constitution. Poetry existed before distinct genres came into existence, and prose later split off from it.[8] Lyrical poetry developed as a consequence of "the distinction of

7 "The paradox disappears only if we make a radical break with the idea that language always functions in one way, always serves the same purpose: to convey thoughts—which may be about houses, pains, good and evil, or whatever" (Wittgenstein, *Philosophical Investigations*, para. 304).

8 "The Greek word *poiesis*, which was first used to designate poetry in the first half of the fifth century BCE was in fact more akin to our idea of literary fiction than to that of poetry proper [. . .] Greek prose, which developed much later than the traditional poetic genres, specialized in [. . .] forms of non-fiction and identified itself, in a conscious contrast to poetry, as 'the language of truth'. Well beyond the end of the classical period, the distinction of 'fiction' and 'non-fiction' coincided for all purposes with that between poetry and prose" (Margalit Finkelberg, "Poetry Versus Prose in Ancient Greece," in *Wool from the Loom: The Development of Literary Genres in Ancient Literature*, ed. Nathan Wasserman [Jerusalem: Magnes, 2002], English abstract: pp. VI–VII).

'fiction' and 'non-fiction,'" and Plato placed "nonmystical lyrical poetry at the apex of the genres."[9] Aristotle reversed this hierarchy, and did not even include lyrical poetry in his *Poetics*, but in this book we return to the Platonic hierarchy. This is not for the purpose of determining what is ideal poetry, as did Plato, but because the focus of lyrical poetry on the inner world of the "I"-speaker is an "order" (in the Wittgensteinian sense) that directs us to the processes of self-constitution.[10] The boundaries between the genres have unquestionably become blurred since their division by the Greeks into mystical degrees, but I maintain that in these corpora we can see the dominance and distinctness of the poetics of reflective self-constitution.

The book begins by examining the poetic characteristics of poetic language, and in the first stage will therefore discuss poetic grammar. In the next stage, continuing Wittgenstein's argument that language can also show and not merely say, I will clarify the ways of movement beyond the limits of language in the poems. And finally, I will explore the actual, dialogic plane that, by means of its varied tools, constitutes the ways in which the language of the poem acts as it strives, poetically, toward the limits of language. Wittgenstein viewed his philosophical investigations as an expression of inner dialogue.[11] This insight also captures the quality of lyrical poetry: the speaker's inner dialogue might create and conduct a dialogue in the soul of the reader as well.

Self-constitution is problematic, both substantively and methodologically. Since the self is dynamic and cannot be "frozen" and scrutinized from the outside, it is unclear how a person can clarify the features of his selfhood and consciously choose how to fashion them. The methodological difficulty results from the question of how a person can formulate his individual characteristics in public language. In light

9 Finkelberg, "Poetry Versus Prose," p. 39.

10 In terms of the "map of genres—epos, lyric, and drama—that is accepted to this day [. . .] [we see that] nonmystical speech, that is limited solely to the 'I' of the author, represents the lyrical genre" (Finkelberg, "Poetry Versus Prose," p. 40).

11 "Nearly all of my writings are private conversations with myself. Things that I say to myself tête-à-tête" (Ludwig Wittgenstein, *Culture and Value: A Selection from the Posthumous Remains*, ed. Georg Henrik von Wright, trans. Peter Winch [Oxford: Basil Blackwell, 1998], p. 77).

of the fact that the very expression is part of self-constitution, then the use of common language a priori includes both linguistic and spiritual conventions.

Despite these two pitfalls, we succeed in expressing ourselves, in formulating our personality traits, and in employing judgment and selection in the use of language. The book will demonstrate how lyrical poetry is especially suited to contend with this complexity, since it offers a certain answer to these two problems, because its two main characteristics are reflective self-examination and the formulation of a unique individual expression.

The examination of the four processes of self-constitution in the poetic language of lyrical poetry includes a number of possible features of such self-constitution: the process can be retrospectively and comparatively examined and described; it is more distinct in poetic language, in which special attention is paid to individual expression; and finally, lyrical poetry, as a genre devoted to the self-examination of the speaker, at times while detached from the world, can illuminate self-constitution better than other genres.

Wittgenstein's insights, which guide my research, combine the cultural and the universal. Form of life is a universal possibility of controlling language, and the masters of this create possibilities of expressing and constituting identity. Notwithstanding this, Wittgenstein also used the "form of life" concept to denote a set of specific cultural conditions of which we must be aware in order to understand what is said in the language of that culture. I attempted to look at the poets I chose in this integrative way. Twentieth-century Hebrew poetry possesses a specific, and intriguing, characteristic, namely, the revival of Hebrew and its transformation from a language reserved for religious rituals to a living and lively everyday language. The revival of Hebrew that began in the nineteenth century included its influence on fashioning consciousness (especially in the context of immigration to the Land of Israel). It was only in the twentieth century, however, that Hebrew poetry became an integral part of the public consciousness.

It is accepted in scholarly research to view the emergence of the *Likrat* group, which included Yehuda Amichai, as the transition from the fashioning of collective consciousness to the expression of individual consciousness in Hebrew literature. Zelda's poetry, however, is no less distant from the "poetry of the Palmach generation" than from that of Amichai, and it, too, focused on individual self-constitution. Zelda and Amichai wrote in the same period, in Jerusalem; each came from a religious home, and both were masters of the Hebrew language, with its wealth of language-games. These lines of "family resemblance" justify a comparison that reveals profound and intriguing differences between the two corpora.

Admiel Kosman and Shimon Adaf, too, share a "family resemblance": both grew up in religious families and exhibit a command of all the strata in Hebrew; both are critical of traditional conventions in a manner direct yet complex and sophisticated, poetical, and existential. Each in his own way fashions a different, and unique, poetical voice rich in expressions and ideas that exemplify an identity that is both clearly Jewish and universal.

Mention should be made of a feature common to Wittgenstein's thought and the corpora chosen for this book: on the one hand, Wittgenstein stressed that language can be understood only within the context of the form of life in which it acts. On the other hand, the concept of form of life is also interpreted as denoting universal categories of thought. I will show how the works of these four poets all reflect this complexity: Hebrew, which is renewed with their help as well, is created and understood on the context of a concrete reality, while at the same time the questions and problems with which the poems wrestle are universal, both in their formulation and in the response to them—questions of suffering, loneliness, love, and the individual's alienation from the world cross all the corpora.

Two factors influenced the selection of the poems: Wittgenstein's statement that "the limits of my language mean the limits of my world" applies to both the poet and the reader, who feels how his world expands and his identity is enrichened in the encounter with the masters of language. "Grammar is not accountable to any reality"[12] opens the

---

12 Ludwig Wittgenstein, *Philosophical Grammar*, ed. Rush Rhees, trans. Anthony Kenny (Oxford: Basil Blackwell, 1974), p. 184.

possibility of poetic language influencing our identity. The various types of grammar created in the language of poetry (which will be detailed below) create a dynamic essence that accompanies our lives in various settings, whose nature and "point" it illuminates.[13]

My decision to analyze self-constitution in the poetry of Zelda, Amichai, Kosman, and Adaf under the influence of Wittgenstein's concept of grammar came primarily from the desire to refrain from theoretical categorization. Chana Kronfeld was the first, in the spirit of Wittgenstein's concept of "family resemblance," to suggest refraining from categories in her book *On the Margins of Modernism* (1993). The concepts of "family," "game," and "thread" exemplify how final limits for a concept cannot be defined, with the consequent inability to provide a complete definition for a literary movement such as "modernism."[14]

Wittgenstein did not often relate to aesthetic judgment in his writings, but scholarly research from the middle of the 1990s to the present contains many discussions of the methodological characteristics that can be gleaned from his work in order to propose a methodology for such judgment. In the aesthetic expanse, I will focus exclusively on literary works, from a perspective that examines the linguistic processes that take place within them and create its uniqueness. This singularity also includes a series of tensions characteristic of verbal language and its relationship with the world. Wittgenstein addressed the confusion and questions that arise from the action of language in all manner of ways, often simultaneously, such as how is an inner process described, or when it seems to a speaker that a certain picture blocks, or even prevents, his use of a word. His relating to these issues reflects his awareness of the tension that always arises due to the simple fact that the sense of a disparity between language and a person will always remain. We can never even want to "interpose"[15] between the two, let

13 "So I am inclined to distinguish between essential and inessential rules in a game too. The game, one would like to say, has not only rules but also a *point*" (Wittgenstein, *Philosophical Investigations*, para. 564).

14 Chana Kronfeld, *On the Margins of Modernism* (Berkeley: University of California Press, 1993), pp. 28–30.

15 Wittgenstein, *Philosophical Investigations*, para. 245.

alone cancel this gap. This, for me, is the focal point emphasized in what Wittgenstein says about pain: unlike the prevalent position that pain fuels creativity or kindles the creative urge, we could say, influenced by Wittgenstein, that the gaps between language and other things in our world fuel the need to again and again formulate and verbalize. And thus the need to bridge the break between the given language within which we live our lives, on the one hand, and, on the other, the desire to be precise regarding personal meaning and our individual will.

A historical-cultural perspective is not relevant to this book, which seeks to focus on the question of the relationship between language mechanisms and the expressions of universal existential questions. Such a discussion is not exempt from exploring questions from within the culture in which they were written; these, however, will be examined from an existential linguistic viewpoint.

I therefore propose a possible mode of judgment that is not based on existing models, but rather unites three types of Wittgensteinian grammar, all of which are based on grammatical expression: poetical grammar, mystical grammar, and dialogic grammar.

I will show, for each of these language-games, how the creative process acts in each of these ways. Each of the latter reflects the desire to contend with the gap that will always remain in the encounter with the poem, between what is evident in the poem and what is explicitly verbalized, between the eternal craving and the momentary sense of realization. Generally speaking, each of the grammar types to be examined might also be characteristic of expressions in everyday statements, but the combination of the three types is especially characteristic of poetic language. The book's methodology offers a literary examination that describes poetry as functioning in a number of ways concurrently, and therefore reflects aesthetic worth, alongside ethical (dialogical) and (self- and socially) critical value.

Each in its own way, the corpora I choose in order to exemplify the actual meaning of aesthetic judgment are milestones of the longing for a complex Jewish identity. This identity cannot be classified in any sociological category, but rather begins from the starting point of individual will. This will is motivated by the relationship between poetical language and events and things in the world, and not by dictates or conventions, although at times this expression takes form when facing conventions, or in opposition to them.

The first three chapters of the book present the theoretical basis for my interpretation and comparison of the corpora of poetry, and each of the following four chapters is devoted to an analysis of a specific poet's work.

It is my pleasurable duty to thank the individuals without whom this book could not have been written.

This research had its beginnings in my PhD dissertation, which was submitted to Bar-Ilan University in the Program for Hermeneutics and Culture Studies. The program was founded and headed for many years by Prof. Avi Sagi, an outstanding intellectual and unparalleled teacher, whose inspiration is evident in many studies, including this book. I am grateful to him for the encouragement and support he has given to this day. I am also grateful to Prof. Dov Schwartz, who, as head of the Interdisciplinary Studies Program, encouraged my research and was always willing to offer advice that expanded my research directions.

My PhD dissertation was supervised by Prof. Tamar Sovran and Prof. Avidor Lipsker, who greatly enriched my knowledge. Prof. Sovran introduced me to the study of language, and her insights and advice accompanied, and still accompany, my scholarly and personal path in unparalleled fashion.

I am indebted to my students in the Program for Hermeneutics and Culture Studies, who for more than a decade have added challenge to my research. Their enthusiasm and active participation in class and in their diverse studies, and the active dialogue they conduct with my studies, have been of mutual benefit.

A singular component of this book is the dialogue I conducted with two of the poets whose work I examine. My thanks to Prof. Admiel Kosman, who always found time to engage in dialogue that expanded my horizons and warmed my heart and combined the forte of the scholar and poet with rare openness. My special thanks, more than words can express, to Shimon Adaf, who is peerless both as person and poet, for the riveting dialogue that, time and again, took me to the boundaries of language and beyond, and deepened my understanding of the beauty and truth of poetry. Special thanks to my devoted and exacting translator Edward Levin, for hearing the inner voice of the text, which he deftly conveyed into English.

Last, but not least, my thanks to the members of my family—Momi, Yehonatan, Rivki and Shira, Daniel and Noa, and Adi and Michael—for their endless love, understanding, and support.

CHAPTER 1

Poetic Grammar: Three Aspects of Aesthetic Judgment

> Essence is expressed in grammar.[1]
> Grammar tells what kind of object anything is. (Theology as grammar).[2]

One of the central and new elements of the linguistic turn in Wittgenstein's thought was his methodical directive to completely refrain from theoretization and to focus on the comparative examination of the ways in which language works.[3] Wittgenstein was consistent in this, despite the presence of metalinguistic expressions here and there in his books, which we could understand as cognitive expressions meant to clarify a certain issue. Wittgensteinian terms such as "picture," "language-game," "rule," and "form of life," for example, are still the subject of scholarly research, are given new interpretations time and

1 Wittgenstein, *Philosophical Investigations*, para. 371.
2 Wittgenstein, *Philosophical Investigations*, para. 373.
3 "We may not advance any kind of theory. There must not be anything hypothetical in our considerations. All *explanation* must disappear, and description alone must take its place [. . .] These are, of course, not empirical problems; but they are solved through an insight into the workings of our language" (Wittgenstein, *Philosophical Investigations*, para. 109). "The language-games stand there as *objects of comparison* which, through similarities and dissimilarities, are meant to throw light on features of our language" (*Philosophical Investigations*, para. 130).

again, and do not disappear after Wittgenstein finished clarifying some question. His consistency is therefore expressed in the absence of a coherent "method" or "theory," while the terms that he proposed, as well as his unique formulations, continue to intrigue us.

Wittgenstein formulated the motivation for his investigations differently than Hegel.[4] While the latter sought to show the similarity between things that seem different, Wittgenstein suggested comparing language-games and concentrating specifically on heightening the differences between them. Since we cannot find a commonality for language-games in any context, it is similarly impossible to present a shared basis for poetic works. At best, we can speak of a "family resemblance." Such a study depicts a network of similarities that reflects such a resemblance of language-games:

> Consider, for example, the activities that we call "games" [. . .] What is common to them all?—Don't say: "They *must* have something in common, or they would not be called 'games'"—but *look and see* whether there is anything common to all.—For if you look at them, you won't see something that is common to *all*, but similarities, affinities, and a whole series of them at that [. . .] And we can go through the many, many other groups of games in the same way, can see how similarities crop up and disappear [. . .] And the upshot of these considerations is: we see a complicated network of similarities overlapping and criss-crossing: similarities in the large and in the small. I can think of no better expression to characterize these similarities than "family resemblances"; for the various resemblances between members of a family—build, features, color of eyes, gait, temperament, and so on and so

4 "Hegel seems to me to be always wanting to say that things which look different are really the same. Whereas my interest is in showing that things which look the same are really different. I was thinking of using as a motto for my book a quotation from *King Lear*: 'I'll teach you differences'" (*Recollections of Wittgenstein*, ed. Rush Rhees [Oxford: Oxford University Press, 1984], p. 157).

> forth—overlap and criss-cross in the same way.—And I shall say: "games" form a family.[5]

The characteristics of the term "family resemblance" enable us to understand Wittgenstein's methodical avoidance of definitions and generalizations. This said and done, a certain tension is to be found between this abstention and Wittgenstein's desire to indicate the differences between situations or between language-games, since his description contained the locating of a "network of similarities."[6] The tension can be resolved by proposing a methodology based on the locating of both differences and similarities; in this spirit, I wish to connect Wittgenstein's discussions of aesthetic judgment to an examination of the ways in which poetic identity is established.

Wittgenstein proposed a number of features regarding aesthetic judgment, and our discussion of the language-games of the poets to be examined in the current work will be based on "family resemblance" on three planes: the poetic, the mystical, and the dialogic. Each of these three has its own characteristic rules of grammar, which constitute its nature, such that "*essence* is expressed by grammar." But how is "essence" expressed, if Wittgenstein opposed the possibility of articulating it, and how can we suggest a comparative methodology to formulate aesthetic judgment?

Wittgenstein's later investigations, and especially his book *Philosophical Investigations*, were highly influential on scholars in England and the United States who explored aesthetic judgment.[7] In his *Philosophical Investigations*, Wittgenstein formulated modernist features, such as refraining from theoretization and focusing on examining the ways in which language works. This orientation continued in the research of his thought as a whole, and serves as the basis for the study of *Philosophical*

5 Wittgenstein, *Philosophical Investigations*, para. 66–67.

6 The series of terms that Wittgenstein coined in his discussion can be considered to be "tools" needed to analyze differences in reality in general, and especially between different uses of language; see the detailed discussion below.

7 For an extensive discussion, see Benjamin Tilghman, *Wittgenstein, Ethics, and Aesthetics: The View from Eternity* (Albany: SUNY Press, 1991).

Investigations, specifically.[8] Wittgenstein stressed the significance of external criteria in order to be able to speak of meaning, and the need to set forth one of many possible orders in order to conduct a comparative examination of language-games.[9] Poetic creations and aesthetic judgment come into existence within the cultural context, and constitute the language-games that are to be studied within their context:

> The words we call expressions of aesthetic judgment play a very complicated role, but a very definite role, in what we call a culture of a period. To describe their use or to describe what you mean by a cultured taste, you have to describe a culture.
>
> What we now call a cultured taste perhaps didn't exist in the Middle Ages. An entirely different game is played in different ages. What belongs to a language game is a whole culture. In describing musical taste you have to describe whether children give concerts, whether women do or whether men only give them, etc., etc.[10]

Even if we will never be able to relate to all the cultural characteristics that encompass the work or the aesthetic judgment, the terminology of such judgment has a distinct role. "Poetic grammar," "mystical grammar," and "dialogic grammar" are examples of terms that enable aesthetic judgment, and that will be applied in the analysis of poetic word-games. Wittgenstein did not clearly distinguish between aesthetic judgment in general and that of a specific artistic realm.

8 "We may not advance any kind of theory. There must not be anything hypothetical in our considerations. All *explanation* must disappear, and description alone must take its place. And this description gets its light [. . .] from the philosophical problems" (Wittgenstein, *Philosophical Investigations*, para. 109).

9 "An 'inner process' stands in need of outward criteria" (Wittgenstein, *Philosophical Investigations*, para. 580); "Our clear and simple language-games are not preliminary studies for a future regimentation of language—as it were, first approximations, ignoring friction and air resistance. Rather, the language-games stand there as *objects of comparison* which, through similarities and dissimilarities, are meant to throw light on features of our language" (*Philosophical Investigations*, para. 130).

10 Ludwig Wittgenstein, *Lectures and Conversations on Aesthetics, Psychology, and Religious Belief*, ed. Cyril Barret (Berkeley: University of California Press, 1967), p. 8.

The choice of the term "poetic" denotes a focus on the language-games of poetry, but is certainly valid for other literary genres as well. The examination of the language-games of poets aims to present different possible contemporary identities that do not fit into categories prevalent in the Israeli literary expanse. Definitions such as "religiosity," "Easternism," or "modernism" overlook the complexities of identity to be found in these corpora, while, in contrast, the methodological terms that were inspired by Wittgenstein allow us to more clearly delineate the uniqueness of the poets we will discuss in contemporary Hebrew literature. The theoretical principles that will be set forth in the introductory chapters will guide our study of the thematic moves reflected in these poets' works, along with an examination of the grammar that makes this possible.[11]

Like every language-game, poetic judgment is based on rules that can be retrospectively described after their use in the judgment process.[12] Notwithstanding this, if these rules were not learned at some time, aesthetic judgment could not be conducted. Learning the rules improves the quality of the aesthetic judgment, but the nature of this judgment is also dependent on the capabilities of the judge. These features form the underpinning for the central argument of the current book: that grammatical rules that establish the poetical qualities of a literary work can be identified within the work. Aesthetic judgment therefore contains an examination of relevant rules, a description of the thematic move that is grammatically fashioned, and, finally, an indication of the manner of functioning within a certain culture.

11 "Rule" is a central term in *Philosophical Investigations*; see below.

12 "(1) Lewy says: 'This is too short.' I say: 'No. It is right. It is according to the rules.' (2) I develop a feeling for the rules. I interpret the rules. I might say: 'No. It isn't right. It isn't according to the rules.' Here I would be making an aesthetic judgment about the thing which is according to the rules in sense (1). On the other hand, if I hadn't learnt the rules, I wouldn't be able to make the aesthetic judgment. Learning the rules actually changes your judgment. [Although, if you haven't learnt Harmony and haven't a good ear, you may nevertheless detect any disharmony in a sequence of chords]" (Wittgenstein, *Lectures and Conversations*, p. 5).

I will therefore offer the term "poetic grammar" as a metaphorical "ladder."[13] The significance of such a ladder is that the poetics of a work are embodied in grammatical rules that, according to Wittgenstein, enable examination and judgment. Wittgenstein drew a sharp distinction between philosophical discussion and poetic expression, while believing that the two types of expression should be drawn closer, so that philosophical writing would be characterized by poetic elements:

> One should write philosophy only as one writes a poem. That, it seems to me, must reveal how far my thinking belongs to the present, the future, or the past. For I was acknowledging myself, with these words, to be someone who cannot quite do what he would like to be able to do.[14]

Wittgenstein formulated an analogy between poetic and philosophical writing: poetry, like philosophy, can yield self-consciousness and an awareness of the sources of influence that fashion man's personality (the past's tradition, the present's circumstances, and one's aspirations for the future). In this manner, a person can correctly assess his abilities and limitations. Wittgenstein's proposal to write philosophy as a poem is based on poetry's ability to cause a person to come to know himself, while at the same time the very words by means of which this reflective thought occurs attest to man's limited ability to know himself.

Poetic language functions in this context as the driving force for self-knowledge, but actually we do not know what is special about poetic language so that it makes this journey of discovery possible. If we apply another suggestion by Wittgenstein, to examine whether

13 At the end of his *Tractatus*, Wittgenstein used the metaphor of a ladder to argue that the sentences of a book must function as stages of understanding, and that after this understanding has been attained, the ladder is superfluous: "My propositions are elucidatory in this way: he who understands me finally recognizes them as senseless, when he has climbed out through them, on them, over them. (He must so to speak throw away the ladder, after he has climbed up on it)" (Ludwig Wittgenstein, *Tractatus Logico-Philosophicus*, trans. D. F. Pears and B. F. McGuiness [London: Routledge & Kegan Paul, 1961], para. 6.54).

14 Wittgenstein, *Culture and Value*, p. 28.

certain words at a certain juncture effect something of significance for the person who understands them, we can say that he saw the function of poetic language as enabling the reader to see the meaning of moments of life in different periods.

Wittgenstein's philosophical writing was indeed characterized by poetic elements of two types: the first includes the features of Wittgensteinian language itself—abbreviation, conciseness, figurativeness, and dialogic nature. The second type (listed below) comprises the manner in which "things are done" in poetic language.[15] Austin's terms, which describe the ways in which language actions are performed, will aid us in resolving the questions that Wittgenstein addressed in his depiction of poetic language: What generates poetic language? What does it make possible, as opposed to everyday language? How does it stimulate the reader's emotions, and what questions does it arouse?[16] Examining poetic grammar means clarifying the grammatical ways that make poetry possible, from one (or more) of the following aspects:

1. The ability of an aesthetic work *to effect a person's reflective introspection* of his life by arousing sentiment that causes the reader to scrutinizer his life, in the past, the present, or in regard to his future will.

---

15 Inspired by Austin's well-known book: John L. Austin, *How to Do Things with Words: The William James Lectures Delivered at Harvard University in 1955* (Oxford: Oxford University Press, 1962).

16 These questions were formulated in accordance with three of Austin's terms—"locutionary act," "illocutionary act," and "perlocutionary act"—as he defined them: "The act of 'saying something' in this full normal sense I call [. . .] the performance of locutionary act" (*How to Do Things*, p. 94); "'illocutionary' act, i.e. performance of an act *in* saying something, as opposed to performing of an act of saying something (p. 99); "There is yet a further sense in which to perform a locutionary act, and therein an illocutionary act, may also be to perform an act of another kind. Saying something will often, or even normally, produce certain consequential effects upon the feelings, thoughts, or actions of the audience, or of the speaker, or of other persons: and it may be done with the design, intention, or purpose of producing them; and we may then say, speaking of this, that the speaker has performed an act in the nomenclature of which reference is made either, only obliquely, or even, not at all, to the performance of the locutionary or illocutionary act. We shall call the performance of an act of this kind the performance of *perlocutionary* act or *perlocution*" (p. 101, emphases in the original).

2. The ability of an aesthetic work *to express individuality, and to effect a change in aspect*, to show something else.
3. The ability of an aesthetic work *to present a symbolic structure that cannot be directly verbalized*, but can only make itself "manifest." The "logical form" can be interpreted in two ways: form as the inner, hidden, structure of the work, or form as a symbolic array that represents the ineffable.

The theoretical detailing of these aspects requires a clarification of how Wittgensteinian aesthetic judgment can be described, in light of the fact that he placed aesthetics, along with logic, ethics, and belief, beyond the bounds of language.[17] Continuing in this vein, throughout his thought, Wittgenstein based his philosophical investigations on the manner in which language works in different contexts, and not on judgment grounded in external or substantive criteria. It therefore would seem that any move in language, including poetic-aesthetic language-games, can be judged in the context of the language-game in which it is created.[18]

1. Examination and Judgment of Aesthetic Language: The Fundamental Tension

> Art is a kind of expression. Good art is complete expression. The work of art is the object seen sub specie aeternitatis; and the good life is the world seen sub specie aeternitatis. This is

17 "Logic is not a body of doctrine, but a mirror-image of the world. Logic is transcendental [. . .] It is clear that ethics cannot be put into words. Ethics is transcendental. (Ethics and aesthetics are one and the same.) [. . .] There are, indeed, things that cannot be put into words. They make themselves manifest. They are what is mystical" (Wittgenstein, *Tractatus Logico-Philosophicus*, para. 6.13, 6.421, 6.522).

18 Aesthetic judgment was never a central concern in Wittgenstein's investigations, but despite Wittgenstein's few direct references to the issue, Garry L. Hagberg already identified elements of aesthetic judgment in Wittgenstein's philosophical writings ("Wittgenstein's Aesthetics," *Stanford Encyclopedia of Philosophy*, 2007). Hagberg drew parallels between the way language works and the act of poetic creativity. He asserts that this similarity must be expressed in judgment, and therefore we cannot speak of the causes of creativity, while we can examine a poetic work and indicate its innovativeness and, accordingly, its creativity.

> the connexion between art and ethics. The usual way of looking at things sees objects as it were from the midst of them, the view sub specie aeternitatis from outside.[19]

Wittgenstein used the Latin expression "sub specie aeternitatis" to present the goal of a work of art: making it possible to view the world from outside it, as a whole, as complete. In ordinary language, states of affairs are portrayed in a certain context, "from the midst of them." A work of art, in contrast, can show the boundaries of language by showing the rules that enable the expression of a certain content and, consequently, that of the wholeness of content and form.

What is the meaning of sensing "the world as whole," and how does a work of art produce such a feeling? Is this a feeling of holistic merging with the world? A sense of wholeness in the encounter with or the creation of a work of art, because the artist or observer/reader can formulate the rules for himself? Does a work of art allow us to disregard verbal language, and accordingly creates a sense of wholeness (due to the possibility of avoiding the distinctions, boundaries, and definitions that language requires)? Does a good work of art generate a sense of "connection to life" and thereby touch upon the "wonder" at the world's existence?[20]

19 Ludwig Wittgenstein, *Notebooks 1914–1916*, ed. Georg Henrik von Wright and Gertrude E. M. Anscombe, trans. Gertrude E. M. Anscombe (Oxford: Basil Blackwell, 1961), p. 83.

20 Aesthetic judgment that is based on the work's effect on the viewer/reader as a criterion of the work's quality was formulated by Ray Elliot, following Wittgenstein: "This may be thought sufficient reason for understanding aesthetic contemplation, in Wittgenstein's aesthetic, as resulting in an experience of wonder at the existence of the object; which is also wonder at the existence of the world, since (a) the object *is* my world; (b) it is seen together with the whole of logical space; and (c) every object is capable of being seen in this way. This wonder belongs to the aesthetic 'significance' we have been looking for. Since aesthetic contemplation involves the contemplation of the world as a limited whole, and 'the feeling of the world as a limited whole is the mystical feeling' (*Tractatus*, para. 6.45), aesthetic contemplation involves the mystical both as a feeling of the oneness of the world, and of wonder at its existence" (Ray Elliot, "Wittgenstein's Speculative Aesthetics in Its Ethical Context," in *Beyond Liberal Education: Essays in Honour of Paul H. Hirst*, ed. Robin Barrow and Patricia White [London: Routledge, 1993], pp. 159–60). This viewpoint was followed and developed by Malcolm Budd,

Wittgenstein's assertion "Good art is complete expression" presents the quandary at the basis of the review of poetry in the current book. On the one hand, he describes a feeling of certainty regarding the existence of good art that embodies a certain type of completeness, while, on the other, the descriptive words of aesthetic judgment are not suitable for detailing the nature of this completeness, since a description of wholeness requires an external perspective, while our vision is limited to seeing only certain aspects, and not the entirety of the aspects. Throughout his thought, Wittgenstein set forth two major reasons for the lack of such a possibility.

The *first reason* is that aesthetic expression cannot be described, because of the positioning of aesthetics beyond the boundaries of language. This argument appears in Wittgenstein's early thought, in which he formulated the boundaries of language. In the first stage, he placed logic beyond these bounds, and in the second stage, he compared ethics to aesthetics, and stated that both lie beyond the bounds of human expression. Notwithstanding this, in his diaries, which were written during those years and contain many parallels to *Tractatus*, Wittgenstein expanded his discussion of aesthetics, and asserted that art is a type of expression, and that good art is complete expression. Taking these two statements together and the tension that this produces inspires the current discussion: on the one hand, good art exists in the world and therefore can be assessed; on the other hand, its inherent ability to present the world as total completeness does not actually exist in language (since this ability cannot be verbalized, continuing the parallel of ethics—that cannot be verbalized—to aesthetics), which focuses on objects and not on comprehensive introspection from without.

The *second reason* for the problematic nature of aesthetic judgment is the absence of dedicated terminology. A speaker can indicate the distinctness of an aesthetic object and portray its influence on him, but such a discussion is based on first-person certainty. The discussion of first-person certainty and its consequences is one of the most studied

"Wittgenstein on Aesthetics," in *Aesthetic Essays* (Oxford: Oxford University Press, 2008), pp. 252–77.

topics in Wittgenstein's thought and is basic to our inquiry: on the one hand, the speaker's affinity to the aesthetic object, and the latter's effect on him, occur in the emotional plane and cannot be described empirically. On the other hand, the terms of emotion (such as "pleasant," "moving," and the like) are public, general terms and expressive tools at the disposal of the speaker, and do not express the uniqueness of his aesthetic experience. In summation, the possibility of aesthetic judgment, according to Wittgenstein, is in doubt, in terms both of the ability to describe the features of the aesthetic object itself, and of the ability to depict its influence on the speaker and his examination of it.

Despite these difficulties, attempts have been made to describe Wittgenstein's notion of aesthetic judgment. Like the effort made in the current book, they can be explained by citing two "Wittgensteinian" reasons: the first is the importance of aesthetics in our lives, and especially for Wittgenstein.[21] The second reason is the centrality of the aesthetic aspect in Wittgenstein's philosophical writing, so that the uniqueness of his writing is evident. The care he took regarding the quality of the expression of his ideas includes aesthetic features such as metaphors, the use of dialogue, and additional aesthetic means; his concern for the aesthetic also finds expression in his editing and reediting of his writings.

In his book on metaphor in Wittgenstein's writings, Jerry Gill finely showed how the choice of metaphors is not an attempt to create a second-order language, to which Wittgenstein was explicitly opposed; rather, the metaphors are intertwined within and throughout his investigations as a philosophical method.[22] This methodology is based on the use of metaphor for different purposes, after the attainment of which it

---

21 Many scholars teach of the importance of aesthetics in Wittgenstein's life. See, e.g., Budd, "Wittgenstein on Aesthetics"; Garry L. Hagberg, *Art as Language: Wittgenstein, Meaning, and Aesthetic Theory* (Ithaca, NY: Cornell University Press, 1995); Peter B. Lewis, ed., *Wittgenstein, Aesthetics, and Philosophy* (Aldershot: Ashgate, 2004); and Richard Allen and Malcolm Turvey, eds., *Wittgenstein, Theory, and the Arts* (London: Routledge, 2001).

22 Jerry H. Gill, *Wittgenstein and Metaphor* (Atlantic Highlands, NJ: Humanities Press, 1996).

is no longer necessary.[23] Gill lists uses such as substitution, constitution, and metaphor, and examines the metaphorical usages in Wittgenstein's three central works.[24] The problematic nature, throughout Wittgenstein's writing, of the discussion of the aesthetic aspect remains, since, in actuality, everyday language cannot be absolutely distinguished from aesthetic language.

The presumed "solution" is to be found in *Philosophical Investigations*, in which Wittgenstein stressed that the language of logic is based on the mechanisms of regular, everyday language, which, he maintains, has the potential to serve all human needs.[25] Aesthetic judgment is a common practice, and therefore, despite the perception of aesthetics as existing beyond language, it can be formulated in routine expressions. The use of super-concepts must be truly humble, just like the use of words that denote ordinary objects. Aesthetics, or aesthetic judgment, certainly can be thought of as "*super*-concepts." The question arises: what is the meaning of the "humble" or routine use of terms that are meant to organize a certain praxis, and not only denote some object?

A possible direction to resolve this question can be found in Wittgenstein's few discussions of "poetics." In his later writings Wittgenstein took note of the fact that we use poetic means in everyday language as well, in several ways. For example, poetics can be expressed in a "poetic mood," that recalls the mimetic criterion set forth by Aristotle:

> Schiller writes in a letter (to Goethe, I think) of a "poetic mood." I think I know what he means, I think I am familiar

23 Gill, *Wittgenstein and Metaphor*, pp. 150–51.

24 Wittgenstein, *Tractatus Logico-Philosophicus*; Wittgenstein, *Philosophical Investigations*; Gertrude E. M. Anscombe and Georg Henrik von Wright, eds., *On Certainty*, trans. Denis Paul and Gertrude E. M. Anscombe (Oxford: Basil Blackwell, 1969).

25 "The sense in which philosophy of logic speaks of sentences and words is no different from that in which we speak of them in ordinary life" (Wittgenstein, *Philosophical Investigations*, para. 108). "We are under the illusion that what is peculiar, profound and essential to us in our investigation resides in its trying to grasp the incomparable essence of language. That is, the order existing between the concepts of proposition, word, inference, truth, experience, and so forth. This order is a *super*-order between—so to speak—*super*-concepts. Whereas, in fact, if the words 'language,' 'experience,' 'world' have a use, it must be as humble a one as that of the words 'table,' 'lamp,' 'door'" (*Philosophical Investigations*, para. 97).

> with it myself. It is the mood or receptivity to nature & one in which one's thoughts seem as vivid as nature itself.[26]

A second method of poetic use depicts the way in which an imaginary picture is created, as a spontaneous occurrence:

> "If I shut my eyes, there he is in front of me."—One could suppose that such expressions are not learned, but rather poetically formed, spontaneously. That they therefore "seem just right" to one man and then also to the next one.[27]

A third sort of poetic use consists of transmitting a message by means of a picture, instead of words:

> I might get an important message to someone by sending him the picture of a landscape. Does he read it like a blueprint? That is, does he decipher it? He looks at it and acts accordingly. He sees rocks, trees, a house, etc. in it. (The situation here is one of practical necessity, but the means of communication is one that has nothing to do with any previous agreement, definition, or the like, and that otherwise only serves quasi-poetic purposes. But on the other hand normal speech also serves poetic purposes.)[28]

Beyond the fact of Wittgenstein's clarification of the incorporation of poetic language in regular language and the use of poetic means for the needs of "normal speech," and vice versa, I wish to emphasize the importance of Wittgenstein's repeated use of the picture. Not only can it replace words; it does not need agreement or definition, which are

26 Wittgenstein, *Culture and Value*, p. 75.

27 Ludwig Wittgenstein, *Remarks on the Philosophy of Psychology*, ed. Georg Henrik von Wright and Heikki Nyman, trans. C. G. Luckhardt and Maximilian Nyman, trans. C. G. Luckhardt and M. A. E. Aue (Oxford: Basil Blackwell, 1980), vol. 2, para. 117.

28 Wittgenstein, *Remarks*, vol. 2, para. 447–48.

necessary when we use words.[29] This means that, despite the combination of routine and poetic language, poetic language retains its uniqueness in Wittgenstein's later writings as well.[30] This singularity also retrospectively sheds light on the picture in *Tractatus*, and justifies our reliance on Wittgenstein's early works in formulating the methodology of aesthetic judgment.

An additional direction in his early writings illustrates the distinctiveness of the aesthetic perspective in the sense of "the world as a whole." This singularity lies in the possibility of aesthetics to generate experience enveloped in the sense of the miraculous:

> Aesthetically, the miracle is that the world exists. That there is what there is. Is it the essence of the artistic way of looking at things, that it looks at the world with a happy eye? Life is grave, art is gay. For there is certainly something in the conception that the end of art is the beautiful. And the beautiful is what makes happy.[31]

The encounter with the aesthetic produces an experience of wholeness and completeness—as if the entire world merges with and is included in the work of art. We can speak of two opposing experiences in this context: a work of art is likely to arouse joy and wonder at the world's very existence or, alternately, a sense of "the end of the world." In both instances, the world is epitomized by a somewhat general experience in which the work of art expresses or creates a feeling of "the world as a whole." While Wittgenstein portrays an experience of wonder and happiness, a literary work can also be used to illustrate the opposite general experience, of the "end of the world." Children or adolescents are more readily inclined to perceive a certain experience as fateful and

29 "It is not only agreement in definitions, but also [. . .] agreement in judgments that is required for communication by means of language" (Wittgenstein, *Philosophical Investigations*, para. 242.

30 For a comprehensive discussion of Wittgenstein's various uses of the term "picture" throughout his writings, see David Egan, "Pictures in Wittgenstein's Later Philosophy," *Philosophical Investigations* 34, no. 1 (2011), pp. 55–76.

31 Wittgenstein, *Notebooks 1914–1916*, p. 86.

determining the nature of the world for them. An outstanding example of this appears in the classic work *Winnie-the-Pooh*. When Piglet runs and falls, his balloon explodes, resulting in his thinking that the world came to an end: "he thought that the whole world had blown up."[32] The sensation of "the world as a whole" is possible in the variants of both an experience of joy and wonder and a negative experience of terror and incomprehension of events.

The possibility of "seeing as a whole" is problematic because it cannot be verbalized. Later, in his book *Philosophical Investigations*, Wittgenstein centered the philosophical problematic around the difficulty of seeing things "es an Ubersichtlichkeit":

> A main source of our failure is that we don't have *an overview* of the use of our words.—Our grammar is deficient in surveyability. A surveyable representation produces precisely that kind of understanding which consists in "seeing connections." Hence the importance of finding and inventing *intermediate links*.[33]

The parallelism between Wittgenstein's early and later thought is evident: it is not only the work of art that cannot be described as a whole; this same difficulty exists for grammar. Wittgenstein's writings exhibit methodological continuity on this point because, despite the transition to describable phenomena in *Philosophical Investigations*, the

32 "While all this was happening, Piglet had gone back to his own house to get Eeyore's balloon. He held it very tightly against himself, so that it shouldn't blow away, and he ran as fast as he could so as to get to Eeyore before Pooh did; for he thought that he would like to be the first one to give a present, just as if he had thought of it without being told by anybody. And running along, and thinking how pleased Eeyore would be, he didn't look where he was going . . . and suddenly he put his foot in a rabbit hole, and fell down flat on his face. BANG!!!???***!!! Piglet lay there, wondering what had happened. At first he thought that the whole world had blown up; and then he thought that perhaps only the Forest part of it had; and then he thought that perhaps only *he* had, and he was now alone in the moon or somewhere, and would never see Christopher Robin or Pooh or Eeyore again" (Alan Alexander Milne, *Winnie-the-Pooh* [New York: Penguin, 2009], pp. 83–84). I am grateful to my student Naphtali Yisraeli for the reference.

33 Wittgenstein, *Philosophical Investigations*, para. 122.

desire and inability to comprehensively describe from the outside remains.[34] After explaining the tensions underlying the discussion of aesthetic judgment in Wittgenstein's writings, his methodological goal can be put as follows: a description of poetic grammar should explore the ways in which this grammar functions. I will suggest three possible ways that can be described and evaluated, while not ruling out the existence of additional ways of functioning that create poetic grammar.

2. The First Aspect: A Poetic Work as Driving Reflective Introspection

> The works of the great masters are stars which rise and set around us. So the time will come again for every great work that is now in the descendent.[35]
> Scientific questions may interest me, but they never really grip me. Only conceptual & aesthetic questions have that effect on me. At bottom it leaves me cold whether scientific problems are solved; but not those other questions.[36]
> We feel that even when all possible scientific questions have been answered, the problems of life remain completely untouched.[37]

Wittgenstein contends that classic works of art are both eternal and of dual aspect: in a certain period, they might illuminate our world as stars, while in periods of decline they "await" the time in which they can once again shine. Beyond the constant quality of these works, they also have a cognitive facet that is dependent on reality. This aspect is

34 Notwithstanding this, Marjorie Perloff pointed to an exceptional passage in Wittgenstein's thought in which he argues for the possibility of perceiving the world "sub specie aeternitatis," not only by means of a work of art. That is, the work of art is the default for such a perception, and para. 122 is not a wish, but a realistic possibility. See Marjorie Perloff, *Wittgenstein's Ladder: Poetic Language and the Strangeness of the Ordinary* (Chicago: University of Chicago Press, 1996), p. 79.

35 Wittgenstein, *Culture and Value*, p. 23.

36 Wittgenstein, *Culture and Value*, p. 91.

37 Wittgenstein, *Tractatus*, para. 6.52.

embodied in the communicative feature of poetic grammar: the work might influence people, but not necessarily. Its effect depends on the period and on the individual. By proposing to write philosophy as poetry, Wittgenstein attests of himself that an aesthetic work is capable of generating reflexive introspection in his life. This introspection comes about by arousing sentiment that causes man to examine his life in the present, or as regards his will for the future. How, then, does poetic grammar enable the creation of such introspection that is dependent on the period and the individual?

Wittgenstein bound together conceptual and aesthetic questions, and those two types together with "problems of life." Such problems are insoluble, nonetheless—and perhaps because of this—they repeatedly ignite his consciousness. Throughout Wittgenstein's thought, there is constant tension between two types of inquiry: "scientific" investigation, which relates to the regulative nature in which language works; and "conceptual and aesthetic investigation," that pertains to the meaning of life, and that generates "subjective enthusiasm towards life." Wittgenstein asserted that aesthetic and cognitive questions warmed his heart, while he was indifferent to scientific ones. The ability of poetic language to arouse feeling stands in opposition to scientific inquiry, which does not touch upon the problems of life; nonetheless, scientific language and poetic language share the same linguistic mechanism. Furthermore, the way in which we understand ourselves is verbalized in language. Consequently, the way how poetic language effects reflective introspection and formulates a response to life's questions is closely linked to the manner in which meaning is understood, in its simple, ordinary sense:

> The idea of the human soul, which one either sees or doesn't see, is very similar to the idea of the meaning of a word, which stands next to the word, whether as a process or an object.[38]

38 Ludwig Wittgenstein, *Last Writings on the Philosophy of Psychology*, ed. Georg Henrik von Wright and Heikki Nyman, trans. C. G. Luckhardt and Maximilian A. E. Aue (Oxford: Basil Blackwell, 1982), vol. 1: *Preliminary Studies for Part II of the Philosophical Investigations*, para. 979.

When we attempt to understand an abstract idea such as "the human soul," we would be well advised to think of the distinction between "meaning" and "word." Meaning is illusory, since, on the one hand, it cannot be separated from the word:

> People say: it's not the word that counts, but its meaning, thinking of the meaning as a thing of the same kind as the word, even though different from the word. Here the word, there the meaning. The money, and the cow one can buy with it. (On the other hand, however: money, and what can be done with it.)[39]

On the other hand, since use is generally not dictated, a number of meanings can be attributed to every word, and therefore a specific meaning is not a necessary component of the word.[40] Bar-Elli portrayed different possible uses or interpretations, as a sort of reservoir of possibilities that he called "rich use."[41] This reservoir exists virtually, in the consciousness of the speaker, from which he instinctively selects a certain interpretation. This description, however, does not explain Wittgenstein's express distinction between "meaning" and "word." In the following citation, for instance, Wittgenstein clearly distinguishes between the two, being compelled to use the word "meaning":

39 Wittgenstein, *Philosophical Investigations*, para. 120.

40 This ensues first and foremost from the rules paradox, which is one of the most extensively researched issues of Wittgenstein's philosophy; "This was our paradox: no course of action could be determined by a rule, because every course of action can be brought into accord with the rule. The answer was: if every course of action can be brought into accord with the rule, then it can also be brought into conflict with it. And so there would be neither accord nor conflict here" (Wittgenstein, *Philosophical Investigations*, para. 201).

41 Bar-Elli proposes the expression "rich use": "The concepts of use [. . .] are rich and replete with meanings to the extent of the horizons of concepts and meanings that they contain [. . .] action and use are always perceived *in a certain way*, which itself is teeming with meaning and conceptuality" (Gilead Bar-Elli, *The Fathers of Analytic Philosophy: Frege, Russell, Wittgenstein* (Tel Aviv: Goryn, 2009), vol. 3: *Wittgenstein: Language, Mind, Reality*, p. 162 (Hebrew, emphasis added).

> When I pronounce this word while reading expressively, it is completely filled with its meaning. "How can this be, if meaning is the use of the word?" Well, what I said was intended figuratively. Not that I chose the figure: it forced itself on me [. . .] But if a sentence can strike me as a painting in words, then it is no more astonishing that a word uttered in isolation and without purpose can seem to carry a particular meaning within itself.[42]

Wittgenstein explicitly related to the possibility of distinguishing between "meaning" and "word," employing metaphors such as "soul," "character," "face," and "picture":

> Though one would like to say every word can have a different character in different contexts, at the same time there is a single character it always has—a face. It looks at us, after all.[43]

These metaphors denote the word's unique "character" that creates a sort of meeting with the reader that leads him to understand the word in a certain manner.[44] This stance resembles that of Charles Sanders Peirce, the founder of modern semiotics, who argued that every sign possesses qualia, quality that is indefinable but constitutes the foundation and source of the process of understanding and interpretation.[45] Bar-Elli noted Wittgenstein's use of metaphors to denote a fixed aspect of the use of words, which remains in all instances, the perception of which is dependent on experiential and psychological factors.[46] I wish

---

42 Wittgenstein, "Philosophy of Psychology—A Fragment," part 2 of the 2009 edition of *Philosophical Investigations*, henceforth *PPF*, para. 265, 267.

43 Wittgenstein, *PPF*, para. 38.

44 An additional example of the claim that a word also embodies a fixed meaning, like a face: "The familiar face of a word, the feeling that it has assimilated its meaning into itself, that it is a likeness of its meaning" (Wittgenstein, *PPF*, para. 294).

45 See Charles Sanders Peirce, *Philosophical Writings of Peirce*, ed. Justus Buchler (New York: Dover, 1955), pp. 80–87. Susan Langer, whose views I will relate below, already incorporated Peirce's concept of the sign in the formulation of Wittgenstein's aesthetic judgment.

46 Bar-Elli, *Wittgenstein*, p. 131.

to differ with Bar-Elli's claim that these factors, too, are components of the concept of "use," and are not external to it. Wittgenstein showed differences in the use of the same words in order to illustrate introspective processes. In such processes, a word can be experienced in different ways, with an expanse of *spontaneity* that cannot be anticipated even in the framework of "rich language." This expanse expresses the new and the "spontaneous," and, in practice, establishes a language-game, since expression in language can exist only within the context of a "language-game":

> We don't notice the enormous variety of all the everyday language-games, because the clothing of our language makes them all alike. What is new (spontaneous, "specific") is always a language-game.[47]

The "inner," as Sandra Laugier finely showed, is logically dependent on the concept of the "outer," but this does not allow us to negate the existence of the "inner"; the opposite is the case.[48] The fact that at times the "inner" seems hidden from us, or concealed "behind" an outer expression, does not justify the reduction of the "inner" to the "outer."[49] Wittgenstein argues that, actually, these are two different (and legitimate) uses of language.[50] Wittgenstein coined the term "gappy space" to illustrate the existence of an irreducible gap between the "outer" and the "inner" (which he expressed also in his

47 Wittgenstein, *PPF*, para. 355.

48 Sandra Laugier, "The Myth of the Outer: Wittgenstein's Redefinition of Subjectivity," in *Perspicuous Presentations: Esssays on Wittgenstein's Philosophy of Psychology*, ed. Daniele Moyal-Sharrock (Basingstoke: Palgrave Macmillan, 2007), pp. 151–71.

49 "(As one can sometimes reproduce music only in one's inward ear, and cannot whistle it, because the whistling drowns out the inner voice, so sometimes the voice of a philosophical thought is so soft that the noise of spoken words is enough to drown it and prevent it from being heard, if one is questioned and has to speak)" (Ludwig Wittgenstein, *Zettel*, ed. Gertrude E. M. Anscombe and Georg Henrik von Wright, trans. Gertrude E. M. Anscombe [Oxford: Basil Blackwell, 1981], para. 453).

50 Wittgenstein, *Philosophical Investigations*, para. 304.

discussion of pain, in *Philosophical Investigations*, para. 245).[51] I will show that the personal interpretation of a literary work is established within that gappy space. A gap exists between the continuity of events (past-present, and the anticipation of the future) in the speaker's life and the encounter with the work. If a significant meeting occurs, in which one or more aspects of the work function as a "significant face" for the reader, then reflective introspection regarding the reader's life is possible. In order to understand the possibility of some type of change, we must explain the metaphorical field created by Wittgenstein that centers around the term "aspect" and contains a range of its applications.

3. The Second Aspect: Conscious Change as the Key to Aesthetic Judgment

> But the application, after all, is completely different in aesthetics and descriptive geometry. In aesthetics isn't it essential that a picture or a piece of music, etc., can change its aspect for me?—And, of course, this is not essential for that topological demonstration.[52]

The ability of an aesthetic work to change the person who experiences it is depicted by Wittgenstein as "essential." For our purposes, one of the features of poetic grammar is its ability to effect change. The preceding discussion spoke of the intent of the reader/observer to comparatively examine different times in his life. Such an exploration is possible, inter alia, because an aesthetic work is characterized by a broader range of meanings, or perspectives, from which it can be interpreted. First, however, we must understand how Wittgenstein describes the nature of the introspection that would enable a person to discern the change that occurs in his consciousness.

---

51 "One language-game analogous to a fragment of another. One space projected into a limited extent of another. A 'gappy' space. (For 'inner and outer')" (Wittgenstein, *Zettel*, para. 648).

52 Wittgenstein, *Last Writings*, vol. 1, para. 634.

Wittgenstein speaks of two uses of the wording “to see.”[53] One type of usage relates to seeing something and describing it, while the other is expressed in a comparative view of things. He claims that the object of seeing is totally different in every instance, even if two people are seemingly looking at the same object. The “first looker” might create an exact copy of the two faces, while the second would emphasize the similarity between the two faces to which the first relates.

On the one hand, Wittgenstein compares seeing (*Sehen*) to interpretation (*Deuten*). We can see the same illustration in different ways, meaning that seeing is actually interpretation. On the other, he argues that seeing is a passive situation, while interpretation is an active effort.[54] In the interpretive process we create hypotheses that are liable to prove false, while seeing is a process of direct impression. This comparison reflects the connection between Wittgenstein’s study of language and aesthetic judgment: he compared the image that arises as a result of the meeting with the word with the visual image (between seeing an object [such as a prism, for example] and interpretation of a word). The image aroused as a result of a meeting with words is “interpretation,” while one that is brought about by a visual encounter is direct.[55] The term “poetic grammar” that I propose in this chapter as a methodological “ladder” comprises two ways of seeing in the process of interpreting poetry: at times what happens is portrayed “by itself,” while in other instances a comparison will be conducted between poetic events, either to describe a change, or to compare different poems (by the same or different poets).

Wittgenstein also demonstrated what is common to the two types of seeing by arguing that words have physiognomy, based on which the self-meaning of the word can be understood. The importance of “physiognomy” (along with the fixed nature of the word, as mentioned above) lies in its being the basis for the individual process of examination and judgment:

53 Wittgenstein, *PPF*, para. 111.
54 Wittgenstein, *PPF*, para. 117.
55 Wittgenstein, *PPF*, para. 117.

> Meaning—a physiognomy.[56] The familiar face of a word, the feeling that it has assimilated its meaning into itself, that it is a likeness of its meaning—there could be human beings to whom all this was alien. (They would not have an attachment to their words.) And how are these feelings manifested among us?—By the way we choose and value words.[57]

The visual imagery of meaning (image—*Ebenbild*) directs the viewer to normative seeing, in the framework of which the word appears as possessing a certain fixed physiognomy, and seeing of this sort is likely to establish an interpretive path. Continuing in this vein, it could be said that action in accordance with a rule is the basis common to seeing and interpretation. Action in accordance with a rule is not conducted by itself, but is always part of the praxis of social customs and institutions:

> An intention is embedded in a setting, in human customs and institutions. If the technique of the game of chess did not exist, I could not intend to play a game of chess.[58]

Meaning for Wittgenstein, therefore, is not a substantive concept, it rather is revealed in the language-game, in the context of a certain form of life:

> The word "language-*game*" is used here to emphasize the fact that the *speaking* of language is part of an activity, or of a form of life.[59]

Interpretation—that is, an action of imparting meaning—is conducted within this framework. This is not the cryptological uncovering of meaning but application. The verbal application of a rule is done within

56 Wittgenstein, *Philosophical Investigations*, para. 568.
57 Wittgenstein, *PPF*, para. 294.
58 Wittgenstein, *Philosophical Investigations*, para. 337.
59 Wittgenstein, *Philosophical Investigations*, para. 23.

the framework of a certain praxis, and cannot be private.[60] At this juncture, Wittgenstein's discussion of the multimeaning nature of language joins the possible multiplicity of aspects in the process of understanding the meaning of a specific situation. Although meanings and rules are always understood within the context of the underlying form of life, a number of understandings are always possible in the interpretation of a given situation.

A number of perspectives are possible even within the context of an individual's interpretive view; furthermore, change is made possible and is perceived by a comparison between them. Accordingly, when a poetic work influences the reader and fosters ferment within him, in practice, it leads him from one perception to another. Wittgenstein calls the range of viewpoints "aspects," and creates a "semantic field" of aspect terms that constitutes the variations of use within the context of aesthetic judgment (and in general). His four basic terms are: "noticing an aspect," "'continuous seeing' of an aspect," "an aspect's 'lighting up,'" and "the change of aspect."[61] These terms will be examined in detail below, in the chapters that analyze the poetry. At this point, I wish to explain their contribution to understanding the action of "poetic grammar": the ability of an aesthetic work to express a certain aspect, on the one hand, and, on the other, to effect change in the aspect is dependent on the preparedness of the reader or viewer. This fitness includes the ability to distinguish between observation and description, and to identify an act of imaging in the poetic work. Such identification means spotting the creativity that comprises aesthetic examination and judgment:

> I learn the concept "seeing" along with the description of what I see. I learn to observe and to describe what I observe. I learn the concept "to have an image" in a different context [. . .] the concepts are thoroughly different. The concept of

60 Wittgenstein, *Philosophical Investigations*, para. 201–2. This approach is prevalent in the study of Wittgenstein's thought on rules; other approaches, however, also exist, and I will present them in the chapters on Zelda and Adaf.

61 Wittgenstein, *PPF*, para. 113, 118, 129.

> imaging is rather like one of doing rather than receiving. *Imagining might be called a creative act. (And is of course so called.)*[62]

The parallel that Wittgenstein draws between the act of imagining and creativity leads to the conclusion of his discussion of the aspect-changing action of poetic grammar, using his distinction between "taste" and "creativity." Wittgenstein deemed such a distinction necessary to describe two different ways in which language works, with no causal relationship between them. Man's having aesthetic tastes is not connected to his creativity. Nonetheless, we can compare taste and creativity, and thereby understand the sum total of language actions in the process of aesthetic judgment:

> The faculty of "taste" cannot create a new organism, only rectify one that is already there. Taste loosens screws & tightens screws, it doesn't create a new original work. Taste rectifies, it doesn't give birth [. . .] The most refined taste has nothing to do with creative power [. . .] I cannot judge whether I have only taste, or originality as well. The former I can see distinctly, but not the latter, or only quite indistinctly. And perhaps it has to be like that, & you see only what you have, not what you are [. . .] Taste can delight, but not seize.[63]

Creativity means making something new that was not there before. Taste, in contrast, is an ability that refines aesthetic sensitivity, but is based on something already in existence. Wittgenstein illustrates this with a house that he built. As, however, regards his writing, he wonders whether it can be defined as creative or only as possessing taste.[64] He suggests an intriguing psychological distinction: that a person can see what he possesses, but not what he is; accordingly, an individual cannot

62 Wittgenstein, *Zettel*, para. 637 (emphasis added).

63 Wittgenstein, *Culture and Value*, p. 67.

64 "You can as it were restore an old style in a new language; perform it afresh so to speak in a manner that suits our times. In doing so you really only reproduce. I have done this in my building work" (Wittgenstein, *Culture and Value*, p. 68).

judge whether or not his work is original. For our purposes, I maintain that Wittgenstein's distinction between creativity and taste does not attest solely to the possibility of aesthetic judgment (which is actually "taste"), it also is indicative of the ability to detach oneself from a certain form of life and create something new and original, which did not exist before. I wish to connect this to Wittgenstein's discussion of the possibility existing in language to exceed what can be verbalized within it, and to argue that poetic creativity is an example of such surmounting.

4. The Third Aspect: Showing What Cannot Be Said

> What finds its reflection in language, language cannot represent. What expresses itself in language, we cannot express by means of language.[65]
> What can be shown, cannot be said.[66]

When Wittgenstein indicated in *Tractatus* the possibility of seeing in language what cannot be said in it, he referred to language in general, and not necessarily to poetic language. Nonetheless, placing aesthetics beyond the bounds of language, as was mentioned above, raises the question of the difference between what cannot be expressed in everyday language and the way in which aesthetic language works. The ways of action discussed above—the possibility of creating introspection, and the possibility of effecting change—are conducted within the boundaries of language and are understood by means of external criteria. But aesthetic language, too, has ways of working that arouse a response to the "beauty" that is present in these manners of acting or in the meaning that is expressed. From these aspects, Wittgenstein's philosophical language is frequently fashioned as a poem, such that the metaphors that he used continue to be points of reference in the annals

65 Wittgenstein, *Tractatus*, para. 4.121.
66 Wittgenstein, *Tractatus*, para. 4.1212.

of philosophy. The most common of these is "language-game," which also encompasses the various types of aesthetic language-games.[67]

I will attempt to demonstrate throughout the book that a poetic language-game comprises, on the one hand, the ways in which grammar that is in everyday use works and, on the other, "poetic grammar," which enables us to discern the boundaries of language. In order to determine the boundary, Wittgenstein argues in *Tractatus* for the need to examine what lies beyond the boundary as well. Poetic grammar will likely effect such an understanding by means of a double action of language, in which a certain meaning is expressed in one plane, with this meaning also reflected in an expression of form or rule. The form or the rule are not explicitly stated and, in actuality, cannot be verbalized, but they enable the expression of the meaning, as well as the reader's "crossing" the boundary.

Susanne Langer was the first to develop a theory of aesthetic judgment inspired by *Tractatus*.[68] In her book, which was concerned with the ways of symbolization, and mainly with aesthetic expressions, she defined meaning as function, and stated that three factors are at work in every meaningful expression. One of these is "a pattern, in which the term itself holds the key-position," accompanied by intent expressed in functioning, and the factor/person to whom the meaning is directed.[69] Langer maintained that the pattern cannot be verbalized, but it clearly is to be heard in the function of aesthetic expression. Based on Wittgenstein's locating aesthetics beyond the boundaries of language and

67 "But how many kinds of sentence are there? [. . .] There are *countless* kinds [. . .] And this diversity is not something fixed, given once for all; but new types of language, new language-games, as we may say, come into existence, and others become obsolete and get forgotten [. . .] The word 'language-*game*' is used here to emphasize the fact that the *speaking* of language is part of an activity, or of a form of life. Consider the variety of language-games in the following examples, and in others: [. . .] Describing an object by its appearance [. . .] Reporting an event [. . .] Making up a story; and reading one [. . .] Acting in a play–Singing rounds [. . .] Requesting, thanking, cursing, greeting, praying" (Wittgenstein, *Philosophical Investigations*, para. 23).

68 Susanne K. K. Langer, *Philosophy in a New Key: A Study in the Symbolism of Reason, Rite, and Art* (New York: New American Library, 1954 [1942]).

69 Langer, *Philosophy*, p. 44.

his distinction between showing and telling, Langer suggested a way to describe, after the fact, what the creative process constitutes.

In her next book, Langer connected the pattern that cannot be verbalized with the expression of feeling. She examined the action of the aesthetic pattern in a series of aesthetic practices such as poetry, dance, and theater.[70] An aesthetic work, for Langer, is a "symbol of sentience," and it thereby shows the ineffable: the sentiment or inner process from which the work issues. Langer coined a statement that became a milestone in the history of the research of aesthetics: "Art is the creation of forms symbolic of human feeling."[71] She formulated a criterion for aesthetic judgment, writing that an aesthetic work is founded on the ability to present emotion that cannot be verbalized. The goal of an aesthetic work is not to "invent," but to express feeling that cannot be put in words.[72] This declaration leads us to ask: what is the source of that feeling that cannot be verbalized, as well as the source of the form, pattern, or symbol that the artist used in his work? As Wittgenstein puts this, we can ask, what is the connection between the aesthetic manner of organization and the reality. Langer argues that the quality of a poetic image is dependent specifically on its detachment from the reality of physical or causal order by being "an abstraction."[73]

70 Susanne K. K. Langer, *Feeling and Form: A Theory of Art Developed from Philosophy in a New Key* (New York: Scribner's, 1953).

71 Langer, *Feeling and Form*, p. 40.

72 "The concept of significant form as an articulate expression of feeling, reflecting the verbally ineffable and therefore unknown forms of sentience (capable of feelings) [. . .] All articulation is difficult [. . .] the making of a symbol requires craftsmanship [. . .] The fundamental technique of expression—language—is something we all have to learn by example and practice, by conscious or unconscious training. People whose speech training has been very casual are less sensitive to what is exact and fitting for the expression of an idea than those of cultivated habit [. . .] a utilitarian object may also be a work of art [. . .]: *Art is the creation of forms symbolic of human feelings* [. . .] Not the invention of new original terms, not the adoption of novel themes, merits the word 'creative,' but the making of any work symbolic of feelings, even in the most canonical context and manner" (Langer, *Feeling and Form*, pp. 39–40; emphasis added).

73 "Detachment from actuality, the 'otherness': The true power of the image lies in the fact that it is an abstraction, a symbol, the bearer of an idea [. . .] Something that exists only for perception, abstracted from the physical and causal order is the

While *Tractatus* is Langer's starting point, in practice she formulates a substantive criterion for aesthetic judgment, in a way that is closer to another source of inspiration for her, Peirce.

Summation

To sum up the nature of poetic grammar, we should indicate how Langer and Wittgenstein differ or agree on the relationship between "form" and "content." Wittgenstein, as does Langer, argues that the rules of grammar do not result from any relationship to the actuality, nor do they owe any loyalty to such a relationship. Grammatical rules are arbitrary, and they alone establish the meaning that is created within the context of their application. Such an assertion gives the artist unlimited freedom, and joins the possibility of creativity discussed above. Creativity is possible, according to Wittgenstein, because grammatical rules are not subject to any element external to them.[74]

Poetic grammar is therefore grammar within which something new and previously unknown can be identified. For Wittgenstein, this grammar is characterized by a number of features, none of which can be limited: its rules can be learned only after the fact, since the artist himself cannot be aware of his creativity during the process, nor even afterwards; there is no possibility of establishing any clear criterion for determining whether any specific expression is erroneous or correct, only that it is "another"; and finally, it is especially noteworthy that Wittgenstein did not erect any barrier between everyday and poetic language.[75] To the contrary, his philosophical writing brims with

artist's creation [. . .] The forms in a design [. . .] have a *life*" (Langer, *Feeling and Form*, pp. 46–47).

74 "Grammar is not accountable to any reality. It is grammatical rules that determine meaning (constitute it) and so they themselves are not answerable to any meaning and to that extent are arbitrary" (Wittgenstein, *Philosophical Grammar*, p. 184).

75 "There cannot be a question whether these or other rules are the correct ones for the use of 'not' (that is, whether they accord with its meaning). For without these rules the word has as yet no meaning; and if we change the rules, it now has another meaning (or none), and in that case we may just as well change the word too. 'The only correlate in language to an intrinsic necessity is an arbitrary rule. It is the only

creativity and aesthetic quality, and he encourages such creativity outright.

By offering the term "poetic grammar," I am not ignoring Wittgenstein's thinking that no orderly and fixed methodology of aesthetic judgment could be advanced. Although he opposed aesthetic judgment based on substantive principles, he nonetheless personally experienced the importance of the aesthetic in life, and the will to choose, evaluate, and judge aesthetic works. He consequently formulated a series of methodological proposals that cannot be united into a single uniform methodology. The notion of "poetic grammar" has judgment mainly in describing the word's place within a certain field, that is, its grammatical function that creates aesthetic quality that can be identified, evaluated, and judged. Words influence behavior, and establish for the reader "internal speech" that might generate reflection, change, and crossing the border toward what cannot be said in regular language:

> A *great deal* can be said about a subtle aesthetic difference—that is important.—The first remark may, of course, be: "*This* word fits, *that* doesn't"—or something of the kind. But then all the widespread ramifications effected by each of the words can still be discussed. That first judgment is *not* the end of the matter, for it is the *field* of a word that is decisive.[76]
>
> What is going on in my mind at this moment? That is not the point at all. Whatever went on was not what was meant by

thing which one can milk out of this intrinsic necessity into a proposition.' Why don't I call cookery rules arbitrary, and why am I tempted to call the rules of grammar arbitrary? Because I think of the concept 'cookery' as defined by the end of language. You cook badly if you are guided in your cooking by rules other than the right ones; but if you follow other rules than those of chess you are playing another game; and if you follow grammatical rules other than such and such ones, that does not mean you say something wrong, no, you are speaking of something else" (Wittgenstein, *Philosophical Grammar*, pp. 184–85).

76 Wittgenstein, *PPF*, para. 297.

that expression. What is of more interest is what went on in my behavior.[77]

Silent, "inner" speech is not a half hidden phenomenon, seen, as it were, through a veil. It is not hidden *at all*, but the concept may easily confuse us, for it runs over a long stretch cheek by jowl with the concept of an "outer" process, and yet does not coincide with it.[78]

77 Wittgenstein, *PPF*, para. 298.
78 Wittgenstein, *PPF*, para. 301.

CHAPTER 2

Dialogical Grammar: Variations of Dialogue in Wittgenstein's Methodology as Ways of Self-Constitution

In the preceding chapter I drew a parallel between philosophy and poetry as the basis for aesthetic judgment. In this chapter we will take another step in understanding Wittgenstein's methodology by examining the dialogic aspect of his language, as the key to understanding a poem as dialogue. A poem, even when it concentrates on the "I"-speaker, addresses the other and communicates with him, both directly and obliquely; Wittgenstein's philosophical language in his *Philosophical Investigations* acts in the same manner.[1]

Wittgenstein shed light on the dialogic aspect of every language-game, from the language of builders and shopping lists to that of poetry

1 The references are to the fourth and revised edition of Wittgenstein, *Philosophical Investigations* (2009). In addition to the new translation and reediting, this edition contains an important new feature: the second part (*PPF*) was reordered and divided into sections. It is also noteworthy that the title given to the second part: "Philosophy of Psychology—A Fragment" reflects a trend that began in the 1980s and intensified in the last decade, namely, that Wittgenstein was occupied, in a focused and intentional manner, with the psychology of the individual, in order to understand the activity of language. For our purposes, it will be important to examine the psychology of the individual within the creation and existence of fertile dialogue.

and philosophy.[2] In order to understand how that dialogic language acts in the interpretation of poetry, we must first closely examine the types of dialogic grammar in *Philosophical Investigations*. Such inquiry is necessary, because poetry uses these types indirectly, while Wittgenstein's *Philosophical Investigations* enables us to examine them directly, as we look at the use of dialogism in clarifying the features of various concepts. We will see how Wittgenstein enrichened the concept of "dialogue" in a manner relevant to interpretation in numerous realms, in addition to that of poetry.

Dialogism is not only a methodology; it is also a fundamental position by which meaning is constituted in a dialogic process, including the meaning of inner mental processes. In his later work, Wittgenstein extensively discussed the nature of states of consciousness, in an attempt to characterize the differences between them, while at the same time contending with the instances in which they can hardly be distinguished. To this end he employed a range of dialogues, each of which embodies a different aspect of the action of language. I will then seek to show that his range of dialogical usages is not incidental. Rather, an examination of the nature of the dialogue aids in clarifying the nature of the action that is conducted, or that of the state of consciousness, when at times a number of actions are conducted in tandem, or a number of states of consciousness occur in parallel, as, for example, pain and hope, or longing and understanding. Wittgenstein thus created a methodology of reflective dialogue that is likely to aid us in understanding complex situations by examining the grammatical rules that establish them.

The discussion of Wittgenstein's contribution to clarifying the nature of dialogical usage is of importance for two reasons. One is that the first part of Wittgenstein's magnum opus, *Philosophical Investigations*, is written in dialogical fashion (he did not compile the second part). In the introduction to the fourth edition, the editors went so far as to stress the need for a new translation, to adapt its grammatical

2 Wittgenstein, *Philosophical Investigations*, para. 1, 2, 130, 531.

usages to the conversational character of the book.[3] In practice, during the Vienna Circle period Wittgenstein had already employed a dialogical method of conversation, questions and answers, and the use of dialogical terminology such as "aspect" and "game," which will be discussed below.[4]

Furthermore, his students composed additional books as conversations, which reflect the manner in which Wittgenstein would teach and talk with them.[5] In light of this being both a writing method and a method of oral teaching, it seems that a separate discussion, beyond the scholarly discussion up to now, is needed regarding the relationship between the dialogical nature of writing and teaching and its content, that is, the ways in which language works.[6] Although much has been written about Wittgenstein's philosophical language, his choice of a dialogical method is perceived as a rhetorical technique meant to convince us of the correctness of a certain position, as an example of what can be said in language or to dispel disquietude and illusions.[7] Such uses certainly exist, and will be exemplified below; in the current book I wish to show that Wittgenstein's methodology contains a dominant aspect of "dialogical grammar," in two senses: the first includes

3 "We have also favoured colloquial compression, as in 'I'm,' 'I'll,' 'he'd,' 'we'd,' 'isn't,' 'aren't,' 'won't' and 'wouldn't,' rather more than Anscombe, in order to bring out the conversational tone of the writing" (p. xiii).

4 Ludwig Wittgenstein and Friedrich Waismann, *The Voices of Wittgenstein*, trans. Gordon Baker et al. (London: Routledge, 2003).

5 One of the major relevant works is *Wittgenstein's Lectures on Philosophical Psychology 1946–1947* (1988), from which we will exemplify dialogical usage; see also Wittgenstein, *Lectures and Conversations.*

6 See Beth Savickey, *Wittgenstein's Art of Investigation* (London: Routledge, 1990), who relates to Wittgenstein's manner of teaching, and cites testimonies by his students to his lectures having the nature of meetings and lengthy conversations, and not that of frontal instruction (pp. 58–59).

7 An outstanding example of this is provided by the scholarly reference to Wittgenstein's recurring discussion of the relationship between "picture" and "use." Marie McGinn, *Routledge Philosophy Guidebook to Wittgenstein and the Philosophical Investigations* (London: Routledge, 1997), for instance, presents the awareness of the difference between picture and use as being conscious of the existence of a number of uses (p. 85). In the current book, however, I will argue that this does not refer to a number of alternate uses, but to a dialogue between simultaneously functioning states of consciousness.

the technical plane of punctuation marks that denote addressing another, such as quotation marks, question marks, and exclamation points, all of which belong to "surface grammar." The second sense is in the plane of "depth-grammar," which includes Wittgenstein's references to sources of influence, whether explicit (Frege, Augustine, James, Plato) or implicit (either conscious or not, with which he became acquainted in the context of his "form of life").

A second aspect that requires a discussion of the connection between manner and content in dialogical methodology is a series of terms based on "dialogical consent" that Wittgenstein coined in order to understand the action of language, such as "rule," "family resemblance," "form of life," and more. In order to describe the nature of dialogue from a linguistic perspective, we will argue that Wittgenstein created a "strategy of understanding" in which the use of language is not based solely on technical capability or, alternately, on mystic ability, but on mutual understanding that is expressed in agreement on definitions and judgments.[8] The above terms have been intensively discussed in the scholarly literature, and I do not intend to elaborate on them, only to argue that the dialogical nature of *Philosophical Investigations* is the basis that facilitates them all. In his dialogical format Wittgenstein delineated a triad (meaning-creature-understanding) each of whose three elements participates in the conduct of a meaningful linguistic activity. This move is based on the need for justification, under certain conditions and circumstances that always include the discourse (a potential one, which is not necessarily expressed and vocal) of more than a single person. Since Wittgenstein mentioned Platonic dialogue in his *Philosophical Investigations*, we should begin by comparing

8 This argument was raised by Herman Parret, "Contexts as Constraints on Understanding in Dialogue," in *Dialogue: An Interdisciplinary Approach*, ed. Marcelo Dascal (Amsterdam: Benjamins, 1985), p. 167, who continued to develop it following John Searle, and claimed that it is possible to distinguish between "shared intentionality" and "shared awareness of the context of discourse" (p. 168). In contrast, I wish to argue that, in addition to the existence of agreed-upon meaning in dialogue, Wittgenstein's thought also contains an irreducible aspect of solipsism that also functions as dialogue. Marcelo Dascal, *Dialogue*, p. 3, called this "semantic solipsism"; I will expand on this below.

Wittgensteinian dialogues with those of Plato, especially in light of Wittgenstein's methodological directive to examine philosophical questions by a comparison between language games.[9]

The discussion and its aims will proceed as follows: in the first stage, we will examine what Wittgenstein adopted and what he rejected from among the features of Platonic dialogue; in the second, we will see how language functions as the foundation for thought in the Platonic dialogues, and especially in soliloquy; in the third, how dialogue between states of mind is generated in Platonic dialogue; and finally, I will propose a Wittgensteinian methodology that is based on features of Platonic dialogue, and that includes three types of dialogue: rhetorical, conversational, and reflective dialogue, each of which will be described in detail, in order to understand its uniqueness. We will end the discussion by showing how the different dialogue types are used and adapted for the various goals of self-constitution. Since each type enables different actions and certain states of mind, we will see in the continuation of the book, in the analyses of the poems, how their dialogical grammar constitutes the states of mind that facilitate self-constitution.

1. "Family Resemblance" between the Platonic Dialogue and Wittgenstein's Methodology

1.1. Wittgenstein's Critique of Socrates

Plato's dialogues have been the subject of broad and diverse scholarly attention, beginning in the nineteenth century, with emphasis placed on the division into three periods, with the dialogues in each being of completely different nature. An alternate interpretation for the division into periods that is relevant for a study of Wittgenstein was offered by Charles Kahn, who proposed viewing the differences between the types of dialogue in Plato's writings as reflective of transitions between different directions in the positions he held.[10] We can see the similarity

9 Wittgenstein, *Philosophical Investigations*, para. 130.

10 Kahn presents Plato as critical of his own writings. And this is not all: he regards the significant change that occurred in Plato's dialogues as forgoing the pretension

between Kahn's interpretation of the way in which the dialogues function in Plato's writings and Wittgenstein's discussion in the second part of the *Philosophical Investigations* of "changing aspect" (as will be exemplified below), but we should first scrutinize the seeming difference between them.

In the few instances in which Wittgenstein used the term "dialogue," he did so to express his vigorous opposition to the Platonic dialogue, both as didactic and scholarly method and as content:

> I can characterize my standpoint no better than by saying that it is the antithetical standpoint to the one occupied by Socrates in the Platonic dialogues. For if I were asked what knowledge is, I would enumerate instances of knowledge and add the words "and similar things." There is no shared constituent to be discovered in them since none exists. The traditional conception of the use of concept-words hangs together with the idea that the meaning of a word is something that must be present at the same time as meaningful use is made of the word. It is as if words were labels of bottles with particular contents, and if I take down the bottles, I thereby have my hands on the stated fluid contents as well. If it is objected that the words "and similar things" do not give the concept a boundary, I can only say that the application of concept-words is in most cases actually not bounded. If one compares a concept, as Frege did, with an area in the plane, one could say that the use of a concept corresponds to an area with blurred boundaries.[11]

Wittgenstein is critical of the Socratic concept of "forms" that appears in the Platonic dialogues. He uses the bottle and fluid metaphor to

of imparting knowledge and teaching, *in favor of the transition to the rhetoric of persuasion* (Charles Kahn, *Plato and the Socratic Dialogue* [Cambridge: Cambridge University Press, 1996], pp. 376–77, emphasis added). This transition can be seen as paralleling that between the *Tractatus* and *Philosophical Investigations.*

11 Wittgenstein, *Voices of Wittgenstein*, pp. 33–34.

illustrate the perception of content as form, and its applications as fluid. Wittgenstein claims that knowledge cannot be bounded; it is possible only to show its expressions, and therefore no narrower concept can be bounded. All that is possible is to show the various embodiments of any concept, without any possibility of setting its boundaries. The methodology that Frege already proposed is comparative, and waives essentialism. In effect, this is another formulation of the "family resemblance" in *Philosophical Investigations*, or of Wittgenstein's critique in *Blue and Brown Books* of the "craving for generality."[12] Wittgenstein clearly opposed the attempt—that he found reflected in the Platonic dialogues—to clarify the nature of things by means of the relation between a concept and its embodiment. This disagreement is implied in the negation of the very dialogical method as a key to understanding or explanation.[13]

1.2. Similarities between Wittgensteinian and Socratic Dialogue

Along with this, in a number of passages in *Philosophical Investigations* Wittgenstein cites the dialogue *Theaetetus*, in a way that attests to his acquaintance with complex conceptions of language in the Platonic dialogues.[14] In para. 46, for example, he raises one of the fundamental questions that explain the transition from *Tractatus* to *Philosophical Investigations*: "What lies behind the idea that names really signify simples?" In response, Wittgenstein cites Socrates in *Theaetetus*, as asserting that *primary elements* cannot be defined (emphasis in the original). He continues to quote Socrates, who discusses the boundaries of a name, which cannot determine if something exists or not, and

12 See Wittgenstein, *Philosophical Investigations*, para. 66–67; Ludwig Wittgenstein, *The Blue and Brown Books* (Oxford: Basil Blackwell, 1969), p. 17.

13 "Reading the Socratic dialogues, one has the feeling: what a frightful waste of time! What's the point of these arguments that prove nothing and clarify nothing" (Ludwig Wittgenstein, *The Collected Works of Ludwig Wittgenstein* [Oxford: Basil Blackwell, 1931 (Internet version)], p. 55).

14 Wittgenstein, *Philosophical Investigations*, para. 46, 48, 518. Maurice Drury even quoted Wittgenstein, who claimed that "Plato in this dialogue is occupied with the same problems that I am writing about" (Maurice O. Drury, "Some Notes on Conversations," in *Recollections of Wittgenstein*, p. 149).

therefore, in practice: "It is impossible to give an explanatory account of any primary element." In the end of the section, Wittgenstein compares Socrates' position to "Russell's 'individuals' and my 'objects' (*Tractatus Logico-Philosophicus*)." Then, in para. 48, he analyzes the action of calling by name and demonstrates its role in the language-game of "representation." These sections can be seen as an expansion and exemplification of para. 43: giving names is one way to impart meaning, alongside others. This does not mean that it is faulty, merely that it is part of a language-game (just as presenting Augustine's stance regarding children's learning of language is not refutable, but only partial).[15]

Beyond Wittgenstein's directly quoting the Platonic dialogues, maintaining their original wording, I wish to indicate additional points of similarity between the conception of language in those dialogues and Wittgenstein's study of language in *Philosophical Investigations*. I will show below how this family resemblance is a basis for understanding the importance of dialogue in *Philosophical Investigations*, not only as a methodology, but also as cognitive content, in the instances in which Wittgenstein examines concurrent states of consciousness. After exploring the types of dialogue in *Philosophical Investigations*, I will propose the term "aspects-dialogue" to describe dialogue between two distinct states of consciousness. The singularity of such dialogue lies in its inclusion of more than a single state of consciousness by the same speaker, and in its action, which transforms the dialogical method into an expression of content, and not only of manner.

15 In para. 518, too, Wittgenstein quotes a dialogue from *Theaetetus* that discusses the relation between image and picture, and between "something" and "something real" as the starting point for proving the necessity of grammar for understanding during the course of visual perception. Actually, Wittgenstein continues the Platonic dialogue in a formulation similar to what was described above, with the dialogical method illustrating the process of clarification that exists within the context of the reality of a conversation between people, and not as theoretical thought.

Savickey already indicated the methodological similarity between *Philosophical Investigations* and the Platonic dialogues, in, for instance, examining the conduct of children to understand the use of language (Savickey, *Wittgenstein's Art of Investigation*, p. 75).

1.3. Language as a Medium of Thought: Soliloquy as Ordinary Language

In the first stage, I will seek to demonstrate how the dialogical perception of thought was already embraced by Socrates, in, for instance, the dialogue *Theaetetus*, which portrays language as a substrate for thought.[16] Socrates depicts the thought process as founded in an inner cognitive dialogue that is composed of questions and answers, affirmations and oppositions. This process continues until thought reaches something clear, whether as a result of the inner conversation or as a "leap." This process ends as an inner process, when, either gradually or suddenly, a person formulates a judgment by means of a statement. This statement is not intended for another person, nor is it formulated vocally:

> Socrates: A talk which the soul has with itself about the objects under its consideration [. . .] The soul when it thinks is simply carrying on a discussion in which it asks itself questions and answers them itself, affirms and denies. And when it arrives at something definite, either by a gradual process or sudden leap, when it affirms one thing consistently and without divided counsel, we call this its judgment [. . .] to judge is to make a statement, and a judgment is a statement which is not addressed to another person or spoken aloud, but silently addressed to oneself.[17]

Two points are important for our discussion: first, the dialogical process set forth here is not rhetorical (in order to persuade of the rightness of a certain claim), nor is it based on agreement between individuals. Second, formulation in language is a condition for the implementation of a process within the consciousness. Such formulation is not intended

16 David Sedley used the phrase "Language as the Medium of Thought" as a subtitle for his "Plato on Language" (in *A Companion to Plato*, ed. Hugh H. Benson [Oxford: Wiley-Blackwell, 2009], p. 214).

17 Plato, *Plato: Complete Works*, ed. John M. Cooper (Cambridge: Hackett, 1997), *Theaetetus*, pp. 189e–90a.

for any communicative act, but for a person's reflective activity within himself. This reflectivity is comparable to Wittgenstein's discussion of the will in *Tractatus*: a person can know his will; it is the will that gives meaning to the individual's world, so that he will be happy or wretched, but he can formulate it only within the boundaries of his language, and he cannot influence facts that are formulated in the general language.[18] While Socrates formulates this dialogical method as a response to the question of what is thought, for Wittgenstein in *Tractatus*, reflective thought has the nature of soliloquy. In *Investigations*, in contrast, reflective thought is clarified by means of dialogue, and while soliloquy exists, it is expressed by general language, which is not limited by the boundaries of a certain person. This view is stated concisely in the latter work:

> A human being can encourage himself, give himself orders, obey, blame and punish himself; he can ask himself a question and answer it. So one could imagine human beings who spoke only in monologue, who accompanied their activities by talking to themselves.[19]

Wittgenstein concludes by denying the existence of an individual criterion that cannot be known by another person. At the same time, soliloquy occurs in the reality, and the language used by the speaker is "ordinary language." That is to say, Socrates and Wittgenstein concur that even if the speaker chooses not to vocalize his thoughts, this is not due to the impossibility of expression in general language, it rather is a choice that has its source in the speaker's intent to refrain from vocal expression.

18 "If the good or bad exercise of the will does alter the world, it can alter only the limits of the world, not the facts—not what can be expressed by means of language. In short the effect must be that it becomes an altogether different world. It must, so to speak, wax and wane as a whole. The world of the happy man is a different one from that of the unhappy man" (Wittgenstein, *Tractatus*, para. 6.43).

19 Wittgenstein, *Philosophical Investigations*, para. 243.

1.4. Reflective Dialogue: Dialogue between Sense-Perception and Image

In the second stage, I will attempt to show how a more complex cognitive reality is portrayed in the dialogue *Philebus*, which can be characterized as a dialogue between states of consciousness. Socrates portrays for Protarchus a situation in which different states of consciousness appear concurrently in the consciousness, and lead to the conclusion that there is more than a single factor responsible for creating cognitive content. The dialogue between Socrates and Protarchus is completely rhetorical, but the content of what Socrates says indicates a cognitive dialogical method that might pose an obstacle to judgment:

> Socrates: If memory and perception concur with other impressions at a particular occasion, then they seem to me to inscribe words in our soul, as it were. And if what is written is true, then we form a true judgment and a true account of the matter. But if what our scribe writes is false, then the result will be the opposite of the truth. [. . .]
> Socrates: Do you also accept that there is another craftsman at work in our soul at the same time? [. . .] A painter who follows the scribe and provides illustrations to his words in the soul. Protarchus: How and when do we say he does this work?
> Socrates: When a person takes his judgments and assertions directly from sight or any other sense-perception and then views the images he has formed inside himself, corresponding to those judgments and assertions.[20]

I will show below how Wittgenstein related to this difficulty and resolved the tension. At this juncture, however, I want to conclude the comparison between the Socratic dialogical method and that of Wittgenstein, taking note of the similarity between the directives for examining meaning in accordance with the use made of the word, since

20 Plato, *Complete Works*, *Philebus*, p. 38c.

the same word could naturally have different meanings.[21] In both instances, dialogue functions as a method that enables both its use and its understanding in relation to other possible uses. In the dialogue *Euthydemus* Plato shows how to use "learning" to denote opposites, and energetically advises examining the manner in which the word is used in order to decide upon its meaning (as does Wittgenstein in *Philosophical Investigations*, since the verb "use" appears in countless passages in the book):

> You must learn about the correct use of words [. . .] You did not realize that people use the word "learn" not only in which a person who has no knowledge of a thing in the beginning acquires it later, but also when he who has this knowledge already uses it to inspect the same thing, whether this is something spoken or something done. (As a matter of fact, people call the latter "understand" rather than "learn," but they do sometimes call it "learn" as well.) Now this, as they are pointing out, had escaped your notice—that the same word is applied to opposite sorts of men, to both the man who knows and the man who does not.[22]

The possibility of using the same word to denote something and its opposite (learning refers both to the acquisition of knowledge without any prior basis and to the acquisition of already existing knowledge) requires us to conduct a meticulous examination of the specific manner of use in order to determine meaning. We cannot make do with knowledge of the "inherent" meaning of a word, for even if a person knows all the meanings of words (as Socrates later argues), he cannot predict the nature of a certain use. The parallelism to the concept of use in *Philosophical Investigations* is clear: Wittgenstein, too, bases any

21 See Sedley, "Plato on Language," pp. 214–27, for an exhaustive examination of Plato's discussions on the nature of language, and particularly on equivocation.

22 Plato, *Complete Works*, *Philebus*, pp. 277e–78c.

examination of meaning on the nature of its use, even if it seems to us there is some preexisting picture or attempt.[23]

This parallelism is supported by an additional argument, based on the considerable differences between people: in the dialogue *Sophist*, the guest says to Theaetetus that, even if there is agreement on a certain name for something, each of them might view it differently; consequently, the agreement concerning the essence of the matter must be specified verbally, and they should not make do merely with agreement on the name (*Sophist*, p. 218). This view regarding use parallels Wittgenstein's argument on the need to agree concerning definitions and judgments in order to conduct fruitful communicative actions.[24] In summation, we see a series of parallels between the Socratic dialogues and the conception of language in *Philosophical Investigations* that is reflected in dialogical grammar, with these parallels sharing an inherent linkage between grammar and everyday life: language reflects human conduct, which is dynamic, cannot be defined on the basis of "quantitative scientific knowledge," is mainly dialogical, and is based on agreement.

2. Wittgensteinian Dialogical Grammar in the *Philosophical Investigations*: Rhetorical, Conversational, Reflective

2.1. Dialogism in the *Philosophical Investigations*: "A Surveyable Representation"[25]

> Almost the whole time I am writing conversations with myself. Things I say to myself tête-à-tête.[26]

23 See, e.g., Wittgenstein, *Philosophical Investigations*, para. 59 and many others.

24 "'So you are saying that human agreement decides what is true and what is false?' What is true or false is what human beings *say*; and it is in their *language* that human beings agree. It is not only agreement in definitions, but also (odd as it may sound) agreement in judgments that is required for communication by means of language" (Wittgenstein, *Philosophical Investigations*, para. 241–42).

25 Wittgenstein, *Philosophical Investigations*, para. 122.

26 Wittgentein, *Culture and Value*, p. 88 (December 26, 1948).

Although Wittgenstein's methodology that uses dialogue with another in *Philosophical Investigations* is unmistakable, Wittgenstein research relates to it only infrequently, and emphasizes the rhetorical effect of dialogue, to convince us of Wittgenstein's unequivocal stance on central issues, such as the possibility of private language, or the possible existence of second sense.[27]

Actually, when Wittgenstein uses the word "dialogue," he generally is critical of Plato's usage (as in the passage from *Voices* cited above). When, however, he portrays conversations that he conducted with his fellows, or routine communicative acts between people, he uses the words *Gesprach*, *Gesprachen* (conversation). In practice, Wittgenstein regarded conversation as a central medium in human activity, and as the key to understanding our use of language.[28] Indicating the regulatory nature of the conduct of a conversation, in the course of which it seems to us that the listener perceives the meaning of what is said by the encounter with the manner in which he perceives this meaning in his own mind, Wittgenstein created defamiliarization of a routine everyday activity (the language-game of reporting). He did so in order to argue that the process of transmitting meaning in a

27 A prevalent contemporary scholarly view relates to dialogue only incidentally, within other discussions, as, for example, in the context of private language when dialogue is harnessed in support of the position attributed to Wittgenstein (McGinn, *Routledge Philosophy Guidebook*, pp. 134–35). Even in works that give pride of place to interpersonal discussions, as Rush Rhees, *Wittgenstein and the Possibility of Discourse*, ed. Dewey Z. Phillips (Cambridge: Cambridge University Press, 1998), that describes dialogue as essential, not only as a expression of control of the technique of language, but also for understanding the nature of the discussion, the nature of dialogue is shunted aside in favor of the underlying clarification of the way in which what is understood is distinguished from what is not (*Routledge Philosophy Guidebook*, pp. 90–91). In the final analysis, we conclude that speaking in language does not always entail discussion (*Routledge Philosophy Guidebook*, p. 94).

28 "What is the language-game of communicating something? I'd like to say: you regard it too much as a matter of course that one can communicate anything to anyone. That is to say, we are so much accustomed to communicating in speech, in conversation, that it looks to us as if the whole point of communicating lay in this: that someone else grasps the sense of my words—which is something mental—that he, as it were, takes it into his own mind. If he then does something further with it as well, that is no part of the immediate purpose of language" (Wittgenstein, *Philosophical Investigations*, para. 363).

conversation is complex, and its success is not self-understood. Notwithstanding this point, this language-game reflects the fact that speech, conversation, is the "straight highway" for the transmission of meaning between two people.

The original word that Wittgenstein used in the above passage, *Selbstgesprache*, illustrates, without irony or any rhetorical interest, the nature of the Wittgensteinian dialogue in *Philosophical Investigations*. He would customarily write his works as a conversation with himself, conducted in private. Wittgenstein's reflective awareness of the manner of his writing did not prevent him from typifying it as the key to understanding his future activity, that is, he did not give priority to what is said in the first person when someone is speaking to himself.[29] This said and done, he applied this dialogical method in *Philosophical Investigations* in such a way that at times it is difficult to determine whether he is documenting an inner dialogue, or one with another person. In any event, by using the term "dialogical grammar," I wish to argue that we can find in Wittgenstein's depth grammar a range of rules that are based in dialogue: context-grounded conversation of (at least) two principals, mutual recognition (by one factor of the other), and agreement regarding its regulatory nature.[30] On the surface-grammar level, at times these rules are invisible or are only alluded to, but in any event they allow us to base the discussion on them, as was noted by Jane Heal.[31] The understanding of dialogical grammar, even if the reader

29 The following passage is an important example of this: "At the question 'Why don't I infer my probable actions from my talk?' one might say that it is like this: as an official in a ministry I don't infer the ministry's probable decisions from the official utterances, since of course I am acquainted with the source, the genesis of these utterances and of the decisions.—This case would be comparable to one in which I carry on conversations with myself, perhaps even in writing, which lead me to my utterances out loud in conversation with other people; and now I say: I shall surely infer my future behavior, not from these utterances, but from the far more reliable documents of my inner life" (Wittgenstein, *Remarks*, para. 711).

30 See Wittgenstein, *Philosophical Investigations*, para. 664. Gordon Baker, "Wittgenstein's 'Depth Grammar,'" *Language & Communication* 21 (2001), pp. 3003–19, already pinpointed the connection between depth grammar and the form of life which conditions its overall understanding.

31 "The fact that the dialogue element in the *Investigations* is introduced so inexplicitly and is not signposted by some uniform devise enables Wittgenstein to

faces it on his own, entails a waiver of unequivocal conclusions and the constant movement between one aspect and another, in the attempt to clarify the connections between mental processes and the language in which they are fashioned.

The dissimilarity between the manner of argumentation in *Tractatus* and that of *Investigations* is already evident from a comparison of the introductions to the two books. In *Tractacus* Wittgenstein argues:

> The truth of the thoughts that are here communicated seems to me unassailable and definitive.[32]

In his introductions to *Philosophical Investigations*, in contrast, he presents the book as an album that evades the possibility of indicating a single coherent and clear direction.[33] Furthermore, the presence of an interlocutor is pronounced in the latter, both formally and rhetorically. On the formal level, many sections in the book raise or answer a question. Rhetorically, this fashions a conversation. While Wittgenstein's statements in *Tractacus* are formulated as logical arguments, with an unequivocally declarative tone that brooks no dispute, only rarely do we find in *Philosophical Investigations* emphatic claims that do not develop into a renewed discussion. To this we should add Wittgenstein's methodological directives to avoid definitions and to accept the impossibility of unequivocal definitions (and therefore we must make do with indicating the "family resemblance" between things). I will attempt to show how the dialogical method suits Wittgenstein's arguments, following his claim that there is no difference between method

foreground it or background it to the extent that seems most appropriate to him at any given stage of the discussion" (Jean Heal, "Wittgenstein and Dialogue," in *Philosophical Dialogues*, ed. Timothy Smiley [Oxford: Oxford University Press, 1995], p. 72).

32 Wittgenstein, *Tractatus*, para. 24.

33 "My thoughts soon grew feeble if I tried to force them along a single track against their natural inclination. And this was, of course, connected with the very nature of the investigation. For it compels us to travel criss-cross in every direction over a wide field of thought [. . .] So this book is really just an album" (Wittgenstein, *Philosophical Investigations*, pp. 3–4).

and content, because there is no "second-order language."[34] At the same time, however, I wish to demonstrate how we nevertheless can distinguish between the various ways of language use that represent different ways in which the language functions, further to Wittgenstein's argument that language functions in different ways.[35] This differentiation between ways of usage is made possible methodologically by the dialogue that facilitates the fashioning of a distinct intersubject process that is not subservient to another or prior order. This illustrates how language enables the expression of a singular encounter between two factors that are not subject to generalization, definition, or standardization. There are all manner of types of duality: two people, two aspects in the experience of a conflict by a certain person or by two parties. In any event, in some instances we can speak of duality that is regulative, and not a one-time occurrence, and that cannot be reduced to an unequivocal description.

I chose as examples three aspects that appear more than others, and that concretely illustrate the function of the dialogical method, with these aspects being part of a broader array of differences between the language of *Tractatus* and that of *Philosophical Investigations*.

2.2. Aspects of Dialogism

The first prevalent aspect, which is technical-rhetorical, is often used by Wittgenstein to present one of the frequent arguments in *Philosophical Investigations*, such as the need to examine meaning in the context of use, the inherent connection between language and everyday actions, the avoidance of theories, second-order language, and more. The second aspect relates to instances in which Wittgenstein mentions, either directly or incidentally, the conversants with whom he conducted discussions, such as Frege and Ramsey, or virtual conversants such as Plato, Augustine, and William James. The third aspect concerns

34 Wittgenstein, *Philosophical Investigations*, para. 121.

35 "The paradox disappears only if we make a radical break with the idea that language always functions in one way, always serves the same purpose: to convey thoughts which may be about houses, pains, good and evil, or whatever" (Wittgenstein, *Philosophical Investigations*, para. 304).

dialogue between states of consciousness. In my survey of this aspect I will attempt to show how, even when Wittgenstein eventually casts the die in a certain manner, the dialogical method reflects the possible existence of two parallel states, even if these are two concurrent states of consciousness. Above I reviewed the characteristics of the dialogical method, which enables us to see the great similarity to Wittgensteinian dialogue, more than Wittgenstein and his researchers have shown.

2.3. Dialogue as Technique

The dialogical format of most of *Philosophical Investigations*, as well as many passages in Wittgenstein's books that were published posthumously, is at the center of the affinity between Platonic and Wittgensteinian dialogue. Furthermore, dialogue is most frequently used (both by Plato and by Wittgenstein) to clarify commonly used terms or conceptions, with dialogue functioning as a technique for shaking off an illusion pertaining to the nature of language. In Wittgenstein's first use of the word *Technik*, in the sense of a system of rules governing a game, he argues that even though we establish a "technique," it does not enable us to control the conduct of the game.[36] The result is a contradiction between what we expected would happen and what actually took place; consequently, we say: "That's not the way I meant it."[37] On the level of surface grammar, except for the sentence enclosed in quotation marks (as in a conversation), the dialogical grammar is expressed in the recurring use of the first-person plural. This creates the sensation that all the readers are participating in joint activity, and they all sense the contradiction between individual intent and the actual activity in the game. On the depth-grammar level,

36 "Here the fundamental fact is that we lay down rules, a technique, for playing a game, and that then, when we follow the rules, things don't turn out as we had assumed. So that we are, as it were, entangled in our own rules. This entanglement in our rules is what we want to understand: that is, to survey. It throws light on our concept of meaning something. For in those cases, things turn out otherwise than what we had meant, foreseen [. . .] That is just what we say when, for example, a contradiction appears: 'That's not the way I meant it.' The civic status of a contradiction, or its status in civic life—that is the philosophical problem" (Wittgenstein, *Philosophical Investigations*, para. 125).

37 Wittgenstein, *Philosophical Investigations*, para. 125.

Wittgenstein offers the ultimate example of tension in a dialogical context, when there is a differential or contradiction between the speaker's intent and his action in the context of the shared language. Wittgenstein returns in para. 664, too, to the example of intent in order to illustrate the role of depth grammar, and—which is important—emphasizes the gap between the two types of grammar that emerges in dialogical application, between a person's wording when speaking to himself and the use of agreed-upon rules in actual speech. The dialogue between the two uses preserves the possibility of distinguishing between depth and surface grammar, and therefore is a technique for the expression of the philosophical "problem."[38]

Wittgenstein's depiction of the attempt to distinguish between fantasy and reality is an outstanding example of the function of dialogue as technique. This is a rare instance of Wittgenstein's use of the word "dialogue" to denote an effective technique, and not as a critique of Plato. Along with the use of dialogical grammar on the surface level (the directing of questions, quotations), Wittgenstein used the writing of dialogue as a technique for exploring the nature of his thought activity. As I argued above, dialogue functions as an imagined technique that allows us to determine whether the speaker is fantasizing or not.[39]

This passage also indicates two additional functions of dialogue. One, self-dialogue, between a dreamer and himself, which Wittgenstein presents as "quite imaginable"; and the other, "dialogue of a play," that reveals the possibility of a gap between language games. In the dialogue of a play, the playwright does not attest to his intent in the reality, but only to the intent of the speaker in the play. While the

38 Wittgenstein, *Philosophical Investigations*, para. 664.

39 "Suppose it were part of my day-dream to say: 'I am merely engaged in phantasy,' would this be true? Suppose I write such a phantasy or narrative, an imaginary dialogue, and in it I say 'I am engaged in phantasy'—but, when I write it down,—how does it come out that these words belong to the phantasy and that I have not emerged from the phantasy? Might it not actually happen that a dreamer, as it were emerging from the dream, said in his sleep 'I am dreaming'? It is quite imaginable that there should be such a language-game. This hangs together with the problem of 'meaning.' For I can write 'I am healthy' in the dialogue of a play, and so not mean it, although it is true. The words belong to this and not that language-game" (Wittgenstein, *Zettel*, para. 397).

inner dialogue in a dream does not display any specific technique, dialogue in a play, in contrast, is an example of dialogue as an agreed-upon technique in the context of a literary-artistic language game. Dialogue similarly serves as a function for clarifying a series of "problems and disquietudes."[40] Following Augustine, Wittgenstein argues that it is the simple things that are hidden from sight.[41] Just like Platonic dialogue, Wittgensteinian dialogue creates defamiliarization that makes it possible to examine the simple things, since dialogical grammar contains addresses to another and the asking of questions, techniques that require a reexamination of the instinctive manner in which we generally act in language. Dialogue as technique is not only a rhetorical means, it also is a psychological instrument (in the Wittgensteinian sense, in which psychological terms aid in distinguishing between different uses of language). By means of dialogue, a person may extricate himself from a linguistic move that seems necessary when communicating with himself, and correctly understand it with "external criteria" that make this possible.[42] At times, however, dialogue with a conversant is required to illuminate a certain understanding.

2.4. Conversational Dialogue

From the beginning of and throughout his philosophical career, Wittgenstein constantly engaged in conversations and correspondences, in the first stage with his teachers, Frege and Russell, and afterwards with his students and colleagues.[43] He mentioned these dialogues both

40 Wittgenstein, *Philosophical Investigations*, para. 111.

41 Wittgenstein, *Philosophical Investigations*, para. 90.

42 Wittgenstein, *Philosophical Investigations*, para. 580.

43 In the introduction to *Tractatus*, Wittgenstein seemingly negated the importance of finding the sources of intellectual inspiration for what he wrote. In the introduction to *Philosophical Investigations*, in contrast, he makes the ability to understand the problems in the former, as well as the stimulus and clarification at the basis of the book, conditional upon his conversations with his colleagues Ramsey and Sraffa:

> For since I began to occupy myself with philosophy again, sixteen years ago, I could not but recognize grave mistakes in what I set out in that first book.

generally, and in *Philosophical Investigations*, also during the formulation of specific arguments. To this we should add testimonies to the clear influence of thinkers to whom he related (Kierkegaard) or whom he cited (James, Augustine). Whether or not Wittgenstein agreed with them regarding any specific argument, we can see the very citation as presenting their argument as a challenge worthy of consideration and response.[44] His dialogue with Frege is an outstanding example of this. On the one hand, Wittgenstein disputes Frege's claim that the ability to be formulated means a move in language.[45] In another place, on the other hand, he agrees with Frege that a name is insufficient to mean something, since a name has meaning only in the context of a sentence.[46]

The meaning of "dialogical grammar" is that dialogue is conducted as conversation with another philosopher (either real or virtual), colleague, or student-colleague. In this "conversation" Wittgenstein contends with his conversant's position or question, since it allows for the clarification of a difficulty in comprehending the action of language. In *Philosophical Investigations*, when Wittgenstein mentions Augustine, Frege, or James, he does not present the thinker as having raised the

> I was helped to realize these mistakes to a degree which I myself am hardly able to estimate—by the criticism which my ideas encountered from Frank Ramsey, with whom I discussed them in innumerable conversations during the last two years of his life. Even more than to this—always powerful and assured a criticism, I am indebted to that which a teacher of this university, Mr P. Sraffa, for many years unceasingly applied to my thoughts. It is to this stimulus that I owe the most fruitful ideas of this book (Wittgenstein, *Philosophical Investigations*, p. 4).

See also para. 81 n.

44 Russell Goodman, *Wittgenstein and William James* (Cambridge: Cambridge University Press, 2004), already suggested this interpretation, and offered a comprehensive examination of Wittgenstein's dialogue with James. His position, however, is not representative of most scholarly opinion.

45 "Frege's opinion that every assertion contains an assumption, which is the thing that is asserted, really rests on the possibility, found in our language, of writing every assertoric sentence in the form 'It is asserted that such-and-such is the case'. But 'that such-and-such is the case' is *not* a sentence in our language—it is not yet a *move* in the language-game" (Wittgenstein, *Philosophical Investigations*, para. 22).

46 "With the mere naming of a thing, nothing has yet been done. Nor *has* it a name except in a game. This was what Frege meant too when he said that a word has meaning only in the context of a sentence" (Wittgenstein, *Philosophical Investigations*, para. 49).

issue to his own consciousness, but as one who engaged this matter anyways, and formulated an expression (such as James's "if-feeling") or prevalent insight (such as learning by ostensive definition, as in Augustine). It therefore is not surprising that the prevalent scholarly view maintains that in his deliberations with other thinkers, Wittgenstein was not actually influenced by any of them, but rather used their statements to justify his own stance.[47] Since, however, Wittgenstein himself wrote *Philosophical Investigations* in dialogue format, while including statements by these philosophers, this question should be reexamined.

Unlike this widely held view, I maintain that in *Philosophical Investigations* and additional late writings, as in his activity in the Vienna Circle, Wittgenstein frequently referred to other positions, not only to dispute them or as rhetoric, but also as a catalyst for a more precise formulation of his arguments, or as a source for important, major questions to be discussed. Wittgenstein expressed complete agreement with his conversant only infrequently, but this does not detract from the importance of the conversation. In this sense, there is a marked resemblance to the Platonic dialogues, each of which is named after the main speaker who converses with Plato. This "other speaker," whether fictitious, representing Plato himself, or an actual speaker, fills a similar function: revealing (generally dialectically) the various facets of the discussion, which usually does not arrive at an unequivocal definition of a concept, even if consensus is obtained.[48]

47 "Wittgenstein rarely quotes other authors and when he does so, he brings attention to where he differs rather than where he agrees with them" (Todor Polimenov, "Wittgenstein in Conversation with His Sources: *Anspielungen und Zitate im Werk Ludwig Wittgensteins* by H. Biesenbach," *Nordic Wittgenstein Review* 1 [2012], p. 200). See also Jackman's thorough discussion and conclusion: "In conclusion, in spite of the fact that James was one of the most frequently cited authors in the *Investigations*, he was not one [sic] 'a classical opponent of the tradition in the philosophy of mind that [Wittgenstein] was opposing.' There remain, of course, serious differences between the two philosophers, but in terms of what was central to their outlook, Wittgenstein and James were far less apart than has been commonly assumed" (Henry Jackman, "Wittgenstein and James's 'Stream of Thought,'" *Meeting of the Society for the Advancement of American Philosophy* [2004], p. 9).

48 This position is represented, e.g., by Sedley, "Plato on Language," who divided the Platonic dialogues into periods, with the later dialogues characterized by discourse

Another example of conversational dialogue can be seen in dialogues that were not edited by Wittgenstein, in the collection of his lectures on psychological concepts that mainly documents dialogues between Wittgenstein and his students.[49] Wittgenstein begins his attempt to describe "motive," in contrast with "reason," with the reservation that we cannot automatically assume that all humans learn and know how to use all language-games. Notwithstanding this, in the context of the description of a motive or reason for action, a person elucidates, not only for himself, but also for his surroundings, why he performed a certain action.[50] A reason is given or a factor is described in dialogical fashion, since at least in this conversation, a person does not have to explain to himself, but only to another, why he performed a certain act. A linguistic-ethical discussion as well, ensues from this question, since Malcolm suggests that if a person offers an absurd reason for murder, it cannot be defined as a motive. Intriguingly, Wittgenstein himself, as a teacher, struggles with the question of when different terms should be used to describe the background for a certain action ("It's not clear to me")[51] and, mainly, how his students' questions lead him to the cardinal distinction between the reason for an action and the motive. As regards the former, a person can explain to himself the connection between two moves (for instance: I remain in my work, because I need money.)[52] As for the latter, Wittgenstein draws a parallel between the murderer's explanation and a bull's response to a red flag: the connection between the facts is evident, but cannot be justified ethically or causally by the person; it "just happens."

lacking unequivocal answers/definitions. See also Samuel Scolnikov, *Idea and Method: Thirty-Three Studies in Plato* (Jerusalem: Magnes, 2008), pp. 301–7 (Hebrew), on Plato's two different perceptions of language that create an open, skeptical, and reserved dialogical language.

49 Ludwig Wittgenstein, *Lectures on Philosophical Psychology 1946–1947*, ed. Peter Geach (Chicago: University of Chicago Press, 1988).

50 Wittgenstein, *Lectures on Philosophical Psychology*, pp. 82–84.

51 Wittgenstein, *Lectures on Philosophical Psychology*, p. 83.

52 Wittgenstein, *Lectures on Philosophical Psychology*, p. 83.

2.5. Reflective Dialogue

Reflective dialogue is the third type of dialogue, and is the most complex and vaguest of the three types presented here. This is so because it is mixed together with dialogues of other types and because it combines a person's inner conversation, which is fashioned by public criteria so that it will be comprehensible to someone else. A person's choice not to share this conversation with another ensues from the need for privacy, embarrassment, or shame, but not from a lack of linguistic possibility.[53] Language functions as a mechanism that enables reflection, self-examination, and self-knowledge, as Wittgenstein uses dialogue numerous times in the course of the *Philosophical Investigations* to describe self-observation (*Selbstbeobachtung aussprechen*).[54] For example, when the speaker portrays longing and expectation, which he experiences as an inner process:

> "I've heard he is coming; I've been expecting him all day." This is a report on how I have spent the day. In conversation, I come to the conclusion that a particular event is to be expected, and I draw this conclusion in the words "So now I must expect him to come." This may be called the first thought, the first act, of this expectation.
>
> The exclamation "I'm expecting him—I'm longing to see him!" may be called an act of expecting. But I can utter the same words as the result of self-observation, and then they might amount to: "So, after all that has happened, I'm still expecting him with longing." It all depends on what led up to these words.[55]

53 In his discussion of Wittgenstein's notion of private language, Norman Malcolm, *Ludwig Wittgenstein: A Memoir* (Oxford: Oxford University Press, 1984), coined the term "contingent private language." This means that a person can conduct a conversation that, for various reasons, is wholly inner, and therefore his language seems private (but it is possible that other people will understand what is said in this conversation if the speaker chooses to include them). Such use of language ensues from the need for privacy, and Wittgenstein himself exemplified this when he wrote "secret diaries" while a prisoner of war during the First World War.

54 Wittgenstein, *Philosophical Investigations*, para. 586.

55 Wittgenstein, *Philosophical Investigations*, para. 586.

This passage graphically illustrates the role of dialogue, since Wittgenstein lists both the surface-grammar function and the depth-grammar role, thereby shedding light on the use of *Selbstbeobachtung*. Wittgenstein wrote of the process that occurs on the surface level in the consciousness of the speaker, in the description of the process from expression to conclusion, when these take place "in conversation" in the individual's consciousness. He then distinguishes between "first thought" and "exclamation," that expresses "an act of expecting." Here we have two types of "self-observation": the first watches the actions of language: reporting, conversation, contemplation, and expectation. The second is also directed to a certain conclusion beyond the distinction between the actions of language. The conclusion contains a sort of self-criticism ("After all that has happened, I'm still expecting him with longing"). Wittgenstein next seeks to clarify the nature of "the process of introspection." This process functions as a reconstruction of past states of consciousness, and differs from self-observation in the present. It is noteworthy that Wittgenstein uses dialogical language only in relation to the present (and not to the past) to depict a situation of indecision followed by decision.[56]

An additional example of introspective activity formulated in dialogical grammar is when self-observation facilitates distinguishing between levels of intent:

> "When you were swearing just now, did you really mean it?" This amounts to something like: "Were you really angry?" And the answer may be given on the basis of introspection, and is often some such thing as "I didn't mean it very seriously," "I meant it half jokingly," and so on. There are differences of degree here.[57]

Self-observation enables the detection of differences of degree in the speaker's intent. Such distinction is made possible by the inner dialogue by means of which the speaker clarifies the degree of seriousness of his intent.

56 Wittgenstein, *Philosophical Investigations*, para. 588.
57 Wittgenstein, *Philosophical Investigations*, para. 677.

Wittgenstein's discussions of memory constitute an additional example of an inner dialogue in which two states are compared. Wittgenstein does not directly relate to the dialogue *Meno*, in which Socrates portrays search and learning as recollection, which is dependent on a person's courage and continual quest, but we can see the similarity.[58] These three actions—searching, learning, and recollection—are characteristic of Wittgenstein's investigation of the traits of inner processes in which memory is a participant.[59] In this context he also raises the need for an external criterion to indicate an action of memory; at the same time, "we *bear in mind*" the model we select to determine whether we remember it. That is, a reflective dialogue is conducted between the remembered model and a specific use in the present, such as the attribution of a certain color to an object.[60]

An additional point of similarity between the depiction of recalling in *Meno* and the description of inner processes is to be found in the argument that the occurrence of an individual process is based on a potential mental mechanism that can be spotted only when an action is conducted in the context of general, public language. Socrates' claim that "the soul has learned everything," and man can consequently recall specific things when he learns them is analogous to Wittgenstein's argument that the pedal action is based on the existence of an entire mechanism that, despite being hidden from sight, is necessary for a concrete action to take place.[61] Moreover, this context, too, is identical to that in *Meno*: Wittgenstein uses the metaphor of pedal and mechanism in order to depict a process of learning by ostensive definition.[62]

A completely different type of dialogical mutual relationship that is reflected in the use of language in the speaker's consciousness already appeared in *Notebooks 1914–1916*, and in matching arguments in

58 Plato, *Complete Works*, *Meno*, pp. 81c–d.

59 See, e.g., Wittgenstein, *Philosophical Investigations*, para. 53, 56, 166.

60 Wittgenstein, *Philosophical Investigations*, para. 56.

61 "'I set the brake up by connecting rod and lever.'—Yes, given the whole of the rest of the mechanism. Only in conjunction with that is it a brake-lever, and separated from its support it is not even a lever; it may be anything, or nothing" (Wittgenstein, *Philosophical Investigations*, para. 6).

62 Wittgenstein, *Philosophical Investigations*, para. 6.

Tractatus. These works contain inner-conscious dialogue of two types: the first, dialogue between what is present within the bounds of language and what definitely exists, but is situated beyond the bounds of language (and the world);[63] and the second, the dialogue between what is said and what is shown, which cannot be explicitly expressed.[64] In this context, we can distinguish between two rule types that establish the use of language: normative-consensus rules, and logical rules that are independent of human consent.[65] Here, as well, we are speaking of reflective dialogue in which a person accepts his decisions in the realms of ethics, aesthetics, and belief when, according to Wittgenstein, these decisions cannot be justified on a factual basis, and therefore cannot be justified in general language. Nonetheless, instead of remaining silent, as Wittgenstein suggests at the end of *Tractatus*, we could say that in order to make conscious decisions in these realms, a reflective dialogue occurs in which the possibilities are examined.

In conclusion, Wittgenstein's dialogical notion of language can be illustrated by his anthropomorphization of the word as having a face that looks at us and seemingly requests a response, like a face in a painting. Continuing in this vein, the statement creates a "group-picture." Notwithstanding this, the existence of factors that might engage in dialogue with each other does not excuse us from the question of how meaning comes into existence, but rather directs our attention to the boundaries between which meaning is created:

> While any word—one would like to say—may have a different character in different contexts, all the same there is one character—a face—that it always has. It looks at us.—For one

63 Wittgenstein, *Notebooks 1914–1916*, pp. 72–73.

64 "Propositions cannot represent logical form: it is mirrored in them. What finds its reflection in language, language cannot represent. What expresses itself in language, we cannot express by means of language. Propositions show the logical form of reality. They display it [. . .] What can be shown, cannot be said" (Wittgenstein, *Tractatus*, para. 4.121, 4.1212).

65 Wittgenstein's statement "Grammar is not accountable to any reality" (Ludwig Wittgenstein, *The Big Typescript 213*, ed. and trans. Grant Luckhardt and Maximilian Aue [Oxford: Blackwell, 2005], p. 185) demonstrates the claim for linguistic independence.

> might actually think that each word was a little face; the written sign might be a face. And one might also imagine that the whole proposition was a kind of group-picture, so that the gaze of the faces all together produced a relationship among them and so the whole made a significant group. But what constitutes the experience of a group's being significant? And would it would be necessary, if one is to use the proposition, that one feel it as significant in this way?[66]

A study of the wealth of dialogic features in *Philosophical Investigations* and in other late writings by Wittgenstein produces a central conclusion and a number of secondary ones. My major conclusion is that dialogue, in all its types, contends with the tension resulting from the gaps between, on the one hand, public language which is not dictated by and/or subject to the individual speaker and, on the other, the speaker. At times this tension raises difficulties (in the use of language, conflict between states of mind), while in others it encourages creativity in language (as the motive force of fashioning and of the inclusion of more than a single state of mind).

On one level, our study offers a hierarchy of dialogue types, in which rhetorical dialogue is the most technical and straightforward, followed by conversational dialogue and, finally, reflective dialogue, which is composed of all three types and contains contradictions, thereby most successfully reflecting the features of self-consciousness as it acts within the context of public language.

On another level, the three types of dialogue can be seen as acting simultaneously in many language uses, with different degrees of dominance. This integrative action well illustrates how language has been a medium for thought from the time of Platonic dialogue to Wittgenstein. Our most important conclusion, therefore, is in the realm of psychology: the need to accept the mediation of dialogic grammar, in its various types, in any use we make of language.

66 Wittgenstein, *Remarks*, para. 322.

CHAPTER 3

Self-Constitution through Mystical Grammar: The Urge and Its Expressions

> There are, indeed, things that cannot be put into words. They make themselves manifest. They are what is mystical.[1]
>
> What can be shown, cannot be said.[2]
>
> The urge towards the mystical comes of the non-satisfaction of our wishes by science.[3]
>
> Grammar is not accountable to any reality.[4]

The question of Wittgenstein's influence on mysticism, religion, and spirituality began to significantly enter Wittgenstein research only in the 1990s. Despite the explicit mention of the mystical in *Tractatus*, Wittgenstein's "warning" to remain silent about what lies beyond the boundaries of language was taken seriously by Wittgenstein scholars. The research follows two main directions (that at times are combined): the first examines Wittgenstein's personal position on these questions, the sources that influenced him, and his personal decisions. The second

1 Wittgenstein, *Tractatus*, para. 6.522.

2 Wittgenstein, *Tractatus*, para. 4.1212.

3 Wittgenstein, *Notebooks 1914–1916*, p. 51.

4 Wittgenstein explains this statement as he continues: "It is grammatical rules that determine meaning (constitute it) and so they themselves are not answerable to any meaning and to that extent are arbitrary" (Wittgenstein, *Philosophical Grammar*, p. 184).

direction contends with the problematic presence of metaphysical elements in Wittgenstein's thought, in light of what is perceived as a declaration to discuss only what can be verbalized, only within the boundaries of language. My central argument in this context is that the mystical traits characteristic of the poetry of Amihai, Kosman, and Adaf have not been given the exhaustive discussion they deserve. The adaption of Wittgenstein's arguments to such an analysis follows from the "family resemblance" between his approach to mysticism and the mystical features of these corpora of poetry: the mystical springs flows out of the game within the boundaries of language, and does not emerge from a metaphysical position that precedes experience (the Hasidic-mystical ideas in Zelda's poetry have been subjected to scholarly inquiry, but not in the manner that I propose).

The mystical, like other Wittgensteinian terms in this work, sheds light on an important and central aspect of longing, in the Platonic sense.[5] This longing for the possibility of seeing the world as "sub specie aeterni" and to comprehend the meaning of "problems of life" is based on the unjustifiable confidence in the possibility of such understanding.[6] This self-consciousness is not based on logical proof, but on a "gamble" (as Blaise Pascal asserted), or a "leap" (as was stated by Kierkegaard, who greatly influenced Wittgenstein). The choice of the mystical, as it emerges from the above passage by Wittgenstein, begins as the urge to explore the boundaries of language.[7]

5 I wish to stress that in my discussion of mysticism in Wittgenstein's writings, I do not relate to the question of the centrality of mysticism in his thought as a whole.

6 Wittgenstein, *Tractatus*, para. 6.45, 6.52.

7 "I see now that these nonsensical [ethical or religious] expressions were not nonsensical because I had not yet found the correct expressions, but that their nonsensicality was their very essence. For all I wanted to do with them was just *to go beyond* the world and that is to say beyond significant language. My whole tendency and I believe the tendency of all men who ever tried to write or talk Ethics or Religion was to run against the boundaries of language. This running against the walls of our cage is perfectly, absolutely hopeless [. . .] But it is a document of a tendency in the human mind which I personally cannot help respecting deeply and I would not for my life ridicule it" (Ludwig Wittgenstein, *Philosophical Occasions 1912–1951*, ed. James C. Klagge and Alfred Nordmann [Indianapolis, IN: Hacket, 1993], p. 44).

Two constitutive and active types of world in the consciousness of the subject, as set forth by Wittgenstein in *Tractatus*, are of great importance for analyzing the corpora of poetry that I will examine: the factual world, which can be described in language, and the mystical world—which contains the will of the subject, ethics, aesthetics, and religious belief, and is encapsuled in the term "mystical." The latter, for Wittgenstein, comprises all that cannot be verbalized, but whose existence might be a certainty.[8] At times, this can be partially shown, while in other instances it is a basis for action. On occasion tension arises between what can be verbalized and what the speaker wants to perceive or express. The main point that I wish to show is that the complexity of the mystical sphere longs, at heart, to give meaning to life. This thirst is not dictated, nor does it come from any tradition, it rather results from a lack of emotional and experiential satisfaction from what the world of science has to offer, as Wittgenstein declares. This lack of satisfaction meets language, and finds its indirect expression by means of grammar.[9] Language can act independently of the factual world, and therefore enables the subject who thirsts for the mystical to express this longing. Language's ability to express the world of the subject includes decisions that exceed the boundaries of factual language and is summed up in the statement: "The limits of my language mean the limits of my world."[10] This assertion has a dual function: on one level, the boundaries of the language of the subject *limit* the

8 I do not intend to argue that Wittgenstein was a "mystical type," in the sense of studying mystical texts or engaging in mystical practices, as was already emphasized by his direct students. I maintain that he constituted mystical grammar, that includes the grammar of everyday language and that relates to life in this world and its meaning. See, e.g., the testimony of his friend Paul Engelmann: "Above all, he was never a mystic in the sense of occupying his mind with mystic-gnostic fantasies. Nothing was further from his mind than the attempt to paint a picture of a world beyond (either before or after death), about which we cannot speak. (He says in the *Tractatus* that the fact of a life after death could explain nothing)" (Paul Engelmann, *Letters from Ludwig Wittgenstein*, trans. L. Furtmuller, ed. B. F. McGuinness [Oxford: Basil Blackwell, 1967], p. 79).

9 "What finds its reflection in language, language cannot represent. What expresses itself in language, we cannot express by means of language. Propositions show the logical form of reality. They display it" (Wittgenstein, *Tractatus*, para. 4.121).

10 Wittgenstein, *Tractatus*, para. 5.6.

boundaries of his world; while, on the other hand, the flexibility of language enables it to be used *in accordance* with the boundaries of the subject.

These two possibilities, of setting limits or of adapting the boundaries of language to the world of the subject, will serve our discussion of the mystical. Following Wittgenstein, I will attempt to show three possible meanings of the mystical that will be relevant for our analysis of the poems. All three exhibit influences by philosophers such as Augustine, Kierkegaard, and William James, but Wittgenstein is unique, beyond the fine polishing and conciseness of his arguments, in his enabling us to examine the embodiment of the different forms of the mystical experience *in language*. Accordingly, his position is more suitable for literary analysis.

Three Channels of Mystical Grammar

Mystical expressions, in Wittgensteinian meanings, typify the poetry of Zelda, Amihai, Kosman, and Adaf, and are a major element in constituting the subject-speaker in the poems. The four poets are far removed, each in his or her own way, from the conventional conceptions of mysticism, although, on occasion, we find features of such notions in their poetry. The "family resemblance" between them is based mainly on the individual feeling of longing for a meaningful expanse that cannot be described verbally, as Wittgenstein presented this at the end of *Tractatus*. Notwithstanding this point, such sentiment is indirectly expressed by linguistic means, so that we can indicate its visibility in the grammar that I call "mystical grammar." This sentiment includes a number of expressive channels, three of which I wish to examine.

The *first channel* is religious, in the sense that it is centered around some conception of God. This stance has paradoxes or tension that can be contained by means of mystical grammar (unlike the logical grammar that demands their resolution). For example, the paradox of commitment to a general system of values, as opposed to commitment to personal authenticity, or the paradox of belief in revelation in a world of what cannot be located and proven.

The *second channel* is based on containing the paradox of the "I": on the one hand, a person does not identify the "I" when he speaks in the first person, while, on the other, certainty and privileged access to the innermost realms of his psyche are ascribed to the one speaking in the first person. This paradox is contained in the mystical plane in which, while everyday language cannot contain the subject, who is the limit of the world, mystical language is capable of relating to him. Many discussions have been devoted to this issue; I will base my analysis of the self-constitutive exploration of poetry on a discussion of self-constitution as object and as subject. This is based on the distinction between "I as object" and "I as subject" that was first made by William James (see below). Notwithstanding this, in the philosophical discussions of self-constitution in language, Wittgenstein is considered to be the first to show the relevance of this distinction for understanding the use of the first person in language. In order to examine self-constitution in poetic language, I suggest using these methodical terms to show when the speaker bases his self-constitution on verifiable description and, in contrast, when a move that is primarily mystical is depicted. The category of "I as subject" includes subjective expressions of decisions that are not a result of causal rationalization and that are described as nouns which express drastic change that cannot be foreseen, such as "leap," "epiphany," or "conversion."[11]

The *third channel* is poetic writing as an act of self-mending on the ethical plane by means of inner contemplation, confession, and cultural criticism. These are evident in the writing indirectly, and not as an intentional, direct declaration. Additionally, the source of the motivation for self- and cultural mending is inner, in the will of the subject that Wittgenstein placed beyond the boundaries of the world and language.

11 John Churchill drew a parallel between the epiphany scene in *The Wind in the Willows* by Kenneth Grahame and Wittgenstein's description of aspect-drawing, which he connected to religious belief (see below for an extensive discussion of this connection). See John Churchill, "Rat and Mole's Epiphany of Pan: Wittgenstein on Seeing-Aspects and Religious Belief," *Philosophical Investigations* 21, no. 2 (1998), pp. 152–72.

Actually, the three grammatical channels (also) direct social criticism at the prevalent culture: the first channel presents an alternative to scientific supremacy, the second emphasizes the constitution of subjectivity in an era of blindly following societal conventions, and the third is directed to constant self-criticism against the temptations in language, which also represent the countless seductions of culture.

1. Preliminary Considerations: Theology as Grammar and the Metaphysical Subject

Wittgenstein argued that the mystical, the logical, and the aesthetic are beyond the boundaries of language, so that they all lack the possibility of verbalization. Together with this, we can find a few distinctions that enable us to differentiate between the three planes by paying attention to what each allows to be shown during the use of language. The logical plane contains the grammar that enables the creation of sensible propositions in language.[12] The realm of the aesthetic, as was discussed at length in the preceding subsection, makes possible the presentation of linguistic creativity along with aesthetic expressions that only personal taste can assess. The mystical sphere, which is of concern to us here, enables us to explore the emotional and mental processes that represent the longing for a spiritual expanse that gives meaning to the individual's life, along with various ways and degrees of the realization of this yearning.

Wittgenstein spoke of the mystical only infrequently, but I maintain that his thought contains comments that if collected will produce a mystical grammar.[13] What Wittgenstein sees as the three central

12 "When something falls under a formal concept as one of its objects, this cannot be expressed by means of a proposition. Instead it is shown in the very sign for this object. [A name shows that it signified an object, a sign for a number that it signified a number, etc.]" (Wittgenstein, *Tractatus*, para. 4).

13 Almost every scholarly discussion of this issue in Wittgenstein's thought begins by mentioning this fact, since Wittgenstein engaged in few direct discussions of the mystical, in its various aspects. Nevertheless, Wittgenstein's arguments regarding the mystical continue to be of interest, and a number of studies on this issue have been published. See, e.g., Fergus Kerr, *Theology after Wittgenstein* (Oxford: Basil Blackwell, 1986); Norman Malcolm, *Wittgenstein: A Religious Point of View?*, ed. Peter Winch (Ithaca, NY: Cornell University Press, 1993); Tim Labron,

features of the mystical appear in the above passage: some things cannot be formulated in language, but nevertheless are embodied in it; we long for the mystical results because scientific inquiry fails to satisfy our aspirations (as Wittgenstein attests about himself, which was already mentioned in the discussion of aesthetic judgment, above); and language can act (also) unrelated to the reality. Grammar's freedom from the reality allows language to also embody contents that are not based in logical grammar, but rather are grounded in a consistency of another sort that at times is paradoxical. In comparison with the lack of satisfaction from scientific research that results in an aesthetic creation, a different sort of dissatisfaction arises in a mystical context. The mystical urge ensues from the desire to locate and express the essence of our experience and existence as individuals in the world. This need finds expression in the drive to understand the essential nature of the world that awakens during logical study, when the investigation of the facts does not suffice for man, and he seeks to understand what enables these facts in his thought and in the world.[14]

Wittgenstein's Religious Point of View (London: Continuum, 2006); Genia Schonbaumsfeld, *A Confusion of the Spheres: Kierkegaard and Wittgenstein on Philosophy and Religion* (Oxford: Oxford University Press, 2007); and Tim Labron, *Wittgenstein and Theology* (New York: Continuum, 2009). Additionally, Stephen Mulhall (a leading Wittgenstein scholar) highlighted the importance of Wittgenstein's discussions for a contemporary definition of religiosity: "It is rare to find a philosopher of religion who does not define her own position, at least in part, by specifying the nature of and the grounds for her rejection of work carried out under the Wittgensteinian banner. In this respect, that work continues to function as an essential reference point in the discipline" ("Wittgenstein and the Philosophy of Religion," in *Philosophy of Religion in the Twenty-first Century*, ed. Dewi Zephaniah Phillips and Timothy Tessin [Houndmills: Palgrave, 2001], p. 95).

14 "For logic seemed to have a peculiar depth [. . .] logical investigation explores the essence of all things. It seeks to see to the foundation of things [. . .] It arises neither from an interest in the facts of nature, nor from a need to grasp causal connections, but **from an urge to understand the foundations, or essence, of everything empirical.** Not, however, as if to this end we had to hunt out new facts; it is, rather, essential to our investigation that we do not seek to learn anything *new* by it. We want to *understand* something that is already in plain view. For *this* is what we seem in some sense not to understand. Augustine says in *Confessions* XI.14, 'quid est ergo tempus? si nemo ex me quaerat scio; si quaerenti explicare velim, nescio' [. . .] Something that one knows when nobody asks one, but no longer knows when one is asked to explain it, is something that has to be *called to mind*"

Many studies assume a distinction between the early and late Wittgenstein regarding, inter alia, the relation between what can be said and what we must pass over in silence when examining how language works. A minority of scholars find continuity between *Tractatus* and *Philosophical Investigations*, and show how arguments that can be deemed metaphysical are formulated within the boundaries of language.[15] I wish to add to this interpretive direction a similarity between the two books that affords us an intriguing perspective on poetic language. I cited the passage containing Wittgenstein's main innovation, which is at the center of *Philosophical Investigations*, to introduce my discussion of poetic grammar. Now I wish to turn to a parenthetical statement of his: "Grammar tells what kind of object anything is. (Theology as grammar.)"[16] Wittgenstein parenthetically takes note of a realm that in *Tractatus* was presumably set beyond the boundaries of language: theology. Now we learn that theological propositions, too, can be formulated, and they constitute a representative example for the central principle in *Philosophical Investigations*. In this clause Wittgenstein brings theological propositions, too, within the bounds of grammar, and applies to theology the argument that grammatical rules reflect the essence of what is said in them. Along with this, it is noteworthy that this is the only positive reference to theology in the book. To explain its presence at such a central junction in the book, we should return to *Tractatus* (while embracing Wittgenstein's directive regarding "theology as grammar"):

> Thus there really is a sense in which philosophy can talk about the self in a non-psychological way. What brings the self into philosophy is the fact that "the world is my world." The philosophical self is not the human being, not the human body, or

(Wittgenstein, *Philosophical Investigations*, para. 89; (here and below, when a quotation contains two types of emphasis, italics are in the original, bold has been added).

15 The first significant discussion of this possibility (and the most comprehensive to the present) is to be found in John Webber Cook, *Wittgenstein's Metaphysics* (New York: Cambridge University Press, 1994).

16 Wittgenstein, *Philosophical Investigations*, para. 373.

> the human soul, with which psychology deals, but rather the metaphysical subject, the limit of the world—not a part of it.[17]

Wittgenstein's main aim in *Tractatus* was to indicate the boundaries of language: what can be said, and what we should pass over in silence. As was mentioned above, Wittgenstein argued that ethics, aesthetics, and the mystical lie beyond the boundaries of language, and therefore silence is fitting for them. Notwithstanding this, he asserted that the subject that is the boundary of the world is a metaphysical subject. What is the meaning of this "metaphysical" quality, and how can it be resolved with the commitment (that Wittgenstein scrupulously observes in all his discussions) to say only what can be uttered within the boundaries of language?

If we are faithful to Wittgenstein's statement in *Tractatus* that the subject is metaphysical, this means, in short, that he embodies a will that is beyond the boundaries of language. This will constitutes the meaning of the world for the subject, and can be divided into various planes that are outside the limits of language: the ethical, the aesthetic, and the mystical. Despite their being beyond the boundaries of language, there might be linguistic creations that show them, even if they do not verbalize them.

This starting point develops as a consequence of one of the features of poetic grammar: the preceding discussion spoke of the possibility of an aesthetic creation to show a form without verbalizing it, and thereby producing a sort of "container" for the reader's emotional identification with the description. I now wish to argue that this is the first stage of the possibility inherent in language of exceeding the bounds of what may be said in it. In the second stage, movement is made toward the mystical. The poet delineates rules for the expression, not only of the aesthetic, but also of the mystical. This is possible, first and foremost, due to the autonomy of language.

The movement toward the mystical is also driven by additional factors (see below). I wish to show how the mystical expresses a holistic

17 Wittgenstein, *Tractatus*, para. 5.641.

perspective that facilitates a "surveyable representation" of events in the world.[18]

It should be stressed that language is the medium by means of which the mystical can be indicated, even if it cannot be directly verbalized; otherwise, Wittgenstein's insights could not aid us in analyzing poetic language. Language acts in all manner of ways, and can accompany all our activities, including moods that have no external expression and states of consciousness that can be verbalized only after the fact.[19] These characteristics chart the boundaries of the coming discussion of the presence of the mystical in poetic language.

2. The Mystical-Religious Channel: The Religious Aspect of Mystical Grammar

> My type of thinking is not wanted in this present age. I have to swim so strongly against the tide. Perhaps in a hundred years people will really want what I am writing [. . .] I am not a religious man but I cannot help seeing every problem from a religious point of view.[20]

By saying this, Wittgenstein connected the religious aspect that characterized his perspective on the world with his critique of the age in which he lived. He claimed that there was an inherent difficulty in understanding the way he thought in his time, and he felt completely opposed to the prevailing *Zeitgeist.* He immediately continued by specifying the uniqueness of his way of thinking, in that he was fated to view every question from a religious perspective, despite his not being

18 Wittgenstein, *Philosophical Investigations*, para. 122.

19 Wittgenstein frequently portrayed language's powerlessness, for example, in the context of pain (*Philosophical Investigations*, para. 245, cited above), or when the picture that remains in our consciousness prevents us from seeing the use of words (*Philosophical Investigations*, para. 306). At the same time, language enables our attesting to such situations, and thereby accompany them, as it accompanies all our actions (*Philosophical Investigations*, para. 23).

20 Quoted in Drury, "Some Notes on Conversations," p. 79.

a religious man.[21] The sense of inner necessity expressed in this statement reflects a Wittgensteinian paradox typical of mystical grammar: the lack of commitment, in contrast with an inner need for some commitment. This tension already appeared in Wittgenstein's early writings, enabling us to indicate an interesting relation between *Notebooks 1914–1916* and *Tractatus*. In the former, Wittgenstein formulated a series of arguments that constitute mystical grammar, in the religious sense.[22] He began with a claim of knowledge of the existence of the world, continued by mentioning the problematic nature of giving meaning to the world from within it, followed by drawing a parallel between the meaning of life and God:

> What do I know about God and the purpose of life? I know that this world exists [. . .] That something about it is problematic, which we call its meaning. That this meaning does not lie in it but outside it. That life is the world [. . .] The meaning of life, i.e. the meaning of the world, we can call God [. . .] To pray is to think about the meaning of life.[23]

Wittgenstein depicts in his *Notebooks* how God emerges during the search for the source of the meaning of life. In *Tractatus*, however, he chose to do this only partially and in abbreviated fashion, in a manner that created immanent tension. There are three such tensions. The first is the tension between two types of meaning: the meaning within the limits of language and the world and that beyond. Consequently, the goal of philosophy is paradoxical: it must show what can be said, its meaning lies specifically in what cannot be verbalized.[24] The second is

21 Norman Malcolm was the first to speak of the meanings of this declaration. See Malcolm, *Wittgenstein*.

22 For a detailed description of this issue, see my article: Dorit Lemberger, "Wittgenstein and Religious Belief: Between 'Theology as Grammar' and 'A Religious Point of View,'" *Iyyun* 52 (2003), pp. 399–424 (Hebrew).

23 Wittgenstein, *Notebooks 1914–1916*, pp. 72–73.

24 "It will signify what cannot be said, by presenting clearly what can be said" (Wittgenstein, *Tractatus*, para. 4.115); "The sense of the world must lie outside the world" (*Tractatus*, para. 6.41).

the tension between the present and eternity: meaning can be constituted only in the present, but a sense of the eternal is embodied in this activity.[25] The third is the tension between immanence and transcendence: meaning is discussed throughout *Tractatus* as a function of logical grammar, and the term "God" is mentioned three times, simply to denote a type of belief that is not relevant for understanding meaning in the world. Toward the end of the book, God is mentioned in another way, with His existence linked to certainty in the existence of the mystical and the possibility of viewing the world as a whole.[26] Taking into account the meticulous editing of *Tractatus*, we can wonder why Wittgenstein chose to place these tensions at the end of the book. We already mentioned Wittgenstein's argument (para. 4.115) on the way to achieve the aim of philosophy, but it could be further argued that Wittgenstein wanted in this manner to distinguish between the grammar of mystical-religious arguments and the grammar of everyday language. Based on this, we can understand Stephen Mulhall's portrayal of how Wittgenstein developed the "grammatical investigation" of religious expressions.[27] Wittgenstein's important contribution is the argument that religion, too, has grammar, syntactical rules that constitute deep grammar and surface grammar, which act differently from and independently of the working of the grammar of everyday language, or that of scientific or historical research. This said and done, this grammar has practical consequences. The point I wish to make is that religious grammar places at its center a conception of God that gives meaning to the world, but this is a personal notion that cannot be directly verbalized. Mulhall maintains that religious grammar is not committed to a historical or empirical mechanism, and therefore can speak of God

25 If we take eternity to mean not infinite temporal duration but timelessness, then eternal life belongs to those who live in the present" (Wittgenstein, *Tractatus*, para. 6.4311).

26 "How things are in the world is a matter of complete indifference for what is higher. God does not reveal himself in the world" (Wittgenstein, *Tractatus*, para. 6.432); "It is not how things are in the world that is mystical, but that it exists. To view the world sub specie aeterni is to view it as a whole—a limited whole. Feeling the world as a limited whole—it is this that is mystical" (*Tractatus*, para. 6.44–6.45).

27 Mulhall, "Wittgenstein and the Philosophy of Religion."

as a possibility, not necessary as actually existing, but rather "what it would be like if there were (or if there were not) such a thing as God."[28]

The religious and personal semantic field is based on emotion and imagination. The figurative language of poetry offers it a fertile expanse for fashioning, because it is designated, from the outset, for representing others, comparisons, and the intentional creation of expanse. Unlike everyday language, with its practical goals, poetical language is directed to the search for meaning that originates beyond the boundaries of practical language. In the following chapters I will attempt to show how each of these poets fashioned the features of language that is capable of portraying existential meaning that lies beyond the boundaries of language. We will conclude the discussion of the religious aspect of mystical grammar by relating to a controversial question, in the context of Wittgenstein's conception of religiosity, one that is important both for understanding his religious stance and for comprehending its application in the study of poetry: the question of fideism.[29] The possibility of understanding a religious position from "outside" is bound up with a profound understanding of its inherent commitment, and it is far from being self-understood as are other common language-games (such as marriage or inheritance procedures, as John Austin explains). As I demonstrated, Wittgenstein's view is complex, but in the final analysis, even if the personal aspect in a religious position that cannot be verbalized is emphasized, when its expression is created in language, it may be understood. Mulhall stresses in his discussion of religious grammar that, not only is it possible to understand this position, the Wittgenstein researcher is duty-bound to do so.[30] Understanding this grammar means comprehending the manner in which concepts of religiosity are incorporated in and influence daily practices. Application,

28 Mulhall, "Wittgenstein and the Philosophy of Religion," p. 99.

29 For a comprehensive discussion, see Lemberger, "Wittgenstein and Religious Belief."

30 "A Wittgensteinian is committed [. . .] to the clarification of the grammar of the words [. . .] What provides that clarification in the case of religious belief is [. . .] how they in fact employ religious concepts in the practices which go to make up their lives" (Mulhall, "Wittgenstein and the Philosophy of Religion," p. 108).

for our purposes, means the attempt to understand how the concepts of religiosity are included in poetical practice.

The analogy that Mulhall sets forth, in the name of Norman Malcolm, between Wittgenstein's notion of grammar and his religious conception is of especial importance. Mulhall finds four similarities: an endpoint for explanations (in which we must accept the fact that no further explanation is possible), the element of surprise, the use of the term "illness" for a function that does not correspond to the criteria of the system, and priority of action over intellectual understanding and justification.[31] These features are possible only if we assume that language has boundaries, while at the same time there is a possibility of the indirect linguistic expression of everything that lies beyond these boundaries. While it is possible to view function in language from an autonomous viewpoint, the analogous points between language and religious belief cannot be explained. At this juncture the discussion branches off in another direction, in which the mystical is an expression of subjectivity in language. On the one hand, language is general and common, and every first-person expression is not an individual product, but, at most, an individual use of language. On the other hand, the subject that, according to *Tractatus*, is the boundary of the world is capable of looking beyond this limit and identifying its will, even if this cannot be uniquely verbalized. Furthermore, in poetry, the unique poetical language of the poet can be characterized. This is the basis for the basic argument of *Tractatus*: that singular self-constitution can be identified in the poetical language in these corpora. How, then, are we to characterize the subjective aspect of language?

3. Who Is Experiencing? The Paradox of the I and the "Solution" of the Mystic Subject

> *I am my world.* (The microcosm.) There is no such thing as the subject that thinks or entertains ideas [. . .] The subject does not belong to the world: rather, it is a *limit* of the world.

31 Mulhall, "Wittgenstein and the Philosophy of Religion," p. 111.

> Where in the world is a metaphysical subject to be found? You will say that this is exactly like the case of the eye and the visual field. But really *you do not see the eye.* And nothing in the visual field allows you to infer that it is seen by an eye.[32]

The paradox of the "I" underlies the discussion in the philosophy of religion of knowledge and self-constitution. On the one hand, the first-person speaker attests to his mental states (feelings, emotions, thoughts, positions),[33] while, on the other, the "I" cannot be separated from the mental state. This is acutely problematic in poetry, as we attempt to determine the nature of the speaker in a poem, apart from the situation that is portrayed. For instance, how can we distinguish between the "I" who is the speaker and what is said about him, when the speaker in Zelda's poem *About Facts* describes the disagreement between her soul and her senses:

> My soul says: / "Facts conceal the sea." / My senses say: / "Facts are an island in the ocean."[34]

One possible answer is that the dialogue between the soul and the senses presents different facets of the "I" who is the speaker, and when many details are pieced together, the poetical identity of the poet can be described phenomenologically. This answer, however, does not address the paradox: grammatically, the first-person speaker can be mentioned by himself, while, in practice, he cannot be separated from the described event.

This paradox is connected to another that is especially relevant for an analysis of the constitution of identity in poetry. Wittgenstein described this in his discussion of the existence of inner processes: on

32 Wittgenstein, *Tractatus,* para. 5.63–5.633." In *Philosophical Investigations* Wittgenstein continued to exemplify the paradox of the "I," e.g., in his discussion of the meaning of first names (para. 406).

33 In his later writings, Wittgenstein suggested this division for mental states. For two major discussions, see *Zettel*, para. 472; and *Remarks*, vol. 2, para. 63.

34 Zelda, *The Spectacular Difference*, trans. Marcia Falk (Cincinnati: Hebrew Union College Press, 2004), p. 237.

the one hand, the existence of such processes is undeniable, while, on the other, even when a certain subject depicts what is happening within him, the subjective features of the process cannot be discerned in language.[35] Consequently, it seems that all pains are similar, all loves are similar, and for our purposes, self-constitution cannot be discerned in language as a singular and individual process, but, at best, as a pattern than can characterize many people. In practice, different poetical identities can be distinguished even when the poets depict similar states of consciousness. The question then arises: how is subjective expression possible in public language?

Wittgenstein asserted that language can work in all kinds of ways, including those of conventional expression or, alternately, those of personal-subjective expression.[36] This understanding resolves the paradox in which language can express a personal inner process and at the same time—and in the very same words—a general mental process that is characteristic of many people. This fact, however, does not resolve the first paradox: that the "I" cannot be differentiated from the mental state that it experiences. David Hume, the eighteenth-century British philosopher, articulated this problem quite lucidly:

> When I enter most intimately into what I call *myself*, I always stumble on some particular perception or other, of heat or cold, light or shade, love or hatred, pain or pleasure. I never can catch *myself* at any time without a perception, and never can observe anything but the perception.[37]

35 Wittgenstein, *Philosophical Investigations*, para. 289.

36 "'But you will surely admit that there is a difference between pain-behavior with pain and pain-behavior without pain.' Admit it? What greater difference could there be?—'And yet you again and again reach the conclusion that the sensation itself is a Nothing.'—Not at all. It's not a Something, but not a Nothing either! The conclusion was only that a Nothing would render the same service as a Something about which nothing could be said. We've only rejected the grammar which tends to force itself on us here. The paradox disappears only if we make a radical break with the idea that language always functions in one way, always serves the same purpose: to convey thoughts—which may be about houses, pains, good and evil, or whatever" (Wittgenstein, *Philosophical Investigations*, para. 304).

37 David Hume, *Treatise of Human Nature* (Oxford: Clarendon, 2011), p. 165, sec. 3.

Following this line of thinking, if a person cannot distinguish between his self and his mental state, we must ask: how does language nevertheless reflect the identity of a specific author, and more generally, how can a subjective voice be heard in public language? Wittgenstein merely sharpened this problem when he wrote in *Philosophical Investigations*:

> An "inner process" stands in need of outward criteria.[38]

This means that inner processes exist, but in order to express them, they must be adapted to "outward" criteria, namely, public language's rules of meaning. I will use what Wittgenstein wrote in *Tractatus* to overcome this problem.

Following Wittgenstein's assertion in *Tractatus* that the subject is the boundary of the world, this duality (that an expression is, at one and the same time, both personal and general) can be explained by the expression's "showing," on the one hand, and on the other, "saying": it could express subjective emotion by the seeing inherent in general expression. This showing could occur in a number of ways, such as, for example, the erroneous reading of a word, as Wittgenstein showed in *Philosophical Investigations* as well.[39] In that discussion he distinguished between people who experience the meaning of a word and those who lack such experiential capability; he thereby demonstrated the possibility of distinguishing between people in the subjective experiential plane.[40] Since rules or criteria for subjective expression cannot be found, I will argue that this is one of the directions of mystical grammar, differing from that of everyday language.[41] Each of the poets we will

38 Wittgenstein, *Philosophical Investigations*, para. 580.

39 Wittgenstein, *PPF*, para. 264–65.

40 Wittgenstein, *PPF*, para. 261.

41 The interpretation that criteria for subjective expression cannot be determined is accepted by all Wittgenstein researchers. When the speaker utters a sentence that expresses subjective emotion, he creates a grammatical fiction, since expression in language that can be repeated and understood by someone else could also represent the latter, thereby negating the possibility of its "uniqueness." For a discussion of the emotion of fear, see John Canfield, "The Self and the Emotions," in *Emotions and Understanding: Wittgensteinian Perspectives*, ed. Yiva Gustafsson, Camilla

examine makes singular use of this direction, which constitutes the subjectivity of the speaker.

For Wittgenstein, the mysticism in subjectivity is embodied in the claim that the subject is the boundary of the world. Just as we cannot see the eye that sees, but its existence is proven by the data of the reality, so, too, we cannot locate the mystical subject. This said and done, the expressions of the subjective will give meaning to the world in many diverse ways, thus enabling us to deduce the existence of a subject that desires and chooses, even if its reality in the world cannot be located. As Norman Malcolm already demonstrated in the 1950s, Wittgenstein forcefully negated in *Philosophical Investigations* the possibility of a discussion not employing language. Garry Hagberg showed, in his discussion of the relevance of Wittgenstein's methodology for analyzing literary works, that the metaphysical subject continued to occupy Wittgenstein in his later writings as well.[42] I see no point in examining whether Wittgenstein himself was troubled by this, or whether he felt that the methodical move than he attempted to establish remained incomplete. In either event, what is most important is that the personal, metaphysical experience also emerges in routine contexts and, more outstandingly, in literary contexts.[43] Hagberg especially emphasizes the relevance of "experience" in Wittgenstein's discussions.[44] Wittgenstein asked how the content of personal experience

Kronqvist, and Michael McEachrane (New York: Palgrave Macmillan, 2009), pp. 102–12.

42 Garry Hagberg, "Autobiographical Consciousness: Wittgenstein, Private Experience, and the 'Inner Picture,'" in *The Literary Wittgenstein*, ed. John Gibson and Wolfgang Huemer (London: Routledge, 2004), pp. 228–50.

43 "The sense that the *content* of lived experience, whatever one says (or whatever Wittgenstein has said), is, as a brute fact of life, metaphysically private, is one that seems to want to survive Wittgenstein's reflections to this point, and there is good reason to think that this sense, however incompatible with all the ground Wittgenstein has covered and however clearly picture-driven in all the ways heretofore considered, was felt by Wittgenstein himself. For after finishing Part I of *Philosophical Investigations* in 1945, he turned (in 1946) to problems exclusively in the philosophy of psychology, to which he devoted the following three years almost without interruption" (Hagberg, "Autobiographical Consciousness," p. 240).

44 "And it is not too long before the question of the content of experience comes up. In *Remarks on the Philosophy of Psychology*, vol. 1, para. 109, Wittgenstein asks 'Where do we get the concept of the "content" of an experience from?' This idea,

could be identified, and, under the influence of Schopenhauer's concept of "will," spoke of a private object.[45]

As regards personal experience, most Wittgenstein scholars argue that personal experience is inaccessible to man, in opposition to Ned Block's view that a person can identify change in his personal experience, thus allowing us to speak of such experience.[46] Block used Pierce's term "qualia" to describe the experiential expanse that cannot be verbalized, and therefore is accessible only to the individual himself. Thus only the individual himself can identify changes in this expanse. According to Block, a person can discern changes in his experience and express them in language because language enables us to see the nonverbal stratum of the experience (the qualia). It nonetheless is noteworthy that spotting qualia in language is retroactive, after the change has been effected.[47] What we should take from this disagreement between Block and his opponents is that, according to Wittgenstein, reduction to the existence of private experience is impossible; nor,

of course, co-conspires with those guilty conceptions and pictures, and in giving us a dualistic conceptual model for the content of experience, at the same time gives us a conceptual model for the content of autobiography" (Hagberg, "Autobiographical Consciousness," p. 240).

45 "He writes—giving voice to his early way of thinking even now, only a few years before his last writings in *On Certainty*—'Well, the content of an experience is the private object, the sense datum, the "object" that I grasp immediately with the mental eye, ear, etc.' That private object would be the inner object upon which the private diarist introspects, and (for our present concerns) it would be the inner representation of world-constituting Schopenhauerian significance, knowable only to the autobiographer, and upon which that self-describing, self's-world-defining author introspects in order to capture the inner content for which the autobiographical writing serves as external descriptive-narrative counterpart. Thus Wittgenstein adds the phrase, 'The inner picture.' Reminding himself, and us, once again of the gulf that separates this picture from the particularities of our practices, he then asks 'But where does one find one needs this concept?'" (Hagberg, "Autobiographical Consciousness," p. 240).

46 Ned Block, "Wittgenstein and Qualia," *Philosophical Perspectives* 1, no. 21 (2007), pp. 73–115.

47 As was noted, this position is controversial, with the most direct and most forceful attack upon it launched by John Canfield, "Ned Block, Wittgenstein, and the Inverted Spectrum," *Philosophia* 37 (2009), pp. 691–712. Canfield, based on *Philosophical Investigations*, para. 580 (cited above), totally negates the possibility of discerning qualia.

however, can it be expressed in public language. Block's solution accords with Susanne Langer's view (see above) that the possibility of symbolization in poetry enables the expression in everyday language of emotion that cannot be verbalized.

To summarize the aspect of poetry's possibility of expressing a subjective aspect, I will argue that poetical language can be fashioned in ways that make possible the expression of metaphysical subjectivity. This lies beyond the boundaries of language, and therefore is included within the mystical. The embodiment of this subjectivity is expressed, in practice, in the resolution of life's problems in the plane of depth grammar, since the meaning of things for the subject is examined in this plane:

> Words are probes; some reach very deep; some only to a little depth.[48]
> If we understand a sentence, it has a certain depth for us.[49]
> The problems of life are insoluble on the surface, & can only be solved in depth. In surface dimensions they are insoluble.[50]

The depth-grammar plane acts in both the contexts of life's problems and everyday language. Wittgenstein spoke of an aspect of subjectivity in the everyday use of language, and used the concept of intent to exemplify the difference between "surface grammar" and "depth grammar,"[51] which are mentioned only once in *Philosophical Investigations*.[52] The term "depth" appears only an additional four times, in most of which it can be understood ironically, or as critical of the conception of depth.[53] Notwithstanding this approach, we can see in each instance

48 Wittgenstein, *Notebooks 1914–1916*, p. 39.
49 Wittgenstein, *Philosophical Grammar*, p. 147.
50 Wittgenstein, *Culture and Value*, p. 84.
51 For a development of the argument on how the distinction between Wittgenstein's two types of grammar contributes to understanding a religious stance, see Dorit Lemberger, "Depth Grammar and Surface Grammar of Religious Belief," in *Knowledge and Belief*, ed. Winfried Loffler and Paul Weingartner, *Contributions of the Austrian Ludwig Wittgenstein Society* 9 (2003), pp. 202–4.
52 Wittgenstein, *Philosophical Investigations*, para. 664.
53 Wittgenstein, *Philosophical Investigations*, para. 89, 111, 241, 594.

that Wittgenstein alludes to the simultaneous action of two functions in language: the expression of content and the expression of the speaker's intent in relation to the content of what is said. Consequently, it is possible to distinguish between speakers, and there is a possibility of assessing and judging the degree of intent in speech.

The psychoanalyst Donald Meltzer attests to the inspiration he gained from Wittgenstein's work, especially as regards language's ability to express intent, which is of great value in psychoanalysis.[54] Meltzer writes explicitly that he developed his view of language, following Wittgenstein and Langer, as moving between two planes, depth and surface. Under Wittgenstein's influence, Meltzer indicates two ways in which language functions: signs, which indicate something; and symbols, which can contain subjective emotion. The problem is that most of the symbols that we use are given to our consciousness as conventions. The dream state of consciousness, however, facilitates the generation of new symbols, as can be seen also in works by poets, and in psychoanalytical treatment. Meltzer maintains that we can determine when a symbol bears an emotional charge (based on the work by Susanne Langer that we mentioned in the subchapter dealing with aesthetic judgment).

He develops this notion, and adds that these planes are musical in essence, and they function in a developmental sense, for the communication of moods by means of a mechanism described by Bion as projective identification.[55] Meltzer consciously joined Langer's open discussion of the manner in which musicality enables symbolism, and Wittgenstein's private discussion with his friend Maurice Drury on the importance of music in his life.[56] Wittgenstein voiced his frustration at his lack of success in showing this in *Philosophical Investigations*, and

54 Donald Meltzer, "Temperature and Distance as Technical Dimensions of Interpretation," in *Sincerity and Other Works: Collected Papers of Donald Meltzer*, ed. Alberto Hahn (London: Karnac, 1994), pp. 374–86.

55 Wilfred Bion, "Attacks on Linking," *International Journal of Psycho-Analysis* 40, no. 5–6 (1959), p. 308.

56 "It is impossible to say in my book one word about all that music has meant in my life [. . .] How then can I hope to be understood?" (Rush Rhees, *Ludwig Wittgenstein: Personal Recollections* [Oxford: Basil Blackwell, 1981], p. 94).

this frustration finely exemplifies the basic claim that will is situated beyond the boundaries of language, and at most, can be expressed within it only indirectly. The mysticism of Wittgensteinian musicality can be seen in the inability to directly mention it, but, unlike what Wittgenstein thought, rhythmical musical motifs are evident in *Philosophical Investigations*.[57]

Meltzer channels the discussion of the two planes of language in order to improve therapeutic technique. Wittgenstein's great contribution, for Meltzer, consists of honing the distinction between saying and meaning. As was noted above, the depth level can be distinguished from the surface level, with the former expressing meaning. Meltzer develops the methodological aspect of the Wittgensteinian discussion by explaining that meaning cannot be found as a condition or result of any action. Moreover, at times the patient develops symbolization that cannot be interpreted, and that might definitely be a private language. He totally disagrees on this point with the accepted view in Wittgenstein research: that private language is an impossibility. Meltzer asserts that such a language is the province of poets, writers, and twins or, as a rule, among children.[58] Of importance for our discussion is the impression he gained, as a therapist, of his patients' capability for private symbolism and his amazement at this ability by a poet in therapy.[59] This

57 Shimon Adaf drew my attention to the musical features in *Philosophical Investigations*, from the division into sections and the dialogues that create rhythm, continuing with metaphors like the fly in the jar, to the sensation of flow while reading the text.

58 For a detailed description of privacy that can be identified, but not comprehended, by another, both in poetry and in psychological therapy, see Donald Meltzer and Meg Harris Williams, *The Apprehension of Beauty: The Role of Aesthetic Conflict in Development, Art, and Violence* (London: Karnac, 1988).

59 "While it is true that the analyst may introduce into the discourse with the patient a certain amount of his own poetry, his own symbol formation, the discourse between analyst and patient, in so far as it is creative, is largely of the patient's creation through the symbol formation that is conveyed in his dream structures. One of the most important indicators of analytic progress, to my mind, is the progress in the nature of the patient's dreaming. The general development is from long anecdotal dreams to short condensed symbolic dreams. The one rather famous poet I had as a patient from the very beginning amazed me with the bombardment of the autonomous condensed symbolic formations in his dreams.

ability can be located only by its results, and thereby reflects the working of the depth grammar that produces surface grammar.

Another aspect that may be attributed to depth grammar is of especial importance for describing the constitution of identity, namely, the state of consciousness in which the subject undergoes sudden change. This phenomenon has been studied in many fields (including poetry, psychology and psychoanalysis, and the study of religion) and is not necessarily related to other states of consciousness or to specific biographical events. Many terms portray such a change, like "leap," "conversion," or "epiphany," all of which—besides the suddenness of their appearance—cannot be predicted or given a retroactive causal explanation. Change of this sort is an ultimate expression of mystical subjectivity, and it finds expression in a person's powerful emotional movement to an idea, event, or experience in a life-changing manner, or one that at the very least gives his life new meaning. I regard the sudden transition in which God appears in *Tractatus* as a grammatical expression of such a change, and the mention without any prior warning of "theology as grammar" in *Philosophical Investigations* can be seen in a similar light.

Wittgenstein held Augustine, Kierkegaard, and James in high regard, for all three attested to a change of this type and added significant elements to its discussion in the study of religion. For our purposes, James is most relevant, since he starts from a psychological viewpoint that was not preceded by any religious belief. This is of importance, because the "leap" does not retroactively justify a certain religious path:

> If it comes, it comes; if it does not come, no process of reasoning can force it. Yet it transforms the value of the creature loved as utterly as the sunrise transforms Mont Blanc from a corpse-like gray to a rosy enchantment; and it sets the

---

Patients who do not progress in analysis demonstrate this by the continuing lengthy anecdotal dreams which are hardly distinguishable from daily life" (Donald Meltzer, "Concerning Signs and Symbols," *British Journal for Psychotherapy* 14, no. 2 [1997], p. 175).

> whole world to a new tune for the lover and gives a new issue to his life. So with fear, with indignation, jealousy, ambition, worship. If they are there, life changes.[60]

The manner in which James formulated the features of conversion in *The Varieties of Religious Experience* is still inspiring for the way in which he presents a significant change in man's psyche, such that it gives new meaning to his life.[61] Suddenness, the inability to indicate causality, and a series of emotions that produce a significant change in one's way of life are characteristic of a change of consciousness, marks of which are evident in the way a person describes his life. The leap happens without prior notice, and it changes the colors of the subject's world, the quality of his world. This cannot be caused in some way or another, but its influence is felt both in the emotional plane and in the manner one looks at the world.

In the more general discussion of the nature of humanism in his article "On a Certain Blindness in Human Beings," James was critical of people's difficulty to experience the world deeply. As a consequence of this difficulty, they miss the ability to identify a surprising possibility of deepening the meaning of their lives.[62] The leap effects an awareness of inner meaning that changes the subject's historical consciousness of himself, and is more significant than any of his experiences prior to its occurrence.[63] James calls this a mystical experience and argues that at

60 William James, *The Varieties of Religious Experience* (London: Routledge, 2002), p. 120.

61 James, *Varieties of Religious Experience*, chaps. 9–10.

62 William James, "On a Certain Blindness in Human Beings," in *Writings 1878–1899* (New York: Literary Classics of the United States, 1992), pp. 841–60.

63 "This higher vision of an inner significance in what, until then, we had realized only in the dead external way, often comes over a person suddenly; and, when it does so, it makes an epoch in his history. As Emerson says, there is a depth in those moments that constrains us to ascribe more reality to them than to all other experiences. The passion of love will shake one like an explosion, or some act will awaken a remorseful compunction that hangs like a cloud over all one's later day. This mystic sense of hidden meaning starts upon us often from non-human natural things" (James, "Certain Blindness," p. 847).

times it can begin even from something natural and not human, although it influences the human subject.[64]

Now, back to *The Varieties of Religious Experience*. Importantly for our needs, James connected the subjective experience that constitutes individuality (including unique poetical identity) with religiosity. In his conclusion, James changed his personal attitude to the mystical phenomenon, from the perspective of a psychologist who is empathetically attentive to the mystical experiences of his patient and records them, to a judgmental stance that favored the religious experience with an emotional basis.[65]

James criticizes the apple of the eye of the pragmatists, the practical interest, and argues that understanding and changing man's humanity depends on the experience that is beyond any experience in the present. He finds no point to the question of God's existence, and asserts that our very occupation with religious questions constitutes the realization of our task as humans, which cannot be limited to what is present in our consciousness. Openness to God is the way to constitute the human experience, and this belief is ingrained in every man.[66]

Notwithstanding this, a person's emotions, like the mystical experience that takes place within them, are subjective, and even if we

---

64 "Yet so blind and dead does the clamor of our own practical interests make us to all other things, that it seems almost as if it were necessary to become worthless as a practical being, if one is to hope to attain to any breadth of insight into the impersonal world of worths as such, to have any perception of life's meaning on a large objective scale. Only your mystic, your dreamer, or your insolvent tramp or loafer, can afford so sympathetic an occupation, an occupation which will change the usual standards of human value in the twinkling of an eye, giving to foolishness a place ahead of power, and laying low in a minute the distinctions which it takes a hard-working conventional man a lifetime to build up. You may be a prophet, at this rate; but you cannot be a worldly success" (James, "Certain Blindness," p. 851).

65 James, *Varieties of Religious Experience*, pp. 385–87.

66 "God is the natural appellation [. . .] for the supreme reality, so I will call this higher part of the universe by the name of God. We and God have business with each other; and in opening ourselves to his influence our deepest destiny is fulfilled. The universe, at those parts of it which our personal being constitutes, takes a turn genuinely for the worse or for the better in proportion as each one of us fulfills or evades God's demands [. . .] I only translate into schematic language what I may call the instinctive belief of mankind" (James, *Varieties of Religious Experience*, pp. 398–99).

assume, following James, that every man has this potential, the question that is of acute interest for us is: what enables us to identify such an experience? What are the features of the mystical grammar of the descriptive "leap" or of any subjective experience? If an experience of this sort can be described after the fact, and can even be understand by one who did not experience it, what is the grammatical difference between the understanding of the speaker, who portrays the experience in the first person, and that of the listener, psychologist, or anyone else, who comprehends the experience, but does not sense it himself?

4. I as Object—I as Subject: From James to Wittgenstein

First-person speech is a common grammatical occurrence in poetry. One of the striking features of figurative speech is new metaphorical fashioning, which has a dual function: generating emotion for the reader, and expressing the speaker's subjectivity. This use of metaphor represents, and at times, creates an unverifiable mental reality and does not presume to represent an actual specific reality. When, however, we speak of constituting a subject, we must ask: Should we explore the connection between the grammatical expression that constitutes the subject during the poetical process and its result? Can we point to the "success" or "failure" of constituting the subject?

For example, how can we distinguish between an ironic expression that indicates the failure of self-constitution and a grammatical expression that embodies an actual description? If every metaphor can, in the final analysis, be contained in everyday language, as Donald Davidson suggests, can the poet create a personal code and express a stance that escapes from everyday language?[67] In his discussion of first-person authority, Davidson, influenced by Wittgenstein, maintains that a criterion for identifying error can be devised only within public language. This is so because we can indicate an exception—namely, an error—only when it diverges from a fixed rule.[68] Can there be a private

67 Donald Davidson, "What Metaphors Mean," *Critical Inquiry* 5, no. 1 (1978), pp. 31–47.

68 Davidson, "What Metaphors Mean."

code that is understandable only to its creator, in which there is no possibility of error, that is dependent upon the existence of an "other"?

Wittgenstein proposed two methodological directions for a discussion of subjective expressions. His first follows his statement in *Tractatus* that the subject is the boundary of the world. Continuing in this vein, every expression of subjective will is situated beyond the boundary of language, in the sense that it cannot be expressed by means of language. Taking this as a given, such will is inherently of great importance, since it constitutes man's happiness or wretchedness.[69] An expression of will, according to *Tractatus*, is therefore included within the realm of the mystical, and it affects the boundaries of the world, but not facts. Although it is inexpressible in language, traces of it can be identified because they fashion the world as happy or wretched. This fashioning is not included in the grammatical rules of regular language, since it originates outside the boundary of language, and therefore can be called (a manner of) mystical grammar. Wittgenstein averred the certain existence of a "willing subject," despite its mysterious nature.[70] This certainty will be the basis for the third type of mystical grammar (see below).

Wittgenstein formulated a second methodological solution inspired by James's distinction between "I as object" and "I as subject." James set forth this distinction in a psychology textbook:

> Whatever I may be thinking of, I am always at the same time more or less aware of *myself*, of my *personal existence*. At the same time it is *I* who am aware so that the total self of me, being as it were duplex, partly known and partly knower,

69 "If the good or bad exercise of the will does alter the world, it can alter only the limits of the world, not the facts—not what can be expressed by means of language. In short the effect must be that it becomes an altogether different world [. . .] The world of the happy man is a different one from that of the unhappy man" (Wittgenstein, *Tractatus*, para. 6.43).

70 "The thinking subject is surely mere illusion. But the willing subject exists. If the will did not exist, neither would there be that center of the world, which we call the I, and which is the bearer of ethics. What is good and evil is essentially the I, not the world. The I, the I is what is deeply mysterious!" (Wittgenstein, *Notebooks 1914–1916*, p. 80).

> partly object and partly subject, must have two aspects discriminated in it, of which for shortness we may call one the *Me* and other the *I*. I call these "discriminated aspects," and not separate things, because the identity of *I* with *me*, even in the very act of their discrimination, is perhaps the most ineradicable dictum of common-sense.[71]

This passage by James is the key to the ongoing discussion of the paradox of self-knowledge: on the one hand, the first-person speaker is the knowing subject, while on the other, the knowledge that is acquired is self-knowledge. How, then, can the knower also be the known? James suggests distinguishing between two aspects of knowledge. He says that a person can know himself as object and as subject, with these two sorts of knowledge being the two sides of the same coin.

Following James, Wittgenstein drew a distinction between the two main ways in which a person describes himself in language: in the first, he makes verifiable claims, and therefore relates to himself as an object. In the second, a person makes subjective claims that are neither verifiable nor refutable, and thus describes features of himself as a subject.[72]

Up to now, the discussion of Wittgenstein's distinction between "I as object" and "I as subject" has been the starting point for the discussion of first-person certainty.[73] In analyzing poetry, and especially in the

71 William James, *Textbook of Psychology* (London: Macmillan, 1892), p. 176.

72 "Now the idea that *the real I* lives in my body is connected with the peculiar grammar of the word '*I*,' and the misunderstandings this grammar is liable to give rise to. There are two different cases in the use of the word 'I' (or 'my') which *I* might call 'the use as object' and 'the use as subject.' Examples of the first kind of use are these: 'My arm is broken,' 'I have grown six inches,' 'I have a bump on my forehead' [. . .] Examples of the second kind are: 'I see so and so' [. . .] 'I think it will rain,' 'I have a toothache.' One can point to the difference between these two categories by saying: The cases of the first category involve the recognition of a particular person, and there is in these cases the possibility of an error [. . .] *I could*, looking into a mirror, mistake a bump on his head for one on mine. On the other hand there is no question of recognizing a person when I say *I* have a toothache. To ask 'are you sure that *it's you* who have pains?' would be nonsensical" (Wittgenstein, *Blue and Brown Books*, pp. 66–67; emphasis added).

73 This discussion became the starting point for all the major discussions of self-knowledge in the philosophy of language, without mentioning that Wittgenstein took this distinction from James. This omission misses James's psychological

context of self-constitution, this distinction is of great importance for determining when we have a general statement, and when the speaker's self-constitution. The problem is that when we relate to the "I" as subject, we seemingly discern a bodiless entity, as when we speak of mental activity, but actually, when we employ terms, we do not explain the use, with the consequent possibility of erring with a metaphysical claim. We should instead focus on the grammatical plane, and aim to discern within it when the speaker in the poem depicts subjective situations, and when objective ones. This discrimination will draw into sharp focus the mystical direction chosen by the speaker to fashion its subjectivity.

5. From Perfectionism to Confession: Work on Oneself

> A man will never be great if he misjudges himself: if he throws dust in his own eyes.[74]

> Work on philosophy—like work in architecture in many respects—is really work on oneself. On one's own conception. On how one sees things. (And what one expects of them.)[75]

> Words are deeds.[76]

The third channel of mystical grammar is based on the first two. In the first channel, we saw how grammatical autonomy makes it possible to constitute theological grammar that includes belief and religiosity arguments that cross the boundaries of language. In the second channel, we showed how Wittgenstein adopted James's distinction between objective and subjective use in statements about

---

context. See, e.g., Sidney Shoemaker, "Self-Reference and Self-Awareness," *Journal of Philosophy* 65, no. 19 (1968), pp. 555–67; Gareth Evans, *The Varieties of Reference*, ed. John McDowell (New York: Oxford University Press, 1982), pp. 217–20; and Jose Luis Bermudez, *The Paradox of Self-Consciousness* (Cambridge, MA: MIT Press, 1998), p. 5.

74 Wittgenstein, *Culture and Value*, p. 49.

75 Wittgenstein, *Culture and Value*, p. 24.

76 Wittgenstein, *Culture and Value*, p. 53.

the "I," and presented the possibility of immunity to error that is not subordinate to a logical verification principle. The third channel unites the Wittgensteinian conception of religious morality with the subjective will that is guided by a person's individual conscience. Thus unification creates a third direction for mysticism in Wittgensteinian grammar: in the thematic plane, this refers to self-correction, and in the methodical one, this process occurs by means of confession.

The relation between man and God is embodied in two conceptions of meaning that Wittgenstein formulated in *Tractatus*: the linguistic meaning that is revealed when language is used that is present in the world. The subject is the boundary of the world, and the subject's will, which Wittgenstein mentions as a certainty, gives meaning to the world as a whole. The subject's will derives from his conscience, which reflects the voice of God. Consequently, man's consciousness contains both linguistic and metaphysical meanings, the latter being beyond the boundary. Working on myself means action that follows my conscience, that expresses the voice of God in the subject's soul.[77]

For Wittgenstein, a person's working on himself is both a reevaluation of the common use of terminology and confessional writing. These two methodologies illustrate language's being a vehicle for expression, either verbalized or perceived, of the possibility of self-correction. The methodologies are mutually dependent, since the confessional process includes recognition of the lack of correspondence between what is formulated in language (as expressing the "I") and the reality, to the same degree that a critical examination of the use of language requires the act of confession.

Wittgenstein compared the work of philosophy with that required of a person on himself. He said to scrutinize the manner in which we see things and our expectations regarding them. All this is embodied in

77 "Certainly it is correct to say: Conscience is the voice of God" (Wittgenstein, *Notebooks 1914–1916*, p. 75); "It would be possible to say (à la Schopenhauer): It is not the world of Idea that is either good or evil, but the willing subject" (*Notebooks 1914–1916*, p. 79); "To believe in God means to see that life has a meaning" (*Notebooks 1914–1916*, p. 74).

words, and therefore, an examination of the way language is used is philosophical work that functions as self-examination. At times the way in which a person acts may contradict his expectations of himself in the spiritual-moral realm, and philosophical work facilitates the encounter between a person's expectations of himself and his actual life. This self-correction takes place in two connected planes. The first is the intellectual sphere, in which a person makes incorrect use of language, or is captured by the illusions that are created during the processes of understanding language. The second realm is the existential-emotional, in which Wittgenstein identified a number of modern man's distresses, such as guilt feelings, the loss of self-respect, infantile weakness, aloofness and alienation from others, and loneliness. Confession is the way to deal with the forms of distress in both planes:

> The whole Earth cannot be in greater distress than one soul [. . .] Someone who in this way opens his heart to God in remorseful confession opens it for others too. He thereby loses his dignity as someone special & so becomes like a child. That means without office, dignity & aloofness from others [. . .] Of course you must continue to feel ashamed of what's within you, but not ashamed of yourself before your fellow human beings. There is no greater distress to be felt than that of one human being. For if someone feels himself lost, that is the ultimate distress.[78]

Wittgenstein links religious, everyday confession with philosophical confession by setting up a single criterion for both: truthfulness. This criterion differs from the logical criterion for the truthfulness of a sentence, and is based on the practical outcome of such behavior:

> The criteria for the truth of the *confession* that I thought such and such are not the criteria for a true *description* of a process. And the importance of the true confession does not reside in

78 Wittgenstein, *Culture and Value*, pp. 52–53.

> its being a correct and certain report of some process. It resides, rather, in the special consequences which can be drawn from a confession whose truth is guaranteed by the special criteria of *truthfulness*.[79]

Wittgenstein thereby joins Augustine and Kierkegaard, who demanded that every man seek and find the authentic inner truth, confronting the majority and even in opposition to the prevalent truths, thus creating the foundation for confession based on the discovery of the truth by means of language. Augustine depicted the motivation for knowing what happens in the mind of another, which makes man attest to himself as the sole possible representative of his inner truth.[80] Wittgenstein opened *Philosophical Investigations* with a seeming critique of Augustine's conception of language, but all his citations from the latter in the course of the book are cast in a positive light and attest to Augustine's influence on him, especially in his discussions of confession as self-criticism. Thus, for example, the following citation of Augustine by Wittgenstein can be seen as inspiring the examination of everyday language and the discovery within it of the surprising (a directive that parallels Kierkegaard's praise of the routine; see below):

> Here it is easy to get into that dead end in philosophizing where one believes that the difficulty of the problem consists in our having to describe phenomena that evade our grasp, the present experience that slips quickly by, or something akin—where we find ordinary language too crude, and it looks as if we were dealing not with the phenomena of everyday conversation, but with ones that "are evanescent, and, in their coming to be and passing away, tend to produce those others."

79 Wittgenstein, *PPF*, para. 319.

80 Augustine writes in his *Confessions*: "How do they know, when they hear from me about me, whether I am telling the truth, since no one knows what is going on in a human being except the spirit of the human being, which is in him?" (*The Confessions of Saint Augustine*, ed. P. M. Parker [San Diego: ICON, 2005], 10:3:3, p. 162).

> (Augustine: Manifestissima et usitatissima sunt, et eadem rursus nimis latent, et nova est inventio eorum.)[81]

Actually, we can say that Augustine established within Western philosophy a methodology of self-constitution by means of the action of speech. The dominant act of speech is confession, but it is accompanied by actions such as declaration, the expression of emotions, and philosophical clarifications. The sum of these actions constitutes the Augustinian subject-speaker, and paves the way for self-constitution that seeks constant correction and improvement. Augustine portrays a process of conversion that is mainly religious, that comes about by addressing God. Concomitantly, he legitimizes turning to the mystical by undermining and refuting the methodologies of human knowledge, in both the rational sphere and the physical realm, namely, life's pleasures.

Kierkegaard, in contrast, placed greater emphasis on the need to contend with, and at times, oppose prevalent conventional ways of thinking when they clash with the individual's subjective truth. He followed this with a vigorous critique of most people's inclination to accept their mental exile, presenting instead the model of the "knight of faith" who finds the sublime, even in daily life.[82] Cavell viewed this in an anachronistic light, as Kierkegaard's religious interpretation of the Wittgensteinian term "ordinary": Wittgenstein, who proposed returning to the rough ground of everyday speech, saw Kierkegaard's attempt to extract the sublime from the everyday as religious.

In the third meaning that we will explore, the mystical embodies the constant aspiration for correction and perfectionism within philosophical investigation. Wittgenstein, most likely influenced by Augustine, regarded philosophical writing as a type of confession, both

---

81 Wittgenstein, *Philosophical Investigations*, para. 436.

82 "Most men live in relation to their own self as if they were constantly out, never at home" (Soren Kierkegaard, *On Authority and Revelation: The Book on Adler, or a Cycle of Ethico-Religious Essays,* trans. Walter Lowrie [Princeton, NJ: Princeton University Press, 1955], p. 154); "to transform the leap of life into a walk, to express the sublime in the pedestrian absolutely—that only the knight of faith can do" (Kierkegaard, *Fear and Trembling*, trans. A. Hannay [London: Penguin, 1985], p. 52).

in the sense of an attempt to clearly express the truth, and in that of the verbal expression of remorse and correction.[83]

In expressions such as "[a] confession has to be part of one's new life"[84] and "[s]omeone who in this way opens his heart to God in remorseful confession opens it for others too,"[85] Wittgenstein connected the religious practice of confession before God with the human. The practice of confession expresses remorse and the desire for correction, but does not suffice by itself; it rather should be part of a new and proper way of life. Different formulations of this directive appear in *Philosophical Investigations*, when Wittgenstein relates to philosophical distresses as wounds, or to a philosophical question as an illness.[86] In both instances, the healing of the symptom is not enough. We must understand how language bewitched thought and created the problem. This problematic is not expressed in the realm of the logical meaning, in which the criterion of a sentence being sensible is its truth value, but rather in the autonomous domain of the ethical, in which an inner demand is constituted in man's innermost being to be faithful to himself, in the sense of truthfulness (as was discussed above, following *PPF*, para. 319). At this point, we should distinguish between the manner in which *Philosophical Investigations* was written, including conversations and discussions between Wittgenstein and his friends and family, and the difficulty of finding examples of confessions by Wittgenstein in the book. Moreover, I maintain that there is not necessarily any connection between the praxis of confession, in the prevalent religious sense of describing sin, on the one hand, and, on the other,

83 Along with the fact that Wittgenstein mentions or cites Augustine nine times in *Philosophical Investigations*, Ray Monk describes at length Wittgenstein's profound esteem for Augustine, and the latter's influence on what Wittgenstein deems to be the proper way to write philosophy. See Ray Monk, *Ludwig Wittgenstein: The Duty of Genius* (London: Vintage, 1990), pp. 282–83.

84 Wittgenstein, *Culture and Value*, p. 16.

85 Wittgenstein, *Culture and Value*, p. 52.

86 "The results of philosophy are the discovery of some piece of plain nonsense and the bumps that the understanding has got by running up against the limits of language. They—these bumps—make us see the value of that discovery" (Wittgenstein, *Philosophical Investigations*, para. 119); "The philosopher treats a question; like an illness" (*Philosophical Investigations*, para. 255).

the philosophical confession that Wittgenstein wanted to fashion in *Philosophical Investigations*, and which is relevant for the following analyses of poetry. The latter sort of confession reflects a recurring examination of the concepts and principles by which man fashions his life, in accordance with their meaning for him. This issue was discussed in the section devoted to poetical grammar, based mainly on the sense of inner commitment that Wittgenstein sought to arouse, one that aims to constitute a meaningful life. Such a life could be regarded as improper or irrational by another person, yet this does not detract from its worth. The problematic ethical condition (that requires confession) arises within a person, and does not result from confrontation with an external norm. Such a confrontation occurs, for instance, when a person's values contradict the way he lives his life.

Michael Peters portrayed various facets of the Wittgensteinian confession, and showed how it functions in Wittgenstein's philosophical writing as a self-constitutive mechanism.[87] Inter alia, Peters illustrated the contents of Wittgenstein's own confession, which expressed the inner compass that led to confession: Wittgenstein confessed to concealing his Jewish origins, and the incident in which he hit a pupil in the high school he attended (and for which he apologized).[88] Since, for Wittgenstein, concealing biographical details

---

87 Michael Peters, "Writing the Self: Wittgenstein, Confession, and Pedagogy," *Journal of Philosophy of Education* 34, no. 2 (2000), pp. 353–68.

88 "Ray Monk (1990: 367–72) reconstructs the extraordinary events that surrounded his preparation for his own confession which he undertook in 1936 at the same time as completing sections 1–188 of what was to become the *Investigations*. The confession was to be read to a circle of close friends (Maurice Drury, G. E. Moore, Paul Engelmann, Fania Pascal and Francis Skinner) and family. He delivered his confession (*read* and *recited* it) to family and close friends in Vienna around Christmas 1936, and to intimate friends at Cambridge in the New Year. There were a number of minor sins describing his weaknesses and two major 'sins' remembered by Fania Pascal: what Wittgenstein saw as his attempt to cover up his Jewish ancestry (a sin of omission, as Monk notes) and the action where he lied to his school headmaster denying he hit a girl pupil in his charge. Wittgenstein surprised the villagers of Otterthal by appearing on their doorsteps that same year (i.e., 1936) to apologize personally to children he had hurt. Monk (1990: 372) quotes Wittgenstein's reflections on his confessions as bringing him 'into more settled waters, into a better relation with people, and to a greater seriousness,' and he suggests that

ran counter to his value of candor, he felt the need to confess things that someone else might find natural, and that certainly were not opposed to ethical norms or even to any religious law. As was already argued, we should separate a frank confession of personal misdeeds from confession in the sense of mystical grammar that serves as an interpretive methodological tool for determining how the speaker constitutes his self in the poems. Confession in the latter sense means a manner of formulation that constitutes self-correction by exploring how concepts are conceived in language, and the attempt to alter them in order to effect general cultural change. On a number of occasions Wittgenstein voiced his unease at the *Zeitgeist* and his attempt (that was doomed to failure) to exert influence by means of his philosophical work, because his criticism was not understood. Thus, for example, his partner to these conversations, Maurice Drury, relates:

> Throughout his life Wittgenstein was convinced that he could not make himself understood [. . .] When he was working on the latter part of the *Philosophical Investigations* he told me: "It is impossible for me to say in my book one word about all that music has meant in my life. How then can I hope to be understood?" And about the same date: "My type of thinking is not wanted in this present age, I have to swim so strongly against the tide."[89]

The scholar and philosopher Stanley Cavell linked the way that Wittgenstein wrote philosophy as confession, in the sense of exploring the way words are used, with self-examining cultural criticism. Under the influence of the nineteenth-century philosopher Emerson, Cavell coined the term "moral perfectionism," and sought what united a series of "perfectionist" philosophers:

Wittgenstein considered confession 'as a kind of surgery, an operation to remove cowardice'" (Peters, "Writing the Self," p. 355).

89 Peters, "Writing the Self."

> Perfectionism [. . .] is not a competing theory of the moral life, but something like a dimension or tradition of the moral life that spans the course of Western thought and concerns what used to be called the state of one's soul, a dimension that places tremendous burdens on personal relationships and on the possibility or necessity of the transforming of oneself and of one's society.[90]

Cavell wrote that Emerson and Wittgenstein share a notion of philosophical work that expresses a sense of confusion, self-exile, and loss of one's way. The philosophical method for dealing with these feelings is based on a type of autobiographical confession that characterizes Wittgenstein's writing in *Philosophical Investigations* and in other works. Stephen Mulhall, Cavell's student and the editor of his *Reader*, proposed viewing this direction of Wittgenstein as an expression of religiosity, since what drives him is located beyond the limits of language.[91] Mulhall explained the manner in which Cavell formulated Emerson's perfectionism:

> Emersonian perfectionism [. . .] embodies an idea of the individual's truth to herself or to the humanity in herself; it is an understanding of the soul as on an upward or onward journey that begins by finding oneself lost to the world and requires a refusal of society in the name of some further, more cultivated or cultured, state of society and the self. As the myth of the journey would imply, talk of perfectionism here does not entail an idea of perfectibility, as if Emerson conceives of there being any given state of the self that is final, unsurpassable rather than simply unsurpassed; it rather captured the idea that each given and attained state of the self is final, in that each constitutes a world that the self can and does desire, to which

90 Stanley Cavell, "Moral Perfectionism," in *The Cavell Reader*, ed. Stephen Mulhall (Malden, MA: Blackwell, 1996), p. 355.

91 Mulhall, "Wittgenstein and the Philosophy of Religion," pp. 95–118.

> it is (and is always at risk of remaining) attached—a world that is, one might say, self-sufficient.[92]

Emerson's criteria contain two features that were also formulated by Kierkegaard, both of which are important for the study of the mystical in poetry in the third channel: the first feature is the need to go beyond accepted conventions, while clearly personally identifying with them. The second feature is the inability of formulating any justification for going beyond the limits of language. Both features are based in the feeling of exile and distance, and the desire for authentic self-constitution. As Emerson puts this:

> These are the voices which we hear in solitude, but they grow faint and inaudible as we enter into the world. Society everywhere is in conspiracy against the manhood of every one of its members. Society is a joint-stock company, in which the members agree, for the better securing of his bread to each shareholder, to surrender the liberty and culture of the eater. The virtue in most request is conformity. *Self-reliance is its aversion.*[93] The great man is he who in the midst of the crowd keeps with perfect sweetness the independence of solitude.[94]

Cavell unites the notion of the development of the soul held by Plato, Kierkegaard, and Wittgenstein with Emerson's portrayal of the dual nature of this journey: the relation to the self and to others is that of possible representation, so that each individual's potential might be found and seen by his fellow.[95] He offers the clearest formulation of

---

92 Stephen Mulhall, *Stanley Cavell: Philosophy's Recounting of the Ordinary* (Oxford: Clarendon, 1994), p. 265.

93 Ralph Waldo Emerson, "Self-Reliance," in *The Collected Works of Ralph Waldo Emerson* (Cambridge, MA: Harvard University Press, 1980), vol. 2: *Essays, First Series*, p. 29 (emphasis added).

94 "The objection to confirming to usages that have become dead to you is, that it scatters your force [. . .] under all these screens I have difficulty to detect the precise man you are" (Emerson, "Self-Reliance," pp. 31–32).

95 "Being one [. . .] who represents for each of us the height of the journey, to the idea of each of us being representative for each of us [. . .] Emerson study [. . .] comes

perfectionism, based on the self's constant movement from one state to another, together with an awareness of its ad hoc perfection.[96] Perfection is therefore a constant aim; at the same time, it is constituted in the consciousness in the world itself, with no need of the metaphysical. This is the meaning of the process that Cavell calls "having 'a' self."

To come full circle, let us return to James, who directed Emerson's humanistic position to the mystical dimension.[97] James, following Emerson, argued that at times a mystical revelation occurs by means of an encounter with a literary work that generates it or with another person. The mystical is that moment of change that enables one to see the otherness beyond himself as illuminating something within him. James's depiction of the religious experience is evidently linked with his stance regarding the "I as subject," since in his discussion of this experience, he repeatedly emphasized the dominance of the emotional experience that cannot be verbalized in the present tense. That is, it evades general language, and remains as a conscious private experience. In, however, his discussion of a "certain blindness," in which the mystical functions as the key to fathoming otherness, some difficulty arises in determining, from the outset, if a certain experience is

up [. . .] under the head of 'standing for' [. . .] as a relation we bear at once to others and to ourselves: if we were not representative of what we might be [. . .] we would not recognize ourselves presented in one another's possibilities; we have no 'potential'" (Cavell, "Moral Perfectionism," p. 361).

96 "Having 'a' self is the process of moving to, and from nexts. It is [. . .] the work of (Emerson's) writing to present nextness, a city of words to participate in [. . .] our position is always (already) that of an attained self; we are from the beginning, that is from the time that we can be described of having self, a next, knotted. An Emersonian sally at this idea is to say that we are (our thinking is) partial [. . .] That the self is always attained, as well as *to be* attained [. . .] you are left precisely in the negation of the position he calls for, left in conformity [. . .] *Each* state of the self is final, one we have desired, in this sense perfect, kept, however painful, in perfect place for us. In this dire sense [. . .] Perfectionism implies Perfectibility" (Cavell, "Moral Perfectionism," p. 364).

97 James, "Certain Blindness."

objective or subjective, as William Barnard showed.[98] It is only after the fact that we can indicate objectivity or subjectivity.[99]

James joins the mystical occurrence with logical grammar and pragmatism: the manifestation of the mystical can be seen in language, not only in the first person, if it influences the overall experience of the one undergoing it. This offers us a criterion for identifying the mystical in poetry. Poetry does not stand in and of itself; it rather functions deeply in the process of constituting identity, just as Wittgenstein would have philosophy function:

> What is the use of studying philosophy if all that it does for you is enable you to talk with some plausibility about some abstruse questions of logic, etc., and it does not improve your thinking about the important questions of everyday life [. . .] You see, I know that it is difficult to think well about "certainty," "probability," "perception," etc. But it is, if possible,

98 "Unlike most other theorists, James does not believe that the decision as to whether an experience is 'subjective' or 'objective' is predetermined. This understanding that experience is classified as subjective or objective according to its context or function, rather than according to its inherent, predetermined qualities, has important implications for the reality status that is assigned to mystical experiences. From a philosophical perspective that accepts the subject/object distinction as a given, mystical experiences are inevitably seen as 'subjective' because they occur within an individual's psyche and cannot be observed, weighed, measured, and quantified like other more overtly 'objective' aspects of our experience. Unfortunately, from this particular philosophical perspective, when an event is determined to be 'subjective,' it is also, by default, 'illusory,' 'arbitrary,' 'unreal,' and so on" (G. William Barnard, *Exploring Unseen Worlds: William James and the Philosophy of Mysticism* [Albany: State University of New York Press, 1997], p. 146).

99 "From a Jamesian perspective, however, the reality status of mystical experiences is not preordained. If it can be demonstrated that mystical experiences have important effects on other aspects of our experience, if it can be shown that they heal, they enliven, they guide, they inspire, they illuminate, then we have every right to claim that they are 'objective' or 'real.' On the other hand, James would say that if mystical experiences make no viable connections with the rest of our experience, then we can and should shrug them off as being nothing more than fanciful products of our imagination" (Barnard, *Exploring Unseen Worlds*, pp. 146–47).

> still more difficult to think, or try to think, really honestly about your life and other peoples' lives.[100]

In summation, Wittgenstein saw philosophy's primary goal as directed at improving man's ability to sincerely look at himself and at others. Such observation is not based on an improvement in the methodological tools of linguistic research, but on the constitution of the mystical dimension in man's soul, in the Wittgensteinian sense: the development of the meaning of life, understanding of the subjective dimension of how man leads his life, and the constant desire for improvement are the three mystical channels that cross the boundaries of language, but are embodied and expressed in our linguistic choices, as in the poetical fashioning of the language of poetry.

100 Quoted in Malcolm, *Ludwig Wittgenstein: A Memoir*, p. 93.

CHAPTER 4

Zelda: The Complex Self-Constitution of the Believer

A poem, as a manifestation of language and thus essentially dialogue, can be a message in a bottle, sent out in the—not always greatly hopeful—belief that somewhere and sometime it could wash up on land, on heartland perhaps. Poems in this sense too are underway: they are making toward something. Toward what? Toward something standing open, occupiable, perhaps toward an addressable Thou, toward an addressable reality [. . .] who goes toward language with his very being, stricken by and seeking reality.[1]

What is your aim in philosophy?—To show the fly the way out of the fly-bottle.[2]

---

1 Paul Celan, "Speech on the Occasion of Receiving the Literature Prize of the Free Hanseatic City of Bremen," in *Selected Poems and Prose of Paul Celan*, trans. John Felstiner (New York: W. W. Norton, 2001), p. 396. Celan was thought by many, both in Germany and outside it, to be the most important post-Second World War poet (by, for example, Heidegger and Derrida). Celan was personally acquainted with Yehuda Amichai, and in my chapter on the latter's poetry, I will relate to a poem that he published after Celan's death. An additional fact of importance for our discussion is Celan's reliance on the Buberian terms "meeting" and "conversation" for describing the action of language, an application on which I will base my analysis of these motifs in Zelda's poetry.

2 Wittgenstein, *Philosophical Investigations*, para. 309.

The poetry of Zelda (1914–1984) was warmly received during her lifetime, and is highly thought of by her readers and the scholarly community, although it has been the subject of relatively few studies. Literary criticism of and scholarly research on her work emphasized the connection between the story of her life and the content of her poems. Despite the existence of such strong links, the universal aspect of her poetry, notwithstanding its centrality in her corpus—which I will examine and exemplify—has attracted relatively little attention. The traits of the "I" that are fashioned in the poetry of Zelda reflect a singular poetic grammar that incorporates everyday language with lofty, and at times archaic and inaccessible, language, thereby creating poetry that, in Wittgensteinian terminology, "shows" sources of meaning beyond the world with which we are familiar. Her singular relation to nature and her ability to give oneself over to the natural foundation of all existence, in tandem with her poetry's piercing and sophisticated criticism of modern humanity, were harbingers of the current awareness of such concerns. Along with its extraordinary aesthetic quality, with its capacity for movement between diverse cultural contexts, Zelda's poetry offers a significant possibility of existence, which I will attempt to uncover in my analysis of her poems. This constituted selfhood can be seen as addressing the audience, and as a suggestion to include meditative contemplation of both simple and uplifting human and natural phenomena in life's daily struggles.

These statements by Celan and Wittgenstein, taken together, concisely sum up the complexity of the self-constitutive act in poetry: the poem addresses the "Thou," and seeks to reach the "heartland," in order to use poetic language to constitute the speaker's reality. The speaker, "stricken by and seeking reality," constitutes his existence by means of language, but this constitutive act is possible only in the process of addressing the audience. The possibility of the message not arriving or not being understood, too, is inherent in Celan's "message in a bottle" metaphor. This means that the very formulation in language, and especially in poetic language, does not ensure the success of "the speech-act of self-constitution." This is the place for Wittgenstein's metaphor that guides his methodological goal: philosophical inquiry is meant to show the fly how to leave the bottle, to explicate the "bumps" in understanding,[3] and to facilitate dialogue between the speaker and the audience.

1. Expression and Conversion between Everyday and Poetic Grammar

The boundary between everyday and poetic language, for Wittgenstein, is indefinable, which leads to the problematic nature of judging aesthetic language, as was discussed in chapter 1. Nonetheless, while reading poetry we can identify the special attention paid to poetic grammar, so that the choice of words and their grammatical fashioning will express irreplaceable meaning. Wittgenstein formulated the criterion for distinguishing between an everyday sentence and poetry as follows:

> We speak of understanding a sentence in the sense in which it can be replaced by another which says the same; but also in the sense in which it cannot be replaced by any other. (Any more than one musical theme can be replaced by another.) In the one case, the thought in the sentence is what is common to different sentences; in the other, something that is expressed only by these words in these positions. (Understanding a poem.)[4]

The comparison between a musical composition and a poem is based on the special pictoriality that is created by irreplaceable grammar.[5] This grammar produces a picture that "tells me itself," with the consequent

3 "The results of philosophy are the discovery of some piece of plain nonsense and the bumps that the understanding has got by running up against the limits of language. They—these bumps—make us see the value of that discovery" (Wittgenstein, *Philosophical Investigations*, para. 119).

4 Wittgenstein, *Philosophical Investigations*, para. 531.

5 "'A picture tells me itself' is what I'd like to say. That is, its telling me something consists in its own structure, in *its* own forms and colours. [What would it mean to say 'A musical theme tells me itself'?]" (Wittgenstein, *Philosophical Investigations*, para. 5).

difficulty that traps the fly in the bottle in the attempt to interpret poetry: poetic language is based on dialogic communication, on shared and public rules, while at the same time it employs unique, irreplaceable grammar that produces a picture that is to be understood as it is. Alongside the interpretive difficulty, Wittgenstein's position sheds light on the possibility of originality in poetry, since poetic grammar can produce something new in the connections between words and semantic fields, and is not bound by the possibility of replacement that is characteristic of everyday language.

The following "impression" by Zelda on the nature of poetry exemplifies the language-game that expresses transitivity between everyday and poetic language. Zelda wrote many "impressions," some of which contain motifs that were later incorporated in her poems.[6] This passage can be classified as a work that moves on the boundary between everyday grammar and poetic grammar, and therefore is more accessible for understanding the place of poetry in Zelda's self-constitution:

> Poetry is the light of sunset
> Poetry is the cry "Help"
> It is a cheer
> It is
> I want to die
> It is
> Be good to me
> It is
> You don't know who I am
> It is
> I don't need anyone
> It is

6 *Reshimah* (translated here as "impression"), in this sense, is the term coined by Zelda for writings "that need not be polished, and are natural," in contrast with poems (Zelda, *An Enchanted Bird: Writing and Art*, ed. Reuven Kassel, Yunadav Kaplun, and Rivka Goldberg [Jerusalem: Keter, 2014], p. 6 [Hebrew]). Many such "impressions" were edited from manuscripts and collected in this volume.

> the golden butterfly
> It is
> the beggar
> It is my childhood [. . .]
> one foot of poetry in the whirlpool of fate, and the other in the stillness beyond [. . .]
> Is the wordless silence, which is the subtle stillness,
> actually, the self of the eternal?[7]

Why doesn't the "addressable Thou" know the identity of the speaker? How does the "addressable reality" connect with the nature of poetry?

The direct description of the essence of poetry for Zelda in this "impression" is exceptional, since she only infrequently related to the nature of poetry or to her creative process. The above "impression" appears in a collection of writings and drawings that was published only in 2014, thirty years after her death. This collection includes "impressions" and personal letters, along with unpublished poems, that teach of the need for a discussion of self-constitution in her work.

This poem-"impression" highlights the connection between the nature of poetry for Zelda and the central features of her life and personality. Zelda insisted on maintaining her privacy, and gave few interviews. Her need for intimacy also encapsuled the downplaying of her ars poetica stance and direct and poignant expressions of loneliness (such as "Poetry is the cry 'Help' [. . .] I want to die"). Such expressions are also to be found in the poems that she chose to publish, but none appear in an ars poetica context.[8]

The outstanding motif in this "impression" (which Zelda herself did not publish) is the correlation and identity between the nature of

---

7 Zelda, *Enchanted Bird*, pp. 134–35. It seems that some of the statements in this posthumously published "impression" would have been too intimate an exposure for Zelda during her lifetime. The book's editors mentioned her request to publish the works she had kept away from the public eye only twenty years after her death.

8 See, e.g., the poems in Zelda, *The Spectacular Difference: Selected Poems of Zelda*, trans. Marcia Falk (Cincinnati: Hebrew Union College Press, 2004): *All Night I Wept* (pp. 144–45); "I awoke—the house was lit" (pp. 172–73); *Who Can Resist the Beauty of the Light* (pp. 198–99).

poetry and that of the speaker. This correlation illustrates the centrality of language in Zelda's poetic identity, such that the poetry compresses the essence of all aspects of the speaker's existence. Its lines touch on everything: both what happens in the word (the "addressable reality") and what lies beyond the real world. Furthermore, it allows her to be in the real world and in the mystical world, at one and the same time. Poetry also includes silence, which expresses her ability to touch "the stillness beyond," and movement on the axis between the routine and the mystical.

The poetic language is omnipotent, and is capable of expressing all the intentionalities of the "I," whether positively ("I want to die") or negatively ("I don't need anyone"), as Wittgenstein argued as he linked intent with language:

> It is only in a language that I can mean something by something.[9]

John Searle formulated this argument as the expressibility principle:

> Whatever can be meant can be said.[10]

Since the speaker's intent also includes movement to the mystical, the poetic grammar in this poetic passage comprises both everyday, understandable language and features that go beyond the reality and are metaphorically fashioned. An additional example of intent that exceeds the speaker's routine existence is embodied in the transition from the use of the first person, which, in the Hebrew, does not reflect gender identity ("Be good to me"; "You don't know who I am") and the use of the masculine ("I want [*rotze*, m.] to die"; "I don't need [*tzarikh*, m.] anyone"). Poetry, in contrast, is presented in feminine language that emphasizes the return to the copulative "It [*hi*, literally, "she"] is." The poetic grammar contrasts the gender identity of the poetry with that of

9 Wittgenstein, *Philosophical Investigations*, para. 35.

10 John R. Searle, *Speech-Acts: An Essay in the Philosophy of Language* (Cambridge: Cambridge University Press, 1969), p. 19.

the speaker in this passage, and constitutes an androgynous poetic identity.[11]

This choice joins together with the absence of feminine physical characteristics in Zelda's poetry. Even when the speaker uses feminine language, it generally refers to character traits that could pertain to men, and she refrains from describing physical traits characteristic of women, such as the ability to give birth, breasts, and the like. This is especially marked in the poems that Zelda wrote to her husband, such as *When You Were Here* (*Spectacular Difference*, pp. 110-11) and *Yom Kippur Eve* (pp. 156-57), but is also present in a poem such as *When Yearnings* (pp. 232–33), in which the speaker is betrothed to a river, and not to a man. Consequently, in English translation, since English lacks such gender-specificity, the speaker's expression is asexual. This also holds true for many of Zelda's poems in the original Hebrew, which are written in the first person, leaving the reader without the ability to identify the speaker as woman or man. We therefore should argue that the erotic dimension is hidden, and almost absent, from the poetry of Zelda. Her modest behavior and low-key personality might explain this absence, but cannot explain the use of the masculine when she speaks of her poetic self. This might be connected with poetry both expressing, and not expressing, the "I" of the speaker. Poetry expresses external objects such as a beggar, a butterfly, and childhood experiences, but it cannot express the "I."[12] Nonetheless, the speaker

11 The "impression" mentions items from Zelda's poetic biography (butterfly, beggar, childhood), so that she clearly refers to herself, and not another, male speaker.

12 A similar feeling is expressed in the poem-"expression" *For the Sin*:

> For the sin of not drawing my soul from my abyss, from my night, from my splendor, from my dross
> For the sin of concealing my thousands of "I" from the fire of song in the marketplaces and the caves.
> For the sin of not smacking with my fingertips the flame of mystery in each word and in each letter.
> For the sin for fleeing in wonder from the magical music in my veins.
> For the sin of thinking that the melody of the seraphim separated me from the universe.
> For the sin of calling the temple of the Infinite *Ein Sof* blood and ashes and dung (Zelda, *Enchanted Bird*, p. 34).

possesses first-person authority that constitutes her complex attitude to her poetic ability.[13] In his book *Expression and the Inner*, David Finkelstein showed how linguistic usage can be viewed as an expression of the speaker's innermost self, despite its functioning within the context of general language. Finkelstein argued that the self-attribution of mental states commands first-person authority, and there is no sense or need to confirm logically whether the speaker's self-testimony is genuine.[14]

The authority attributed to first-person testimony about what happens in the speaker's consciousness teaches of the self-constitution that occurs in the seam between everyday language and the poetic grammar. This transition is already exemplified in the title of the following poem, and during its course:

The anaphora "For the sin" constitutes a completely different consciousness, reflecting semantic change from the original meaning of this phrase in the Yom Kippur confession. In the dialogue in the poem, the speaker contrasts two aspects of her soul: the creative side, which embodies her individual uniqueness, and the side that represses, that is ashamed and subdues that singularity. The speaker expresses the conflict between these aspects, and in the process formulates the message that the creative individual must be committed, first and foremost, to the realization and expression of his creative powers. If he sins by not giving full expression to his creative vitality, then he must confess—to himself, not to God or to society.

13 Crispin Wright described Wittgenstein's contribution to understanding self-constitution through the first-person account of beliefs: "The authority standardly granted to a subject's own beliefs, or expressed avowals, about his intentional states is a *constitutive principle*: something that is not a by-product of the nature of those states, and an associated epistemologically privileged relation in which the subject stands to them, but enters primitively into the conditions of identification of what a subject believes, hopes and intends" (Crispin Wright, "Wittgenstein's Later Philosophy of Mind: Sensation, Privacy and Intentions," in *Privileged Access: Philosophical Accounts of Self-Knowledge*, ed. Brie Gertler [Aldershot: Ashgate, 2003], p. 154).

14 "An avowal of happiness [such as "I'm so happy!"] typically performs two functions: it expresses the speaker's happiness, and it says something true—that the speaker is happy [. . .] It is only when we take note of the way in which mental-state self-attributions are akin to smiles and winces that first-person authority can come into focus as an unsurprising concomitant of the fact that one of the ways in which a person may express her state of mind is by commenting on it" (David H. Finkelstein, *Expression and the Inner* [Cambrige, MA: Harvard University Press, 2003], pp. 101–2).

The Good Smell of Far Away
Something within me
Lifted its head from the sea
Longing to be in words.
I stand like that beggar
With a song inscribed on my heart
Telling every passerby
Every runner
of the hidden regions in the heart—
what madness
what shame
to lead strangers there.
The song, too, wants to die,
for trees and stones touched roughly
the melody.
The song inscribed on my heart
signals to me
that the sunset threw it
a golden drop
So that I would once again rejoice,
once again rejoice
in the rain that falls on a sunny day.
The song whispers to my soul:
Don't flee,
I hear the steps of my friends.

To the end of the world and back
Wander songs
of every people and tongue
parables and signals come,
The good smell of far away
radiates from them
If on their way they don't touch
the stench of standing water
or blood.

But finer than all the songs
is the white curtain
on which is embroidered in white thread:
Praise befits you.[15]

The poem begins with the initial formation of the poetic expression: "Something within me / Lifted its head from the sea / Longing to be in words." An inner emotion that does not yet have form and nature signals its desire to be embodied in words. This same something continues to be hidden within us, but it seeks an audience to share the experience of the hidden regions "in the heart." The poem exemplifies the difficulty inherent in its nature as a "message in a bottle," in Celan's imagery, because revealing oneself before others entails madness and shame. The connection to the act of poetry itself, in contrast, is instinctive and makes possible the speaker's spiritual elevation in the direct encounter with nature. Along with its charm, this meeting is merely an "object of comparison"[16] with the encounter with the mystical that suddenly arises in the end of the poem. In many of Zelda's poems, her poetic grammar includes a turning point at the end of the poem that, along with the element of surprise, also creates a new hierarchical balance: in this poem, the beauty of the curtain, which symbolizes the finest of all poems, lessens the beauty of nature and the poem that verbalizes it.

The poem preserves the tension between what is hidden in the soul of the speaker and what is evident to all, which "needs" the poem to express its worth in the eyes of the speaker. We understand, retrospectively, that she seeks the mystical beauty of the curtain, which dwarfs the beauty of nature, and which longs to exist in words. The turning point in the end of the poem embodies poetic grammar that "shows" the mystical, even though it cannot be verbalized. The mystical longing is the motive force behind the poetic act that produces the grammar of

15 Zelda, *Zelda's Poems* (Tel Aviv: Hakibbutz Hameuchad, 1985), pp. 200–201 (Hebrew; the original translations of Zelda's poems in this chapter are by Edward Levin).

16 Wittgenstein, *Philosophical Investigations*, para. 130.

"showing," in the same turn that demands of the reader to discern the dramatic difference between the relation to nature and that to the mystical.

Together, however, with the desire for the mystical that is hidden from all and visible only to the speaker herself, the poem also contains a magical universal depiction of poems and signals from all the world that come in a procession from far away. This inner mystical movement is aroused by relation to poetic expressions from the whole world, a relation that in the end of the poem is funneled into the mystical expression of the Jewish *parokhet*, the curtain that serves to shield the holy (see, e.g., Exodus 26:31). The poetic act occurs as a conversation between relations, and is dependent upon them. Thus, for example, poems from throughout the world give off a good smell only if not harmed by the ravages of reality. The inner poetry is rescued from the shame in exposure to all, and joins other poems by means of synesthetic fashioning: the poems give off a good smell and connect with the sight of the curtain. This poem exemplifies the centrality of language (expression of intent in words, a symposium between poems from different cultures), with the poetic ability at its best being embodied in the smell of far away, in the mystical showing.

A completely different example of a conversation with the world is provided by the following powerful poem, which is the opposite of the usual low-key manner of Zelda's poetry:

> *From His Tales, from His Contempt*
> From his tales, from his contempt, from the depths of his
> inner eye
> A breath of wicked nard
> luxuriant, lawless
> My shuttered chambers
> were invaded by the torrents of his spirit.
> My ancient woe, persecuted.
> To every thought he gave a new name
> awful as the ocean.

My soul—what's with you?
You've become a blind handmaiden.
Roar: I will see you, happiness.
Shout: The seraph shines.
Every bound is vanity.[17]

The object of the poem is unknown: the title and the first line refer to someone who might be known to the speaker, but not to the reader, thereby producing a sense of unease, of flinching from the negative act of tale-telling and contempt. This negative feeling is intensified in the second line, when the tale-telling and contempt are linked to wickedness, that is, to intentional immorality. The poem takes an unexpected turn in the third line, when the element that appears in the world as a breath is "luxuriant, lawless."

This nard penetrates the inner being of the speaker, forces itself on her soul, and causes a tempest to rage within by cursing the ancient woe and giving names to her thoughts. As a baby learns to know the world by ostensive definition,[18] so, too, the speaker comes to know her innermost thoughts by means of the power that seemingly comes from an external source and verbalizes the hidden chambers of her soul.

This unnamed external force also arouses an inner reflective dialogue within the speaker's soul, and gives her the possibility of happiness. The inner dialogue reveals that the bounds on the way to happiness are meaningless; nonetheless, the outcome of the inner struggle is unclear. The poem fashions an "I" that is split and torn between depressive acceptance of ancient woe and freedom with inherent evil, which is liable to harm the speaker's everyday life by removing the bounds of her life that she has erected. The speaker's soul

17 Zelda, *Zelda's Poems*, p. 48.

18 Wittgenstein begins his *Philosophical Investigations* with a quotation from the *Confessions* of Augustine in which he portrays how, as a child, he learned language by ostensive definition. While Wittgenstein is critical of the claimed exclusivity of this way of learning, and maintains that it does not enable learning all language skills, he nevertheless admits that this is one of the ways to understand meaning (see, e.g., *Philosophical Investigations*, para. 43). Zelda's poetry exhibits a special attitude to names (see below).

is fashioned (following James's "I as object"—"I as subject" distinction) as an object that she scrutinized from the outside. She portrays the inner struggle from a position of first-person certainty which allows for no doubt, while at the same time she fashions a battle that goes beyond the private sphere and reflects a universal state of consciousness of "being torn from the lost unity."[19]

It is intriguing to see how this poem converses with the following poem, in which faith is fashioned as the inner source of self-confidence that cannot be undermined by any external source. Faith is a bulwark against "floating in space" and the intermingling of good and evil:

> *I Shall Not Float Unreined*
> I shall not float unreined
> in space
> lest a cloud swallow
> the thin band in my heart
> that separates good from evil.
> I have no existence
> without the lightning and thunder
> that I heard at Sinai.[20]

Being chained to the earth and the preclusion of good and evil intermingling are founded on the thin band in the speaker's soul, so that she is totally aware of its limited power and the threat that lurks without. She nevertheless formulates in poetic grammar first-person testimony to revelation, which is mainly the giving of the commandments and the agreement of each individual in Israel to accept them. She uses metaphorical grammar to establish the element of faith in her self-constitution, so that this poem, more than others, clearly expresses the first-person certainty that is based on a mystical experience.

As is typical of many of Zelda's poems, the last line guides us to reread the poem retrospectively in order to understand the starting

19 Georg Wilhelm Friedrich Hegel, *Hegel's Preface to the Phenomenology of Spirit* (Princeton, NJ: Princeton University Press, 2005), p. 76.
20 Zelda, *Spectacular Difference*, pp. 230–31.

point of its entire course. This starting point, the mystical experience of hearing the lightning and thunder at Sinai, fashions a specific faith that is based on the observance of the commandments. This faith also includes a certain inner line that distinguished between good and evil, and therefore prevents free and boundless movement. It seems that the speaker in this song is at peace with her choice of limiting her mental freedom and of connecting the Revelation at Sinai with the distinction between good and evil.

If, however, we compare this poem with others by Zelda, we find here a more complex conversation between the different facets of the speaker's soul. This conversation questions the function of boundaries in the process of creating poetry, and, accordingly, in the process of self-constitution in poetic language. Besides the inner indecision regarding the proper relation between freedom and creativity, we find in Zelda's poetry a diversity of fashionings of dialogic grammar in which she is uncertain in her attitude to human nature in general, and to her character, specifically. For instance, in the poem *All This Misery—When Will I Die?*, we are unclear as to the identity of the person to whom the rhetorical question is directed, but, patently, the death-wish is at least in tension with (if not in total contradiction to) the commandment: "Choose life" (Deuteronomy 30:19) and all that is derived from it in Jewish tradition.

All This Misery—When Will I Die?
All this misery—When will I die?
My folly—a heavy burden;
tenderness—a heavy burden.
In vain, the sea wind kisses my eyes
and the grasses of Mount Carmel
pamper me with honey and myrrh.
I scorn the hopes of the sun
and the promises of blossoms.[21]

The speaker vocally expresses her wish to die, because she is weary of the suffering in her life. Nothing consoles her, certainly not human

21 Zelda, *Spectacular Difference*, pp. 60–61.

traits that might make the difficulty more bearable, nor the elements of nature and their features, which in many other poems offer balm for the soul, even in its most difficult moments. The poem questions, or at the very least offers an alternative to the accepted interpretation of the conception of art in Zelda's poetry, and courageously and sincerely presents the difficulty of being consoled. This and other poems, such as *From His Tales, from His Contempt*, transform the dialogic grammar from a figurative technique into an existentialist element, in the spirit of Wittgenstein and Buber: the relation of the speaker in the poetry of Zelda splits into different directions—to nature, to people, and to the mystical dimension.

In his later *Philosophical Investigations*, Wittgenstein based the moves of his philosophical inquiry on realistic or imaginary dialogues, since he wanted to examine intermediate cases, compare various examples, and study different aspects of situations.[22] I wish to add to Wittgenstein's systematic methodology Buber's existentialist conception regarding the three areas of relation that he defined in regard to language. These methodologies complement each other in our study of Zelda's poetry, since Buber explains the areas of relation and defines them as regards language, while Wittgenstein offers the methodical tools that facilitate their study, and does not remain in an abstract and vague plane.

2. Dialogic Grammar: Internal and External Observations

The transition that Wittgenstein made from the methodology of *Tractatus* to that of *Philosophical Investigations* is based on a dynamic methodology that creates meaning and its comprehension. As I showed in detail in the discussion of dialogic grammar, Wittgenstein attempted to show how language-games accompany all our activities, and how the various types of states of consciousness are verbalized. The dynamic nature of language-games and the tension between inner states of consciousness, on the one hand, and, on the other, their formulation in

22 Wittgenstein, *Philosophical Investigations*, para. 122; *PPF*, para. 113.

public language are preserved throughout his thought, from beginning to end, and the seeming "resolution" of this tension is always temporary and ad hoc. This tension is finely exemplified in the various types of Zelda's dialogic poems that will be presented below. Before this, however, I wish to support Wittgenstein's methodological decision with Buber's existentialist conception of dialogue.

Buber viewed language as the stage on which dialogue occurs. While Wittgenstein concentrated on what takes place on the stage, Buber was concerned with the existential movement that produces dialogue. Wittgenstein and Buber presumably belong to two diametrically opposed philosophical schools: Wittgenstein comes from analytic philosophy, while Buber has his roots in continental philosophy. Notwithstanding this, both were troubled by the question of how meaning is constituted in the world, and how man can perceive this meaning; in the ethical sphere, they placed responsibility on the shoulders of the individual. Each of them, in his own way, denied external authority, and formulated a type of perfectionism as an eternal, never-ending task. This task is based on dialogic methodology, and at this juncture we should indicate a significant difference between the two philosophers.

From *Tractatus* throughout all his writings, Wittgenstein consistently removed the mystical from the context of the philosophical discussion. This said and done, the importance and very existence of the mystical for Wittgenstein is acknowledged in recent studies as well, to the extent of describing "his whole philosophy as a kind of mystic revelation, remembering that mystic *means* what cannot and should not be spoken."[23]

Buber, as well, exhibited a similar relation between the mystical and language, but unlike Wittgenstein, for Buber the mystical is one of the types of relation that he lists as the underpinning for the desideratum of man's existence. In a paraphrase of the wording that begins Genesis and John, Buber declares: "In the beginning is relation."[24]

23 Originally stated by B. McGuiness in 1988; quoted in Newton Garver, *Wittgenstein and Approaches to Clarity* (Amherst, NY: Humanity Books, 2006), p. 99.

24 Martin Buber, *I and Thou*, trans. Ronald Gregor Smith (Edinburgh: T. & T. Clark, 1937), p. 18.

Unlike Wittgenstein's assertion that it is possible to speak and investigate only in public language, Buber spoke of three types of relation: the relation with nature acts below language, the relation with people is formed in language in the world, in the sphere-in-between, and the relation to the spiritual is sensed, but cannot be expressed in language.[25] The nature of relation to the mystical is the same for Wittgenstein and Buber, with the latter's starting assumption being given a more complex formulation, making use of Wittgenstein: there is relation and there is language, with differing relations between them, in accordance with the object of the relation. The three-relation model will enable us to deepen our examination of the various aspects of Zelda's poetic character, since it includes a complex attitude to nature, people, and the mystical—which remains nonverbalized, sublime, at times an object of longing and consolation, and at other times, not. Additionally, these relations are fashioned in the inner space that at times engages in a dialectic with itself.

The conversation that drives the poem *About Facts* is an example of such an inner conflict. The nature of faith is clarified in the inner debate conducted within the poem, with the certainty of faith fashioned as a derivative of the argument between the soul and the senses. Unlike the previous poems, in which the speaker expresses the experience of the "I" that is united, as regards both the acceptance of the Torah and the desire to die, the current poem presents a split within the speaker's soul. This rupture is between two manners of consciousness: the sensory system, which discovers the world empirically and draws according conclusions; and the soul, which intuitively reveals its inner

25 "The spheres in which the world of relation arises are three.

"First, our life with nature. There the relation sways in gloom, beneath the level of speech. Creatures live and move over against us, but cannot come to us, and when we address them as *Thou*, our words cling to the threshold of speech.

"Second, our life with men. There the relation is open and in the form of speech. We can give and accept the *Thou*.

"Third, our life with the intelligible forms. There the relation is clouded, yet it discloses itself; it does not use speech, yet begets it. We perceive no *Thou*, but none the less we feel we are addressed and we answer—forming, thinking, acting. We speak the primary word with our being, though we cannot utter *Thou* with our lips" (Buber, *I and Thou*, p. 6).

truth and is also based on metaphysical experiences that are beyond the bounds of the empiric world and everyday language:

About Facts
My soul says:
"Facts conceal the sea."

My senses say:
"Facts are an island in the ocean."

My soul says:
"Facts are a wall around the self."

My senses say:
"Facts are a window lit in the dark,
a lens into my core."

And from the beginning,
the abyss said:
"Facts are a lion
roaring in space
existing
existing
existing."[26]

The speaker consciously describes the split in her soul between the senses and the soul in relation to the manner in which events in the world are justified. The starting point is the attitude to the fact, and the disagreement is whether facts conceal what they attest to, or whether they constitute a sea of certainty regarding the world. This age-old discussion concerning the relationship between language and reality is concisely, and masterfully, stated by Wittgenstein in his description of the manifold ways in which language acts: it enables the presentation of states of

26 Zelda, *Spectacular Difference*, pp. 236–37.

affairs that contain facts, but obviously, it is not identical with the facts, but rather accompanies them, at times in the form of pictorialization, and on other occasions as delineating the manner of action. The poetic grammar employed by the speaker, when she says: "Facts are a wall around the self," portrays the feeling of enchainment and repression of the self, when it is forced, at times, to contend with facts that are contrary to its will. The poem finely illustrates Wittgenstein's argument that language bewitches us,[27] so that we attribute failures to it, while the failure of comprehension ensues from our thought. Facts clash with the speaker's self-perception, since they repress her erupting faith. The turning point at the end of this poem, too, compels us to read it anew: already, from the outset, the lion within her soul roars the existence of the mystical. That is, the seeming disagreement was resolved before it began. Since, however, this revelation makes itself known only at the end of the poem, the tension of the senses-soul chasm is preserved. The inner dialogue in the poem embodies the speaker's relation to the world of facts and to the mystical world.

Nature is metaphysically fashioned here: the sea, the island, and the lion express inner voices within the speaker's soul, and exemplify Buber's assertion of the existence of such voices "beneath the level of speech." This fashioning attests to relation to the natural world, but this relation is fashioned in a much more meaningful way in other poems. In *Heavy Silence*, for instance, the speaker expresses the death experience, which is beyond the bounds of language and cannot be expressed as embodied within the activity of nature. Actually, the poem speaks of the death of the speaker herself and its consequences for her relation to nature: the verbal ability that includes classification and the giving of names to objects in nature and animals will cease to function. Thus the poem fashions the relationship between language and nature in the speaker's consciousness as one of dependency: without verbal capability, it is impossible to perceive the meaning of the details of nature:

---

27 "Philosophy is a struggle against the bewitchment of our understanding by the resources of our language" (Wittgenstein, *Philosophical Investigations*, para. 109).

Heavy Silence
Death will take the spectacular difference
between fire and water
and cast it to the abyss.

Heavy silence
will crouch like a bull
on the names we have given
the birds of the sky
and the beasts of the field,
the evening skies,
the vast distances in space,
and things hidden from the eye.

Heavy silence will crouch like a bull
on all the words.
And it will be as hard for me to part
from the names of things
as from the things themselves.

O Knower of Mysteries,
help me understand
what to ask for
on the final day.[28]

The speaker magnifies the importance of language to the extent that she describes her relation to names as that to the things themselves. Language exceeds its representative role to that of substance itself and the substance that finds expression in the poetic grammar. The poem opens with a statement that death expunges the differences between things. Death is depicted as embracing all, despite this actually being the personal viewpoint of the speaker, who sees death approaching, and in her perception of the world, it will encompass the entire world.

28 Zelda, *Spectacular Difference*, pp. 220–21.

Jacobson understood the speaker's difficulty as that of casting off the human distinctions that give meaning to life, inspired by the biblical narrative in which Adam gives names to the living creatures (Genesis 2:19).[29] But an additional, more obscure tension is concealed in this allusion. The speaker wonders at the reason for the constitution of the human world (inter alia, by the classification and naming of the living creatures), if, in the end, death lies in wait for it. This existential question, which was most strongly formulated by Heidegger, is quite clearly at loggerheads with the conception of religiosity honed so sharply in the poem *I Shall Not Float Unrefined*. A relation is fashioned universally to whatever exists in nature, in face of the fashioning of the religious relation in the national context of the Giving of the Torah, and in the face of death.

Already in the first line the speaker returns the reader to the reality that preceded Creation, before the separation between water and water in Genesis 1:6. The phrase that stands out is "spectacular difference," since the distinction in language functions as world-creator. Intriguingly, God is absent from the picture: death will remove the differences between things that God traditionally created. There is a certain degree of correlation between the course of the poem and the biblical chronology: in Genesis, Adam gives names to all the beasts, and the Bible emphasizes: "and whatever the man called each living creature, that would be its name" (Genesis 2:19). The speaker returns to this point in history when, in the second stanza, she describes in the first-person plural how the "heavy silence" threatens to negate man's contribution to Creation. The personal stance of the speaker is fashioned only in the third stanza, when she confesses her difficulty in parting from the names, no less than from the things themselves. The poem's gradual movement to its focus on the personal experience is obviously connected to its beginning, in circular fashion, and sheds light on the death that opens the poem as a private experience.

The dialogic relation is fashioned in a complex and fascinating way: in the first phase, the speaker applies her private experience to the

29 David Jacobson, *Creator, Are You Listening? Israeli Poets on God and Prayer* (Bloomington: Indiana University Press, 2007), p. 39.

world as a whole, and then gradually exposes her feeling of partnership with the world from its beginnings, until she reaches her inner, personal point and bemoans her taking her leave. Her relation is to things "beneath the level of speech"—to nature, to things above the level of speech, to death, and to the Jewish idea of the creation of the world. These two, both those below and those above, are expressed in the sphere-in-between of human grammar, in poetic language. Even if it seems that nature dominates language and erases the distinctions of the latter, in practice, experience is fashioned in language that does battle with death, making use of the will to live embodied in the relation to names.

The motif of giving a name in the existential constitution of something was discussed above in the analysis of *From His Tales, from His Contempt*, in the context of uncovering hidden thoughts that are exposed against the speaker's will. In that analysis, we mentioned the reference to Augustine's discussion of the way in which children learn their mother tongue, in order to state that Wittgenstein saw this as the manner of representation of things.[30] Wittgenstein's critique of Augustine was that this did not suffice to describe emotions and experiences, and he therefore proposed adding to the "ostensive definition" observing the use of the word in its concrete context.[31] Zelda's poetry exemplifies how poetic grammar, without stating this outright, shows how the two rules for imparting meaning that Wittgenstein formulated are combined (and exemplifies his claim of language's ability to present the rules that facilitate its action).

The concrete context is the death experience, in the composing of which the speaker returns to her search for the source of the feeling of difficulty in parting from the world. This clarification touches upon the basis of the relation to the world that she feels: the sensation of her partnership with God and with Adam in giving names and in distinguishing between things. At this juncture, an important central element in Zelda's poetic self comes to light: the feeling of omnipotence that gives her poetic skill. The ability to give names, to distinguish between

30 Wittgenstein, *Philosophical Investigations*, para. 1.
31 Wittgenstein, *Philosophical Investigations*, para. 2, 7.

things, and to sense their essence is distinctive of her attitude to the world and fashions the approaching death experience.

The sense of ownership imparted by her poetic ability is more indirectly fashioned in the concrete context of the city of Jerusalem, while incorporating a metaphorical dialogue in the speaker's thought between her and some unnamed soldier:

> sapphires, turquoise, and rubies
> the silver treetops tremble like my heart.
> And when a foreign, enemy king
> crushes our awesome love
> for the City of David,
> the roots of the olive tree
> hear the small soldier's blood
> whispering to the earth:
> "The city is crouching on my life."[32]

Unlike the death experience that is crafted as splendid isolation, in this poem Zelda fashions a counter-character that reinforces her experience regarding the city: "The city is crouching on my life." The experience is formulated as a first-person expression spoken by the soldier, but it can also be interpreted as joining the soldier's feeling with that of the speaker. The latter's emotions regarding Jerusalem are fashioned as metaphors of precious stones from the biblical word-game. The wealth of gems, in all their varied colors, creates an atmosphere of erotic relations in which the beloved receives this collection of jewels as a gesture from her lover. The speaker expressly uses the word "love," and personifies her attitude to Jerusalem, so much so that it seems that the city is a substitute for human love. This feeling is strengthened in the words of the soldier, with their almost obsessive resonance, as if it is impossible to escape or free oneself from the city's domination of the soul of whoever is devoted to it, as the soldier devoted himself to its defense.

32 Zelda, *Spectacular Difference*, pp. 148–49.

The highlighting of the dialogue by the use of quotation marks draws into sharper focus the lack of dialogue on the contentual level: the city influences the speaker and the soldier directly, with no need for dialogue. Even so, the poetic grammar constitutes an inner, and not necessarily conscious, dialogue: the speaker fabricates what happens in the soldier's soul, to reflect the contrast in her soul between love of the city and the anxiety that it creates in the frequent wars that take place in it. Her fascination with the city and the difficulty are not resolved, they rather act in parallel, and the poem facilitates the simultaneous fashioning of contradictory emotions, which is difficult to describe in everyday language.

At the beginning of this chapter we mentioned how Celan developed the idea that a poem is a message directed to an interlocutor. The dialogic nature of Zelda's poetry, however, is fashioned in many directions, between which an inner dialogue is conducted, in which the speaker encounters different facets of her personality. I will preface our discussion by adding two terms that Celan uses to shed light on the action of the poem: encounter and conversation. Celan apparently formulated these terms under the influence of Buber, whom he knew personally, along with his familiarity with Buber's writings.[33] What is pertinent for our purposes is Celan's adaption of the Buberian term encounter for the poetic act:

> The poem is lonely [. . .] Its author stays with it. Does this very act not place the poem already here, at its inception, in the **encounter**, *in the mystery of encounter*? The poem intends

33 "I have already drawn attention to the fact that the solitary category 'man' is to be understood as a working together of distance and relation. Unlike all other living beings, man stands over against a world from which he has been set at a distance and, unlike all other living beings, he can again and again enter into relationship with it. This fundamental double stance nowhere manifests itself so comprehensively as in language. Man—he alone—speaks, for only he can address the other, as the other standing at a distance over against him; but in addressing it, he enters into relationship" (Martin Buber, "The Word That Is Spoken," in *The Knowledge of Man*, ed. Maurice Friedman, trans. Maurice Friedman and Ronald Gregor Smith [New York: Harper & Row, 1965], p. 117).

> another, needs this other, needs an opposite. It goes toward it, bespeaks it [. . .] The attention which the poem pays to all that it encounters, its more acute sense of detail, outline, structure, color, but also of the "tremors and hints"—all this is not, I think, achieved by an eye competing (or concurring) with ever more precise instruments, but, rather, by a kind of concentration mindful of all our dates [. . .] The poem becomes—under what conditions—the poem of a person who still perceives, still turns towards phenomena, addressing and questioning them. **The poem becomes conversation**—often desperate conversation. **Only the space of this conversation can establish what is addressed, can gather it into a "you" around the naming and speaking I.**[34]

At times the dialogic grammar in Zelda's poems creates an encounter with an (at least seemingly) external element when the encounter generates a conversation that exposes the speaker's selfhood. As Celan stresses, it is only in the dialogic expanse of the conversation that the poem can create the identity of the "I" who speaks. I will exemplify three types of an expanse that creates self in Zelda's poetry: a rhetorical dialogic conversation, a conversation of struggle and conflict with the world, and a conversation in which an actual encounter occurs. Two poems with the word "Dialogue" in their title are examples of the rhetorical dialogic expanse.

In these two poems the dialogic grammar depicts inner dialogue that reaches an impasse. Nonetheless, each poem constitutes an expanse in which the speaker's desires are formulated, so that the speaker becomes "Thou" for the reader.

Dialogue
The old bird heard
The stifled wail

34 Paul Celan, "The Meridian," in *Collected Prose*, trans. Rosmarie Waldrop (New York: Routledge, 2003), pp. 49–50.

Strangest of all that is known
the cry of the gold mines:
—How shall we play with the sun
in flickers
How shall we answer it
with sparks—
For we are kept apart
by a thousand inkwells of dust.
How can we make each other whole?[35]

The poem opens with a picture of an old bird that hears concealed wailing. The bird does not respond, and, in the spirit of Buber and Celan, the dialogue is conducted in the sphere-in-between in which words are uttered in poetry. The bird hears the complaint of the gold mines, that they cannot play with the sun and thereby respond to it by actively participating in a dialogue. In practice, the poem presents the desire for dialogue and the inability to take part in it, because of opposing forces in nature: the dust is more powerful that the flickers, and therefore they cannot conduct with the sun the dialogue that would lead them to wholeness. The poem *Two Elements* contains a dialogue that, too, is unilateral: the title of this poem, as well, promises a dialogue between two, while in the poem itself, only the moon speaks, and the cypress is silent ("The cypress does not answer [. . .] But the flame will not understand").[36] These poems eloquently present dialogue as a means for self-fashioning by creating the third expanse, that of conversation between two, so that even if one of the participants does not respond, something, nonetheless, is created.

In contrast, the poem *Savage Dialogue*, even though in it, too, the two participants do not speak in a dialogue, the speaker seemingly forces the sun to respond to her profound grief, and to deport itself accordingly:

35 Zelda, *Spectacular Difference*, pp. 174–75.
36 Zelda, *Spectacular Difference*, pp. 234–35.

Savage Dialogue
A savage dialogue
between a woman wrapped in grief
and the sun above
in the delicate, trembling tongue
of light rays,
in the secret
of the rainbow's colors—
And when she shuts her eyes,
suddenly
a red torrent rushes towards her
and blots out the peacock's feathers
painted by the air.
And when she shuts her weary eyes,
a dark sea swallows
the world.[37]

The savagery is expressed both in the intensity of the address to the sun and in the act of consciousness that this encounter creates: a beautiful vision of a peacock. The peacock, however, appears for just a moment only in order to vanish again when the speaker closes her eyes and the darkness of sadness dominates her consciousness and ends the poem. The sphere-in-between that the dialogue created in its compulsive savagery cannot last, and dissipates. Nonetheless, the poem reflects how the speaker uses her relations to nature in an imaginary process to overcome the darkness of depression, and does not rely on other factors such as people or God. Nature apparently is an element with which the speaker feels most instinctively connected, in anguish as in normal times, as is evident in the following poem. I think this is the most caustic poem that Zelda composed, in which she gives expression to the distance and alienation that she felt toward the modern world in all its manifestations. The poem embodies conversational dialogue, since the speaker—against her will—is situated firmly within the generation

37 Zelda, *Spectacular Difference*, pp. 114–15.

about which she writes. The poem is an attempt to create a sphere-in-between that could contain two diametrically opposed types of will, so that the dialogue is conducted between the will of the speaker and the motivation that drives the generation and fashions the world in which she lives:

A Drunk, Embroiled Will
A drunk, embroiled, bleeding will
that imposed itself on constellations,
on the world's secret,
is blazing in my generation's heart.
Fettering the free, festive air,
with a strict hand.
The sun and the deeps are wheel horses
on its farm.

It is strange to be a woman,
simple, domestic, feeble,
in an insolent, violent generation,
to be shy, weary,
in a cold generation, a generation of wheelers and dealers,
for whom Orion, Pleiades, and moon
are advertisement lights, golden marks, army badges,
To march in a shaded street
reflecting, slowly, slowly,
to taste China
in a perfumed peach,
to look at Paris
in a cold movie theater,
while they fly
around the world,
while they fly in space.
To be among conquerors
and conquered,
while every creature is ashamed, afraid,
alone.

It is strange to wither before clouds of enmity,
while the heart is drawn
to a myriad of worlds.[38]

The poem is scathingly critical of the nature of the will that drives the people of her generation. The dialogic grammar presents two possible ways of existence, but the encounter between them is forced, without conversation, rather in opposition: the generation acts in a fast, forceful manner and silences any possibility of spiritual or mystical expression. Facing this reality, the speaker wants to go about slowly and enjoy the taste of a simple fruit that connects her imagination to China, or to sail in her imagination to Paris, when she watches a movie in a theater. The poem ends with harsh criticism—that is not typical of Zelda's low-key poetry—within the context of a social critique: the entire world acts in the binary pattern of conquerors and conquered, and this pattern pushes man as such to a place of shame and fear, and mainly, solitude.

We find an interesting tension between the adjectives used by the speaker in the third-person description, which are biting and uncharacteristic of Zelda's poetic way, and the hedging "strange" to which she returns when she depicts her feelings in the first person. In my opinion, the force of this opposition ensues from the differences in the ways the speaker conducts her life: in her outward behavior, she is a shy and weary character, who does not directly challenge the people who act violently and clash with each other; in the realm of her consciousness, however, she totally rejects their way of life. The poem thereby fashions a reflective dialogue in which the speaker's self is fashioned in two different and parallel ways, which is possible in the poem's sphere-in-between.

I want to digress from Zelda's poetry, and compare this poem to one by Shimon Adaf that is included in his latest prose work, *The Wedding Gifts*.[39] The similarity between the poems by Zelda and Adaf

38 Zelda, "Seven Poems by Zelda," trans. Varda Koch Ocker, The Free Library, http://www.thefreelibrary.com/Seven+poems+by+Zelda.-a0138949899.
39 Shimon Adaf, *The Wedding Gifts* (Or Yehuda: Kinneret Zmora-Bitan Dvir, 2014) (Hebrew).

is arresting: in each, the speaker faces the world in which he or she lives, and refuses to cooperate and obey basic norms, such as the rule of force and repression, self-definition in accordance with given patterns, and the race after achievements. The encounter between the speaker and the world is inevitable, but the confrontation draws into sharper focus the distinct "I" of the speaker. In Zelda's poem, her heart longs for the celestial spheres, while Adaf's speaker insists on remaining outside the world, "before the hinge," and not adopting one of the supports that the world proffers in order to constitute identity and function in the world.

Zelda's and Adaf's poems differ in many ways, from their disparate relationship to Jewish tradition to other relationships between experience and emotion, on the one hand, and, on the other, philosophical rationalism. Notwithstanding this, the stance taken toward the world that Kierkegaard formulated as "subjectivity is truth," and the desire to express a distinct "I," in contrast to all the norms by which life is evaluated, offer a similar path to self-constitution. The latter uses poetic grammar to create ways of life and judgment that do not exist in the real world in which the speaker lives. Adaf's poem presents a "negotiation" between the world and the speaker, but employing irony to draw into sharp focus the world's coercion of any individual who does not accept its dictates:

I encountered the world
At an outer point that faces
a hinge
How dark
is the space
not the darkness of outer space
Perhaps as children

Who were abandoned to the forests
To grow up among a wolf's
fangs, his teeth
And a touch or voice returned

to them, years later,
Their humanity
(Loss that grieves momentarily
for a pattern of acknowledgment)
Yes
perhaps that moment
(That is, like it
was)

And the world said, Bring it in
The world said, airports, tracks
of metal and electricity
I said, No
I said—No.

And the world said, Bend your knee,
The world said, Sex!
I said, No
No.
And the world said, Sleep, my wine
The world said, Cities
Large and fortified.
I said, No
I said—No.
And the world said, Superposition, man, the wisdom
Of old women,

I will be
the door, I will be the reality.
I said, no
At the outer point before
hinge, I said
No
No
Leave me be

And the world said, See what this is
in the middle of speaking, how much
of you I already have, how much
of you is already
Here.[40]

The poem sets forth an imaginary possibility of consciousness: the speaker encounters the world before he enters it, so that he cannot truly confront his distinct self with the manner in which the world demands that he conduct himself. If we use this poem as the key to understanding the poetry of Zelda, we may state that Zelda's speaker, as well, refused to conform to the world's dictates, as if she had been created outside it, based on another way of acting. In each of the poems the speaker objects to the mores prevalent in the world, which are based on force and achievement. "The world" wants to be the compass, the reality space by which every individual is given his worth, but the speaker refuses to comply. While in Zelda's poem the individual remains alone and ashamed, Adaf's character succeeds in inserting his self in the world, despite its different nature. The world cannot prevent the penetration of the different self that even, while speaking, expands into the world. Here we have an actual dialogue in which the influence of the distinct "I" on the world happens within a dialogue. Zelda's poem, in contrast, presents her existential alternative in the act of poetry that finds its place in the world, even if it does not penetrate into the general discourse.

The comparison of the poems leads to a discussion that concludes our examination of the various types of dialogic grammar by comparing Buber's terms "meeting" and "mismeeting" (as he invented a new German word: *Vergegnung*, as distinct from *Begugnung*). Buber coined this term in his autobiographical *Meetings*, when he distinguished between a successful meeting and one that is confused or missed.[41] In

40 Adaf, *Wedding Gifts*, pp. 7–8.

41 "The house in which my grandparents lived had a great rectangular inner courtyard surrounded by a wooden balcony extending to the roof on which one could walk around the building at each floor. Here I stood once in my fourth year with a girl

comparison with the metaphysical thought in Adaf's poem in which the speaker stands outside the world, Buber portrays the mystic leap that occurs in the course of the meeting with another person. This description is based on Buber's own experience, in which he changed his concept of conversion: instead of using it to refer to religious revelation, he began to employ it for the sense of illumination in human encounter, which is the forum for understanding between two conversants that exceeds words.

Buber told of an autobiographical experience of a conversation during the course of which and consequent to which illumination occurred, which he called "a conversion." For him, a routine event of meeting and conversation became the revelation of what is true religiosity. This everyday occurrence raises to his consciousness the division in his life, causing a healing conversion. This conversion occurs in an actual meeting in which questions of the meaning of life are discussed.[42]

several years older, the daughter of a neighbor, to whose care my grandfather had entrusted me. We both leaned on the railing. I cannot remember that I spoke of my mother to my older comrade. But I hear still how the big girl said to me: 'No, she will never come back.' I know that I remained silent, but also that I cherished no doubt of the truth of the spoken words. It remained fixed to me; from year to year it cleaved ever more to my heart, but after more than ten years I began to perceive it as something that concerned not only me, but all men. Later I once made up the word 'Vergegnung'—'mismeeting,' or 'miscounter'—to designate the failure of a real meeting between men. When after another twenty years I again saw my mother, I could not gaze into her still astonishingly beautiful eyes without hearing from somewhere the word 'Vergegnung' as a word spoken to me. I suspect that all that I have learned about the genuine meeting in the course of my life had its first origin in that hour on the balcony" (Martin Buber, *Meetings*, ed. Maurice Friedman [La Salle, IL: Open Court, 1973], pp. 18–19).

42 "In my earlier years the 'religious' was for me the exception. There were hours that were taken out of the course of things. From somewhere or other the firm crust of everyday was pierced [. . .] 'Religious experience' was the experience of an otherness that did not fit into the context of life [. . .] The 'religious' lifted you out. Over there now lay the accustomed existence with its affairs, but here illumination and ecstasy and rapture held without time or sequence. Thus your own being encompassed a life here and a life beyond, and there was no bond but the actual moment of the transition. The illegitimacy of such a division of the temporal life [. . .] was brought home to me by an everyday event, an event of judgment [. . .] I had a visit from an unknown young man, without being there in spirit [. . .] I did not treat him any more remissly than all his contemporaries who were in the habit of seeking me out about this time of day as an oracle that is ready to listen to

Buber did not indicate a specific cause of his conversion regarding the young man who came to visit him, but he attests to a sudden illumination, the likes of which are to be seen also in Zelda's poetry: within routine, everyday experience, when he did not act any slower than usual towards this young man, his attention was suddenly riveted in the depths of the human encounter. Buber concluded that a true mystical experience is not bound up with the relation between man and God, but with conversation between people, to be more precise, with conversation that enables true encounter.

The poem *Shaded by Oak* paints a picture of an encounter with a beggar woman who distinguishes between two sides of the speaker's behavior: compassion and lovingkindness externally, in contrast with the refusal to give friendship. The speaker portrays a meeting that, in real time, was partial, and in a certain sense missed, but in retrospect, seems to have led the speaker to a tangible and true human encounter. Zelda's poetry depicts some meetings with those whom life has treated harshly, whether real or imaginary (including Mephibosheth, a crippled beggar, and in the current poem, a beggar woman). Her relation to people is directed especially to those on the fringes of society, as a precis of humanity lacking ulterior motives; a humanity that originates in a sensitive and attentive gaze, but nonetheless is neither pathetic nor totally devoted, but rather aware of the chasm between herself and the person whom she meets:

> *Shaded by the Oak*
> An old woman, with sick legs
> Her hand outstretched for alms in the street
> Drinking tea in the paved courtyard
> Shaded by the oak.
> It's a wonder to me how she breaks through
> from the terrors of angry fate

---

reason. I conversed attentively and openly with him—only I omitted to guess questions which he did not put. Later, not long after, I learned from one of his friends—he himself was no longer alive—the essential content of these questions. I learned that he had come to me not casually, but borne by destiny, not for a chat but for a destination" (Buber, *Meetings*, pp. 45–46).

to refined etiquette
to royal manners that spread their wings
In a life of all good, in a comely life.
The light that shines in her brown eyes
Saw Job in the heart of the tempest.
The shame of the gutter did not keep her
from the fear of the heavens.
Suddenly, she said to me:
"Did you see the man who sells pins and needles in the cellar
at the corner of the street?
Did you see his gazes?"
I was amazed
for within the desolation of the shadow of death she can
behold
the visions of life.
It was only when her heart was overflowing
and she offered me a jar of honey
she had been given in some alley
I discovered, bewildered, my love was still in the lower
spheres
For I had to smash seven walls of refusal
so that I could receive from her
the honey, the gift of friendship.[43]

The beggar woman introduces the speaker to old age, sickness, and want, while, surprisingly, exhibiting noble behavior that rises above the vicissitudes of fate. In expressing her wonder, the speaker already includes her empathetic worldview: a poor and sick person in one who has suffered a bitter fate, which could happen to anyone. She looks at the beggar woman with wonder, and not only with empathy; furthermore, she sees in the beggar woman's eyes the light that shined in Job's eyes. Job's insight after God reveals Himself was "fear of the heavens," that is, the acceptance of the kingdom of

43 Zelda, *Zelda's Poems*, p. 210.

Heaven out of fear. Job understood (according to the interpretation of the poem) that the ravages of his fate are part of a greater plan that he cannot perceive, and therefore all that remains for him is fear of the Lord.

The nobility of the beggar woman in the poem is perceived by the speaker as resulting from an inner balance based on her seeing her fate in proportion to what happens in the world. To this point, the dialogic grammar acts indirectly: the speaker sees the light in the beggar woman's eyes and understands its meaning, that is, something happens in the sphere-in-between of the meeting between two people, but this encounter takes place only in the speaker's consciousness.

In the next stage, a surprising illumination occurs in the direct dialogue between the speaker and the beggar woman, when the latter, apparently admiringly, draws the speaker's attention to the gazes of another beggar. The direct dialogue strikes the speaker like a bolt of lightning, acting both as conversational dialogue and reflective dialogue: the speaker is stunned, first of all, within herself. She appreciates the beggar woman's ability to look upon another person and hold him in esteem. The attempt at conversation, however, does not develop into dialogue between the two woman, but rather is an inner conversation. The speaker understands that she herself has not spiritually risen to receive the jar of honey that the beggar woman offers to her. Despite her esteem for the actions of the beggar woman, she cannot relate to her as a friend, as a person of equal worth.

The meeting in the poem is missed, because the speaker does not respond to the beggar woman, and especially, due to her inner refusal to treat the beggar woman as the speaker herself thought was proper. The poem fashions the fascinating state of consciousness that expresses the tension between behavior in reality and the ethical stance of the speaker, who continually seeks perfectionism. The result is a "genuine meeting," but not a "genuine conversation."[44]

44 "The great characteristic of men's life with one another, speech, is doubly significant as a witness to the principle of human life [. . .] *Genuine conversation*, and therefore every actual fulfillment of relation between men, means acceptance of

Note should be taken of the complex manner in which the faithful position is fashioned in the poem: on the one hand, Job's consciousness is expressed as a faithful ideal that is embraced by the beggar woman. On the other hand, the speaker attests of herself that she is trapped in a sort of haughtiness that does not allow her to accept the beggar woman's proffered friendship, regardless of the esteem in which she holds the latter. Despite the presence of Hasidic motifs in Zelda's work, this poem highlights her individuality and sober self-awareness, which at times is opposed to what she views as values. The authenticity, sincerity, and directness of its self-examination turn this and other poems into a confession of self-constitution with the courage to include its flaws.

The illumination felt by the speaker is one of comprehension, not one of change, and certainly not of divine revelation. This is a conversion in the sense suggested by Buber, in which the consciousness is significantly changed following a meeting, even if the conversation in it did not include the content of the illumination.

The definition of conversion also influenced Buber's definition of the faith experience and his conception of God, which enable us to understand various elements in Zelda's poetry that exceed the conventions of faith commonly ascribed to her writing (such as Hasidic *devekut* [communion with God, or devotion] and Orthodoxy). Buber based his faith on the possibility of a conversation and confession regarding

---

otherness. When two men inform one another of their basically different views about an object [. . .] everything depends so far as human life is concerned, on whether each thinks of the other as the one he is [. . .] The strictness and depth of human individuation, the elemental otherness of the other is then not merely noted as the necessary starting point, but is affirmed from the one being to the other [. . .] Human life and humanity come into being in *genuine meeting*. There man learns not merely that he is limited by man, cast upon his own finitude, partialness, need of completion, but his own relation to truth is heightened by the other's different relation to the same truth—different in accordance with his individuation, and destined to take seed and grow differently. Men need [. . .] to confirm one another in their individual being by means of genuine meeting. But beyond this they need [. . .] to see the truth, which the soul gains by its struggle, light up to the others [. . .] in a different way, and even so be confirmed" (Martin Buber, "Distance and Relation," *Knowledge of Man*, pp. 68–69; emphasis added).

suffering, unlike the faith founded on third-person speech regarding God, or the conception of God as a source of information about future happenings:

> If to believe in God means to be able to talk about him in the third person, then I do not believe in God. If to believe in him means to be able to talk to him then I believe in God [. . .] The God who gives Daniel such foreknowledge of this hour of human history [. . .] is not my God and not God. The God to whom Daniel prays in his suffering is my God and the God of all.[45]

Zelda did not formulate an unequivocal dichotomy as had Buber, who distinguished between "my God" and "not mine." Notwithstanding this difference, we see in her poetry a recurring model of a very personal faith that is born out of subjective and individual experience from which an expression of faith "suddenly" emerges. The poem *I Am a Dead Bird* is a transitional link between the dialogic grammar of the human meeting and the mystical grammar of the encounter with God. This meeting takes place when the speaker does not find her place among human beings, to the extent of feeling dead in life, and only her openness to the mystic succeeds in reviving her:

I Am a Dead Bird
I am a dead bird,
one bird that has died.
A bird cloaked in a gray coat.
A scoffer mocks me as I walk.
Suddenly Your silence envelops me,
O Ever-living One.
In a teeming market, a dead fowl sings:
"Only You exist."

45 Buber, *Meetings*, p. 44.

In a teeming market, a bird hobbles
with a hidden song.[46]

The title chooses to present a mournful side of the bird, which arouses a sense of contrast: birds usually symbolize freedom and liberation, flight and vitality. Zelda chooses to present the possibility of a bird lacking the will to live; nonetheless, the wording "dead bird" preserves the potential for vitality. Death is emphasized additional times in the first two lines, and the triple usage produces a feeling of finitude, in the sense that the reality does not offer the speaker the possibility of a return to life. In the third line, despite all, the bird carries on and goes about wearing a gray coat. The ludicrousness of this image is expressed in the scoffer's mockery, with the grayness of the coat strengthening the stagnation of the everyday.

The fashioning of the bird as lonely to the point of feeling dead and the choice of first-person poetic grammar are reminiscent of a connotation from Psalms 102:6–8: "On account of the voice of my groaning my bones cling to my flesh. I am like a great owl in the wilderness, an owl among the ruins. I lie awake; I am like a lone bird upon a roof." The passage from Psalms aids us in understanding how the experience of death comes about: the groaning out of pain results in her bones clinging to her flesh. The mental feeling is so closely identified with the suffering body that the speaker feels as if she were dead. The speaker in Psalms then compares himself to the owl-bird in the wilderness, who despairs of his condition, and becomes both aggressive and a bird that—with no seeming explanation—experiences loneliness on a roof. The poem expresses identification with nature, certainly in contrast with the human alienation that reigns within it. And then we have the sudden turning point when the speaker, all at once, is enveloped within a mystical experience. The experience is verbalized as a technical dialogue: "Only You exist," but it nevertheless is transformative: it elevates the speaker

46 Zelda, *Spectacular Difference*, pp. 36–37.

and transports her to another dimension, to another poem—a hidden one that embodies her relation to the mystical.

3. Mystical Grammar: Perfectionism and Metaphysics as Zelda's Varieties of Religious Experience

Zelda defined herself as a religious person; in her poetry she expressed both her commitment to observance of the commandments and her profound and intensive spiritual relation to the mystical dimension of the reality. This religious stance, despite her declared and frequent use of the Jewish sources, could also be understood as a holistic-universal approach, of relation to the world.

I propose combining Wittgenstein's methodology for observing and analyzing language with James's contentual insights, which at times are intuitive and in other instances empirical. The correspondence between methodology and content is supported by Wittgenstein's acknowledgment of James's influence on him, which was already mentioned in the introductory chapters. The constitution of the subject for each of these thinkers is based on an exceptional conception of religiosity, internal upheaval, and the constant striving for perfectionism. These three elements are clearly present in Zelda's poetry, and they all derive from the guiding principle formulated by James, as the foundation for understanding this singularity: "I myself believe that the evidence for God lies primarily in inner personal experience"; "Religion is the great interest of my life."[47]

William James's scientific work examines in detail the emotional and experiential behavior of the consciousness. As is accepted in the pragmatic tradition that he firmly grounded, following Peirce, James spoke of the activity of an "inward law" in the constitution of the moral-religious system, which can be discerned only in retrospect:

> Man has an inward law or light telling him what good and evil, truth and falsity, respectively are, and so insuring all the

47 Ralph B. Perry, *The Thought and Character of William James*, 2 vols. (Boston: Little, Brown, 1935), vol. 2, p. 321; vol. 1, p. 165.

> possibilities of his spiritual destiny [. . .] Truth must *reveal itself* if it would be known.[48]

James's own interest in religion came from his father's unshakable faith, which he himself opposed, but in reference to which he felt obliged to formulate his own belief. James passionately criticized his father's religious monism, and suggested replacing it with "pluralistic moralism."[49] This said and done, he completely identified with the centrality of religion in his father's life, and even saw it as a path "to his personal salvation."[50] The change introduced by James consisted of removing metaphysics from the discussion, concentrating instead on the moral and poetical aspects of religiosity.[51] Additionally, as a psychologist, he was very interested in examining the salvation his patients found in religion.[52]

Drawing upon James, I maintain that Zelda's poetry constitutes personal—not necessarily Jewish—religious selfhood, and even when she explicitly (and at times frequently) employs connotations from within the Jewish sources, she is closer to religiosity in the spirit of James and Wittgenstein than that of Orthodox Judaism. In this religiosity, the concept of "God" means setting a goal in life that imparts meaning to the subject, and therefore must ensue from him:

> It is a curious thing, this matter of God! [. . .] As an ideal to attain and make probable, I find myself less and less able to do without him. He need not be an *all*-including "subjective unity of the universe," [. . .] There must be *some* subjective unity in

48 Perry, *Thought and Character*, vol. 1, p. 146. Perry's collection of all of James's writings includes letters that shed more light on his personal thoughts than do his empiric philosophical writings. In light of the current work's focus on self-constitution, the connection between James's philosophical arguments and his own self-constitution is instructive.

49 Perry, *Thought and Character*, vol. 1, p. 164. As James's student and biographer depicts this, "James took the content and rejected the form" (vol. 1, p. 467).

50 Perry, *Thought and Character*, vol. 1, p. 165.

51 "James took the poetic or moral insight, and let the metaphysics go" (Perry, *Thought and Character*, vol. 1, p. 467).

52 Perry, *Thought and Character*, vol. 1, p. 165.

> the universe which has purposes commensurable with my own, and which is at the same time large enough to be [. . .] The strongest. I simply refuse to accept the notion of there being *no* purpose in the objective world. On the other hand, I cannot represent the existence of purpose except as based in a mind. The not-me, therefore, so far as it contains purpose, must spring from the mind; but not necessarily a *one and only* mind. In saying "God exists" all I imply is that my purposes are cared for by a mind so powerful as on the whole to control the drift of the universe.[53]

James's argument is intrinsically paradoxical: on the one hand, he refuses to accept the possibility of a purposeless world, while, on the other, he asserts that interest in any goal that is embodied in some belief in God is conditional upon man's personal consciousness. Couldn't James imagine the possible existence of a nonbeliever, a nihilist whose life does not contain any purpose that gives it meaning? James's pluralism is limited, but its importance lies in presenting the infinite range of possible types of religiosity. The religious stance evident in Zelda's poetry reflects a similar notion: it, too, is based on the existence of a God who imparts metaphysical meaning to the world, including her actions.

This position encourages the inclination for constant perfectionism inherent in self-criticism, including that which entails exposure that she finds embarrassing (see, for instance, my analysis of the poem *Who Can Resist the Beauty of the Light*, below). James divided faith into two main types, both of which are evident in Zelda's poems: "The fighting faith and the comforting faith; or [. . .] the faith upstream and the faith downstream."[54]

---

53 Perry, *Thought and Character*, vol. 1, p. 737.

54 Perry, *Thought and Character*, vol. 2, p. 324. Perry then explains: "The former is the faith that springs from strength. Preferring the good to the evil, the moral person fights for it with the sort of confidence that the brave man feels in himself and his allies, exulting in the danger and in the uncertainty of the issue [. . .] The second is the faith that springs from human weakness, and asks for refuge and security. In the fighting faith religion is a stimulant to the will; the comforting faith, on the

This division would preclude her classification as an "Orthodox poet," no matter how open and diverse, and situate her in a much richer cultural expanse. The philosophical-existential argument is that the religious attitude, in all its variations, is an existential matter—subjective, on the one hand, and universal, on the other—and is not dependent on particularist religiosity. This attitude, as I will show, is not based on "Jewish" conceptions, but on ideas such as the source of meaning for the world, which is outside it, leads to limitless perfectionism, and can be applied within every cultural context.

The subjectivization of faith means that its source is to be found in man's consciousness, and not in tradition, whether externally imposed or consensual. As I argued in Kierkegaard's name in the chapter on mystical grammar, there is a contradiction between personal religiosity and institutionalized religion, and Zelda's poetry is a milestone in Hebrew poetry in the poetical fashioning of the former. The existentialist stance that emerges from the poems presents, at times paradoxically, a combination of certainty and skepticism, understatement and drama, thereby fashioning a private world which on occasion is openly opposed to the world around, or even does not relate to it at all.

The scholarly study of Zelda's poetry devoted some attention to an analysis of the mystical dimension in her poetry, but this dimension was ascribed to her Hasidic roots and the theological-religious plane in her poetry.[55] Hamutal Bar-Yosef, who authored the most comprehensive discussion of Zelda's poetry, suggested six characteristics of what she

---

other hand, is at the bottom of one's heart, relaxing" (*Thought and Character*, vol. 2, p. 324). Perry notes that James himself experienced the need for comforting faith, both in the personal crisis he underwent and in his work as an analyst with many patients who came to him in a state of severe mental crisis.

55 Zvi Mark indicated parallels between poetry and faith in Zelda's poems, focusing on Hasidic-mystical features such as the transition from aesthetic experience to religious experience, and the manner in which her poetry alludes to the presence and existence of God, that are hidden from the nonbeliever. See Zvi Mark, "Faith and Song in the Poetry of Zelda: On the Mystical Elements in Zelda's Ars Poetica Conception and Their Hasidic Origins," in *Faith: Jewish Perspectives*, ed. Avi Sagi and Dov Schwartz (Boston: Academic Studies Press, 2013), pp. 384–416. Mark emphasized the Hasidic influence on Zelda's mystical ideas, while my analysis will concentrate on the universal characteristics of the mysticism in her poetry.

called "religious worldview," and emphasized that "even if a plethora of religious manifestations can be found in modern Hebrew literature [. . .] Zelda's poetry is religious poetry in the fullest sense of the word: all six characteristics are present in Zelda's work."[56] The approach that I will take below, in contrast, is closer to that of Esther Ettinger in her book on Zelda. Ettinger writes:

> All poetry is religious poetry [. . .] the moment that the poet places his words on paper, he performs a religious act, an act of creation, if only by his very belief in the power of words to say something about the world. Every literary work has some revelation and disclosure in language, even if the author is completely secular in his life and worldview [. . .] Zelda is a religious poet, because her poetry is built on foundations of spiritual-religious language and thought that are ceaselessly at work in the poems, and afford them their character, mainly because the religious experience beats in the heart of her poetry.[57]

Ettinger defines religiosity as an expression of language and experience, both of which are drawn from Jewish tradition and create in Zelda's poems the personal expressions of her religiousness. While Ettinger highlights the centrality of the Jewish aspect, on the one hand, and, on the other, the fact of every literary work being "an expression of revelation," I wish to make a different argument. The movement to the mystical can be seen as paying attention to the details of mundane existence so that they reflect meaning that exceeds their routine action, and that we usually ignore. Zelda had a special talent for directing the reader to everyday phenomena, and showing their connection to the

---

56 Hamutal Bar-Yosef, *On Zelda's Poetry* (Tel Aviv: Hakibbutz Hameuchad, 2006), p. 133 (Hebrew). Bar-Yosef lists the following elements: works whose thematic center is theological; works that discuss the relationship between man and God; works that contain a conflict between faith and heresy; works that have an underpinning of religious belief; works that contain words and phrases with religious connotations; works whose imaginary reality is connected to religious life (*On Zelda's Poetry*, pp. 132–33).

57 Esther Ettinger, *Zelda* (Tel Aviv: Mapa, 2007), pp. 104–5 (Hebrew).

meaning of existence that originates beyond the world (this stance is not dependent on any specific religion, even if expressed in Hebrew). In the following poem, the relation to nature rouses the speaker's soul and moves her from looking at the reality of butterfly and flower to mystical relation:

The Delicate Light of My Peace
A butterfly hailing from paradise
clung to the flower I planted
in autumn
letters from on high on its golden wings
signs of God.

In these signs
that before my eyes sank into space
fluttered the delicate light
of my peace.[58]

In the first stanza, the description of the natural event shifts from a realistic presentation to a symbolic one ("Letters from *on high*"). The poem portrays revelation, when the speaker finds signs of God in the butterfly and the flower in which her peace "flutters." This leap is made possible by means of the relation to nature (unlike the leap in *I Am a Dead Bird* [see below], in which the leap is sudden), and is a conversion of a sort different from that of Buber. Buber defined conversion as transformation in human encounter, while James located this mental event on the plane of religious experience. James distinguished between two types of transformation, the sudden and the gradual, and both types are evident in Zelda's poems, where they unite two types of mysticism: the mystical as an expression of subjective experience, and as an expression of religiosity.

In our discussion of mystical grammar, we mentioned James's *The Varieties of Religious Experience* that, inter alia, described cases of

58 Translation by David Jacobson in his *Creator, Are You Listening?*, p. 19.

radical personality change that he encountered in the course of his work as a psychologist. James called such change "conversion," and his thorough and clear definition is relevant for various types of transformation.[59] In his book James set forth the conversion experience as it was portrayed by his patients. Together with this, we also know of James's own transformation, which he refrained from presenting in his book. James speaks of two main features of conversion: the transition from a feeling of fragmentation and wretchedness to one of unification and joy, and an emotional experience of certainty in the existence of a power beyond the individual himself. James distinguished between volitional transformation and that which is neither volitional nor conscious.[60] Barnard, following James, listed all the types of conversion, and noted the factor common to the events included in the category of "conversion" that forms the basis for two types of conversion, the religious and the nonreligious.[61] This shared

59 "To be converted, to be regenerated, to receive grace, to experience religion, to gain an assurance, are so many phrases which denote the process, gradual or sudden, by which a self hitherto divided, and consciously wrong inferior and unhappy, becomes unified and consciously right superior and happy, in consequence of its former hold upon religious realities. This is what at least conversion signifies in general terms, whether or not we believe that a direct divine operation is needed to bring such a moral change about" (James, *Varieties of Religious Experience*, p. 150).

60 "Now there are two forms of mental occurrence in human beings, which lead to a striking difference in the conversion process [. . .] There is thus a conscious and voluntary way and an involuntary and unconscious way in which mental results may get accomplished; and we find both ways exemplified in the history of conversion, giving us two types [. . .] the *volitional type* and the *type by self-surrender* respectively. In the volitional type the regenerative change is usually gradual, and consists in the building up, piece by piece, of a new set of moral and spiritual habits. But there are always critical points here at which the movement forward seems much more rapid" (James, *Varieties of Religious Experience*, pp. 162–63).

61 "James was convinced that dramatic personal transformations often occur when an individual contacts (or is contacted by) the forces that well up from his or her subliminal self by virtue of its contact with the unseen world" (Barnard, *Exploring Unseen Worlds*, p. 179). Barnard argued that James distinguished between religious and nonreligious personal transformation, even though an explicit expression of such a distinction is not to be found in James's writing, since, actually, James described conversion in religious terms: "James is careful to emphasize that conversions, understood in the broadest possible sense, are not necessarily religious (as his own experience demonstrates), but on the whole, James tends to describe

element results from the encounter with the unseen world that leads to significant transformation, which may be called "conversion." The lack of a clear boundary between religious and nonreligious conversion is of especial importance for the current discussion, since one of the traits shared by the corpora of the poets discussed in the current book is the movement from the self to the unseen world, which is neither connected nor committed to a world of religious meanings.

James himself underwent a radical change when he decided to leave his painting studies in Bonn, Germany, and return to Harvard in the United States, to concentrate on scientific studies (chemistry, biology, and the like). We learn from his correspondence with his father that the latter vigorously objected to his son's painting studies, and his intention to devote his life to art in general. James argued with his father for quite a while, but in the end, despite his deep mental affinity for the aesthetic, he realized that it would be preferable to turn to the sciences. The point in a letter to his father in which he explained his decision is definitely a conversion, in the sense of illumination and a diametrical lifestyle change. Perry viewed this turnabout as an expression of James's personal religiousness:

> There is also a close relation between James's view of religious conversion and his own "crisis" in 1870–1872. His sense of black despair and morbid fear is used in *The Varieties of Religious Experience* to illustrate the state of "the sick soul." He tells us that the experience made him "sympathetic with

---

conversion experiences in explicitly religious terms" (*Exploring Unseen Worlds*, p. 182). This said and done, in the above passage James expanded the religious definition of conversion by Augustine and Kierkegaard to include any radical change that enables a person to move from a state of division and depression to one of a sense of unification and joy regarding his life. "The crisis described is the throwing of our conscious selves upon the mercy of powers which, whatever they may be, are more ideal than we are actually, and make for our redemption [. . .] Psychology and religion are thus in perfect harmony up to this point, since both admit that there are forces seemingly outside of the conscious individual that bring redemption to his life. Nevertheless psychology, defining these forces as 'subconscious,' and speaking of their effects as due to 'incubation,' or 'cerebration,' implies that they do not transcend the individual's personality" (*Exploring Unseen Worlds*, pp. 195–96).

> the morbid feelings of others"; and that both his melancholy and his emergence from it had "a religious bearing." *His own "salvation" came through self-reliance and the idea of moral freedom, rather than through a sense of supporting grace*—but he experienced a marked alteration of mood, and a feeling of renewed life similar to that of "the twice born."[62]

The conversion experience joins together with Emersonian perfectionism, which James cited, the parallel to Kierkegaard and Wittgenstein suggested by Cavel in the context of philosophical inquiry as self-correction, and the parallel to the religious option. The poetical grammar in the following poem differs from the usual patterns in Zelda's poems that I indicated above. The turning point occurs in the title of the poem, not in its end, nor even during the course of the work.

The use of quotation marks in this poem emphasizes the dialogic grammar, which is employed for the purpose of trenchant self-criticism that highlights the speaker's ability to examine herself from outside. The inner conversation takes place in conjunction with the speaker's relation to the light that is beyond her and her distresses, and whose beauty is irresistible. The personification of the light and the cruel clarity of its diagnosis ("This must be a lack of love") constitute the speaker's mystical subjectivity in favor of an act of perfectionism, both aesthetic and ethical:

> *Who Can Resist the Beauty of the Light*
> I bore my anger to show to the light,
> seeking comfort in its beauty,
> but I was not worthy in its eyes,
> I was not worthy in its eyes.
>
> "Why is your life dark?" it said.

62 Perry, *Thought and Character*, vol. 2, p. 324 (emphasis added, to indicate the similarity of Barnard's and Perry's characterization of James's conversion as nonreligious).

"You are not in the depths of the pit.
This must be a lack of love."

And I wept.
I wept deeply.[63]

The poem is replete with only-too-human expressions: the inability to resist the beauty, anger and seeking comfort, the darkness of depression, her inescapable need for love, and finally, her flight to the deep weeping that encompasses all. As is Zelda's wont, her attitude to the mystical is always abstract; actually, it is not concretely verbalized, but is only "seen," as the mystical functions in the thought of both Wittgenstein and James. The mystical can be seen by one whose heart is open and turns to it, and its influence is sobering, with acknowledgment of the reality. The speaker seeks comfort, but instead undergoes a transformation, to understand the true reason for her distress and anger. This reason is quintessentially human: a lack of love. We do not know how this upheaval occurs, so that she sees things as they are and gives herself over to weeping, because it remains within her, and the poetic grammar merely shows its results by the subject, with the transformation taking place behind the scenes.

Notwithstanding this, the transformation is volitional. How can the poetical grammar attest to will that is beyond the boundaries of language and that will likely make such a transformation possible? We have mentioned many expressions of will in Zelda's poems, including a will to live and a death wish, the desire to live her life in the face of the embroiled will of the generation. At this juncture, we add to human will, in its various types, the result of conversion, namely, radical change in the speaker's attitude to the world. The next poem includes a rare mention of the connection between looking at nature and her general stance regarding the reality as a whole. A completely natural event links her relation to nature with that to the mystical, and arouses her will:

63 Zelda, *Spectacular Difference*, pp. 198–99.

The first rain—
a plenitude of freshness
with no sign of Cain.
And agony will no longer
whisper to my soul,
"I am the king."
No longer will it say,
"I am the ruler."
Each drop is a link
between me and the things,
a link
between me and the world.
And when night
conjures up the abyss,
the abyss conjures up
fields and gardens.[64]

The Hebrew *zikah* is translated here as "link," but it should rather be rendered as "relation," like Buber's *die Beziehung* in *I and Thou*. The notion in the poem is that every drop epitomizes the relation between the speaker and the world. The mystical in the poem is the sense of unity with the world, as Spinoza first formulated this in the seventeenth century, and as it was developed by Buber three centuries later: the first rain constitutes the speaker's being part of the world, with each drop arousing and creating a connection between her and the things in the world, thereby constituting a connection to the world as a whole. The abyss joining the harmonious communication between the speaker and nature towards the end of the poem is what gives it its special beauty. The abyss—which represents the mystical, the depths of the sadness of despair, or both—joins and unites with the reality of renewal and hope. In this manner, the poem vividly exemplifies Jamesian conversion.

64 Zelda, *Spectacular Difference*, pp. 192–93.

In Zelda's poetry, mystical revelation, in its religious sense, occurs in the world, as well, and as James wrote, is portrayed retrospectively:

> There was something startling
> in the hue of the sky.
> I was amazed that the treetops
> swayed gently
> with no shadow of fear.
> I wanted to flee from the white sky
> but the small garden showed me signs
> that His mercy had not ceased.[65]

The starting point is the speaker's being part of what happens in the world: she is influenced and startled by the color of the sky, but when she turns to look at the treetops, she is amazed by their calm, which interferes with her desire to flee from the sky. At the end of the poem the garden comes into view, and shows her signs of divine mercy. This poem raises the question of the relationship between conscious will with the ability to choose, on the one hand, and, on the other, giving oneself over to the mystical experience of unity, of being part of the world. The poetic grammar gradually moves from passivity to activity in the speaker's feelings ("startling," "amazed," "wanted").

This poetic fashioning leads us to think that will can be brought about, as Wittgenstein suggests:

> In the sense in which I can ever bring about anything (such as stomach-ache through overeating), I can also bring about wanting. In this sense, I bring about wanting to swim by jumping into the water. I suppose I was trying to say: I can't want to want; that is, it makes no sense to speak of wanting to want. "Wanting" is not the name of an action, and so not of a

65 Zelda, *Spectacular Difference*, pp. 204–5.

> voluntary one either. And my use of a wrong expression came from the fact that one is inclined to think of wanting as an immediate non-casual bringing about. But a misleading analogy lies at the root of this idea; the causal nexus seems to be established by a mechanism connecting two parts of a machine [. . .] One imagines the willing subject here as something without any mass (without any inertia), as a motor which has no inertia in itself to overcome. And so it is only mover, not moved.[66]

Wittgenstein explained how will acts: since it is situated beyond the boundaries of language, it is not an entity in its own right that can be discerned or brought about. A person's will is embodied in the action that he takes. Will cannot be brought about, since it is influenced by differing conditions, and is not something distinct. It likewise cannot be perceived as a causal motive. This position clarifies the way in which Zelda fashions the changes in consciousness, whether gradual or sudden, in her poems: the speaker is in a given state when a certain action leads her to a clear understanding of her situation. At times this understanding includes an expression of desire that came to fruition, while in other instances it includes brokenheartedness and anguish, specifically because the will cannot be channeled in accordance with one's wishes, it rather is bound up with a complex reality that at times is immutable.

In the preceding poem the speaker gives herself over to her experience of the world, until it takes her to the desired place in the reality: where she identifies in the world the signs of God's mercy. Once again, we see the indirect verbalization of the object of faith and the caution reflected in the expression of such mercy by nature. The speaker refrains from speculating about God's will or the logic in His actions, and merely attests to their embodiment in the world (that is distinct from God) in practice.

The speaker's will is most evident in the next poem. She realizes the experience that is only a wish in other poems: to be disconnected from the workaday world's demands, and to stay in nature and enjoy all it contains, whether large or small, such as the "beauty of

66 Wittgenstein, *Philosophical Investigations*, para. 613, 618.

grape-leaves." This stay in nature and giving herself over to it leads, in the second stanza, to connection with the mystical ("God hidden and concealed"). Interestingly, human communication is missing from the poem; the speaker does not engage in dialogue with people. Infants surround the speaker as part of the natural world, without verbal dialogue:

At This Thought-filled Hour
At this thought-filled hour
disconnected from everything
I took pleasure in the beauty of grape-leaves—
Only when a shadow of peace
lies on Jerusalem's hills
and waking voices of birds
and infants surround me,
and I have not betrayed
and I have not slandered,
and a dark dread has not bewitched
my senses—
my soul perceives a very faint tremor
passing among the leaves as they meet
the morning light.

God hidden and concealed
save me from evil tidings
that thrust to obscurity
the delicate quiet
of a heart observing from the side.
For what is my house and what is my life
on the day of woe,
the savage day
that casts to the earth
in blinding fury
the delightfulness of the vine
and all my meditations.[67]

67 Translation by David Jacobson in his *Creator, Are You Listening?*, p. 36.

The speaker in the poem is in a sort of sphere-in-between in the world. On the one hand, the poem opens with a declaration of disconnection and a description of thoughtful existence that enables connection to the experience of nature, as Jacobson showed.[68] On the other hand, this disconnection occurs on the background of considered and rational self-criticism that expresses the need for constant perfectionism: "I have not betrayed / and I have not slandered, / and a dark dread has not bewitched / my senses [. . .]." In other words, the attachment to nature and the disconnection from the everyday leads to a turning inward and a self-reckoning. The speaker criticizes her negative tendencies, of which she rids herself during the process of giving herself over to nature. Then, too, she is well aware of the uncertain existence of the "delicate quiet," and she asks God to help her to keep this feeling. She is aware that a day will come that will threaten her present inner tranquility, but her desire is clear: to continue to have the ability for meditations. The speaker is similarly conscious that she will need help from God, the metaphysical source that enables her to merge with the natural world without surrendering to her fears. We see in the poetic grammar how the act of poetry embodies the essence of her desire: the charming portrayal of the elements of nature as they are perceived by the speaker creates a gentle tranquility, for the audience as well, and finely reflects the passive, observing, and devoted stance that is the source of her turning to God, that is opposed to the force-fueled and achievement-oriented positions that the poem then presents and that, among other factors, prevent a connection to nature of this sort.

In order, however, to present a balanced picture of the constitution of self-will in Zelda's poetry, we should examine a diametrically opposing expression of the fervent desire to remain entrenched in sadness and depression, and the refusal to be open to any possible element of positive change:

The Fine Sand, the Terrible Sand
If my soul lies down on its side,

68 Jacobson, *Creator, Are You Listening?*, p. 36.

dug deep into sorrow,
recoiling from violence
in people, snakes, machines,
and does not sail in the secret of the night,
and does not fly through the leaves with the wind,
and is torn from ritual celebrations,
without a path to the living voice,

if my soul lies down on its side
and does not hear a warm voice
whispering its name,
it will forget the mercy of the sun
and the walls of the mountains
and that hidden spring whose name
is conversation
(a spring that once shone in the dark).

If my soul lies down on its side,
wrapped in its webs,
divorced from deed,
expelled from the day-to-day,
a fine sand will come from the shore of the sea
and cover its Shabbaths,
and block to the root its meditations.
The fine, terrible sand
will pierce the mystery of its weeping
before the veiled, hidden God

if my soul lies on its side, dug deep in sorrow.[69]

The speaker's will, in a depressive state, is expressed indirectly: "my soul lies on its side, dug deep in sorrow." The way in which people conduct themselves in the world, like snakes in a mechanistic culture that consecrates technology, does not allow the speaker to find the expanse in which

69 Zelda, *Spectacular Difference*, pp. 128–31.

she can hear and connect to the source of warmth and meaning. The alienation that is imposed by the modern world also comes to dominate the possibility of being amazed by and giving oneself over to the elements of nature: the mountains, the sun, and especially, the "hidden spring whose name / Is conversation." The most tangible conversation that Zelda conducts throughout her poetry is with the elements of nature, through which she locates expressions of God. The "showing," however, does not take place within her soul, but in the poetic grammar: the poem also fashions the sights to which she cannot devote herself, thus situating the mystical stance between the attempt at perfectionism and metaphysics. The poem reflects the constancy throughout Zelda's poetry of her attempt to feel an authentic connection with a world that embodies man's unity with the universe; unity that originates in an external source of meaning—God. At times she is prevented from realizing this desire, but her poetry expresses another possibility, albeit not realized at the time she writes. Thus even in a despairing poem that sinks into agony, we find the metaphysical facet that dominates her poetry: the aspect that includes her perception of God longing for whom gives meaning to the activity, both routine and marvelous, of the natural world. This aspect also contains the speaker's sense of commitment to acknowledge the mercy of this world's beauty and charm by meditative contemplation and giving herself over to the world. Sharp criticism of the human world, too, is present in this aspect, along with empathy and compassion for the weak in this world.

We should conclude our discussion of the process of selfhood constitution in Zelda's corpus with a poem that she published in 1984, which includes the phrase that she chose for the book's title: "Beyond all distance":

> *On That Night of Stars*
> On that night of stars
> my childhood sought
> the Creator of the world.
>
> Years that spill like water,
> sadness,

people—
none of these can make me forget
distances
beyond all distance.[70]

This short and pithy poem masterfully charts the core of selfhood in Zelda's poetry. From the retrospective connection between childhood and adulthood, through all of life's happenings, a single dominant relation emerges: that to the expanses beyond the world. The speaker expresses her desire to reach the expanse with the source of the world's creativity, which is the farthest from the place where she is, but the closest to her heart and desires. The poem expresses what Wittgenstein called "truthfulness," which he found to be the key to meaningful confession.[71] This poem can be viewed as the apex of the long-standing confession that emerges from the journey through Zelda's corpus.[72]

70 Zelda, *Spectacular Difference*, pp. 224–25.

71 "The criteria for the truth of the *confession* that I thought such-and-such are not the criteria for a true *description* of the process. And the importance of the true confession does not reside in its being a correct and certain report of some process. It resides, rather, in the special consequences which can be drawn from a confession whose truth is guaranteed by the special criteria of *truthfulness*" (Wittgenstein, *PPF*, para. 319; emphasis in original).

72 Altieri uses this in the research of poetry to show how a poet invents characteristics of selfhood by a new experiential grammar that is independent of previous experience: "Now I need poetry to display the intricate resources of this grammar. I have to show how authors can establish identifications that do not depend on concepts of the self, and I have to expand my scenario by illustrating what is at stake for readers in attuning to the expressive activity" (Charles Altieri, "Exemplification and Expression," in *A Companion to the Philosophy of Literature*, ed. Garry Hagberg and Walter Jost [Oxford: Blackwell, 2010], pp. 491–506).

CHAPTER 5

Yehuda Amichai: *Amen* and Love

Great Tranquility: Questions and Answers
People in the painfully bright hall
Spoke about religion
In the life of modern man
And about God's place in it.

People spoke in excited voices
Like at airports.
I left them:
I opened an iron door over which was written
"Emergency" and I entered into
A great tranquility: questions and answers.[1]

What is the meaning of modern man's passion to discuss the meaning of his life? What is the place of God in this discourse? Even when Amichai incorporates irony and figurative language that compares this talk to conversations at an airport, existential seriousness is hidden between the lines. Amichai's poetry, throughout his literary career, was occupied with the attempt to clarify the meaning of life for the modern

1 Yehuda Amichai, *Great Tranquility: Questions and Answers*, trans. Glenda Abramson and Tudor Parfitt (New York: Harper & Row, 1983), p. 90.

Jew, a skeptic who poses questions in all realms of existence. His poetical grammar explores the roots of meaning, but always leaves an opening for additional wondering, as is embodied in the title of Amichai's last book, *Open Closed Open*.

Together with the quest for the meaning of life, the title of the poem cited above (also the title of the collection in which it appears) represents the grammatical intonation in Amichai's poetry: a great tranquility that conceals dramas that are formulated as questions, whether big or small. The drama of a twelve-year-old who moved to Israel upon the rise of anti-Semitism in Germany, but who, even in his last book, longs for his childhood girlfriend and wonders why he was so lucky as to be saved from the destruction of the Holocaust; the drama of a fighter in Israel's War of Independence in 1948 who experienced the death of his comrades; the drama of a late return to his birthplace, a visit to the cemetery, and placing on his desk and on the cover of his last book a fragment of a tombstone that bears the word "Amen"; and the drama of the experience of approaching death that closes the life cycle with a finality that is low-key but decisive, as is Amichai's way:

> On my desk lies a stone with the word "Amen" on it,
> a fragment of a tombstone, a remnant from a Jewish graveyard
> destroyed a thousand years ago in the town where I was born,
> one word, "Amen," carved deep into the stone,
> a final hard amen for all that was and never will return,
> a soft singing amen, as in prayer:
> Amen and amen, may it come to pass.[2]

Amichai's poetry, with its wealth of life experiences and diverse fashionings, can be examined from numerous perspectives. I have chosen to examine a small portion of his poems, from the perspective of the process of self-change embodied in his poems. The change in Amichai's poetical consciousness creates the junction at which the grammar of the ways of figurative fashioning meets

2 Yehuda Amichai, *Open Closed Open*, trans. Chana Bloch and Chana Kronfeld (New York: Harcourt, 2000), p. 39.

a philosophical-existential position. In all his poems, what happens in the present is the key to the self-constitution in the poetic grammar whose expressions I will attempt to demonstrate.

Amichai's poetry is not always marked by "great tranquility"; at times it expresses, as in the wording of the poem, an "Emergency," and in other instances, the urgency is tamed. The "family resemblance" throughout his poetry lies in the feeling that Amichai tries to answer basic questions of existence: what is love, what is the meaning of life, how to contend with death, and, mainly, how to accept and contain the frustration of not knowing. The uncertainty about the nature of every aspect of life is accompanied in his poetry by a broad range of emotions, all of which are driven by the urge to ask, to wonder, and to autonomously fashion his experiences. Along with his constant wondering, Amichai does not deny the place and importance of human commitments, such as parenthood and spousal relationships. Together with an acute awareness of the possibility of deconstruction and the fleeting nature of any situation, he also exhibits acceptance, both before and after the fact, of human needs.

The poetry of Yehuda Amichai (1924–2000) enjoys wide popularity, with a large number of translations into other languages.[3] His corpus accompanied Israeli history from the beginnings of the State of Israel, and continues to be relevant into the start of the twenty-first century. Amichai created a special language-game that includes poetical grammar based on the common usage of language, a grammar that conducts dialogues of different sorts, as well as a clear relation to the mystical, in the senses mentioned above in the theoretical discussion. To the present, scholarly research has generally focused on deciphering his figurative language that, on the one hand, uses everyday materials, and, on the other, shows exceptional and arresting originality and

3 In 1994, in honor of Amichai's seventieth birthday, the Institute for the Translation of Hebrew Literature published a bibliography of all of his poems. The introduction stated that Amichai was without doubt the most translated Israeli poet: *To Commemorate the 70th Birthday of Yehuda Amichai: A Bibliography of His Work in Translation*, bibliographer Essi Lapon-Kandelshein, project editor Nava Duchovni (Ramat Gan: Institute for the Translation of Hebrew Literature, 1994), p. III.

force.[4] Although the question of the place of Jewish identity in his poetry was raised, the radical change that this identity underwent so patently in his last book, *Open Closed Open*, was not explained.[5] This change enables us to also retrospectively reexamine positions in his early poetry that present Jewish identity in a positive light, and not only in an ironical and critical fashion.

Our discussion will accordingly examine questions of the constitution of identity with an "overview."[6] We will attempt to identify the "questions and answers" that Amichai poses in his poetry, and examine how they participate in the process of fashioning modern identity that contains relation to and knowledge of the sources of Jewish tradition, which it interprets from an autonomous, critical, and ironic viewpoint. This critical outlook assumes different forms: both low-key tranquility and sharp expressions, since the speaker is in an "Emergency" situation, in which it is incumbent upon him to ask and answer.

Of especial interest for our discussion is the isolation of the subject-speaker in Amichai's poetry from any literary "group" or "school," even if, after the fact, his poetry is seen as belonging to a particular orientation and he is regarded as one of the founders of post-Alterman poetry. I will attempt to show how personal, subjective experience is expressed in Amichai's unique grammar so that it can easily be translated into another language, with the richness of the translation at times exceeding the meanings of the original Hebrew. It should be

4 Exceptional in this respect are the studies by Nili Gold, who offered an impressive and intriguing list of the connections between Amichai's biography and his poems, as the key to understanding Amichai's development as Israel's national poet. See Nili Gold, *Yehuda Amichai: The German-Jewish Roots of Israel's National Poet* (New York: Leo Baeck Institute, 2008); and Gold, *Yehuda Amichai: The Making of Israel's National Poet* (Hanover, NH: Brandeis University Press, 2008).

5 For *Open Closed Open*, see Nili Gold, "Amichai's Open Closed Open and Now and in Other Days: A Poetic Dialogue," in *History and Literature: New Readings of Jewish Texts in Honor of Arnold Band*, ed. William Cutter and David C. Jacobson (Providence: Brown University, 2002), pp. 465–77.

6 "A main source of our failure to understand is that we don't have *an overview* of the use of our words.—Our grammar is deficient in surveyability. A surveyable representation produces precisely that kind of understanding which consists in 'seeing connections.' Hence the importance of finding and inventing *intermediate links*" (Wittgenstein, *Philosophical Investigations*, para. 122).

mentioned that Amichai actively participated in the translation of his books, and therefore the work of translation can be added to his poetical considerations concerning the constitution of the self in his poems. The fashioned situations from the speaker's everyday life in his poetry combine the aesthetic, the dialogic, and the mystical in different levels of presence. The contribution of the current discussion lies in the attempt to connect the three types of grammar, and thus offer an alternative to interpretations that speak of Amichai's "secularness" or "religiosity," or the possibility of finding in his poetry a modern interpretation of Jewish tradition or its subversion.[7]

In his last book, *Open Closed Open*, Amichai offers a simple and clear interpretive key to the movement and changes that the speaker's personality underwent over the course of his poetry: "Change is God and death is His prophet."[8] The idealization of change, and especially its actual application, free the reader from the need to place Amichai in any social, religious, or poetical category. It finely illustrates, time after time, Wittgenstein's central argument as to the manner in which language-games are constituted:

> But how many kinds of sentence are there? [. . .] There are *countless* kinds, countless different kinds of use of all the things we call "signs," "words," "sentences." And this diversity is not something fixed, given once for all; but new types of language, new language-games, as we may say, come into existence, and others become obsolete and get forgotten [. . .] The

7 David Jacobson finely summarized the different approaches for interpreting Amichai's work in such contexts (*Creator, Are You Listening?*, pp. 41–48). I agree with his statement that presenting Amichai as the founder of the secular position, or as criticizing-challenging the tradition in which he grew up at home, does an injustice to his poetry and misses its metaphysical aspect (which is present both in everyday depictions, and in even more pronounced fashion, in his Jerusalem poems and in *Open Closed Open*). While, however, Jacobson focused on Amichai's attitude to God throughout his poetry (and clearly demonstrates the continuity of this attitude), I wish to reveal Amichai's poetic self, including the characteristics of his mystical stance, which also includes his attitude to God.

8 Amichai, *Open Closed Open*, p. 124. This stanza appears several times in the Hebrew original, but not in the English version.

> word "language-*game*" is used here to emphasize the fact that the *speaking* of language is part of an activity, or of a form of life.[9]

Amichai's poetry contains a range of language-games that represent the different periods in his life and in which we can indicate motifs that recur in different periods, as well as intertextual dialogue between the books of poetry, which include repetition and development (such as those, for example, on "little Ruth"). We will focus especially on the grammatical manner in which the main features of the poetical self are fashioned, with emphasis on the relationship between words and the reality. Scholarly research devoted considerable attention to the figurative language in Amichai's corpus; we, however, will examine the philosophical-existential insights that are a consequence of certain uses of grammar. I will seek to show the connections between the perspective of linguistic perception and the main motifs that are woven into the poetical self-constitution, such as change, the intersubjective and intertextual perception of Jewish sources, and the commitment to Jewish history.

1. The Poetics of Change: The Grammaticalization of Experience

The poetics of change, as expressed in the fashioning of various experiences in relation to some context or a certain person, can be examined by comparing poems from different periods while focusing on the "grammaticalization of experience." This term was coined in a discussion of Wittgenstein's later writings that analyzed psychological processes.[10] The term "the third Wittgenstein" was suggested to distinguish those writings from philosophical investigation as therapy and meaning as use (to which the first part of *Philosophical Investigations*

9 Wittgenstein, *Philosophical Investigations*, para. 23.

10 Danielle Moyal-Sharrock, "Introduction: The Idea of a Third Wittgenstein," in *The Third Wittgenstein: The Post-Investigations Works*, ed. Danielle Moyal-Sharrock (Aldershot: Ashgate, 2004), p. 5.

was devoted).[11] In our discussion, I relate to Wittgenstein's philosophy as a single continuum with different emphases, with the incorporation of insights from various periods. Notwithstanding this continuity, it should be stressed, in the spirit of the distinction in the third part of his *Philosophical Investigations*, that Wittgenstein's contribution to literary criticism in the context of the constitution of subjectivity is more noticeable in this phase.[12] This is due to the considerable place he gave in these writings to a discussion of typical grammatical uses that are important for the study of poetry, such as analysis of the difference between the first and other persons, an analysis of states of consciousness, and a comparison of visible and verbalized aspects.

How can we discern and interpret this "grammaticalization of experience"? Michel ter Hark proposed distinguishing between two types of experience, the sensual and the mental:

> Sense-experience is that it should supply information, rightly or wrongly, about the external world (cf. Wittgenstein RPP2, para. 63). By contrast, a mental image tells us nothing about the world.[13]

Mental experience that is fashioned in metaphoric language "tells us nothing about the world," but may set the stage for a mental experience. Only Wittgenstein showed the independence of grammar, that is, the fact that language is not subject to verifiable reality. To the contrary, it makes it possible to exceed the rules of logical grammar on which public language is established, and facilitates the expression of individual mental states that are not subject to grammatical rules:

---

11 The term "the third Wittgenstein" refers to Wittgenstein's latest writings: the second part of *Philosophical Investigations* (which the editors of the last edition called *Philosophy of Psychology: A Fragment*), *On Certainty*; *Remarks on the Philosophy of Psychology*, vols. 1–2; and *Last Writings on the Philosophy of Psychology*, vols. 1–2. All were written between 1946 and 1951.

12 Charles Altieri described and illustrated the unique relevance of the "third Wittgenstein" to literary criticism in his essay "Exemplification and Expression," pp. 491–506.

13 Michel ter Hark, "Coloured Vowels: Wittgenstein on Synaesthesia and Secondary Meaning," *Philosophia* 37 (2009), pp. 589–604.

> Grammar is not accountable to any reality. It is grammatical rules that determine meaning (constitute it) and so they themselves are not answerable to any meaning and to that extent are arbitrary. There cannot be a question whether these or other rules are the correct ones for the use of "not" (that is, whether they accord with its meaning). For without these rules the word has as yet no meaning; and if we change the rules, it now has another meaning (or none), and in that case we may just as well change the word too.[14]

Language, as an autonomous system, acts in accordance with rules, just as logical grammar has rules. Unlike, however, logical grammar, in which the rules are fixed and dictated, the rules of poetical language can be altered. Poetical language, too, must follow rules, otherwise the meaning of its action would be incomprehensible. But since these rules are adjustable, they reflect the movement of change in the speaker's mental world. Thus, for example, the "grammaticalization of experience" aids in understanding how words fashion the picture of the speaker's soul in the following poem:

These Words
These words, like heaps of feathers
on the edge of Jerusalem, above the Valley of the Cross.
There, in my childhood, the woman sat
plucking chickens,
These words now fly all over the world.
The rest is slaughtered, eaten,
digested, decayed, forgotten.

The hermaphrodite of time
who is neither day nor night
has wiped out this valley
with green well-groomed gardens.

14 Wittgenstein, *Philosophical Grammar*, p. 184.

Once experts of love used to come here
to perform their expertise
in the dry grass of summer nights.

That's how it started.
Since then—many words, many loves,
many flowers
bought for warm hands to hold
or to decorate tombs.

That's how it started
and I don't know how it will end.
But still, from beyond the valley,
from pain, and from distance
we shall forever go on calling out
to teach each other: "We'll change."[15]

This poem is exceptional in Amichai's poetry in terms of its direct occupation with language, and therefore invites us to open a discussion of the poetical grammar with its help. Words constitute the concrete reality and the source of the consciousness, while "The rest is slaughtered, eaten, / digested, decayed, forgotten." The attuning of the words to the reality is fashioned under the influence of the feathers metaphor. On the one hand, the words are compared to the feathers of a chicken meant to be slaughtered, while, on the other, they can fly above the world. The private experience of irremediable destruction is fashioned as a general sight that is not necessarily specific to the subject-speaker. The words, however, do not create reality, but only accompany it.[16] In this accompaniment, they generate a language-game that fashions a picture of deconstruction: all is destroyed, with no hope of remedy. The wealth of third-person passive verbs gives the impression of the impossibility of restoration and growth. The words are the sole testimony

15 Yehuda Amichai, *Poems of Jerusalem* (Cambridge: Harper & Row, 1988), p. 91; this poem trans. Ted Hughes.
16 Wittgenstein, *Philosophical Investigations*, para. 23.

to the past, since "The hermaphrodite of time [. . .] has wiped out this valley."

The speaker casts light on an additional function of the words in the past, as a language-game that accompanies human activity, as in Wittgenstein's depiction.[17] The translator elected to omit the wording from the middle of the first line in the third stanza: "Since, many words / and many loves." This line gives voice to the ambivalent connection between language and emotions: on the one hand, according to the poem, it is the nature of emotions of love to be expressed in words; on the other, there is no causal or binding connection between them, nor is it possible to create, maintain, or end love with words. This depiction raises the question of the existence of inner experience that is independent of language, and the need for the concept of mystical grammar. This grammar enables us to discern the experience unique to the speaker that is not dependent on words, while other experiences are dependent on language.

For example: in the end of the poem hope and optimism are embodied in the speech-act of a dialogic call for change. The testimony about the past, the accompaniment in the present, and the mutual prompting for change in the future illustrate the central role of the speech-act in a world without certainly in any realm. The speaker is down-to-earth, and relies on no idea or reality, not even on hope for the future, since he says: "I don't know how it will end." But "these words" allude to a recurring motif that was already mentioned above: the possibility of change.

Throughout his corpus, with varying degrees of confidence, Amichai fashioned changing realities, either after the fact or reflectively in the present. The motif of change apparently could constitute the background for a certain degree of forgiveness and gentleness to all that is human. In any event, the dynamics of emotional change characterizes the poetical grammar by casting light, in both subjective and objective fashion, on the speaker's emotional mechanism. Subjectivity,

17 "The word 'language-*game*' is used here to emphasize the fact that the *speaking* of language is part of an activity, or a form of life" (Wittgenstein, *Philosophical Investigations*, para. 23).

meaning the speaker's personal experience and the possibility of comprehending metaphors, attests to the objective aspect of this emotional experience.[18] In this manner, the grammar unites the shared feature with an element of surprise (the metaphor of words as feathers).

Garry Hagberg, a leading researcher of self-constitution in literary language, following Wittgenstein, showed the complexity inherent in a literary work that facilitates the constitution of self.[19] He portrayed how the fashioning of beliefs and experiences in a literary work expresses the reflection of the characters in a mystical manner that imitates the reader's mental reality and enables him to reexamine his own beliefs and constitute his self.[20] The work arouses self-reflection on

18 The distinction between the objective and the subjective in the current book is based on the following passage by William James, which expresses the second channel of mystical grammar described above: "The world of our experience consists at all times of two parts, an objective and a subjective part, of which the former may be incalculably more extensive than the latter, and yet the latter can never be omitted or suppressed. The objective part is the sum total of whatsoever at any given time we may be thinking of, the subjective part is the inner 'state' in which the thinking comes to pass [. . .] the cosmic objects, so far as the experience yields them, are but ideal pictures of something whose existence we do not inwardly possess but only point at outwardly, while the inner state is our very experience itself; its reality and that of our experience are one [. . .] It is a *full* fact, even though it be an insignificant fact; it is of the *kind* to which all realities whatsoever must belong [. . .] That unsharable feeling which each one of us has of the pinch of his individuality" (James, *Varieties of Religious Experience*, p. 385).

19 Garry Hagberg, "Self-Defining Reading: Literature and the Constitution of Personhood," in *Companion to the Philosophy of Literature*, pp. 120–58.

20 "The literary novel is a complex and extensive web of indeterminate reach that provides the logico-epistemic space within which thoughts, on the part of a character, can be depicted as entertaining thoughts, thoughts themselves made possible by other strands in that background web (roughly, what Wittgenstein, in a related context, called "the scaffolding" of thought) of beliefs. Literature [. . .] can then be seen as mimetic in a somewhat special way: the reader, at the simplest level, sees a narrative world depicted, where the complex web of explicit and implicit beliefs within that world makes thought (and in Davidson's sense, interpretation of speech and action) possible. And then at one higher or second mimetic level the reader of imaginative literature sees belief-neutral thought—often of a self-reflective kind, i.e. where the character, inside his or her imaginative logico-epistemic space, reflects on his or her actions, desires, motives, fears, aspirations, romantic ambitions, and so forth" (Hagberg, "Self-Defining Reading," p. 124). Hagberg discusses prose, but his insights can also be used in the analysis of poetry. Furthermore, in poetry, the singularity of the poetical grammar adds force to the possibility indicated by Hagberg, especially in inwardly contemplative lyrical poetry.

actions, motives, fears, and aspirations by using thought and imagination in a way not done in everyday life.

In the next poem Amichai exemplifies the complexity which was indicated by Hagberg. The speaker contemplates himself and his relationship with previous generations in a manner based on well-known connections, like parent-children relations and the commitment to national history. Together with this, the poetical grammar also creates defamiliarization that causes the reader to examine whether the disposition in the poem also constitutes his consciousness:

All the Generations before Me
All the generations before me
donated me, bit by bit, so that I'd be
Erected all at once
here in Jerusalem, like a house of prayer
Or charitable institution.
It binds.
My name's
my donor's name. It binds.

I'm approaching the age
of my father's death. My last
will's patched with many patches.
I have to change my life and death
daily to fulfill all the prophecies
prophesied for me. So they're not lies.
It binds.

I've passed forty.
There are jobs I cannot get
because of this. Were I in Auschwitz
they would not have sent me out to work,
but gassed me straightaway.
It binds.[21]

---

21 Amichai, *Poems of Jerusalem*, p. 3; this poem trans. Harold Schimmel.

The speaker describes his symbiotically dependent relationship with the previous generations: the generations constitute him, and enable him to flourish in Jerusalem. The comparison to a "house of prayer / Or charitable institution" combines humor and seriousness in a single breath. On the one hand, the speaker illustrates the seemingly formal commitment to his "donors" that is expressed in his being named after them. The fiction is fashioned as realism, and in turn fashions the speaker's personal history. The gap between the speaker, with his individual history, and "All the generations" and the institutions facing which he is constituted, makes the "commitment" ludicrous. The repetition of the wording "It binds" has an ambivalent function, as both acknowledgment and rejection of the bond between the speaker and the preceding generations.

The second stanza channels the humor and the criticism of the imposed bond to the constructive direction of self-constitution, in the spirit of the dominant principle of change in Amichai's poetry: the speaker must change his life daily "to fulfill all the prophecies." It is only in the third stanza that the root of the commitment to prior generations is revealed: the realistic possibility of ending his life in Auschwitz. The speaker connects his rescue from a fate similar to that of his friend Ruth or that of his associate Paul Celan with historic decision that is beyond the merit of the individual, and certainly beyond his power. The speaker's autobiography becomes an object in the service of Jewish history, and he therefore is responsible to adapt himself to the "prophecies." The poem reveals a surprising and intriguing aspect of the motivation for change in the self-constitutive process: this motivation originates in the sense of belonging and representation, of the Jew who was saved and remembers what could have been his personal fate, and what his place is in the historical chain.

The poem in its entirety exemplifies the distinction between "I as object" and "I as subject." The speaker combines first-person speech that expresses his certainty about his place in Jewish history with his relating to himself as an object lacking an identity of its own that is fashioned in accordance with the prophecies and fate that are dictated to him as a Jew. The parallel action of language on the two planes, the general and the individual, is accompanied by macabre humor, with the sense of urgency to fulfill his mission in life formulated under the possible threat of "gassed me straightaway." The poetical grammar includes selected historical facts as the background for the speaker's subjective decision to live in accordance with the feelings of guilt and mission. A striking metaphor in the creation of the picture of these feelings is that of "My last / will's patched with many patches." This seems to be a metaphor, but, in actuality, the speaker creates a quasi-metaphor that presumes to fashion his death, and not only his life as a whole. The desire to fashion death in opposition to the fate forced on the Jews in Auschwitz exceeds the expression of emotion that lies beyond language in the context of the poetical grammar, and is expressed in the mystical desire to connect with the meaning of life and death: "I have to change my life and death / daily to fulfill all the prophecies." The necessary life-death change stands on the boundary that frequently recurs in Amichai's poems, between metaphor and quasi-metaphor: the change of death cannot be simply parallel to the change of life, but it can be perceived as a metaphor for the changed meaning of life that gives meaning to death as well. An obstacle, however, stands in the way of our adoption of this interpretation, since the speaker retrospectively describes the realistic possibility of his death. This description introduces the possibility of death into the realistic world, and transforms the metaphor of changing life and death into a quasi-metaphor.

Important discussions have been devoted to Amichai's art of metaphor, with emphasis on his original fashioning of everyday details along with the element of surprise that awaits the reader. David Fishelov compared Amichai's singular use of simile to the technique of John Donne, the important seventeenth-century English poet.[22] A comparison of the similarity between these two poets in the thematic plane of their conception of death is fascinating: Donne engaged to a great extent in philosophical-poetical writing about death, and wrote a poem

22 David Fishelov, *Like a Rainfall: Studies and Essays on Poetic Simile* (Jerusalem: Magnes, 1996) (Hebrew).

in which he fashioned a scene of his own death.[23] Amichai, in contrast, fashions contending with death in an abstract manner, and the boundary between life and death is a major theme in his work. Nonetheless, the following poem, in which Amichai relates to the suicide of Paul Celan, is an important expression of the fashioning of this boundary, which will open our discussion of quasi-metaphor:

> *The Death of Celan*
> I heard about it in London. They said he killed himself.
>
> The same rope / was tugging lightly at my neck.
> But it wasn't rope: he
> died by water.
> The same water, water, water.
>
> Last metaphor:
> A life like a death.
> (The same water, water, water.)[24]

In this short poem in which Yehuda Amichai tells of the death of Paul Celan, the reader is aroused by the drama of its figurative fashioning, which strikingly differs from the usual minor key of Amichai's poetic language. The opening is as laconic and minimalist as a news report, but nevertheless takes the reader to London, divorced from any Jewish context. And then, in the second line, a dramatic portrayal of a death wish seizes the reader: "The same rope / was tugging lightly at my neck." The speaker is aware of the metaphorical nature of his depiction, and immediately continues by distinguishing between reality and poetics: "But it wasn't rope: he / died by water." The speaker then connects the reality to the poetical plane by saying that the water in

23 Donne's best-known poem on this topic is "Death, Be Not Proud": John Donne, *Holy Sonnets*, no. 6, in *Major Works*, ed. John Carey (Oxford: Oxford University Press, 1990), pp. 175–76.

24 Yehuda Amichai, *The Early Books of Yehuda Amichai*, trans. Harold Schimmel et al. (Riverdale-on-Hudson, NY: Sheep Meadow, 1988), p. 53.

which Celan drowned resembles the water in which the speaker imagines himself to be in now. At the end of this powerful poem, the speaker also presents his awareness of his poetical method by saying: Here, I set before you the last metaphor—water is like death. We, the readers, remain with our confusion: in what sense are the opposites of life and death similar? How does the metaphorical language work here? How is the relationship between reality and imagination woven, when, on the one hand, we are acutely aware of the concrete reality, while, on the other, metaphor unquestionably leads the course of the poem? How does Amichai succeed in linking Celan's fate as a Jew and the speaker's consequent identification with him with the universal idea of life and death as contrast and as completion?

Amichai's poem combines elements of existentialist philosophy with his personal experience: the ability to identify with the other, to the extent of merging with him, and the deterministic influence of the death-experience on life à la Heidegger, which is intensified by his personal relationship with Celan (who also conducted a dialogue with Heidegger). The metaphorical language of this short and powerful poem succeeds in containing all of the above: the general and the concrete, the everyday and the metaphorical, as well as questioning the concept of "metaphor." The speaker's explicit announcement of his presenting the last metaphor raises the question: were metaphors used before in the poem, or do the seeming metaphors actually describe the experience itself? The "grammaticalization of experience" that we presented above functions here in the manner that Altieri described as "making visible something that we have to process as first-person state."[25] In his attempt to depict the experience of suicide, the speaker compares his own feeling, in the first person, with the sense of choking that he imagines led Celan to take his life. The speaker is not explicit in his choice of words, he rather fashions the experience itself so that the reader can imagine it as his own. This subtle grammar of experience is not at all metaphorical. Rather, it constitutes "a shift from treating the self as if it were observable matter and treating the self as something

25 Altieri, "Exemplification and Expression," p. 495.

made visible by the manner of expressive activity."[26] Altieri, following Wittgenstein, emphasizes that the self is not a distinct, observable object; it rather can be made visible by expressive activity that reflects its experience.[27] Thus, in this poem, the speaker who identifies with Celan's feelings does not differentiate himself as a subject who merely feels Celan's distress, but rather portrays it by a description of the same rope around his own neck.

The triple repetition of the word "water" in the middle and end of the poem casts in a new and original light the connotation to the first chapter of Genesis, which relates how God separated water from water on the second day: for the speaker, the water of the river in which Celan drowned joins together with the beginning of Creation, and, after the fact, enables the comparison between life and death. Water is the common denominator, because it symbolizes life (and is essential for life, in the simple and trivial sense), while it also makes death possible, as in Celan's case. In the metaphorical plane, the process of mixture, separation, and comparison repeats itself. This circularity attests to possible connections and relations between the elements of the metaphor.

Metaphor works as semantic change: taking a word or expression from one semantic field to represent something vague in another. Here this also includes connotations from the Bible and the prayerbook that are taken from their original context and "planted" in a modern

26 Altieri, "Exemplification and Expression," p. 496.

27 In *Philosophical Investigations* Wittgenstein deconstructs a series of concepts that are erroneously perceived as possessing independent essence or existence, including the terms "I," "here," and "this": "'I' doesn't name a person, nor 'here' a place, and 'this' is not a name. But they are connected with names. Names are explained by means of them. It is also true that it is characteristic of physics not to use these words. [. . .] Here we have a case of introspection, not unlike that which gave William James the idea that the 'self' consisted mainly of 'peculiar motions in the head and between the head and throat.' And James's introspection showed, not the meaning of the word 'self' (so far as it means something like 'person,' 'human being,' 'he himself,' 'I myself'), or any analysis of such a being, but the case of a philosopher's attention when he says the word 'self' to himself and tries to analyse its meaning. (And much could be learned from this.)" (Wittgenstein, *Philosophical Investigations*, para. 410, 413). Heinz Kohut, the founder of self psychology, similarly described the self (see below).

semantic field. At times a metaphor or connotation is incorporated in ordinary language, so that their origins are hardly distinguishable. This would seem to be the phenomenon known as "dead metaphor." Frank Sibley, however, suggested the term "quasi-metaphor" in his 1959 article, "Aesthetic Concepts," for a metaphor that presumably is incorporated in ordinary language, but in fact retains a unique poetic quality. Sibley writes:

> There does exist [. . .] a large and accepted vocabulary of aesthetic terms some of which, whatever their metaphorical origins, are now not metaphors at all, others of which are at most quasi-metaphorical. Second, this view that our use of metaphor and quasi-metaphor for aesthetic purposes is unnatural or a makeshift into which we are forced by a language designed for other purposes misrepresents fundamentally the character of aesthetic qualities and aesthetic language. There is nothing unnatural about using words like "forceful," "dynamic," or "tightly-knit" in criticism; they do their work perfectly and are exactly the words needed for the purposes they serve. We do not want or need to replace them by words which lack the metaphorical element. In using them to describe works of art, the very point is that we are noticing aesthetic qualities related to their literal or common meanings.[28]

Sibley relates to terms used in aesthetic judgment as a test case. Such terms do not empirically describe what happens in a work of art or its aesthetic quality, and therefore are metaphorical. Sibley, however, argues that they have additional value: they function both literally and metaphorically, and produce a special relation that reflects poetic quality. The "dead metaphor," in contrast, no longer draws the reader's attention to the comparison between the two semantic fields, and already lacks poetic quality. The quasi-metaphor, however, is incorporated in ordinary language in a seemingly natural manner, similar to the

28 Frank Sibley, "Aesthetic Concepts," *The Philosophical Review* 68, no. 4 (1959), p. 441.

dead metaphor. Consequently, Malcolm Budd situated it as an interim metaphorical state, meaning: "Partly metaphorical, the meaning of which is uncertain."[29] Budd indicated a lacuna in Sibley's discussion, namely, his failure to examine the relationship between the literal and the poetic in the case of the quasi-metaphor, and thus missed the manner in which poetic quality is created in the comparison established by the metaphor. Budd, who researches aesthetic qualities from the Greek literature to the present, wrote how the quasi-metaphor creates the relationship between the literal and the poetic:

> The aesthetic term is used precisely to signify a resemblance between what it is applied to in its aesthetic use and what it is applied to in its non-aesthetic use [. . .] *the aesthetic quality it ascribes is the relational property of resembling what is designated by the word used literally.*[30]

In Amichai's poetry we find many instances of original figurative language that employ the language of the classical Jewish sources, and by which they are inspired to express a pluralistic stance. This diverse use also includes references, both direct and indirect, to non-Jewish cultures. In some cases, this use expresses a dual position: on one plane, the linguistic context refers to the Jewish context; while, on the other, it constitutes a multicultural position based on personal experience.

Amichai's poetic language operates on two levels: a dialogue between the sources, both Jewish and non-Jewish, and an event in the speaker's life; and an emblematic pluralistic dimension that constitutes a universal speaker. This dual function is brought about, in many instances, by the use of quasi-metaphor, which is a special type of metaphor.

Different types of dialogic relations can be identified, and I will exemplify three types, each of which ensues from the discussion of the quasi-metaphor: intercultural dialogue, with an aesthetic purpose; intercultural dialogue of a polemical bent; and intercultural dialogue

29 Malcolm Budd, *Aesthetic Essays* (Oxford: Oxford University Press, 2008), p. 143.
30 Budd, *Aesthetic Essays*, pp. 146–47 (emphasis added).

that seeks an encounter between the local and the universal. As a last theoretical introduction, I wish to add the way in which Sam Glucksberg's view of how the quasi-metaphor works with allusion, since this is especially relevant for understanding Amichai's poetry:

> Quasi-metaphorical [. . .] idioms convey meaning via their allusional content. They call to mind a prototypical or stereotypical instance of an entire category of people, events, situations, or actions [. . .] Such metaphors characterize their topics by assigning them to categories that are diagnostic and often evaluative [. . .] Quasi-metaphorical idioms function precisely the same as nominal metaphors. Via the mechanism of dual reference, they can simultaneously refer to an ideal exemplar of a concept and characterize some event or situation as an instance of that concept.[31]

The fashioning of the metaphor also includes an intercultural tie that expresses the speaker's concrete personal experience, which is incorporated within the connotative context of the metaphor. The poem *An Arab Shepherd Is Seeking a Kid* portrays two searches: the Arab shepherd who searches for a lost kid, and a Jewish father searching for his son:

> An Arab shepherd is seeking a kid
> on Mount Zion,
> and on the opposite hill I seek my little son.
> An Arab shepherd and a Jewish father
> Both in their temporary failure.
> Our two voices meet above
> The Sultan's Pool in the valley between.
> Neither of us wants the son or the kid
> To enter the terrible process
> Of the Passover song "One kid."

31 Sam Glucksberg, *Understanding Figurative Language* (Oxford: Oxford University Press, 2001), p. 75.

Afterwards we found them between the bushes,
And our voices returned to us
And we wept and laughed deep inside ourselves.

Searches for a kid or for a son were always
The beginning of a new religion in these mountains.[32]

The kid functions as a quasi-metaphor when, on the one hand, the poem depicts a realistic, commonplace picture of the search for a lost kid, and, on the other, the portrayal of the shepherd searching for the kid is reminiscent of the midrash in *Exodus Rabbah*, in which Moses is presented as a shepherd who searched for and found the lost kid. The importance of this connotation for interpreting the poem becomes stronger at its end, when the speaker mentions the start of a new religion, thereby alluding to Moses, who founded Judaism:

Searches for a kid or for a son were always
The beginning of a new religion in these mountains.

The midrash relates:

> "Moses was tending the flock" [Exod. 3:1]—the Holy One, blessed be He, tested Moses with the flock. Our masters said: When Moses was tending the flock of Jethro in the wilderness, a kid escaped from him. He ran after it until it came to a shady place. When it reached the shady place, a pool of water came to be there, and the kid stopped to drink. When Moses approached it, he said: "I did not know that you ran away out of thirst, you must be weary." So he put the kid on his shoulder and walked along. The Holy One, blessed be He, said: Because you are merciful in leading the flock of a mortal, you will surely tend My flock Israel. (*Exod. Rabbah* 2:2)

32 Amichai, *Great Tranquility*, p. 15.

Moses relates to the kid as a father to his son: he searches for it, understands its needs, and helps it by carrying it on his shoulder. Moses is the premier prophet, a standing he holds in Islam as well. This shared element creates the connotative foundation of the poem, which speaks of a Jew seeking his son and an Arab seeking his kid. Amichai draws a parallel between his personal experience as a father who searches for his lost son and the connotation that functions in a much broader cultural context, which finds special expression in the English version of the poem: in the Hebrew poem, the speaker distinguishes between the *gedi* that the Arab shepherd seeks and the child sought by the Jewish father. The English translation, however, might have two meanings, and "kid," too, could be understood as the shepherd's search for his son.

Thus, the kid and the child merge into a single subject. Moreover, the shepherd and the father share a similar desire: that the object of their search not suffer the fate of the kid in the Passover Haggadah song "One Kid" (that is, death). After both have found their lost ones, both internalize the weeping and laughter within themselves. Amichai created a quasi-metaphor that functions on two planes: on the realistic plane, the shepherd searches for the kid, and the father, his son; on the other level, this search hints at the narratives of Moses and Jesus, and the connection between the two dimensions universalizes, and thereby intensifies, the hidden wish of the shepherd and the father. Following Malcolm Budd, we can indicate three types of relation: similarity (both are searching for something small and weak that became lost; both fear for its fate); difference (in the reality—between the Arab and the Jew; in the history of religion—between Judaism, on the one hand, and Christianity and Islam, on the other); and finally, the connection between the local and other cultures. The Jerusalemite speaker experiences the city from anew as a heterotopic expanse in which the adherents of different faiths can unit in shared search and desire.

The metaphoric also drifts to the New Testament, since Moses looked for the kid in Egypt, and not in the Jerusalem hills, while the connotation of a shepherd in these hills alludes to Jesus, who saw himself, and was perceived by those believing in him, as a shepherd. Thus, for example, the New Testament states (Mark 6:33–34):

> Now many saw them going, and knew them, and they ran there on foot from all the towns, and got there ahead of them. As he landed he saw a great throng, and he had compassion on them, because they were like sheep without a shepherd; and he began to teach them many things.

Such figurative fashioning acts in several ways: the word recalls the original context, imparts new meaning to a modern event or idea, and points to a link or similarity between Jewish and other cultures. This indication of connection is not only referential, to use the terminology of Ivor Richards; it intends to influence and change consciousness.[33] Budd, too, stresses that "'quasi-metaphorical' use" is likely to create a new meaning that is not based on the original one, since we have here fashioning that creates something new and independent.[34] Thus, for instance, we can see the perception of bread in Amichai's poem *Karl Marx, Cold and Bitter One.*

> *Karl Marx, Cold and Bitter One*
> Karl Marx, cold and bitter one,
> A man outside and a Jew in your grave in the foreign rain.

---

33 "It is the supreme agent by which disparate and hitherto unconnected things are brought together in poetry for the sake of the effects upon attitude and impulse which spring from their collocation and from the combinations which the mind then establishes between them. There are few metaphors whose effect, if carefully examined, can be traced to the logical relations involved. Metaphor is a semi-surreptitious method by which a greater variety of elements can be wrought into the fabric of the experience. Not that there is any virtue in variety by itself, though the list of critics who seem to have thought so would be lengthy; a page of the dictionary can show more variety than any page of poetry. But what is needed for the wholeness of an experience is not always naturally present, and metaphor supplies an excuse by which what is needed may be smuggled in" (Ivor A. Richards, *Principles of Literary Criticism* [London: Routledge, 2001 (1926)]), p. 225.

34 "'Quasi-metaphorical' use of a word is not attached to the straightforwardly literal use of the word only historically or by means of resemblances [. . .] For when a word is extended from one domain to another on the basis of recognized similarities between properties of items in the two domains—and then, perhaps, to further domains—if this use becomes standard then it is characteristic for a new sense of the word to be distinguished, one that is not parasitic on the original meaning, so that this sense of the word can be grasped independently of an understanding of what at one time was the word's (only) literal meaning" (Budd, *Aesthetic Essays*, p. 145).

"Man lives by bread alone": yourself
Bread alone, lonely bread that you are,
Round loaf from the last century, A loaf rolling and tumbling the whole world
Upside down.

Here I am on this winter day in Jerusalem
Where tired Jews search the bodies of passerby:
Collarbones, breast, belly, crotch: danger and love.
My skin still protects me against the rain,
But in one of my tears, if I'm still weeping then,
There will remain something of this water
Pouring down now from heaven.

Karl Marx, with a beard like a sage.
Ritual slaughterer of history
So that it can be clean and kosher, according to the Law:
Look, I have put a lamp in my window
To make a field of life for myself.
I pay my rent on time. This too
In some kind of defense line, but directly
In front of it the enemy's armies
Are lined up with rockets and thunder,
Last battle and first death
And nothing after.
Look, my love caresses my breast
Which is the hairy side of my emotions.

Karl Marx, the last drop
Will always be a tear.[35]

Bread functions in the poem as a quasi-metaphor, in four metaphorical planes.

35 Amichai, *Early Books*, p. 162.

In the *historical plane,* Karl Marx fights for the worker's bread, and Amichai transforms bread from a metaphor for the workers' struggle to one for Marx himself, as a person:

> "Man lives by bread alone": yourself
> Bread alone, lonely bread that you are.

Amichai includes the *connotative plane,* and quotes verbatim part of Deuteronomy 8:2: "man does not live by bread alone."[36] The continuation of the verse explains why having bread alone cannot satisfy man's needs, since he is also nourished by the emotional and spiritual realm. In the biblical context, the moral sphere contains God's commandment, and on the universal level, the moral sphere includes compassion and caring for one's fellow, and not only concern for his economic future.

In the third plane, the *personal and local plane,* the speaker situates himself concretely:

> Here I am on this winter day in Jerusalem
> Where tired Jews search the bodies of passerby:
> Collarbones, breast, belly, crotch: danger and love.
> My skin still protects me against the rain,
> But in one of my tears, if I'm still weeping then,
> There will remain something of this water
> Pouring down now from heaven.

Finally, the speaker concludes his attitude to Karl Marx on the *universal plane that results from a depiction within the personal plane*: from within the love scene with the speaker's lover, he reminds Marx that:

> Karl Marx, the last drop
> Will always be a tear.

---

36 "He subjected you to the hardship of hunger and then gave you manna to eat, which neither you nor your fathers had even known, in order to teach you that man does not live by bread alone, but that man may live on anything that the Lord decrees" (Deut. 8:3).

While the above poem exemplified the speaker's ambivalence to Marx's attitude, the following poem shows the internal ambivalence in the speaker's attitude to Jerusalem. Amichai devotes many poems to Jerusalem, some of which were collected in a separate volume, *Poems of Jerusalem*.[37] His last book, *Open Closed Open*, contains a cycle of twenty-eight poems that have Jerusalem at their center. In this cycle, the speaker attempts to examine different aspects of the meaning of his connection with the city, and it seems that he tries to verbalize its mystical power. The city obviously deeply influences him, alongside the tensions that express his inner opposition to the bond with the city that he feels. One of the outstanding features of his descriptions regarding the city is fashioned as a paradox: on the one hand, the city arouses the speaker's sentiments as a Jew, while, on the other, he presents its universal character to create symbols and to be a spiritual home for the members of the three monotheistic religions.

Grammatically, Jerusalem turns everything in it to a symbol, including the specific, private love of two lovers, which functions as a quasi-metaphor in the following poem. The metaphorical fashioning of the act of love is bidirectional: love becomes a symbol, while at the same time the symbol is as hard as rock, as sharp as nails. Love and the mattress on which the act of love takes place symbolize the 613 commandments and their characteristics (Thou shalt-Thou shalt not). At the same time, they reflect what is good for love and its pleasures. The metaphor works in dual fashion, as depicting personal experience, and in parallel, the system of commandments. This exemplifies how love functions as a quasi-metaphor throughout the book, with Amichai suggesting, in other poems as well, to place love at the center of the observance of the commandments.

> *Poem no. 7*
> In Jerusalem, everything is a symbol. Even lovers there
> Become a symbol like a lion, the golden dome, the gates of
> the city.

37 Amichai, *Poems of Jerusalem*.

> Sometimes they make love on too soft a symbolism
> And sometimes the symbols are hard as a rock, sharp as nails.
> That's why they make love on a mattress of six hundred thirteen springs,
> Like the number of precepts, the commandments of Shalt and Shalt not,
> oh yes, do that, darling, no, not that—all for love
> and its pleasures. They speak with bells in their voices
> and with the wailing call of Muezzin, and at their bedside, empty shows
> as at the entrance of a mosque. And on the doorpost of their house
> it says,
> "Ye shall love each other with all your heart and with all your souls."[38]

The lovers are not identified with any specific religion, but with the universal nature of love. Thus, in the continuation of the depiction, their bell-like voices mingle with that of the muezzin. The quasi-metaphor has its greatest effect at the end of the poem: the speaker quotes a biblical verse, with a major alteration, which he highlights by placing the changed section within quotation marks. The verse reads: "If, then, you obey the commandments that I enjoin upon you this day, to love the Lord your God, and to serve Him with all your heart and with all your soul" (Deuteronomy 11:13). Amichai doubles the object of the commandment ("Ye"), so that it can refer both to God and to human beings, who are commanded to love one another.

The English translation of the poem is not accurate, and misses the dual meaning that emerges from this line of the poem in its original Hebrew: ואהבתם בכל לבבכם ובכל נפשכם. Amichai thereby gives us an example of quasi-metaphor, since it preserves the original meaning of the Bible, while adding an additional meaning of the commandment to engage in romantic love (which refers retrospectively to the love scene

38 Yehuda Amichai, "Jerusalem, Jerusalem, Why Jerusalem?," no. 7, in *Open Closed Open*, p. 137.

in the poem). In this manner, we have a dialogue between the universal aspect of love and the Jewish-religious aspect of love of God which is symbolized by the reading of *Shema* ("Hear, O Israel"), from which this verse is taken. We saw how the third type of metaphor, which is an interim type between "live" and "dead" metaphor, functions in Amichai's poetry. This type, the quasi-metaphor, facilitates numerous planes, more than are possible with regular metaphor. This is because it does not merge the semantic fields, but preserves each in its distinctness, thus enabling the author to present different planes and the relations between them. The three functions of quasi-metaphor (aesthetic, polemic, and intercultural) can clarify how Amichai's poetry works in complex fashion, moving between the personal and the general, the Jewish and the universal, and the culture of the place where he lives and other near-at-hand cultures.

Beyond the linguistic strata that Amichai uses in his poetic and dialogic grammar, we should take note of the way in which Amichai's grammar creates an experience of true and profound encounter with the significant "otherness." The following discussion will examine how, in addition to the metaphoric fashioning, the dialogic grammar enables experiencing the fate of another as an integral part of the constitution of self.

2. Dialogic Grammar: The Importance of Otherness

The manner in which Amichai's poetry expresses intersubjective sensitivity to the other is striking, in terms of both scope and quality. The dialogic grammar acts as inner and reflective dialogue with possible destinies and, therefore, as conversational dialogue with significant others, alive or already dead. The poetic grammar is fashioned so that otherness, whether inner or external, arouses a reexamination of values and aspirations. This scrutiny reaches its peak in his last book, *Open Closed Open*, but its early phases are present in his earlier collections. Unlike the preceding discussion, which concentrated on the metaphorical fashioning of experience and change (also) facing others, in the current discussion otherness is the starting point for dialogue.

Additionally, unlike the mystical grammar that makes private and individual positions possible, the dialogic grammar includes features that allow for intersubjectivity.

How does the use of public language, which accompanies all everyday activity and is accordingly accessible to its speakers, differ from the use of intersubjective language, which facilitates the meeting between two individual people? The third Wittgenstein investigated this question at length, and his insights were accordingly incorporated in the therapeutic context, both the psychoanalytic and the cognitive.[39] Amichai's dialogic grammar is based on the fashioning of everyday situations so that they express hidden emotions or meanings that are embedded in the relationships between people. Thus, for example, his feelings for Ruth are fashioned within the experience of waiting for a suitcase at the airport, or the experience of eating and drinking on (the fastday of) Yom Kippur as an expression of the lack of his parents in his life. This fashioning graphically illustrates how the language that accompanies routine actions can also function reflectively, as expressing intentions, emotions, and intersubjective relations.

We will discuss three types of otherness: the otherness that is embodied in the character of "little Ruth," that in his relationship with Paul Celan, and that in the figures of his parents. The "family resemblance" between the othernesses is that they all shed light on the aspect of alternative fate. The dialogic grammar works in a number of ways: in the poems themselves, it expresses the missed meeting with the other, while the poem, at the same time, attests to a significant past meeting. This meeting constitutes the dialogic grammar from which

39 In the psychoanalytical context, see, e.g., Charles R. Elder, *The Grammar of the Unconscious: The Conceptual Foundations of Psychoanalysis* (University Park: Pennsylvania State University Press, 1994); Donna M. Orange, *Thinking for Clinicians: Philosophical Resources for Contemporary Psychoanalysis and the Humanistic Psychotherapies* (New York: Routledge, 2010), pp. 33–54; John M. Heaton, *The Talking Cure: Wittgenstein's Therapeutic Method for Psychotherapy* (London: Palgrave Macmillan, 2010). In the context of cognitive psychology, see Eugen Fischer, "A Cognitive Self-Therapy," in *Wittgenstein at Work: Method in the Philosophical Investigations*, ed. Erich Ammereller and Eugen Fischer (London: Routledge, 2004), pp. 86–126; and Rom Harre and Michael A. Tissaw, *Wittgenstein and Psychology: A Practical Guide* (Aldershot: Ashgate, 2005).

Amichai does not part; nor does he wish to part from it throughout his corpus. This is because the meeting with these others (along with others like Jerusalem, other religions, women, and more) creates existential meanings for him and leaves its mark in his self-constitution.

This position, that interaction with significant others accompanies the process of the subject's self-constitution, was formulated by Heinz Kohut, the founder of the psychology of the self. Kohut coined the term "self-objects,"[40] referring to internalized and external objects, dialogue with which constitutes meaning, because they converse with the speaker's aspirations and ideals.[41] These "hinges" of meaning (to use Wittgensteinian terminology) are possible searches and constitutions of existential meaning that offer an alternative to the speaker's fate and choices. I wish to show how little Ruth, the poet's parents, and Paul Celan function in Amichai's poetry as significant others who are a constant reminder of an alternative fate. Continuing in this vein, the encounter with the otherness joins the mechanism of constant change that guides his worldview.

Heinz Kohut and Stephen Mitchell (the founder of relational psychoanalysis) suggested changing the monadic conception of the psyche that had been formulated by Freud, and examining how a person's self is constituted in interaction with others.[42] According to

---

40 The term "selfobject" was coined by Heinz Kohut in his book *The Restoration of the Self* (New York: International Universities Press, 1977), p. xiii. Kohut immediately underscored the importance of this concept: "The crucial theoretical concept introduced within this framework was that of the *self-object* [. . .] the most important empirical finding in the therapeutic field was the phenomenon to which I refer as *transference to self-objects*" (p. xiii; emphasis in original). Nonetheless, the term was not explicitly defined in the book, but only indirectly, as an alternative to Freud's drive theory meant to show that self-constitution occurs as a result of a relationship, and not as a function of any drives: "From the beginning, the drive experience is subordinated to the child's experience of the relation between the self and the self-objects [. . .] It changes our evaluation of the significance of the libido theory on all levels of psychological development in childhood" (p. 80). (Kohut himself was not consistent in the spelling of this term, and wrote both "selfobject" and "self-object.")

41 Kohut, *Restoration of the Self*, p. 243.

42 "Some outlines of the changes in theory that self psychology is bringing about can already be discerned: a shift from the previous emphasis on quasi-biological 'drives,' and secondarily, from the study of the psychological conflicts that arise

Kohut and Mitchell, the fashioning of selfhood is a dynamic and never-ending process, one that is mainly intersubjective, between a person and external factors that are not subservient to his decisions or desires.[43] An examination in this spirit of the process of self-constitution explains the factors facing which the elements of identity are fashioned, such as historical events, relationships with various people, and ideas and experiences that are imprinted in one's consciousness. Each of these factors is what Kohut called a "self-object." Actually, this is a function that the other fills in relation to the self, in a relation that is characterized by a lack of, or only partial, differentiation between self and object.

The self, therefore, is not a construct of substantive nature, despite people's inclination to experience themselves as possessing a defined personality. Language is the primary substrate in which change occurs in the self, and that includes relational and social contexts:

> In the beginning, we might say, is the relational, social, linguistic matrix in which we discover ourselves, or, as Heidegger put it, into which we are "thrown." Within that matrix are formed, precipitated out, individual psyches with subjectively experienced interior spaces. Those subjective spaces begin as microcosms of the relational field, in which macrocosmic

concerning their expression and their taming to the positing of primary configurations that are already complex from the beginning [. . .] Self-psychology does not work with a framework of biological drives and a mental apparatus. The primary self, in a matrix of empathic selfobjects, is held to be as much a prerequisite of psychological existence as oxygen is for biological life; it experiences *self*object greatness (assertiveness, ambitions), on the one hand, and self*object* perfection (idealization of one's goals, enthusiasm for one's ideals), on the other. Drives are secondary phenomena. They are disintegration products following the breakup of the primary complex psychological configurations in consequence of (empathy) failures in the self-object matrix" (Heinz Kohut, *The Search for the Self*, ed. Paul H. Ornstein [London: Karnac, 2011], vol. 3: *Selected Writings of Heinz Kohut 1978–1981*, p. 236). See also Stephen Mitchell, *Relationality: From Attachment to Intersubjectivity* (Hillsdale, NJ: Analytic Press, 2000), p. x.

43 "Subjectivity always develops in the context of intersubjectivity; we continually process and organize the enormous complexity of ourselves and our world into recurring patterns" (Mitchell, *Relationality*, p. 57).

> interpersonal relationships are internalized and transformed into a distinctly personal experience.[44]

In order to understand how our thought functions as individuals in a general social context and how subjectivity emerges, Mitchell intriguingly refers us to the philosophy of language by quoting "Cavell, drawing on Wittgenstein." Mitchell bases his relational position, that subjectivity is constituted from intersubjectivity, on philosophical insights such as "other minds" and the meaning of skepticism:

> As Cavell (1993), drawing on Wittgenstein, Davidson, and others, has put it, "subjectivity arises along with intersubjectivity and is not the prior state [. . .] doubting the world and other minds, one must be in possession of all one needs to put the doubts to rest" (p. 40). Descartes did not have to derive the external world and other minds from his direct experience of his own mind; the very fact that he had a mind that could raise such questions presumed other minds and an external world they had in common.[45]

Certainty in the existence of a shared world is necessary for a person to doubt, or to assume the existence of other consciousnesses besides his own. Consequently, Mitchell argues, solipsism is a logical possibility, but did not become a philosophical school.[46] In this common world, there is a "family resemblance" between a person and the social system that, as Wittgenstein understands this, includes agreement on definitions and judgments.[47]

The next poem portrays an attempt at existential definition and judgment by clarifying the nature of happiness. The title already begins a reflective dialogue of the speaker with his childhood friend Ruth. The poem's language makes it difficult to distinguish between the

---

44 Mitchell, *Relationality*, p. 57.
45 Mitchell, *Relationality*, p. xii.
46 Mitchell, *Relationality*, p. xii.
47 Wittgenstein, *Philosophical Investigations*, para. 241–42.

realistic figure of Ruth and what she represents in the speaker's self-consciousness, and thereby functions as a self-object, which is both object and subject. The speaker expressed his unrealizable aspiration to speak with Ruth, who is no longer among the living, but he still feels the need to examine existential questions with her, while criticizing the past and the present:

> *Ruth, What Is Happiness?*
> Ruth, what is happiness? We should have
> Talked about it, but we didn't.
> The efforts we make to look happy
> Take our strength, as from tired soil.
>
> Let's go home. To different homes.
> "And in case we don't see each other anymore."
>
> Your bag slung over your shoulder
> made you an efficient wanderer
> without symmetry, with bright eyes.
>
> When the wind, lifting clouds,
> will lift my heart as well and
> bring it to another place—
> that's true happiness.
>
> "And in case we don't see each other anymore."[48]

Ruth Fanny Hanover (1923–1943) accompanies Amichai's work throughout his career, as if his poems were addressed to her,[49] beginning

48 Yehuda Amichai, *Amen*, trans. Ted Hughes (Minneapolis, MN: Milkweed, 1977), p. 96.

49 "These two pages from Amichai's notebook are held in his archive, in the International Modern Poetry division of the Beinecke Rare Book and Manuscript Library of Yale University. These pages were written on the eve of Hanukkah (December) 1990, sixty-seven years after little Ruth died in the Sobibor camp in Poland. Little Ruth is Ruth Hanover, the daughter of Rabbi Dr. Sigmund Hanover of Wurzburg,

with the collection *1948–1962* (1962), continuing with the novel *Not from Here, Not from Now* (1963), the collection of poetry *The Fist, Too, Was Once an Open Hand and Fingers* (1989), to his last book, *Open Closed Open* (1998).[50] The above poem places Ruth in a significant position in relation to the speaker's current life, as regards the question of what is happiness. The question arises as to why the relationship between two children at

---

Germany. Ruth's mother died when Ruth was nine years old. At about that same time, Ernestina, the sister of Ruth's mother, was widowed, and in 1933 she moved to Wurzburg with her children in order to marry her brother-in-law, Rabbi Hanover (Ruth's father). One of Ernestina's daughters, who, too, was named Ruth, was older than Ruth Hanover. In the new family unit that came into being, Ruth Hanover was therefore called "little Ruth," to distinguish her from her cousin and stepsister. Rabbi Hanover's family and the Pfeuffer family lived near each other and were friendly. Friedrich Pfeuffer, Yehuda Amichai's father, was involved in communal affairs, and was one of the pillars of the Jewish community. Little Ruth and Yehuda were together in kindergarten and in the Jewish school, and every day they walked together to and from school, and they spent many hours together after school. [. . .] The members of the two families jokingly called Ruth and Yehuda 'the bride and groom.' When little Ruth was eleven years old, she was run over by an automobile as she was riding her bicycle on a city street. Her leg was amputated above the knee, and she needed a prosthesis. In the above page from his diary, Amichai mentions that the accident that happened to little Ruth occurred a few days before an argument that they had. This is in contrast to the groundless claim made by Nili Gold in her book on Yehuda Amichai, *Yehuda Amichai: The Making of Israel's National Poet* (published by Brandeis University), that the accident happened immediately following the argument between them, and that Amichai therefore felt guilty about little Ruth [. . .] The accident and the amputation, that took place in 1934, sealed Ruth's fate. In 1936 the twelve-year-old Yehuda and his family immigrated to Palestine [. . .] The memory of little Ruth stayed with Amichai his entire life and in all his writing, beginning with the book *Two Hopes Distant* (Hakibbutz Hameuchad, 1960) and the novel that describes his childhood in Germany, *Not of This Time, Not of This Place* (Schocken, 1963), to his last book, *Open Closed Open*. On January 4, 1939, Ruth went to Holland in a children's convoy [. . .] The Hanover family received an entry permit to the United States, that was valid until March 5, 1940 [. . .] Ruth was not permitted to enter the United States due to her disability. Yehuda's father continued, without success, to obtain [immigration] certificates to Palestine. In May 1940 Holland was conquered by the Germans. Some time later, Ruth was transported to the Westerbork concentration camp, and on May 18, 1943, she was sent to the Sobibor extermination camp. She was twenty years old when she was murdered there" (Hanna Amichai, "Little Ruth Is My Private Anne Frank," *Haaretz*, September 12, 2010 [Hebrew]).

50 The years of publication refer to the publication in Hebrew; the years of publication in the footnotes refer to the English translations.

the start of adolescence, even taking into account the traumatic circumstances that put an end to this relationship, still gives the speaker no rest.

The speaker returns to his childhood friend Ruth to give an accounting of his present life ("The efforts we make to look happy / Take our strength"). Presumably, the return to the past will likely provide a sphere-in-between to clarify the cause of the current situation, but the return merely reconstructs the circumstances of the forced parting; it only reopens the wound. Nonetheless, towards its end the poem depicts the possibility of future happiness, in the most abstract manner ("When the wind, lifting clouds, / will lift my heart"). This possibility, as well, is limited by means of the repetition of the sentence that seemingly is said between them, and is proven to be true, since they never saw each other afterwards. The poem attempts to reconstruct a farewell that did not take place, and that he later fashioned as his self-conceptualization of the concept of time, as it relates to Ruth:

> She always returns, for I don't have any early or late. Time is an expanse in which I move forward and back with ease. I don't detach myself from her, just as I don't detach myself from myself [. . .] Maybe I feel guilty about her, just like the guilt of soldiers who return alive from battle, while their comrades were killed [. . .] Now [she] is part of me, my witness, like my parents.[51]

This account by Amichai sheds light on the different aspects of the dialogic nature of the poem: beginning with the title, it is constructed as a seeming dialogue, which is a technical means for the speaker to reevaluate his attitude to his fate.

Ruth is an interiorized self-object to whom the speaker turns in order to conduct a reflective dialogue, with both a possible fate and the question of the existence of happiness in his life. Concealed within this is a conversational dialogue that attempts to argue, as it were, with

51 Dalia Karpel, "Waiting for the Nobel," *Ha-Ir* (November 3, 1989) (Hebrew).

Ruth's fate, especially in the poem's last line. The poem brings Ruth to life in the speaker's memory, and thereby seemingly creates a second chance for the conversation between friends that was abruptly cut off.

While the atmosphere of the first Ruth poem is low-key and allusive, the next poem about Ruth clearly describes the reason for the forced parting. The speaker addresses Ruth by her nickname, and simply and trenchantly depicts her fate:

> *Little Ruth*
> Sometimes I remember you, little Ruth,
> we were separated in our distant childhood and they burned you in the camps.
> If you were alive now, you would be a woman of sixty-five,
> a woman on the verge of old age. At twenty you were burned
> and I don't know what happened to you in your short life
> since we separated. What did you achieve, what insignia
> did they put on your shoulders, your sleeves, your brave soul, what shining stars
> did they pin on you, what decorations for valor, what
> medals for love hung around your neck,
> what peace upon you, *peace unto you.*
> And what happened to the unused years of your life?
> Are they still packed away in pretty bundles,
> were they added to my life? Did you turn me
> into your bank of love like the banks in Switzerland
> where assets are preserved even after their owners are dead?
> Will I live all this to my children
> Whom you never saw?
> You gave your life to me, like a wine dealer
> Who remained sober himself.
> You sober in death, lucid in the dark
> For me, drunk on life, wallowing in my forgetfulness.
>
> Now and then, I remember you in times
> unbelievable. And in places not made for memory

> but for transient, the passing that does not remain.
> Like in the airport, when the arriving travelers
> Stand tired at the revolving conveyor belt
> that brings their suitcases and packages,
> and they identify theirs with cries of joy
> **as at a resurrection and go out into their lives;**
> and there is one suitcase that returns and disappears again
> and returns again, ever so slowly, in the empty hall,
> again and again it passes.
> This is how your quiet figure passes by me,
> this is how I remember you until
> the conveyor belt stands still. *And they stood still, Amen.*[52]

The course of the poem is led by the multitude of questions that have no answer, and they attempt to sketch possible characteristics of Ruth's, and to turn her memory into something substantial, not only an interiorized self-object. In seemingly technical dialogic fashion the speaker constructs the memory of his childhood friend by delving into the details of her being: he wonders what they put around her neck, on her sleeves, what happened to her years that she didn't live, the loves she never had, and if there is some way in which his own life preserves them.

Age, the star, the sleeves, the soul, and the neck are the details from which he tries to construct his childhood friend's final way. The poetic language's autonomy and nondependence on the reality (as Wittgenstein argued) is realized, since it is evident to the speaker and to the reader that what happened to Ruth cannot be reconstructed. The sadness of the deviation from the realistic possibility becomes most intense at the end of the poem, in the mental picture in the hope for the resurrection that was not, in contrast with the picture of the travelers waiting for their suitcases at the airport.

52 Yehuda Amichai, *Even a Fist Was Once an Open Hand with Fingers: Recent Poems*, trans. Barbara Harshav and Benjamin Harshav (New York: Harper Collins, 1991), pp. 42–43.

In addition to the poignant details, the poem contains a significant change from the preceding poem. In the former, the poem is addressed to Ruth, who does not answer the speaker's question. The reason for this is given metaphorically, vaguely: each of them went his or her own way. The danger of the finality of the parting is highlighted, but its circumstances are unclear, and this is even more pronounced regarding the bond between Yehuda and Ruth. In the current poem, in contrast, he calls her by her nickname, which sets her apart from any other Ruth, and looks closely at her fate. The conversation becomes a "conversion," because the speaker enters into the figure of Ruth by means of the precise constitution of her features.

The starting point is the forced departure that returns and raises her memory in his consciousness, but the poem then focuses on what happened to Ruth. The "it" becomes "thou," and the speaker seeks to imagine what could have been, to reach, to feel. The poetic grammar fashions a relationship of dependency between them, when, for example, on the question of the connection between the shortness of her life and the length of his, he asks: "were they added to my life?" and declares: "You gave your life to me."

In his last book Amichai turns once again to little Ruth, in a poem that incorporates the three types of grammar:

> Ruth Ruth Ruth, little girl from my youth—
> now she's a stand-in for Otherness.
> Otherness in death, death in Otherness.
> Will you come back to me the way the dead sometimes
> Come back to the living, as if they were born again.[53]

The poem opens by repeating her name three times, which creates emphasis, as well as "collecting" the three poems that are dedicated to her. In the second poem the speaker expressly presents her figure as a significant other. Ruth's otherness, however, is not limited to the fate that is the alternative to that of the child Yehuda; she symbolizes the

53 Amichai, *Open Closed Open*, p. 131.

otherness that is on the horizon in Yehuda's life—approaching death. The speaker repeats the feeling of anticipation that he portrayed in the preceding poem in the airport scene. While, however, the anticipation of the suitcases is understandable and is fashioned as the opposite of the pointlessness of anticipation for Ruth, the question changes in the current poem. It is unclear whether its fashioning is a metaphor for resurrection in his memory, or an actual question: the poetic grammar wavers in a quasi-metaphor, between consciousness and reality.

The poetic embodiment of significant otherness reaches its peak in Amichai's last book, in which he devotes a cycle of poems to names and their meaning for him. He begins with his own first name, continues with the names of people such as Paul Celan (see below), and dedicates an additional poem to Ruth. The names represent a series of significant others who disappeared from his life. Finally, mystical grammar emerges: the dependency is no longer between Ruth's death and the speaker's life, rather, the demand of responsibility for her life is directed to the ritual of the recitation of the *Shema* ("Hear, O Israel") recited before sleep, which is supposed to guard a person from all evil.[54]

The cycle of poems concerned with names concludes with the speaker's gentle, but piercing, irony regarding the names of God and the sanctity ascribed to them: the closing scene of the cycle is of a nameless women from Rome, whose head, if opened after her death, will reveal the name of the true lover, who certainly is not God.[55] This ending creates a retrospective view of what is common to the figures

54 Ruth Ruth, who died in my youth,
Now the two giants,
Yitgadal and Yitkadash, Magnified and Sanctified,
Will watch over your death
In place of two other giants,
May He Bless and May He Keep,
Who failed to watch over your life (Amichai, *Open Closed Open*, p. 132).

55 In a piazza in Rome, I once saw a woman waiting [. . .]
After her death, God will gently pry open her head, as He always does,
to look for the name of the one she truly loved,
and it won't be His name, it won't be His (Amichai, *Open Closed Open*, p. 132).

in the cycle of poems: each is a significant "other" in the life of the speaker, and the love he feels for them is cut short by the cruel fate for which God is responsible. The metaphor of God functions as an object for the accusation, with Divine Providence becoming responsible for a person's death, as in the case of Celan. In the preceding section we examined the speaker's identification with Celan's fate. Intriguingly, although Celan chose to commit suicide, here, too, the speaker has God as answerable, as in the case of Ruth, who was not responsible for her death:

> Paul Celan. Toward the end, the words grew
> fewer inside you, each word
> so heavy in your body
> that God set you down like a heavy load
> for a moment, perhaps, to catch
> His breath and wipe His brow.
> Then He left you and picked up a lighter load,
> another poet. But the last bubbles
> that rose from your drowning mouth
> were the final concentration, the frothy concentrate
> of the heaviness of your life.[56]

The poem brilliantly develops the connection between the language of the poet and the existential meaning of his life: the speaker portrays how the relation between the words and their meaning changed before Celan's suicide. The words with which he processed suffering and his contending with existence after the Holocaust dwindled, while the burden of life weighed down more oppressively, until his decision to end it. Amichai used the metaphor of God to express the departure of the will to live in the image of Divine Providence, so that it left Celan, allowing him to give himself over to the will to die. Divine Providence chose to turn to another poet, and let Celan drown. The poem ends with a description of chilling significance, albeit, as is usual for Amichai,

56 Amichai, *Open Closed Open*, p. 130.

low-key in its linguistic fashioning: the speaker depicts how Celan's last breaths concentrated all the heaviness of his life. The speaker's "But" in the last part of the poem is puzzling: what happened in the last seconds of Celan's life is not in the least consoling, it rather is the last expression of despair. This expression joins with the lines that end the preceding poem in this cycle and teach that the reality of turning to God happens even when it patently will not bring salvation.[57]

The figure of Celan reappears in the poetic memory of the speaker as a friend who died prematurely, but this memory also contains the self-constitution of the speaker, which considerably exceeds an expression of identification, empathy for his fate, and anger at Providence or at God as a metaphor for ultimate responsibility. Celan chose to process his suffering and his contending in poetic language, as he declared in many places, for example, in a speech he delivered when receiving a literary prize in the city of Bremen:

> Reachable, near and not lost, there remained in the midst of the losses this one thing: language. It, the language, remained, not lost, yes in spite of everything. But it had to pass through its own answerlessness, pass through frightful muting, pass through the thousand darknesses of deathbringing speech [. . .] In this language I have sought, during those years and the years since then, to write poems: so as to speak, to orient myself, to find out where I was and where I was meant to go, to sketch out reality for myself.[58]

The language was the *Sitz im Leben* that enabled "sketching out" a new "reality," while his suicide taught that language as such failed. The

57 praise the Lord who did not save.
But I go back to a weepy pleading *Hoshana*
that turns my mouth into a gaping wound
and may soothe me yet, like an infant crying itself to sleep (Amichai, *Open Closed Open*, p. 128).

58 Paul Celan, "Speech on the Occasion of Receiving the Literature Prize of the Free Hanseatic City of Bremen," *Selected Poems and Prose of Paul Celan*, trans. John Felstiner (New York: W. W. Norton, 2001), pp. 395–96.

disparity between the words and life's experiences is fashioned in reverse ratio: the more difficult the life experience, the more the words decrease and contract into a concentrate that contains all of life's heaviness. Wittgenstein finely expressed the gap between the expression of pain and the actual experience of pain in life: "How can I even attempt to interpose language between the expression of pain and the pain?"[59]

Amichai's poem is concerned with the failure of poetic language to express life's heaviness, while simultaneously talking with Celan by depicting his last moments. The "conversation" with Celan is a type of leave-taking, after the fact, by means of words, but speechless when the depiction of the concentrate of life embodied in the last bubbles tries to "show" the death experience:

> a *conversation* characterized by the need neither to communicate something, nor to learn something, nor to influence someone, nor to come into connexion with someone, but solely by the desire to have one's own self-reliance confirmed by marking the impression that is made, or if it has become unsteady to have it strengthened.[60]

Buber explains the longing of the speaker in Amichai's poem to understand and experience Celan's last moments, even though they can no longer talk to one another. Buber maintains that such a conversation does not ensue from the desire to communicate, learn, or influence, but from the desire to experience the other self without embellishment (which clearly resembles the quest for self-constitution that Cavell formulated, following Emerson).[61] For Buber, dialogic life can continue

59 Wittgenstein, *Philosophical Investigations*, para. 245.

60 Martin Buber, *Between Man and Man*, trans. Ronald Gregor-Smith (New York: Routledge, 2002 [1947]), p. 23.

61 "A dialogical relation will show itself also in genuine conversation, but it is not composed of this. Not only is the shared silence of two such persons a dialogue, but also their dialogical life continues, even when they are separated in space, as the continual potential presence of the one to the other, as an unexpressed intercourse. On the other hand, all conversation derives its genuineness only from the consciousness of the element of inclusion—even if this appears only abstractly as an 'acknowledgment' of the actual being of the partner in the conversation; but this

even when a real conversation is not conducted, in the absence of place and time that would enable it to be held in reality. The criterion for the existence of dialogic life is "the element of inclusion," which characterizes Amichai's attitude to Celan. By means of dialogic grammar, Amichai "speaks" with Celan, in an imaginary conversation.

This element is also present in the poetic fashioning of his attitude to his parents, which changed over the course of time (see below). At this juncture, we should mention the "element of inclusion," that fashions an ambivalent attitude: on the one hand, the need to lie to the parents, and, on the other, bearing the memory of their migration. This reading is markedly different from Dan Miron's interpretation (which is the prevalent scholarly understanding) that finds in the poems idealization based on appreciation for his father's personality.[62]

Some poems exemplify this, but a "perspicuous representation" shows the combination of a reserved attitude and commitment, or in Amichai's wording, "An achievement, a retreat." Amichai's feeling that he will be able to free himself of the burden of historical memory only by his death reflects his parents' dominance as self-objects in the speaker's self-constitution:

> And my parent's migration has not yet calmed in me.
> My blood goes on shaking at its walls
> [. . .]
> Earth forgets the footsteps of those who walk.
> An awful fate. Stumps of talk after midnight.
> An achievement, a retreat. Night reminds
> And day forgets
> [. . .]
> The rules of a game

---

acknowledgment can be real and effective only when it springs from an experience of inclusion, of the other side" (Buber, *Between Man and Man*, p. 115).

62 Dan Miron maintains that Amichai set the father figure as a paragon throughout his poetry. See his detailed discussion in *More! Cognitive Formations in Early Israeli Poetry* (Ramat Gan: Afik, 2013), pp. 264–67 (Hebrew).

> nobody had ever completely explained. The laws of pain and weight [. . .]
> My parents in their migration.
> On the crossroads where I am forever orphaned,
> too young to die, too old to play [. . .]
> Archaeology of the future,
> Museums of what is still to happen [. . .]
> Already my veins, my tendons
> are a tangle of ropes I will never undo.
> Finally, my own death
> And an end to my parents' migration.[63]

The poem gives expression to a singular reflective dialogue, since the speaker does not conduct a dialogue with his parents, but with the experience of their migration. The question arises, why does the speaker portray his parents' migration—in the third person—although he (Amichai) migrated together with them? Apparently, this separation between the migration experiences is meant to place responsibility for the migration on his parents, although the consequences of the family's migration have an impact on him as well. The otherness of the migration experience weighs down so heavily on his life that he feels like an orphan, and he even awaits death that will redeem him from his feeling of rootlessness, from his not understanding the rules of the game that turns alienation and otherness into the way in which he lives his life.

The metaphor of "My blood goes on shaking at its walls" voices a physical sensation of fear, which is also embodied in his footsteps. On the conscious plane, the speaker once again recalls the awful fate, mainly at nights, but the main problem is not memory itself, but the sense of not knowing "The rules of a game" for what governs the experience ("The laws of pain and weight"). The inability to understand them undermines all existence, and the speaker consequently feels like an "orphan": "too young to die, too old to play." How does this

63 Amichai, *Early Books*, pp. 117–18.

situation come about, in which the rules of the reality unravel, and realistic facts assume metaphoric garb?

On Certainty (one of the books belonging to "the third Wittgenstein") examines the nature of certainty in our lives, with an investigation of the conditions that undermine it. The philosophical move is meant mainly to whittle away at skepticism, on both the philosophical plane and that of the everyday:

> I did not get my picture of the world by satisfying myself of its correctness; nor do I have it because I am satisfied of its correctness. No: it is the inherited background against which I distinguish between true and false. The propositions describing this world-picture might be part of a kind of mythology. And their role is like that of rules of a game; and the game can be learned purely practically, without learning any explicit rules.[64]

Wittgenstein uses the term "world-picture" to illustrate his argument that we already live and act within a given system.[65] We also raise doubts about this system, although in everyday life, we do not scrutinize every action and every rule, and actually, this basis of our activity can be seen as a sort of mythology. Accordingly, skepticism is possible only after the fact (doubt can be cast only on something prior, whose existence is therefore certain). This certainty can be subject to change, and does not ensue from some scientific conclusion or from a demonstrable "truth." Explanations that employ language reach a dead end, after which the only basis is the sense of certainty.[66] Wittgenstein adds:

64 Wittgenstein, *On Certainty*, para. 94–95.

65 "All testing, all confirmation and disconfirmation of a hypothesis takes place already within a system. And this system is not a more or less arbitrary and doubtful point of departure for all our arguments: no, it belongs to the essence of what we call an argument. The system is not so much the point of departure, as the element in which arguments have their life" (Wittgenstein, *On Certainty*, para. 105).

66 "We know, with the same certainty with which we believe any mathematical proposition, how the letters A and B are pronounced, what the color of human blood is called, that other human beings have blood and call it 'blood.' That is to say, the questions that we raise and our doubts depend on the fact that some propositions

> The mythology may change back into a state of flux, the river-bed of thoughts may shift. But I distinguish between the movement of the waters on the river-bed and the shift of the bed itself; though there is not a sharp division of the one from the other.[67]

The world-picture can change, but such change is difficult to discern. Wittgenstein asserts that if the change is sudden, it might cause a person to lose his sanity.[68] Amichai portrays the migration of his parents as a destabilizing change, of the sort that illustrates the difficulty in living without knowledge of the rules of the game, the sense of orphanhood, and the death wish felt by someone who lacks such certainty. Additionally, the speaker points an accusing finger at unknown protagonists ("The rules of a game / nobody had ever completely explained"). His implicit claim is that in certain instances, in which a person has to contend with the experience of being uprooted and the threat of destruction, there decidedly should be someone who can explain how to deal with such adversity. Dialogue is definitely reflective, but it expresses the clear need for an "other" who will facilitate dealing with the pain of memory, silence, tiredness, and intensive unrest.

The feelings of being thrown and alienation find expression in a range of fashionings of figurative language, but it should be stressed that the poetic grammar is insufficient for reconstitution of the self. The dialogic grammar works only on the individual plane, and is not realized as a conversation with another, with his parents being the

---

are exempt from doubt, are as it were like hinges on which those turn. That is to say, it belongs to the logic of our scientific investigations that certain things are indeed not doubted. But it isn't that the situation is like this: We just can't investigate everything, and for that reason we are forced to rest content with assumption. If I want the door to turn, the hinges must stay put" (Wittgenstein, *On Certainty*, para. 340–43).

67 Wittgenstein, *On Certainty*, para. 97.

68 In *On Certainty* Wittgenstein mentions, a number of times, the possibility of a loss of sanity, in the context of undermining certainty. He asks rhetorically: "But might it not be possible for something to happen that threw me entirely off the rails? Evidence that made the most certain thing unacceptable to me? Or at any rate made me throw *over* my most fundamental judgments?" (Wittgenstein, *On Certainty*, para. 517; emphasis added).

figures with whom we would expect such a conversation to be conducted. Nonetheless, the speaker has identified with his parents' migration so fully that he is a part of it, it causes him to act, and it directs his life. In light of the fact that he migrated with his parents at a relatively adult age, this interiorization fashioning reflects the complex relationship of dependency between the speaker and his parents: despite the feeling of orphanhood, despite the anticipation of death that will release him from his harsh feelings, his language and silences are all influenced by his parents' migration. That is, his self-identity is based on the figures of his parents as interiorized objects of formative significance.

This poem diverts from the elegiac and chaotic tone that is often to be found in Amichai's poems, as Miron claimed.[69] The poem expresses the indirect conflict with the biography that was forced upon him, and especially with the consequence of the feeling of orphanhood and the desire to die in order to be rid of it.

The following poem formulates a language-game, one that is especially intriguing in the context of self-constitution facing the other. The speaker chooses to methodically and consciously lie to his father. The lie expands until it covers the entire Sabbath eve experience:

Sabbath Lie
On Friday, at twilight of a summer day
While the smells of food and prayer rose from every house
And the sound of Sabbath angels' wings was in the air,
While still a child I started to lie to my father:
"I went to another synagogue."

I don't know if he believed me or not
But the taste of the lie was good and sweet on my tongue.
And in all the houses that night
Hymns rose up with lies
To celebrate the Sabbath [. . .]

69 Miron, *More!*, pp. 275–76.

And since then the lie has been good and sweet on my tongue
And since then I always go to another synagogue.
And my father returned the lie when he died:
"I've gone to another life."[70]

The speaker's father represents two types of otherness: the tradition of Sabbath eve prayer, and the person to whom the speaker must give an accounting. It is not coincidental that Amichai wrote in his last book "My father was God and didn't know it" (see below), because the speaker in *Sabbath Lie* exchanges his father for God as the object of faith. In the poem, a complex self is constituted against the father, because, on the one hand, the need to please his father leads to a lie (which seemingly is difficult for the speaker), while, on the other, the poetic grammar transforms the entire world into one dominated by falsehood, with the Sabbath hymns in all the houses including lies. The speaker goes from the description of the need to lie to the pleasure in the lie, and this portrayal illustrates the autonomy of language to constitute an independent move of its own, without reliance on any external ethical principal: "Lying is a language-game that needs to be learned like any other one."[71] After the speaker becomes accustomed to lying, and even imagines that such a language-game takes place in all the houses, the lie becomes a regulative language-game, since the speaker uses it every Sabbath eve, and shows how this became natural for him.

At the end of the poem, however, two motifs suddenly enter the language-game of the lie, and completely change the speaker's ironic and humorous tone. The father's premature death conceals a lie that had a dual function: in the plane of the father-son relationship, the father paid back the son with a lie more powerful than that of the son; in the existential plane, the speaker must internalize his father's death without the solace and hope offered by the belief in an afterlife. The son is disappointed by the father's assurance that he continues to exist in another world, and this disappointment has a *mysterious* aspect that links this poem with the process of reconciliation between Amichai and his father.

70 Amichai, *Great Tranquility*, p. 59.
71 Wittgenstein, *Philosophical Investigations*, para. 249.

The speaker's self-perception in the traditional plane, as in the existential plane, is formulated in relation to his father, even when there is no direct dialogue between them, and even when the dialogue is based on a lie. The mystery of the threefold connection between the speaker, his parents, and Jewish tradition also finds voice in the next poem:

Yom Kippur
Yom Kippur without my father and without my mother
Is not Yom Kippur.

From the blessing of their hands on my head
just the tremor has remained like the tremor of an engine
that didn't stop after their death.

My mother died only five years ago,
She is still being processed
Between the offices above and the papers below.

My father who died long ago is already resurrected
in other places but not in my place.

Yom Kippur without my father and without my mother
Is not Yom Kippur.
Hence I eat to remember
And drink not to forget
And sort out the vows
And catalog the oaths by time and size.[72]

The speaker conducts a paradoxical dialogue, both with his parents and with Jewish tradition, which is metaphorically represented by Yom Kippur. Yom Kippur, the symbol of holiness in Jewish tradition, creates the context for the poem's language-game, with the speaker using concepts from this holy day (the prohibitions on eating and drinking, the

72 Amichai, *Even a Fist*, p. 71.

wording of the *Kol Nidrei* prayer) to express a controversial position. This stance is puzzling in the autonomous context of the poem, since, on the one hand, the parents' death is absolute, thereby voiding Yom Kippur of its meaning, while, on the other, the death of each parent is presented as an ongoing process: the mother "is still being processed," and the father "is already resurrected in other places." A dialogic-grammar perspective will likely explain this question, since the dominant lack is that of relation. Yom Kippur's dependence upon the reality of the poet's parents does not result from a thematic or traditional context, but from the contact of their blessing hands. Since the intersubjective plane cannot be remedied after his parents' deaths, the speaker chooses to express his attitude to them by the reversal of the praxis of Jewish tradition: instead of fasting, he eats and drinks; instead of canceling the vows and oaths, he sorts out and catalogs them. His fashioning of the memory of his parents through the language of Jewish tradition, even if conducted in a controversial manner, preserves the difficulty of parting from them.

A complex interpretive conclusion emerges from our discussion of the dialogical grammar in Amichai's poetry: on the one hand, the importance of the self-object that takes shape in the dialogic grammar in the process of self-constitution is obvious. On the other hand, in most instances the dialogue is conducted between the speaker and himself, and, above all, expresses yearning for belonging, for interpersonal bond, and for the consolation that the other might offer. Actually, consolation, in the therapeutic sense, is to be found in the act of the poem, although here as well, this is solace in expression, and not emotional consolation. We will end this section with the following poem, which tersely expresses the constant lack of satisfaction in longing, as an existential stance that influences the fashioning of the dialogic grammar:

> I lift my eyes to the mountains. Now I understand
> What it means to lift eyes, what a heavy load
> It is. But those hard longings,
> That pain-never-again-to-be-inside![73]

---

73 Amichai, *Poems of Jerusalem*, p. 13.

The pain of anticipation for something that is beyond the visible world strikes the speaker, against his will. It is already present in the primal feeling of anticipation, and strengthens in the longing to be part of a whole existence. The understanding of the permanency of the state of "thrown-ness," in Heidegger's formulation, constitutes an existential self that cannot find relief for its pain because it no longer believes in the validity and possibility of belief, tradition, or any other affiliation, for they all are transitory.

The stance of longing is alive and well in Amichai's last book as well, but it is limited to a certain perspective, while the book mainly reflects substantive change, mostly in relation to Jewish tradition. Following Wittgenstein, we can state that such change cannot be causally explained. Since it relates to the perception of the world as a whole, we should explain the mystical aspect that is so significantly emphasized here.[74]

3. Reconstruction of the Subject: The Mystical Grammar of *Open Closed Open*

> If we imagine the facts otherwise than as they are, certain language-games lose some of their importance, while others become important. And in this way there is an alteration—a gradual one—in the use of the vocabulary of a language. Compare the meaning of a word with the "function" of an official. And "different meanings" with "different functions." When language-games change, then there is a change in concepts, and with the concepts the meanings of words change.[75]

---

74 Parts of the next section were published in Dorit Lemberger, "Reconstitution of the Subject in Yehuda Amichai's *Open Closed Open*," *Hebrew Higher Education* 15 (2013), pp. 131–59. The article concentrates on a comparison of Amichai's early poetry and his last book. The focus of our discussion, however, is the mystical grammar of self-constitution in the latter alone.

75 Wittgenstein, *On Certainty*, para. 63–65.

How does language express a change in self-constitution? The autonomous nature of language, according to Wittgenstein, is characterized, inter alia, by the fact that a change in language-games could happen as a result of using one's imagination. We can imagine in an alternative way what seem to us to be facts, and thereby alter the language-games. We see in Amichai's direct language how imagination functions by juxtaposing words from distant semantic fields, and this imagination expresses the special power of Amichai's language to effect and present change in self-constitution as well. The more powerful the imagination, the greater the possibility of changing language-games. Wittgenstein additionally stresses that conceptual change also includes change in the field of action, and parallel change in the meaning of words.

The change in *Open Closed Open* is mainly mystical, in the three senses I set forth above: Amichai formulates an individualistic attitude to God, resulting from—as James described—a subjective perception based on personal experience; the paradox of the self as both object and subject occupies a central place in the poems; and Amichai formulates, whether implicitly or directly, an ethical stance of commitment to Jewish historical memory and tradition.

The self that is the speaker in this collection is constituted in a manner that contradicts, continues, and complements his attitudes to Jewish tradition, his parents, and his identity, as they were fashioned in his poems over the years. This is why Chana Bloch and Chana Kronfeld, the book's translators into English, write that it is an autobiographical masterpiece in which Amichai reaches the peak of his poetical powers—expressed, inter alia, in the refashioning of the Jewish sources.[76] Whereas Bloch and Kronfeld highlighted the aspect of continuity in

76 "Composed over nearly a decade, Open Closed Open is the ripe work of the poet in his sixties and seventies—without doubt his magnum opus. Writing at the peak of his powers, and increasingly conscious of his role as a mediator of cultural memory, Amichai pieces together from an intense and strenuously-lived life a poetic biography of our time. As in his earlier books, he writes about language and love, sexuality and mortality, war and memory, Jerusalem and Jewish history. He continues to argue with a God he stopped believing in long ago, and to wrestle with the traditional texts of his Orthodox Jewish upbringing" (Chana Bloch and Chana Kronfeld, "Amichai's Counter-Theology: Opening *Open Closed Open*," *Judaism* 49, no. 2 [2000], p. 153).

the book in relation to Amichai's earlier poetry, I wish to underline the book's difference and distinctiveness, and argue that the subject-speaker in this book is reconstituted.

The poetical and dialogic grammars are at work in this collection as well, but a mystical grammar unfolds alongside them here, one that was shunted aside in his earlier books to an ironical or marginal context, but which occupies center stage in *Open Closed Open*. I will show how the speaker reconstitutes his self from within a conception of the world as a whole, in which memories of the past and traditional texts connect to what is happening in the present, which they refashion. In this sense, the present becomes the "eternal," since it includes the past and the present that are constructed in order to contend with what is expected in the near future: death. Wittgenstein formulated the connection between the conception of the present as eternal and contending with death so that it leads to an awareness of the existence of the mystical:

> Death is not an event in life: we do not live to experience death. If we take eternity to mean not infinite temporal duration but timelessness, then *eternal life belongs to those who live in the present* [. . .] God does not reveal himself in the world [. . .] It is not how things are in the world that is mystical, but that it exists.[77]

This move sheds light on the self-constitution that takes place in the book, and enables us to interpret and understand the significant shift in the self of the speaker. This shift is vividly illustrated in the following poem:

> Now after many years of living I begin to see
> that I rebelled only a little, and I do observe
> all the laws and commandments
> [. . .]
> I abhor the vacuum in my pain and in my joy

77 Wittgenstein, *Tractatus*, para. 6.4311; 6:432; 6:44; emphasis added.

I follow the law of water seeking its own level; past and future
are recycled back to me
[. . .]
I begin to understand, as I would with an old car,
what makes it work, the actions of pistons and brakes,
reward and punishment, be fruitful and multiply,
forget and remember, bolts and springs,
fast and slow, and the laws of history
[. . .]
thus spake my soul unto the parts of my body.
This is the sermon in the synagogue, this is a eulogy
for the dead, this is burial and this
is resurrection. Thus spake the man.[78]

The speaker takes a retrospective look at his life, and reaches a conclusion that seemingly is the opposite of his secular lifestyle: he sees himself as someone who rebelled just a little, and actually observed the laws and commandments. At this juncture he creates a personal grammar that includes terms from the realms of physics ("water seeking its own level"), the Jewish halakhah ("be fruitful and multiply"), as well as existential concerns (body-soul relations, the fear of emptiness, pain and joy). Along with figurative language that combines everyday pictures (an old car, bolts and springs) with terms from the traditional word-game, we can identify a distinct shift in self-constitution by means of the integrative grammar in the poem. The change begins with Amichai's need to reunite with the commandments, to think of himself as someone who abandoned them, and to combine the past and the future with the present ("past and future / are recycled back to me"). The grammar in the poem is mystical, in the three senses mentioned above: the speaker weaves a conception of God before whom one must justify oneself ("I rebelled only a little, and I do observe / all the laws and commandments"); the depiction ranges between the subjective, in the first person, and a depiction of the self as an object that acts in accordance with physical laws; and finally, the present unites with both the past and the future as an

78 Amichai, *Open Closed Open*, pp. 15–16.

expression of will (that exceeds the boundary of language and therefore falls within the realm of the mystical, according to Wittgenstein).

Throughout his corpus, Amichai's poetry is marked by its innovative poetic fashionings of the Jewish sources. These fashionings range from the complete opposite of the original meaning of these sources to personal fashioning and to the use of the sources in a context completely different from the original one.[79] In this poem, however, as in many additional poems in this collection, the sources become part of the self of the speaker, in a process of seeming confession of sin. The speaker, in a certain sense, is remorseful for the impression he created in his earlier poetry, as if he felt alienated and distant from the Jewish sources, while, in fact, they are of existential importance for him, and they are incorporated in his life on all levels.

Throughout the book, the speaker develops a conception of personal belief that includes commitment, to both the Jewish historical memory and Jewish tradition, in both the ritual and textual spheres. All this is expressed in the grammar that engages in correspondence with the past, the present, and the future (the death that is expected shortly) and in which the change is effected, "on the run," in the poems and in the transitions and links between them.

3.1. The Mechanism of Change as the Key to Perfectionism

> So much open that will never close again, so much closed
> that will never open.

---

79 The following two poems clearly exemplify the reversed meaning of connotation:

> God-Full-of-Mercy,
> If God was not full of mercy,
> Mercy would have been in the world,
> Not just in Him (Yehuda Amichai, "God-Full-of-Mercy," trans. Barbara and Benjamin Harshav, http://poemhunter.com/poem/god-full-of-mercy).

> Underneath the world, God lies stretched on his back
> always repairing, always things get out of whack.
> I wanted to see him all, but I see no more
> than the soles of his shoes and I'm sadder than I was before.
> And that is his glory (Yehuda Amichai, "And That Is Your Glory," in *Selected Poetry of Yehuda Amichai*, trans. Chana Bloch and Stephen Michell [New York: Harper & Row, 1986], pp. 11–12).

> [. . .]
> Forgotten, remembered, forgotten.
> Open, closed, open.[80]

The lines that connect the book's title with its content give prominence to the dynamic of change as the key to understanding the world. The change that is expressed in the metaphor of closing and opening is linked to memory and forgetfulness that are at work and create the dynamic of change. In the book change occurs in the positions of the subject-speaker in three main aspects.

The *first aspect* is the dynamic of the speaker's attitude to faith and God, and to Jewish rituals. This is evident from a comparison of the speaker's stances in different phases of his life that illustrate the possibility of change, from ironic distance to experiences of closeness, emotion, and identification.

The *second aspect* is the combination of individual and public elements in the process of fashioning identity. In this fashioning, two hinges of meaning, the meeting of which creates the features of identity, are at work. One is that of the social word-game that constitutes man's surroundings, and therefore its characteristics are dictated to him. In this hinge we can identify factual, objective characteristics such as communal and geographical affiliations and the like (the hinge operates the self-knowledge of "I as subject"). The other hinge includes a person's subjective qualities, aspirations, and values; in this hinge a person identifies himself as a subject. These poems by Amichai present the meeting of these hinges, with the speaker meeting in different ways with contents (figures and events) from Jewish culture. In this encounter, his personal experiences are refashioned with a reinterpretation of the traditional texts.

The *third aspect* is what recent scholarship calls "traditionalism." The traditionalist approach is characterized by a dynamic approach to the sources, in which the legitimacy given to reinterpretation plays an important role in the creation of a pluralistic discourse that enables relation to Jewish tradition without commitment to

80 Amichai, *Open Closed Open*, p. 171.

belong to a specific group. In recent years, this dynamic has been the subject of both philosophical and sociological discussion and development.[81]

3.2. The Conception of an Individual God: God as Change and as Interlocutor

Once I said, Death is God and change is His prophet.
Now I have calmed down, and I say
Change is God and death is His prophet.[82]

The speaker's God changes over the course of time, in accordance with the existential and moral changes that occur in his life: in the past, the speaker perceived death as something divine, whereas at the time he wrote the poem, it is change, the opposite of the cessation of final and absolute death, that is the reflection of God. The death that awaits spurs this change, but it is life that is constant creation by changing what is. The speaker formulates the motivation for change as resulting from disposition, with the will for change ensuing from opposition to the alternative (cessation, death).

The language of the poem that portrays this change is universal, and can be seen as the negative of the poem *God-Full-of-Mercy*, which posits a static divinity who is alienated from the world. The possibility of the transformation of individual experience by its transfer to the poetical plane as self-reconstitution is embodied in the transition from *A World Void of Mercy* in the book *Shirim* (Poems) to *Jewish Travel* in *Open Closed Open*:

God-Full-of-Mercy, the prayer for the dead.
If God was not full of mercy,

81 See Meir Buzaglo, *A Language for the Faithful* (Jerusalem: Keter, Mandel Foundation, 2009) (Hebrew); Yaacov Yadgar, *Masortim in Israel: Modernity without Secularization* (Jerusalem: Shalom Hartman Institute, Keter; Ramat Gan: Bar-Ilan University, Faculty of Law, 2010) (Hebrew).

82 Amichai, *Open Closed Open*, p. 124. The capitalization is in the English translation. This stanza appears several times in the original Hebrew, but not in the English version.

Mercy would have been in the world,
Not just in Him.
[. . .]
I, who must decipher riddles
I don't want to decipher,
Know that if not for the God-full-of-mercy
There would be mercy in the world,
Not just in Him.[83]

Jewish travel. As it is written, "I will lift up mine eyes unto the hills, from whence
cometh my help": not a hike to see a tall mountain in all its glory
nor a climb to rejoice in the vistas of Nature,
but a hike with a purpose, to seek help from high heavens.[84]

The change requested of the self in "Jewish travel" occurs in the fashioning of the experience of a personal trip. In both poems, cultural connotation is fashioned as individual experience, and in both, personal experience is inserted in a traditional context and expresses existential fashioning of the self. While the first poem, however, is pessimistic and fatalistic, the Jewish trip in the second is devoted to receiving help by means of prayer (the continuation of the poem contains a direct reference to God: "as it says, 'Out of the depths have I cried unto thee, O Lord'").

The thematic foundation for this comparison is the two poems' being based on contending with death. While, however, *God-Full-of-Mercy* is defiant, and filled with anger and affront, *Jewish Travel* expresses acceptance, augmented by a portrayal of connection to "a congregation praying with 'clean hands and a pure heart'" and Moses, who ascended Mount Sinai to receive the Tablets of the Covenant, and Mount Nebo, to die. The poems differ in the transition from poetical

83 Amichai, "God-Full-of-Mercy," trans. Harshav and Harshav.
84 Yehuda Amichai, "Jewish Travel: God Is Change and Death Is His Prophet," *Open Closed Open*, p. 117.

grammar that fashions a God detached from the world since He keeps his mercy for Himself, to mystical grammar in which the speaker acts in the anticipation of being answered by God, while crossing the everyday boundaries of the world and language.

This change is not coincidental. It is substantive, and its nature is clarified in the line: "Change is God and death is His prophet." The parallelism between the change and God is an extremely concise embodiment of the change in the speaker's attitude to belief. The deification functions as a bidirectional metaphor as it imparts metaphysical quality to the change, while at the same time presenting the nature of God as changing.[85] Amichai frequently used bidirectional metaphors in his poetry. Unlike the distant and alienated God of his early poetry, it is fascinating to see how God draws close to man in his last book, with Amichai comparing Him to the principle that guided his life (= change) and to his father, the role model in his life. The metaphoric bidirectionality functions as a characteristic of both the poetic and the mystical grammars.

Following the individual perception of God as change, bidirectionality is also present in metaphoric fashioning in the following poem, in which the beloved and the Torah share similar traits:

> The Bible and you, the Bible and you.
> As the Torah scroll is read aloud each year
> from "In the beginning" to "this is the blessing"
> and back to the start, so we too roll together
> and every year our love gets a new reading
> [. . .]
> Sometimes in one night we go through

85 Bidirectionality in poetical metaphors was presented and extensively discussed in the researches of Yeshayahu Shen. This term refers to dual, concurrent movement between the source and the target domains, with each of the metaphor's parts influencing another in certain senses. This transformation is not unfettered, and restraints might prevent it, also in poetical language, which presumably is freer than ordinary language. See Yeshayahu Shen, "Cognitive Constraints on Directionality in the Semantic Structure of Poetic vs. Non-Poetic Metaphors," *Poetics* 23 (1995), pp. 255–74.

what the Torah goes through in an entire year
[. . .]
And each day God says: "And it was evening
and it was morning," but he never says
"twilight." Because twilight is for lovers only.[86]

The speaker's concrete experience in the act of love is fashioned by metaphoric bidirectionality as an experience that other people could have as well. The connection between the language-game of the sexual act and that of the Torah fashions human experience in the world as transcendental. James Olney explained the nature of such a poetical move:

> The poem communicates as experience. It does this, however, not directly but by transforming the experience (itself incommunicable) into a motif available to *more or less* free association, simultaneously limiting the freedom of possible associations by the contextual circumstances under which the motif occurs. Each of us brings to the poem his own experiences, which need not be—indeed, cannot be—the same as the poet's, and there finds these private experiences more or less, depending on the effective power of the motif, conformed to the motif and so expressed in it. Notice that this responsive reading of the poem is a new and creative experience in itself: as much an experience that creates and re-creates the self as any transcendent moment.[87]

86 Amichai, "The Bible and You, The Bible and You, and Other Midrashim," *Open Closed Open*, pp. 19–20. "In the beginning" is from Gen. 1:1, the opening verse of the Torah; "this is the blessing" is from Deut. 33:1, the verse that begins the last weekly portion of the Torah. During the course of the yearly reading cycle, the Torah scroll is rolled in the synagogue. The phrase: "And it was evening and it was morning" concludes the description in Genesis of each of the days of Creation.

87 James Olney, *Metaphors of Self: The Meaning of Autobiography* (Princeton, NJ: Princeton University Press, 1972), p. 267.

The metaphoric fashioning expresses the selfhood of the speaker, on the one hand, while, on the other, the process of reading produced a creative experience for the reader—a sort of "transcendent moment"—that facilitates exceeding the bounds of language and the world, and expressing Jewish subjectivity. The use of traditional language as the metaphoric fashioning of a concrete relationship encompasses the paradox of general and private expression, and stands in opposition to the concrete nature of his previous works.

In her review of the criticism of Amichai's books, Judith Halevi-Zwick showed how the critics highlighted the dominance of concrete poetics in Amichai's works.[88] The focus on everyday experiences and what she claims is "thinghood" often led to his poetry being accused of "lacking meaning," as replete with repetitions and as poetry that is (to say the least) shallow from the perspective of self-constitution. The here-and-now nature of this poetry situated the poetics of the use of traditional Jewish sources as the "poetics of provocation," or at best, as poetics meant to question traditional rituals.[89] Even if these rituals were mentioned in a favorable light, this is because they were presented as characterizing the actions of the father or mother, and not as standing on their own merit. Glenda Abramson goes even further, and maintains that concern with God almost vanishes from Amichai's poetry, beginning in 1968.[90]

In *Open Closed Open*, in contrast, we find a significant shift in his attitude to the Jewish sources, which is expressed in three main phenomena:

The *first phenomenon*, and the most conspicuous, is the wealth of connotations from the Bible, the Jewish prayers, and Jewish ritual as a

---

88 Judith Halevi-Zwick, *Yehuda Amichai: A Selection of Critical Essays on His Writing* (Tel Aviv: Hakibbutz Hameuchad, 1988), pp. 11–13 (Hebrew).

89 Amichai belonged to the 1950s literary group centered around the *Achshav* (Now) magazine, which rebelled against the poetic style and conventions of "the Palmah generation," with its emphasis on the collective, and instead focused on concrete, everyday experiences of the individual.

90 "Amichai's preoccupation with God extends over the early books [. . .] but it disappears almost entirely—with a few exceptions—in later poetry. *It is not only that the value of the entity called 'God' alters substantially as the poetic discourse develops, but also that the intrinsic need for this particular ideological debate diminished* in verse published after 1968" (Glenda Abramson, *The Writing of Yehuda Amichai: A Thematic Approach* [Albany: State University of New York Press, 1989], p. 53; emphasis added).

basis for depicting here-and-now experiences: Cain and Abel, Terah, Abraham, Isaac, Jacob, Sarah, Rebekah, Rachel and Leah, Ishmael, David, Bathsheba, Abishag, Jonathan, Hannah, Samuel, Joseph, Ezekiel, Hulda the prophetess, Joab, Samson, Ruth and Naomi, Psalms, and Ecclesiastes. This surfeit is surprising, even when taking account of the frequency of such connotations in all the periods of Amichai's poetry, especially in light of the next phenomenon. The figurative fashioning plants the biblical reality in modern everyday reality, and this combination infuses the texts with vitality and relevancy. Thus, for example, in the personification of the house of Hulda the prophetess, with the incorporation of modern means of interpersonal communication:

> Here is Hulda's house that knew nights of revelry.
> The sound of music playing, feet dancing, mouths filled with song.
> [. . .]
> In the corners of the rooms, people stood
> and jotted down names, addresses, telephone numbers for each other.[91]

The perception of religiosity expands from the personal conception of the relationship between man and God to a public one, in which the language of the sources is incorporated with daily life. In Wittgensteinian terms, we could say that Amichai combines the conception of faith in *Tractatus*, that belief is subjective and is situated beyond the bounds of language and the world, with that of *Philosophical Investigations*, in which belief is expressed in grammar.[92]

The *second phenomenon* is the change in the attitude of the subject-speaker to religious connotations. The speaker expresses identification with and empathy for David's pain, Moses' fate, Samson in his last moments, and a long list of biblical figures and events. For the speaker, the stories of the Bible symbolize events that occur in cyclical fashion,

91 Amichai, *Open Closed Open*, pp. 77–78.
92 Wittgenstein, *Tractatus*, para 6.432, 6.44; Wittgenstein, *Philosophical Investigations*, para. 373.

also in his own life. Significant change occurs in this stance, from the aloof, critical, and rebellious "I" to the self that belongs in and is committed to Jewish history and its cultural sources. For instance:

> Every year our father Abraham would take his sons to Mount Moriah
> the way I take my children to the Negev hills where I once had a war.[93]

Interestingly, one cycle of poems in the book is dedicated to "Israeli Travel," and a second, to "Jewish Travel."[94] The subtitle of the former is dedicated to love and otherness. The cycle explores pictures from the past of the Israeli experience and records interpersonal experiences and relationships, mainly in the past. The second cycle, in contrast, takes form under the influence of biblical characters and verses, records the religious experience of the speaker, and concentrates on the present.

The *third phenomenon* is the expressions of Jewish identity in the contemplation of Jewish practices (individual and synagogue prayer, the Passover Seder night, the Sabbath, and more) as he experienced them in his childhood. The connection between the subjective private experience and traditional conventions creates an intriguing, complex relation between characteristics that can be objectively identified and the speaker's inner feelings. These experiences are based on the inclusion of additional, similarly fashioned complexities (such as the balance between body and soul, between pain and joy, and between life and death). Thus we see the changed figurative use of a certain image that, in the previous book, illustrated romantic relations, but now expresses identification with a religious ritual. For example, the parachute simile that in a book from 1976 depicts the beloved's face.[95] In *Open Closed*

93 Amichai, *Open Closed Open*, p. 119.

94 Yehuda Amichai, "Israeli Travel: Otherness Is All, Otherness Is Love," *Open Closed Open*, pp. 67–74; "Jewish Travel: Change Is God and Death Is His Prophet," *Open Closed Open*, pp. 117–24.

95 "The distance from where you came is enfolded in your beautiful face, Like a parachute, precisely to open afterwards, in another place" (Yehuda Amichai, "One More Love Poem," *Behind All This Some Great Happiness Is Hiding* [Tel Aviv: Schocken,

Open, however, the parachute functions as a metaphor in two poems, as the connection between a personal experience and a traditional ritual connotation (wrapping oneself in a prayer shawl [tallis], the recitation of laments): in the "Israeli Travel" cycle, the speaker uses language from Ecclesiastes, in the first-person singular, which he links to universal plural language:

> And I said to myself: Everyone is attached to his own lament
> as to a parachute. Slowly he descends and slowly hovers
> till he touches the hard place.[96]

In the next example, as well, the speaker connects his personal experience while putting on a prayer shawl and the experience of the many:

> Whoever put on a tallis when he was young will never forget
> taking it out of the soft velvet bag
> [. . .]
> Then swinging it in a great swoop overhead
> like a sky, a wedding canopy, a parachute.[97]

The parachute metaphor in both poems is surprising, not only because of the distance between the semantic fields, but also, and mainly, since it functions as an intermediary that softens the experience of the speaker. The transition from the use of the parachute as simile in the book from 1976 to its use as metaphor in the book from 2000 illustrates the shift from concrete to more abstract poetry. More important for our purposes, however, is the centrality of the religious language, as if it became part of Amichai's regular language in this book. This language serves as a platform and "world-picture" in which the speaker formulates a diversity of

1976], p. 72 [Hebrew; the original translations of Amichai's poems in this chapter are by Edward Levin]).

96 Amichai, *Open Closed Open*, p. 74.

97 Amichai, *Open Closed Open*, p. 44. For an expanded discussion of the experience of putting on a prayer shawl in the poem, see below.

attitudes to Jewish tradition: from placing his father above God, to the negation of theology after Auschwitz and the connection between God and love.[98]

Connecting these two phenomena, as well as an examination of each by itself, attests to a substantive change in the perception of his self from a speaker who concentrates on the "I" as a prism through which he looks at the world and judges it (as finely described by Boaz Arpaly), to an intersubjective speaker who is amenable to influence and change.[99] The manner in which the sources are employed expresses a desire for harmony and integration between past and future, and between the Jewish sources and the speaker's present life. The central source of influence on this refashioning is the perception of God as a key to a return to the past and as a source for change in the present and in the future. Thus, in the next poem, God is a channel for connection in the present to the past and to the future:

98 See, respectively:

> But when my father prayed, he would stand in his place,
> erect, motionless, and force God
> to sway like a reed and pray to him (*Open Closed Open*, p. 42).
>
> After Auschwitz, no theology
> [. . .]
> From the crematoria of Auschwitz, black smoke rises—
> a sign the conclave of Gods has not yet chosen
> the Chosen People (*Open Closed Open*, pp. 47–48).

99 Boaz Arpaly described the revolution that Amichai effected with his poetry as follows: "The revolution is noticeable in that, of all the 'possible worlds' that poetry can invent or fashion, Amichai chose to represent in his poetry, in the most decisive and consistent manner, 'this world,' 'the world as it is,' and only that [. . .] *Words that mark materials or contexts that belong to other 'worlds' will appear in Amichai's poetic world only in the meanings that can be ascribed to them in this world.* Totally in accord with this, Amichai's poetic hero, too, is created as the image of a person the boundaries of whose power and dream are defined by this world and as the image of a poet who both fashions them and serves as their speaker." In a note Arpaly adds that "this world" is, in the narrow sense, what is perceived by the senses and the intellect, and in the broad sense, whatever can be empirically verified and logically explained" (Boaz Arpaly, *The Joy of Comparing: Transformations in Modern Hebrew Poetry* [Tel Aviv: Hakibbutz Hameuchad, 2004], pp. 296–97 [Hebrew; emphasis added]).

God is a staircase that ascends
to a place that is no longer there or isn't there yet.

The stairs are my faith, my downfall.
Our father Jacob knew it in his dream [. . .]

and the Song of Ascents is a song of praise
to the God of the Stairs.[100]

The metaphor of God as stairs functions mystically, creating a relation to the past and the future, which lie beyond current experience. The poem opens with a third-person metaphorical declaration that gives the impression that God functions in the same way to all humans. The poem then goes over to the first-person singular, to his subjective and personal experience, but afterwards returns and connects his personal experience with "our father" Jacob as a cultural icon. The connotative use of the first-person plural generates a sense of a shared connection to the story of Jacob's dream, and in its wake, a connection to the mystical: Jacob dreams of a ladder and angels, and transcends in his consciousness to a supernal world from which he receives an encouraging message from God.

The linkage to the narrative of Jacob's dream leads to the use of the term "Song of Ascents" from Psalms, and creates a dimension of permanence for the action of addressing God, which receives a positive response. The "God of the Stairs" is given a paean, unlike, for example, the ironic lauding of God in an earlier poem by Amichai, *That Is Your Glory*.

Belief in God assumes the additional aspect of an intersubjective relationship that mutually drives the believer and God. God and man function as a bidirectional metaphor: each creates the other within a cyclical language-game of creativity that illustrates the need for mutual interaction that is realized in a linguistic work:

I don't want an invisible god. I want a god who is seen
but doesn't seem so I can lead him around

100 Amichai, *Open Closed Open*, p. 40.

and tell him what he doesn't see. And I want
a god who sees and is seen.
[. . .]
I declare with perfect faith
that prayer preceded God.
Prayer created God.
God created human beings,
human beings create prayers
that create the God that creates human beings.[101]

The speaker formulates traits of God in accordance with his own personal perception, and creates a paradoxical mystical grammar: on the one hand, he insists on the concept of a God who is abstract, who is the creator of man and sees him, unlike the alienated God who is fashioned in Amichai's early poetry. On the other hand, the speaker personifies God so that all the power that He possesses is also characteristic of man—and man creates. Furthermore, the desire for God that is expressed in the composition of prayers preceded God. At this point, the detachment of the mystical grammar from the logical grammar is intensified, since the man who created the prayers that created God was himself created by God.

The poem expresses the speaker's conscious will, and it accordingly fashions God's characteristics. It should be recalled, however, that the speaker begins the poem with an expression of his awareness that this is solely his desire, and not a faith experience with certainty. In contrast, certainty is expressed in the context of historical memory. The feeling of certitude regarding the speaker's identification with Jewish history is conspicuous throughout the book, with the integration of the past and the present fashioned, at its peak, in the combination of "amen and love."[102] The tombstone fragment that he collected in the city where he was born expresses a fragment of Jewish history that now stands on the speaker's desk and reminds him of the harsh chain of events experienced by the Jewish people throughout history. This new

101 Amichai, *Open Closed Open*, pp. 39–40.
102 Amichai, *Open Closed Open*, p. 173.

consciousness also contains an expression of symbolic commitment that is embodied materially in the stone on which "Amen" is carved, and spiritually, in the book as a whole. This idea is expressed in the circularity of this imagery appearing in the poem that opens the book and in the one that closes it:

> On my desk lies a stone with the word "Amen" on it,
> a fragment of a tombstone, a remnant from a Jewish graveyard
> destroyed a thousand years ago in the town where I was born.[103]
>
> On my desk is a stone with "Amen" carved on it, one survivor fragment
> of the thousands upon thousands of bits of broken tombstones
> in Jewish graveyards. I know all these broken pieces
> now fill the great Jewish time bomb
> [. . .]
> And though I know about all this, and about the end of the days,
> the stone on my desk gives me peace.
> It is the touchstone no one touches, more philosophical
> than any philosopher's stone
> [. . .]
>
> more whole than any wholeness,
> a stone of witness to what has always been
> and what will always be, a stone of amen and love.
> Amen, amen, and may it come to pass.[104]

The tombstone fragment functions as a sort of relic that returns to the speaker's childhood, and passes from there through Jewish history to his desk. Besides memory and testimony, the stone expresses truth and wisdom, wholeness and love, and from all these, it gives the speaker the tranquility that enables him to develop religious openness ("Amen,

103 Amichai, *Open Closed Open*, p. 39.
104 Amichai, *Open Closed Open*, p. 173.

amen, and may it come to pass"). The return to the past not only facilitates understanding the present; it also revives and recreates relations between the subject-speaker and the Jewish fate, the speaker's present and the eschatological End of Days. The tombstone fragment is an object that symbolizes the subject's relations to a national and religious worldview, without a trace of irony or reservation, as an expression of Jewish identity based on choice, and not on habit and necessity. The speaker's identification is emphasized by the romantic tone in which the conception of time enters the metaphysical, and the grammatical expression naturally leads to a declaration that imparts the stone with mythical quality and ends the poem with the language of devotion to the mystical.

3.3. The Encounter with Biblical Word-Games as the Key to the Reconstruction of the Self

> How do the visions of the prophets see me?
> The burning bush sees me as a man extinguished but alive,
> And what does Ezekiel's vision of the chariot say about me?
> Look, down there is a man who has no wings,
> [. . .]
> just a darkness within. That is his soul.[105]

The metaphorical language makes the sources active and the speaker passive (how the visions of the prophets see *me*). The speaker transforms himself into an object (I as object), and therefore his self-knowledge is dependent upon the other's knowledge of him. Amichai, as usual, inserts some humor into his personification of the cherub in Ezekiel's vision, but this humor is present together with the identification of the darkness in the soul of the speaker. The poem fashions the visions of the prophets as a mirror of the speaker's soul, with the spiritual elevation and purity in the prophecy contrasting with his soul and wingless body. This is one of several poems in the book in which the prophet

105 Amichai, *Open Closed Open*, p. 25.

motif appears, with the leading appearance in the "I Foretell the Days of Yore" cycle. In this cycle Amichai describes himself as: "I am a prophet of what has already been."[106] The interaction between the experience of the present and the depiction of a biblical event introduces mutuality into the speaker's relationship with the Jewish sources, and creates the feeling that both are set in the present. The desire for dialogue between the past and the present is explained by the need to give as much meaning as possible to the self, due to the fear of the demolition of the house, a metaphor for the awareness of approaching death:

> And all the while messengers keep running back and forth
> to my childhood to retrieve what I forgot or left behind
> as if from a house that is about to be demolished.[107]

The messengers keep running toward what creates an atmosphere of urgency, as before actual destruction. We realize that the past as a memorial site for significant things that were forgotten or left behind is vital for self-constitution, in order to implant in the present things that could deepen and improve it, as well as inspire the future.

The dialogic grammar in the book incorporates many biblical figures, whose fashioning fundamentally differs from that of the same characters in Amichai's early work. See, for example, the poetical fashioning of Saul and David in relation to the speaker in *The Early Books of Yehuda Amichai*, which expresses distance and even opposition.[108] In

106 Amichai, *Open Closed Open*, p. 12.
107 Amichai, *Open Closed Open*, p. 105.
108 The figure of Saul is fashioned in contrast with the character of the speaker in the poem *King Saul and I*:

> They gave him a finger, but he took the whole hand.
> They gave me the whole hand; I didn't even take the little finger.
> While my heart
> weight-lifted its first feelings
> he rehearsed the tearing of oxen
> [. . .]
> He was my big brother,
> I got his used clothes (translated in Amichai, *Early Books*, p. 96).

contrast, the poetical fashioning of these two kings in *Open Closed Open* is based on the relevance of their characteristics for the reconstitution of the speaker's self—as we see, for instance, in the parallel drawn between the speaker and King Saul:

> Sometimes I am all alone like King Saul.
> I have to play the music for myself, hurl the spear by myself,
> then dodge the spear. And I am also the wall
> in which the spear lodges, trembling.[109]

The dialogic grammar is dedicated to the biblical text, the subject (Saul), and the object (the wall) in it. The parallelism between Saul and the speaker in his loneliness, which uses metaphor, preserves a certain distance between them, but this distance is closed already in the second line, and in the following lines, as the speaker is completely assimilated in the original context and identifies, not only with Saul, but also with the wall in which his spear lodged. The act of hurling the spear is an experience of "agency," since King Saul expresses and represents his self by means of an external action.[110] "Action language" is embodied both actively (hurling the spear) and passively (comparing himself to the wall that is struck by the spear), thereby expressing a split self, with the last word: "trembling" shedding light, after the fact, on the reason

---

The dialogic relationship between the speaker and Saul is evident: on the one hand, the speaker views Saul as his brother, while, on the other, he presents the contrasts between their actions.

109 Amichai, *Open Closed Open*, pp. 23–24.

110 "Agency" means that something (an emotion, an experience, a feeling) occurs by means of something else, another person, or an action which is not the thing itself, but rather its indirect expression. The term "action language" was coined by Roy Schafer, who argues that we create all aspects of our experience through our actions. If we wish to analyze them, then we must analyze the language in which our actions are expressed (the action is the agency of a person's experiences). See Roy Schafer, *A New Language for Psychoanalysis* (New Haven: Yale University Press, 1976). Schafer proposes concentrating the therapeutic process on updating and improving the action language by means of reconstruction that will make it possible to constructively separate the patient from his actions, to ease his adapting them to his will.

for the split: initially, there was a crack in the determination to act. Saul's action is refashioned when it becomes the speaker's action, and it reflects empathy, as the speaker attributes his own feelings to the biblical figure.

Refashioning, in the here-and-now, is evident also in two consecutive poems that are based on the Binding of Isaac. The first portrays two lovers. Despite their physical closeness, each is immersed in his own thoughts. The biblical narrative functions as self-contemplation that reflects uncertainties and doubts that are dramatically intensified under the influence of the biblical story, along with the suggestion of alternative continuations of the plot for the story, and for the lovers:

> Two lovers lie together like Isaac on the altar
> and it feels good. They don't think about the knife
> or about the burnt offering—
> she thinks about the ram and he about the angel.
> Another version: He is the ram and she is the thicket.
> He will die and she will go on growing wild.
> Another version: The two of them get up and disappear
> among the revelers.[111]

The dialogic nature of the poem is graduated and diverse: at the beginning of the poem, the lovers "lie together like Isaac," as the speaker completely identifies them with Isaac. In the second stage, they think about the figures in the narrative (the ram, the angel), and in the third, once again identification takes place: "He is the ram and she is the thicket." The parallelism between the act of love and the thwarted sacrifice (Binding) of Isaac is puzzling, especially in light of two features of the situation: it seems that life is good for the lovers, but they nevertheless connect with the connotation of Abraham's most difficult test. Another feature is their identification with the ram, each in their turn (first she thinks about the ram, and afterwards, he is the ram). The identification with the ram that was sacrificed instead of Isaac

111 Amichai, *Open Closed Open*, p. 24. The Binding of Isaac is the biblical narrative in which Abraham was commanded to sacrifice his son Isaac (Gen. 22).

necessarily raises the questions: whom do the lovers replace, each in turn, and how is the Binding metaphor, which represents a test of faith of father and son, connected to a situation of love?

Lakoff and Turner described four ways in which metaphor functions: extending, elaborating, questioning, and composing.[112] Based on this classification, we can say that the Binding metaphor functions as extending by expanding Abraham's test to the context of romantic love; it elaborates the Binding myth by adding additional possible contexts; it questions the nature of the love between the two by posing scenarios of the death of the lover or of parting; and finally, the Binding metaphor questions the possibility of understanding this prosaic situation, since the sensation of the Binding remains undeciphered and without reason.

In the next poem, in contrast, the parallelism between the Binding and daily routine simplifies our understanding and explains the concrete meaning of the Binding sensation, as all the elements of the biblical narrative are separated and reassembled (in the spirit of the metaphorical composing indicated by Lakoff and Turner):

> Anyone who rises early in the morning is on his own.
> He gets himself over to the altar, he is Abraham,
> he is Isaac, he's the donkey, the fire,
> the knife, the angel,

---

112 *Extending* means that the metaphor does not focus on the transferral of a certain feature from the source realm to the target one; it extends this figurative use to a number of aspects. *Elaborating* refers to an allusion or suggestion in the text to an additional meaning, beyond the regular meaning of the metaphor. *Questioning* means that the bounds of metaphoric understanding in everyday language are examined. *Composing* is the simultaneous allusion to different meanings in the same sentence or paragraph. These functions of metaphor lead Lakoff and Turner to formulate two types of reading a poem: "first-order reading," that is, focusing on each metaphoric expression by itself; and "second-order reading," meaning reading the poem as a whole. See George Lakoff and Mark Turner, *More than Cool Reason* (Chicago: University of Chicago Press, 1989), pp. 138–39. Understanding the overall meaning of the first-order reading enables the reader to comprehend the unique nature of the metaphor, since this is not just a matter of the words, but also a means for social critique, the expression of humor, or the expression of worldview.

he's the ram, he is God.[113]

The Binding narrative is fashioned as a universal metaphor in which "anyone" can identify with any of the figures in the narrative. Most important here, Amichai adds that God's disposition can characterize any of us. Unlike his accusatory stance in *God-Full-of-Mercy*, this poem presents a conception that situates God as commanding the sacrifice as a possibility in the heart of every individual. The metaphorical extending reveals the difference in the attitude to God, from an entity outside man to an inner, integral one.

The Binding narrative is fashioned in the above two poems as an existential metaphor that places in the center the individual's existence, his loneliness, and the reflective awareness of the need to contend with the burden of life, which cannot be shared. The polar movement from the personal to the universal, based on identification, adds an important layer to the fashioning of the subject-speaker due to the extended use of the biblical connotation that encompasses all people, and that depicts the subject-speaker as one who, in his attitude to the Jewish sources, responds to universal regularity (which exceeds the context of the Jewish people), while also expressing mental affinity with the biblical connotation.

A different use of Jewish sources is reflective dialogue with those sources. The speaker contemplates himself, under the inspiration of a biblical character which aids him to understand his own inner processes. In the following poem, the title (*David, King of Israel, Thou Art the Man*) ambiguously uses the wording "Thou Art the Man" so that it could be understood either as a reference to the parable of Nathan the prophet who reproached David for the sin of Bathsheba or as drawing a parallel between David's actions with his wives and the actions of the speaker in this respect.[114] In the body of the poem, David's seemingly strange behavior is the basis for understanding the speaker's actions:

Lately I've been thinking a lot about King David.

113 Amichai, *Open Closed Open*, p. 24.
114 See II Sam. 11–12.

Not the one who is alive forever in the song,
[. . .]
but the one who played and played for Saul
and kept dodging the spear until he became king.
David changed his tune and pretended to be mad to save
his life; as for me, I change my tune and pretend to be sane
to save my life. If he were alive today
he would tell me: No, it's the other way around.
Every nation had a first king once
like a first love. And the other way around.[115]

King David functions as an inner object present in the speaker's mind and, alternatively, as a possible conversant for him in our time. David pretended to be insane when he fled from Saul, while the speaker pretends to be sane in order to survive in contemporary society, which casts out the madmen in its midst. The figure of David functions as a self-object, and allows the speaker to gain a better understanding of his own conduct: at times he feigns some behavior or other for the society to deem him a fit person.

This poem begins a cycle of seven poems that portray different aspects of King David's behavior, especially in his attitude to his wives. In the other poems the speaker does not relate to David from his own personal perspective; instead, the refashioning of the David narratives, from David as a young man to his old age, mirrors in an additional manner the speaker's reflective view of his life. The cycle ends with a stanza full of compassion that presumably forgives the sin of Bathsheba by depicting the poor man's ewe lamb that becomes a flesh-and-blood creature and comes forth from Nathan's parable to warm David, who suffers from the cold in his old age:[116]

I am the poor man's ewe lamb, warm and full of compassion,
I came to him from the pasture
as he came from the pasture to kingship.

115 Amichai, *Open Closed Open*, pp. 50–51.
116 See I Kings 1.

> I am the poor man's ewe lamb that rose out of the parable
> and I am yours until death comes between us.[117]

The speaker's identification with King David and with the poor man's ewe lamb recurs in relation to a series of additional biblical characters, later figures from Jewish culture, such as the poetess Rachel, or from general culture (Paul Celan), or figures from his personal history, such as his friend Dan Omer (p. 129) or Tova's brother, whom he carried wounded from the battlefield (p. 128). The recurring format reflects the sphere-in-between, between the speaker's self and some other character, that enables the speaker to constitute a dialogue in which the other becomes a precondition for the process of recollection. This self-constitution and interaction facilitate the expression of metaphysical subjectivity, because the other is not actually in the speaker's world. Thus dialogic and mystical grammar are combined, since the creation of the dialogue expresses a mystical relation in which the constitution of the self is based on its relations to biblical ideas and events. This mystical position also includes a channel for perfectionism by means of following and developing Jewish values.

The construction of the father's taking his leave of his son before the former's death is a striking example of this. Amichai's father is portrayed as leaving him a subjective way for perfectionism based on a reinterpretation of the Ten Commandments (that become twelve). This interpretation is based on the principle of change, both as a way of life and as the content of the new commandments, with the change formulated in two speech-acts: in the descriptive speech-act, the speaker asserts the importance of change, which is generated in the poetical speech-act. This double grammatical action creates the "poetical" merging of the speaker and his father, to the extent that we find it difficult to determine who came first in teaching the principle of change. The speaker presents his initiative for change, then joins together with his father's testament:

117 Amichai, *Open Closed Open*, p. 53.

I would like to add two more commandments to the ten:
the Eleventh Commandment, "Thou shalt not change,"
and the Twelfth Commandment, "Thou shalt change. You will change."
My dead father added those for me.[118]

In another poem that shows the importance of change, the father and God merge, and thus the mystical subjectivity reaches its sad climax. The father presumably is the source of authority ("Thus spoke my father"), but the contents that he passes over are based on Jewish tradition (including the command to change, which alludes to halakhah [Jewish law as it has evolved over the ages, whose etymological meaning is *halikhah*—walking, that is, adapting the Torah to contemporary needs]):

My father was God and didn't know it. He gave me
the Ten Commandments not in thunder and not in anger,
not in fire and not in a cloud, but gently
and with love. He added caresses and tender words,
[. . .]
and pleaded and wept quietly
between one commandment and the next: Thou shalt not
take the name of thy Lord in vain, shalt not take, not in vain,
[. . .]
And he hugged me tight and whispered in my ear,
Thou shalt not steal, shalt not commit adultery, shalt not kill.
And he lay the palms of his wide-open hands on my head
[. . .]
Then he turned his face to me one last time,
as on the day he died in my arms, and said, I would like to add
two more commandments:
the Eleventh Commandment, "Thou shalt not change,"

118 Amichai, *Open Closed Open*, p. 156.

and the Twelfth Commandment, "Thou shalt change. You will change."
Thus spoke my father, and he turned and walked away
and disappeared into his strange distances.[119]

In his behavior, the father combines expressions of warmth and love with the moral directives of the Ten Commandments. Despite the refashioning of the Ten Commandments, with the insertion of humor and changed emphases, we cannot underestimate the importance of the father's legacy to his son that is based on the heart of the Torah, the Ten Commandments. Amichai clothes his father's entire being in the garb of the Ten Commandments, as if they represent and embody his outstanding traits. This perfect correspondence between the mandates of the Torah and the father's deportment paves the way for complete identification with both.

At this point, the mystical grammar reaches the peak of its individual fashioning: Amichai fashions a conception of faith and God in the image of his father, and these two delineate his notion of continual perfectionism. The wording "disappeared into his strange distances" has a dual function: it is reminiscent of the same wording in an early poem by Amichai (*My Father's Death*), in which the speaker protests God's taking of his father, who went forth to ask for His help.[120] In the current poem, in contrast, this wording functions as a directive for the perfectionism that the speaker needs in order to reach his father's level, so that his "distances" will no longer seem "strange" to him.

The identification with the figure of the father is explained by the speaker's father having given him the Ten Commandments gently, with love, and with "tender words" accompanying the commandments and the promise of reward. The mysticism of the change is ambiguous: change represents the most sublime and is added to the Ten Commandments,

119 Amichai, *Open Closed Open*, pp. 58–59.

120 *My Father's Death*
My father, suddenly, from all the rooms went forth to strange distances.
Once he was going to call upon his God, that He come to our aid now (Amichai, *Poems: 1948–1962*, p. 27).

which represent the bringing down of the word of God to the world. This change is capable of bringing about transitions from the world to what lies beyond and vice versa, and represents both the divine and the human (the speaker and his father effected change by the addition of two commandments). Additionally, we should highlight the end of the poem in which the father takes his leave of his son, along with the mention of two additional commandments. The mysticism is also expressed in the attempt to capture the moment of parting from the father—the transition between life and death that is fashioned with grammar that, on the one hand, is dedicated to the past, and, on the other, opposes it ("Thou shalt not change [. . .] Thou shalt change").

The parallelism between and substitution of the figure of the father with that of God is finely explained in the next poem. Both are perceived as a source of love, both are seen as a source of change that at times seems to be magic, and both appear as figures in the speaker's fantasies who alternatively appear and disappear:

> The sound of a drawer closing—the voice of God,
> the sound of a drawer opening—the voice of love,
> but it could also be the other way around.
> Footsteps approaching—the voice of love,
> footsteps retreating—the voice of God
> who left the country without notice,
> temporarily forever
> [. . .]
> love. A key turning in the door without a sound—
> God. A key hesitating—love and hope.
> But it could also be the other way around.
> A sacrifice of a fragrant scent to God,[121]
> a sacrifice of the other senses to love:
> [. . .]
> But it could also be the other way around.[122]

121 An allusion to the biblical phrase describing the burnt offerings in the Sanctuary and Temple.

122 Amichai, *Open Closed Open*, p. 46.

The conception of God is fashioned in a personal and original manner: the speaker identifies the voice of God both in everyday, tangible, and trivial occurrences, like the sound of a drawer opening, and in the abstract emotion of love. The grammatical rule of the possibility of change is applied sweepingly when God and love influence man in turns, and resemble one another in their appearing and leaving. The ritual of offering sacrifices is stripped of its literal meaning, and it, too, is mixed and interchanged with the scent of love, thereby fashioning a pantheistic reality in which the traditional language-game of divine service is mixed together with public language. The boundaries are blurred, and God is evident in subtle emotions such as hesitation, love, and hope.

Love is fashioned as the most sublime principle of all by means of the grammar characteristic of the moral realm, thereby completing the mystical fashioning of the belief in love.

> For love must be spoken, not whispered, that it may be seen
> and heard. It must be without camouflage,
> conspicuous, noisy, like a raucous laugh,
> [. . .]
> sweet frosting for a bitter life.
> Love is words and flowers that attract insects and butterflies
> [. . .]
> It's the delicate skin of the inner thigh, it's underwear
> down to the bottoms of the soul and overwear up to the
> heavens,
> it's public relations, the pull of earth dwellers to earth,
> Newton's laws of gravity and the law of levity of the divine.
> Hallelujah.[123]

Love is presented as the revelation of all the details of reality, both abstract and concrete, including the laws of physics, the mental and the divine. It does not replace a single one of these realms, but imparts a

123 Amichai, *Open Closed Open*, 165.

special flavor to them that gives meaning to the speaker's life. We see how love breaches the boundaries of diametrically opposed realms of life and is realized in the romantic love of an adult, as in his childhood memories from the synagogue.

3.4. The Refashioning of Religious Rituals as an Expression of Intersubjective Change of the Self

> I studied love in the synagogue of my childhood,
> I sang "Come, O Sabbath bride" on Friday nights
> with a bridegroom's fever, I practiced longing for the days of the Messiah,
> I conducted yearning drills for the days of yore that will not return.
> The cantor serenades his love out of the depth,
> Kaddish is recited over lovers who remain together.[124]

The poem fashions an aesthetic connection between high-register poetic and public language, which provides the basis for the linkage between traditional rituals such as the Sabbath eve prayer service (in which "Come, O Sabbath bride" is chanted) and the recitation of *Kaddish*, on the one hand, and, on the other, love. The speaker, in a natural and personal manner, associates a ritual-cultural convention (the *Lekha Dodi* ["Come, O Sabbath Bride"] liturgical hymn) and the bridegroom's excitement before uniting with his bride. The content of the liturgical hymn, in which the bride is a metaphor for the Sabbath, seemingly invites such an association, but the connection between a "bridegroom's fever" and the excitement at receiving the Sabbath is not self-understood, when we consider poems in earlier books such as *Hanukkah* or *But It Is Our Duty to Praise*, with their critical approach to rituals such as the kindling of Hanukkah lights or the *Aleinu* ("It is our duty to praise") prayer that finds their performance superfluous.[125]

---

124 Amichai, *Open Closed Open*, 47.

125 This year
I did not light candles

In the early poems cited in the preceding note, the speaker voids the ritual language of its content by examining its literal validity: the Hanukkah practices do not reflect his life, and therefore there is no reason to observe them, and the language of the *Aleinu* prayer runs counter to the emotions of loss and distance that he experienced when the beloved left him. In the untitled poem that begins "I studied love" and other poems that record rituals, however, childhood memory enables him to reconstruct experiences of longing and love, not necessarily in a traditional context. Abraham Band argued that the contrast between sacred and profane expresses an epistemological position in which "Amichai preserved the store of words and expressions from the holy books, doing with them as he pleased in writing his poems. It seems that for such a poet, the two realms are not so completely and decisively opposing."[126] Band maintained that the reader who has been religious or secular his entire life would sense a split or tension, but a reader who "passed over" between the cultures would see this as natural. He claimed that Amichai's casting off of religious observance was not done "in Sturm und Drang." Notwithstanding this point, the very preservation and use of the language of the Jewish sources essentially differs from their intersubjective linkage to personal human

---

nor did I place them by the window
[. . .]
nor did I sing
nor did I remember miracles, nor the face of my childhood
[. . .]
nor did I spin a top
I went around in the streets because
I had a reason
I had a lot of reasons (Yehuda Amichai, "Hanukkah," *Poems: 1948–1962*, pp. 223–24; the references in the poem are to Hanukkah practices).

But it is our duty to praise
a familiar night. Gold borrowed from Hades.
Cypresses rose up eternal. Still flowing
Keep long hair away. The Lord of the loss of all (Yehuda Amichai, "But It Is Our Duty to Praise," *Early Books*, p. 246).

126 Arnold J. Band, "Secularization of the Sacred? Forms of Inter-textual Expression in a Poem by Yehuda Amichai," in *Creation and Re-Creation in Jewish Thought: Festschrift in Honor of Joseph Dan on the Occasion of His Seventieth Birthday*, ed. Rachel Elior and Peter Schafer (Tubingen: Mohr Siebeck, 2005), p. 194 (Hebrew).

experiences in a positive context, such as physical and mental love. The language of the *Lekha Dodi* hymn is used as an expression of longing meant to reconstruct moments that were refashioned in the speaker's imagination as moments that express love and a bridegroom's excitement.

A poem of the Passover Seder night is another example of a description of a religious ritual that expresses identification, on the one hand, and, on the other, the desire to change. The Hagaddah recited at the seder enables the speaker to air his existential questions:

> Seder night thoughts, *Mah nishtanah*, we asked
> *Mah nishtanah*—How is this night different from all other nights.
> And most of us grew up and we will ask no more, and others continue to ask all their lives
> [. . .]
> How is this different, everything is different. The change is God.
> [. . .]
> And this is a question without answer, and if it had an answer I wouldn't want to know.[127]

The speaker's attitude to the question of change is answered, on the one hand, by the declaration: "The change is God," while, on the other, the speaker preserves his questioning mode by dismissing the importance of the answer. Beyond change being based on endless questioning, this position is remarkably similar to Wittgenstein's argument concerning questions pertaining to the meaning of life:

> We feel that even when all possible scientific questions have been answered, the problems of life remain completely untouched. Of course there are then no questions left, and this itself is the answer.[128]

---

127 Amichai, *Open Closed Open*, p. 15 (Hebrew edition; not translated in the English edition).

128 Wittgenstein, *Tractatus*, para. 6.52.

The stance of the speaker in this poem, of not wanting to know answers, while equating divinity with the dynamics of change, is quite different from that of the speaker in the poem *God-Full-of-Mercy*, with his inner need to resolve the conundrums of existence.[129] If God is presented in *God-Full-of-Mercy* as detached from the world and as excluding His compassion from it, in *Seder Night Thoughts*, the regularity of the world (the dynamics of change) is equated with God. These two examples of the refashioning of rituals (Sabbath prayers, Seder night) can be understood as an expression of the typical journey of someone who longs for the expanses of his childhood.

Along with the reconstruction of childhood experiences as an expression of longing, the book also, surprisingly, expresses a yearning for religious ritual, such as wrapping oneself in a prayer shawl. The following poem does not relate to the aesthetic plane of prayer, nor is it concerned with the memory of a family experience. Rather, we have here a religious, personal expression that (in the poem) occurs privately. The experience of putting on a tallis is reconstructed as a religious experience that rises above metaphors of the everyday, and creates a picture of spiritual elevation:

> Whoever put on tallis when he was young will never forget
> taking it out of the soft velvet bag, opening the folded shawl,
> spreading it out, kissing the length of the neckband
> [. . .]
> Then swinging it in a great swoop overhead
> like a sky, a wedding canopy.[130]

The experience of putting on the tallis is portrayed in almost erotic terms that engender a sense of elevation above this world and connection to a sublime and mystical spiritual world. This act is broken down

129 I, who must decipher riddles
I don't want to decipher,
Know that if not for the God-full-of-mercy
There would be mercy in the world,
Not just in Him (Amichai, "God-Full-of-Mercy," trans. Harshav and Harshav).

130 Amichai, *Open Closed Open*, p. 44.

into the smallest details of—all positive—feelings and associations that hint of an intimate connection with the ritual, which is the source of feelings of hope, development, and unlimited possibilities. This is not just a reworking of past experience and a mending that expresses acceptance of Jewish culture, it is also a religious experience of a deep and direct connection with religious rituals.

The key to understanding the change expressed throughout the book is longing for the past. The refashioning of traditional aspects can be seen as yearning to return to the past, and to appropriate it from anew for the speaker-self. This is an oblique acknowledgement that opposition, negation, and irony corrode the positive influence of and bond to the childhood experiences, and of identification with the traditional Jewish sources. The desire and will "to speak among the pains" constitute the mystical grammar in the book:

> There's longing everywhere.
> The precision of pain and the blurriness of joy.[131]
>
> The precision of pain and the blurriness of joy. I'm thinking
> how precise people are when they describe their pain in the
> doctor's office.
> Even those who haven't learned to read and write are precise.
> [. . .] I want to describe, with a sharp pain's precision,
> happiness
> and blurry joy. I learned to speak among the pains.[132]

In the Hebrew version of *Open Closed Open*, these lines are immediately followed by a poem that opens with the central synecdoche in the book: the stone that he places on his desk on which the word "Amen" is carved. In the poem that opens and closes the book (in both the Hebrew and English editions), Amichai tells how the stone that he brought from the cemetery in his hometown drives the speaker's memory in the book. Amichai connects the need for precision in

131 Amichai, *Open Closed Open*, p. 101.
132 Amichai, *Open Closed Open*, p. 105.

language with man's eternal longing to seek his roots and complete the puzzle of his personal biography within the broader picture of family and people.

The diverse use of the language of Jewish tradition reflects the dynamics of mystical grammar. The poems, taken as a whole, show how the interpretation of language remains open to the experiences of the subject in the world, so that at times the same image, the same biblical character, and the same ritual assume a completely different meaning in different periods in one's life. This human openness unites the grammar with changing life experience. As Amichai expressed this so well in one of his last poems, which was not included in his books:

> To tell everything:
> Last words, like one condemned to die.
> And to continue to live
> as people live after writing their will.
> To be open as a rose,
> with the possibility of closing again
> [. . .]
>
> A poem is the resurrection of the words.[133]

133 From Amichai's literary estate; published in *Maariv*, "*Sofshavua*" magazine (December 5, 2008) (Hebrew).

CHAPTER 6

Admiel Kosman: We Reached God

The Popping Self

> At prayer,
> the self considers popping like a cork. A cork tossed
> by many waters. Mighty ones.
>
> To anneal feelings of inferiority, and solder, refine them
> into a necklace of silver filigree.[1]

Admiel Kosman's poetry was a milestone in twentieth-century Hebrew poetry, as it crossed the boundaries between traditional religious language and the language of the everyday. The acceptance of his poetry into the heart of the Israeli literary hegemony heralded an openness to a renewed encounter with the sources of Jewish tradition, which was accompanied by the generation of biting criticism of conventions and traditional rituals. This complexity is reflected in Kosman's poetry in a plethora of possibilities of a multifaceted and multiparticipant conversation between the language-games of Hebrew culture through the ages, while creating a subjective, fresh, and challenging voice. Kosman's having studied in a

1 Admiel Kosman, *Approaching You in English*, trans. Lisa Katz and Shlomit Naim-Naor (Boston: Zephyr, 2011), p. 73.

yeshivah (Talmudic academy) before going on to develop an academic career in Talmud leaves him sui generis in comparison with other authors who write out of a religious relation to Jewish tradition.

Kosman developed a voice that expresses an autonomous relation to the sources of Jewish tradition, while using everyday language and post-modernist ideas. Along with the originality characteristic of his poetry, I will attempt to show how it includes existentialist philosophical notions that are finely explained by Wittgensteinian investigation. The self, as in the above poem, is a conscious and alert voice that constantly develops, at times within and at other times beyond everyday activity, and that functions as a self-constitutive speech act: "the self considers popping like a cork" during prayer, to create change that transforms the feeling of inferiority "into a necklace of silver filigree." The wording "the self considers," however, hints at a disparity between what the self wants to generate in its soul by means of prayer and what actually happens. The poem's subtle allusion to the tension between the self and the religious ritual of prayer is an intermediate link in the critique embodied in Kosman's poetry, especially in the first two decades of his poetry (1980–2000). This critique is expressed much more graphically in the poem *I Don't Move during Prayers*:

> I don't move during prayers. I stand still, frozen. Ready
> for what comes. Thoughts creep up on me like an army of
> infiltrators,
> moving nimbly over the sharp stones, and climb onward.
>
> I don't move during prayers. I stand still, frozen. Destruction
> and ruin
> were planted in me a long time ago, and though I said that
> I don't move
> during prayers, yet inside me the earth hard as a rock is rent
> asunder and wails like an impending storm.
>
> I don't move during prayers. I throw my bunch
> of keys upward and pretend to be frozen. Stiff and frozen.[2]

2 Kosman, *Approaching You in English*, p. 71.

The wording "I don't move during prayers" is repeated in the poem's title and in each of its three stanzas, and places the reader in a picture that shows more than it says. The choice of a visual picture instead of an act or a direct statement creates an introspective literary construct. The speaker scrutinizes what happens in his consciousness during prayer and finds a multitude of emotions, all of which show anxiety regarding the future and distance from God.

The poem illustrates a semantic upheaval that recurs, with variations, in many additional poems: the speaker examines a routine situation in the life of the religious Jew, prayer; explores one of its prominent characteristics, movement; and portrays his feelings, which are the opposite of what is expected of him. The contrast between the inner processes and externally imposed conventions creates a grammaticalization experience. The speaker fashions his personal experience in the face of the accepted convention and uses a wealth of conventions (such as "Destruction and ruin") alongside everyday language (such as: "and though I said that I don't move"). This existential move of self-fashioning in the face of, and in opposition to, prevalent norms was described in our discussion above as "perfectionism," a term that Cavell coined under the influence of Kierkegaard and Wittgenstein. Beyond self-fashioning, the grammar created by Kosman also contains features of paradigm shift.[3]

This upheaval is characterized, as Kuhn puts it, by the wearing of "inverted lenses."[4] Kosman's approach to the sources and to discourse with God assumes the garb of a creative, living dialogue that is almost unparalleled in modern Hebrew poetry. At times the dialogue is with God, at other times with the speaker's soul, and in yet other instances with his lover. Notwithstanding the different interlocutors, the dialogue is always charged with the desire to realize the connection with the

3 Thomas Kuhn suggests the term "paradigm," under the influence of the term "family resemblance" coined by Wittgenstein, in *The Structure of Scientific Revolution* (Chicago: University of Chicago Press, 1962), pp. 44–45.

4 "The scientist who embraces a new paradigm is like the man wearing inverting lenses. Confronting the same constellation of objects as before and knowing that he does so, he nevertheless finds them transformed through and through in many of their details" (Kuhn, *Structure of Scientific Revolution*, p. 122).

divine Otherness, an actualization that will lead to the harmonious integration of body and soul, of the spiritual and the tangible, and of sacred and profane. The expressions of this desire in the following poem reflect a recurring pattern in Kosman's poetry of the use of an existing literary form (here, lament; and below, the daily psalm, or sections in the *Shulhan Arukh* [the standard code of Jewish law]) which is infused with new and subversive content.

Lament for the Ninth of Av
For cantor and congregations:
To be sung softly after reading the Book of Lamentations

Hardly any room for the body, my daughter.
The soul has seized nearly everything by force.

Hardly any room left for the body, though
it's true, my daughter, words were etched in stone,
but violently.
Hardly any room for the body. Nearly everything was written.
And all is turned to plunder inside the temple.
The body, torn and split, crumbled from the weight of the
soul
trampling and destroying, spreading fear all around.
Hardly any room left for the body. Crushed, my daughter,
broken, my daughter. Totally destroyed.
And prey for the soul.[5]

Within the literary form of a lament for the Ninth of Av (the fast day that commemorates disasters that befell the Jewish people, including the destruction of both Temples), the speaker laments the—erroneous, in his opinion—body-spirit hierarchy. From Plato's comparison of the soul to a bird imprisoned in a cage to the multitude of prohibitions imposed on the body in the three monotheistic religions, a culture of

5 Kosman, *Approaching You in English*, pp. 20–21.

repression is created: Western culture perceived the body as inferior to the spirit, as Michel Foucault finely described in his essay "Technologies of the Self" and in the three volumes of his *History of Sexuality*.[6] Kosman's poem relates to the religious Jewish experience, while Foucault's writings could offer a broader background: drawing a connection between the body and ethics results in the former's exclusion, or at least, the exclusion of so many of its expressions.

This poem shows how a position of force corrupts and leads the soul to machoistic, ruthless, and destructive acts supported by symbolic and applied practices, as portrayed in the last stanza. The fascinating process of self-constitution, however, peeks though from behind the scenes of the description of trampling underfoot and calamity. This process is intentional and begins with the speaker's addressing his "daughter," with the poem conducted as a conversation between them before it ends with a depiction of his inner recognition. The dialogue is reflective and inner, but also relates to the external cultural concept of "daughter," that could symbolize *Knesset Israel* (the entirety of the Jewish people), the speaker's soul, or the alternative spiritual essence to which he turns in order to extricate himself from his situation, of being imprisoned in a subjugating hierarchy in which the body is silenced and trampled underfoot.

Along with his intimate familiarity with the Jewish sources, Kosman's dialogical poetry generates a sensation of an actual and personal religious experience. This experience is fashioned with the poetic grammar intensively used by all manner of dialogue, both contentually and prosodically, as can be seen in *The Lament*, which is written in a dramatic meter that invites us to read it aloud or set it to music. The theatrical meter illustrates the experience of self-constitution in the world. It creates a new poetical paradigm that expresses individual religiosity that is constituted on the scale of criticism of common

---

6 Michel Foucault, "Technologies of the Self," in *Technologies of the Self: A Seminar with Michel Foucault*, ed. Luther H. Martin, Huck Gutman, and Patrick H. Hutton (London: Tavistock, 1988), pp. 16–49; Michel Foucault, *The History of Sexuality*, vol. 1: *An Introduction*, trans. Robert Hurley (New York: Pantheon, 1978).

religious conventions, such as aggrandizing spirituality at the expense of the body and justifying the forceful imposition of religious principles.

The importance of the conception of paradigm does not lie in its definition, but in understanding the change of consciousness embodied within it: paradigm change does not occur as a result of a causal progression; it comes from the continuing sensation of unease at the dissonance between the conceptual system by which the world is examined and goals and desires. Kosman's discomfort is already evident in the titles of some of his collections of poetry, such as: *After the Horror, the Act of Poetry* (*Ve-Aharei Mora'ot, Maaseh ha-Shir,* 1980); *We Reached God* (*Higanu le-Elohim,* 1998); and *A New Commentary, with God's Help* (*Perush Hadash b.s.d,* 2000).

The methodology of comparing language-games proposed by Wittgenstein is quite suitable for describing this upheaval.[7] Kosman introduced to the poetical expanse an unprecedented range of language-games taken from Jewish tradition, such as the halakhic language-game, the cultural-social language game (which includes conventions of "religiously correct" judgments), philosophical-theological language-games from Maimonides to Hasidism, and more.

Although intertextuality and refashioning of the Jewish sources are clearly present in the poetry of Zelda, Amichai, and other poets, Kosman's poetry—especially in his early books—uniquely forges a lively debate, actual conversation, and self-constitution during the movement of the encounter. As Wittgenstein would put it, the grammar of Kosman's poetry transforms his poetry into language that sets forth self-constitutive alternatives, at one and the same time, in the past, the present, and the future.[8] Thus the grammar changes from descriptive to constitutive, generating a sense of continuing experience and constant

7 "Our clear and simple language-games are not preliminary studies for a future regimentation of language—as it were, first approximations, ignoring friction and air resistance. Rather, the language-games stand there as *objects of comparison* which, through similarities and dissimilarities, are meant to throw light on features of our language" (Wittgenstein, *Philosophical Investigations*, para. 130).

8 See the connection Wittgenstein draws between philosophy and poetry (chap. 1).

examination of the experience of meaning that is constituted in the poetry.[9]

The paradigm of a living conversation with the Jewish sources and with God underwent change during the course of Kosman's poetical career, and if we examine this paradigm, as Wittgenstein advises, by means of "a surveyable representation,"[10] we see a process of significant change in the manner by which the self is constituted: from a monologist position, in which dialogue functions controversially or reflectively, to a dialogical stance, in which the reflection takes place within a dynamic, spousal context. This comparative view shows the singularity of Kosman's poetry, in its ambivalent and paradoxical dialogue that also possesses a mystical dimension, to which the poetical act is directed.

1. The Poetic Grammar of Revolution: The New Believer

> Like everything metaphysical the harmony between thought and reality is to be found in the grammar of the language. Here instead of harmony or agreement of thought and reality one might say: the pictorial character of thought [. . .] Anything can be a picture of anything, if we extend the concept of picture sufficiently. Every projection must have something in common with what is projected no matter what is the method of projection.[11]

How can the relationship between the author's thought and the external reality be verbally described? Wittgenstein argued that thought, like grammar, has a pictorial nature, and therefore grammar

9 "Why should the experience of meaning be important? [. . .] The interest here does not depend on the concept of the 'meaning' of a word, but on the range of similar psychological phenomena which in general have nothing to do with word-meaning" (Wittgenstein, *Remarks*, vol. 1, para. 358).

10 "A surveyable representation produces precisely that kind of understanding which consists in 'seeing connections.' Hence the importance of finding and inventing *intermediate links*" (Wittgenstein, *Philosophical Investigations*, para. 122).

11 Wittgenstein, *Philosophical Grammar*, pp. 162–63.

can reflect the correlation between thought and reality. The verbalized result is indicative, not only of the picture of the thought, but also of the method of reflection. This argument is important in order to understand how poetical language can symbolize the speaker's emotional experience, without fully detailing it. Following Susanne Langer's discussion, based on *Tractatus*, that emphasized the emotional effectiveness of poetry, I will show that this is one of the main features of Kosman's poetry.

The challenge before the literary critic in this instance, under the influence of Wittgenstein, is to uncover "the method of projection" that enables the powerful expression of emotions. "The method of projection" is an outstanding example of a term used by Wittgenstein in the same manner in both *Tractatus* and *Philosophical Investigations*. He maintains that all content is presented in a certain way that enables it to be perceived in a specific manner, with the law of projection paving the way for the translation of the picture, just as the notes delineate the performance of a musical work.[12] He added an important comment in *Philosophical Investigations*: that the understanding of the method of projection cannot be logically imposed, since people might perceive a specific picture differently from its method of projection, due to "psychological compulsion."[13]

The distinction between differing methods of projection enables us to distinguish between different corpora of poetry, and to state that the poetical grammar reflects both the relationship between the author's thought and the reality and the method of projection itself. When a poet creates a new language-game, he expresses a new method of

12 "We use the perceptible sign of a proposition (spoken or written, etc.) as a projection of a possible situation. The method of projection is to think of the sense of the proposition [. . .] There is a general rule by means of which the musician can obtain the symphony from the score, and which makes it possible to derive the symphony from the groove on the gramophone record, and, using the first rule, to derive the score again. That is what constitutes the inner similarity between these things which seem to be constructed in such entirely different ways. And that rule is the law of projection which projects the symphony into the language of musical notation. It is the rule for translating this language into the language of gramophone records" (Wittgenstein, *Tractatus*, para. 3:11, 4.0141).

13 Wittgenstein, *Philosophical Investigations*, para. 140.

projection of the relationship between his thought and the reality. Such a perception is actually metaphysical, since it results from the author's subjective will, and is indirectly reflected, and not verbalized. Nevertheless, every reflection has a method, and the more visual the poem, the easier it is for the reader to characterize the metaphysical stance at the basis of the thought-reality harmony depicted in the poem. We will open our discussion of Kosman's poetry with the striking example of the dramatic visuality in the next poem:

After the Horror, the Act of Poetry
And after the horror, the act of poetry,
after the scandal of its birth, what remains
are graphic signs upon the earth,
the chalk scars the police drew in a circle around
the position of my gunned-down body, a warm bullet
still quivering on the ground, and a few people
whispering about what happened here,
after the terrifying din, after the audience dispersed.[14]

This is the title poem in Admiel Kosman's first book of poetry (1980), and the ars poetical description in it is especially harsh. I chose to present it at the beginning of our discussion of self-constitution in poetical language in order to locate the first pole on the self-constitutive axis, which is the point in which there seemingly is no self-object and no dialogism. The writing of the work has a symbiotic relationship with the life of the poet, which is brutally ended in the completion of the poem. This romantic position is exceptional in his poetry, but additional romantic expressions can be discerned in the poet's relationship with his poetry, in this and in additional books.

The speaker looks at his literary work in the third person, indirectly, as at a picture of an event in which a violent murder was committed. The oblique grammar generates a sensation of distance that, paradoxically, is contrary to the symbiosis between the poet and

14 Admiel Kosman, *After the Horror, the Act of Poetry* (Givatayim: Massada, 1980), p. 11 (Hebrew); trans. for the current book by Lisa Katz.

his poem, perhaps in order to enable him to write it, despite the horror. The murder is reported by means of signs from the crime scene, like the chalk markings around the body, the still-warm bullet, and so forth. The crowd has already dispersed, but the trauma is still powerfully present: the writing of the poem is an act that unavoidably risks the speaker's life.

The poem graphically illustrates a certain aspect of the revolution that Admiel Kosman's poetry caused in the genre usually termed "religious poetry." Without references to Jewish tradition, the poem draws a direct connection to what Kosman sees as the source of poetry: horror and the sensation of murder. Language is merely a collection of graphic marks, and it does not enable actual communication with other people, or with God. Kosman charts the process and the price of writing authentic poetry that verbalizes the speaker's selfhood, and nothing in the world can save him or prevent the paying of the price. The method of projection is the parallel drawn between the process of writing the poem and that of the murder, so that even looking at the process of writing the poem is fraught with danger. Why is this so?

The ars poetica (looking at the poetical act) that is fashioned in the poem corresponds with Hebrew and general poetry. The term "Ars Poetica" (the art of poetry) originates in a poem by the Roman poet Horace (65–8 BCE) written ca. 15 BCE.[15] In this, his longest poem, which is dedicated to the members of the aristocratic Piso family, he sets forth the criteria for writing poetry that looks at itself and relates to the process of its writing.[16] The suffering in Kosman's ars poetica stance in this poem, however, is not the consequence of inner difficulty in the writing process, but results from the clash with external factors. This theme of conflict is dominant in Kosman's early poetry as a whole, and not only in his first book (as is ironically reflected in the book's title, as was mentioned above). Nonetheless, the feeling of danger and

15 Horace, *Satire, Epistles, and Ars Poetica*, trans. H. Rushton Fairclough (Cambridge, MA: Harvard University Press, 1942).

16 See Ruth Kartun-Blum, *Poetry as Its Own Mirror: An Anthology* (Tel Aviv: Hakibbutz Hameuchad, 1982), pp. 9–19 (Hebrew).

horror regarding the very possibility of poetical writing is highlighted in his first book.

At times the connection between the writing process and the sensations of horror and anxiety is fashioned obliquely in the book, in a way that leaves itself open to interpretation. For example, in the following poem, *The First Sights Were Hard*, the portrayal could be interpreted as relating to the writing process, but also as speaking of the process of falling in love. Thus the romantic position (see above) is actualized in two directions:

> The first sights were hard: red canyons of fear fell open
> within me.
> Vast unfallowed areas hardened and closed before the rain.
> The plants withered,
> and before the first tremors within me, before the lava burst
> forth, I was a quiet person.[17]

An additional striking example of the dramatic combined with the romantic, so that they fashion one another, can be seen in the third in a series of poems that portray falling in love:

> And when I heard your voice the earth quaked.
> Roosters crowed bitterly. Machines struck wildly
> on the roads. The streets stormed, filled with people,
> filled with blood, milled with goring bulls.[18]

The emotional storm is embodied both in the words themselves and in alliteration games, in the repetition that develops into a violation of linguistic correctness—a nonsense word ("filled [*malu*] with people / filled [*malu*] with blood, milled [*malhu*—not a Hebrew word] with bulls"). Love comes into being within a world that is shocked by the sights of slaughter and blood. Many expressions of terminality are inserted throughout the book, but it seems that it is only in the two last

17 Kosman, *After the Horror*, p. 30; trans. Edward Levin.
18 Kosman, *After the Horror*, p. 39; trans. Edward Levin.

poems in the book that the cause of the harsh feelings of horror, alienation, and bitterness comes into the open: the clash with one's surroundings, both on the concrete human plane and in the intellectual sphere. The next poem, *You Were Forbidden to Quote from My Poems after My Death*, along with the repetition of the motifs of risk and death, fashions a central theme that would be developed in Kosman's later books, that of surrender to the outer appearance that conceals the continuation of the rebellious act:

> You were forbidden to quote from my poems after my death.
> A poem lasts for a moment
> and is put away
> [. . .]
> But even then, under strict ban, under cover, completely concealed, far from anyone's eyes,
> the echo of its melody continues to resound in the vast cold halls of the dead body.[19]

In the last poem, *The Book's Cover Is Sealed on My Order*, the problem does not lie solely in wrestling with society, contending with the books themselves, with the choking texts of Jewish tradition, is problematic, too:

> The book's cover is sealed on my order.
> I'm choked, by the weight of the pages, too.
> The reader will forgive me for the bitterness of my bile, that sprouted wild
> [. . .]
> The reader will forgive me for my crushed flat, flat-eyed begrudging [. . .]
> for the great conflagration that licked at the edges of my poems. Sorry.[20]

---

19 Kosman, *After the Horror*, p. 58; trans. Edward Levin.
20 Kosman, *After the Horror*, p. 59; trans. Edward Levin.

The choking sensation, which is mentioned both explicitly and indirectly ("by the weight of the pages, too") guides the poem. It expresses an ambivalent mental state, of social and cultural commitment, on the one hand, and, on the other, the need to articulate a personal poetic voice that burns and destroys. The psychoanalyst Melanie Klein explained the movement between the poles of love and hate as a natural movement in the nursing phase, because the mother is the source of both the child's nourishment and its suffering, since she is the one who feeds him, but also delays or withholds care and food.[21]

According to Klein, this ambivalent movement should lead to normal development in which the infant-child learns to differentiate between himself and his mother and to develop an individual personality.[22] When, however, the child is angry, his expressions of hate are liable, first and foremost, to cause him to feel choked.[23] The child's hatred for the mother is also accompanied by the fear that this hate might cause the mother to leave, either temporarily or permanently. Kosman's poem reflects this ambivalent situation of hatred and anger that is acted out in writing poetry. The term "acting-out" was coined by Freud in the context of repressed memory that is expressed as an act of repetition.[24] Klein expanded the term, which she incorporated in the description of the infant's development of love and gratitude.

21 Melanie Klein, "Notes on Some Schizoid Mechanisms," *International Journal of Psychoanalysis* 27 (1946), pp. 99–110.

22 Klein, "Notes on Some Schizoid Mechanisms," p. 100.

23 Melanie Klein and Joan Riviere, *Love Hate and Reparation* (New York: W. W. Norton, 1964), p. 58.

24 "We soon perceive that the transference is itself only a piece of repetition, and that the repetition is a transference of the forgotten past not only on to the doctor but also on to all the other aspects of the current situation. We must be prepared to find, therefore, that the patient yields to the compulsion to repeat, which now replaces the compulsion to remember, not only in his personal attitude to his doctor but also in every other activity and relationship which may occupy his life at the time—if, for instance, he falls in love or undertakes a task or starts an enterprise during the treatment. The part played by resistance, too, is easily recognized. The greater the resistance, the more extensively will acting out (repetition) replace remembering" (Sigmund Freud, "Remembering, Repeating, and Working-Through (Further Recommendations on the Technique of Psycho-Analysis II)," *The Standard Edition of the Complete Psychological Works of Sigmund Freud*, ed. and trans. James Strachey et al. [London: Hogarth, 1958], vol. 12, p. 151).

When the infant has difficulty in integrating the paranoid elements of the psyche with the need to be grateful, he expresses his anxieties as envy.[25]

One of Klein's important contributions in the continuation of her discussion is her distinction between "jealousy," "envy," and "greed."[26] Each of these terms is based on a different configuration of intersubjective relations: greed and envy appear in dyadic relationships (due to the infant's anger at the delay in satisfaction caused by the mother), and express the subject's desire to appropriate for the self parts of various objects. Jealousy is connected to a triangular relationship, and represents the subject's fear of losing the beloved object to a third party. (Klein maintains that jealousy results from an Oedipus complex based on the desire of two for a third object.)[27] In Kosman's poem, the speaker apologizes to the reader for his envy ("The reader will forgive me for my crushed flat, flat-eyed begrudging"), as a continuation to the feelings in the poem of suffocation, anger ("the bitterness of my bile"), and powerlessness. This can be interpreted as Kleinian jealousy: both the speaker and the reader thirst to dominate the poem and possess it; and the speaker is jealous because of the necessity of sharing the poem with the reader, which would take it out of his hands.

25 "In my view *acting out*, in so far as it is used to avoid integration, becomes a defense against the anxieties aroused by accepting the envious part of the self" (Melanie Klein, "Envy and Gratitude," in *Envy and Gratitude and Other Works 1946–1963*, [London: Hogarth Press, 1975], p. 219).

26 Klein, "Envy and Gratitude."

27 Dave Hiles clearly summarized Klein's position: "Jealousy is based on envy, but involves a relation to at least two other people. It pertains to a triangular (oedipal) relationship, i.e. it is whole-object oriented. It is commonly experienced with respect to love that a person feels is their due and has been taken away, or is in danger of being taken away, by a rival [. . .] Jealousy implies envy of the actual or presumed advantages of a rival, especially in regard to the love of an object. Jealousy is often accompanied by suspicion that the loved person favours the other [. . .] The best way to understand envy is to see it as the angry feeling that another (person) possesses, and is *withholding*, or keeping to itself, something one desires for oneself [. . .] Envy is the feeling of conflict that what one desires, and would normally be forthcoming, is being withheld. The envious impulse is to attach, or to spoil the very source that one originally relied upon" (David Hiles, "Envy, Jealousy, Greed: A Kleinian Approach," paper presented to the Centre for Counselling and Psychotherapy Education, London—November, 2007, sec. 5, 6).

The speaker apologizes three times in the course of this short poem: for his anger, for his envy, and most important, "for the great conflagration that licked at the edges of my poems." The multitude of harsh feelings come to a climax in an act of self-destruction, in a way amazingly similar to Klein's depiction of the child's desire to destroy his mother's creativity, as the factor responsible for his distress. The burning of the poems is like the infant's attempt to destroy the mother, and thereby rid himself of his poisonous parts. The speaker's stance in the poem comes from a feeling of distress caused by the threat to dominate the manner in which he writes poetry, to the extent that the speaker is directed to burn his poems himself.

The character of the believer that develops during the course of the book refashions common terms that are known from Jewish tradition, within the experience of a break with the whole world that the speaker senses: a rift from his love, as from the readers of his poems. The drama here, and the force of the anxiety and terror, arouse the reader's identification and compassion, and even the need to defend one who is willing to pay heavy prices in the process of his poetic self-constitution. This controversial position is developed and deepened in Kosman's following books, and splits into a number of paths, running counter to any framework that tries to impose its accepted authority on the speaker and threatens to blur and attenuate his personal characteristics: married life, the halakhic framework, and society as a whole, which defines success in terms of external criteria.

The processes embodied in the poem frequently coincide with the speaker's personal and family history, more conspicuously than in other corpora in the book, and this has poetical consequences. For example, Kosman highlights the plane of personal experience, which includes stormy swings and, under their influence, creates a complex and shifting attitude to the world and to God. This intricacy is involved, inter alia, in the inclusion of poems that depict both minor and acute distress, along with those that experience the gentleness in the reality, a type of compassion and refinement, which, on rare occasions, emerge from within the difficulties of everyday existence:

Inside the uproar, inside crumpled
life, inside the smoking city, suddenly,
without noticing, in an alleyway,
composure will clothe you
in a prince raiment.[28]

At times, princeliness comes to light within life's hardship and tumult, but the experience of princely composure appears only rarely in the first two decades of Kosman's poetry (1980–2000). For the most part, the writing experience is accompanied by an emotional tempest, albeit one less dramatic than the experience of terror in the above poem from his first book but still intensive, fiery, and bound up with inner and outward struggles. At the same time, the ironic and humorous aspect of Kosman's poetical language develops considerably, thus fashioning a voice with the singular ability to incorporate opposites, including dead seriousness and a playful spirit, devotion and detachment, for example. The development of this voice is manifest in the following poem that, on the one hand, is an ars poetica work that continues to fashion the dangerous and dramatic experience of writing; while, on the other, the humor and irony characteristic of Kosman's poetry create a poetical language that crosses the boundary between lyrical poem and minidrama.

Final Corrections to a Poem
My Lilith, are you proofread yet? I wrote "amour"
with an "a" at the beginning of the poem,
and "brilliance" with a "b," tried "cheerful" with a "c,"
"delight"
with a "d," and I haven't conceded the "e's" in "exalt"
"extol," and "exceptional."
Lilith! Look, once again you rise!

You're stepping on my paper! You're really crazy!

28 Kosman, *Approaching You in English*, p. 85.

Have you thought about the question at all? My Lilith
are you proofread yet? I look at you hard through the serifs
of "f," g," and "h," are you paying any attention at all?
My Lilith, what's happening to you?

Look, your mane of wild hair and fiery eyes, your chest
rising and falling. I can't trust you.
I unravel the threads and find your eyes are different now, simple
glass beads. I turned you upside down and spilled
all the details out. Your backpack fell too, everything, all of life,
suddenly becoming a deep pit and a thousand bumps.

Lilith,
tell me, when I write a poem about you,
and hover over the blank page, shaking,
am I being rude, too direct? Perhaps I'm moralistic, suspicious?
Am I still breathing? Do I seem awake to you?
Perhaps you smell the scent of a dead body on me?
Perhaps I'm simply drunk?

Perhaps the opposite is true. I'm alive!
Rather brave? Perhaps a real hero?!
Tell me, Lilith, as a poet—
man or ghost—
perhaps I'm really a bird?[29]

The poem expresses an ars poetica experience with both romanticism and fear on the part of the speaker as regards his muse, the inner Lilith, which is both the condition for writing poetry and the object of the

29 Admiel Kosman, *Perush Hadash b.s.d* (Tel Aviv: Hakibbutz Hameuchad, 2000), p. 46; trans. for the current book by Lisa Katz (with slight changes—E.L.).

struggle in the process of writing the poem.[30] The poetical process is based on dialogue that is both technical and reflective: the speaker repeatedly addresses Lilith in the second person, in order to create the impression of an actual conversation. Even so, I chose to discuss this poem in the context of the poetical refashioning of the stance of the believer, since the speaker does not conduct a dialogue with the inner development of self-fashioning, it rather exposes an eccentric, and even narcissistic side. It expresses his poetical talent as a sort of justification for spontaneous, unbridled, and even harmful conduct, but moves all these negative qualities to a fictional character, so that he is free of any guilt feelings.

The believer's attitude exhibits two main features: allusion to the language of the Jewish sources, and the perception of the ability to write poetry as an inner commitment to an imposed talent, but which was seemingly imposed on the speaker by some external factor. The perception of poetry as a sort of mission, which is actually both inner and external, is expressed by Lilith functioning in different and complementary ways: on the one hand, in various strata of Hebrew language, and on the other, as uncanny.

The word "uncanny" functions in different ways in literary criticism. For our purposes, I will rely on Freud's famous discussion in

30 Admiel Kosman drew my attention to the article in which he interpreted the two versions of the creation of the woman in Genesis. The first version (Gen. 1:27–28) presents an egalitarian creation, while the other (Gen. 2:21–22) has the woman created as part of the man. The first version enables us to understand the woman as a side of the man's personality, while the second subordinates the woman to the man, since she is perceived as one who was created after him, from his body, and therefore is only partial in comparison to the man, to whom she is inferior. See Admiel Kosman, "The Woman as a 'Rib' of the Man: On the Explanations of the Bible Story of the Woman's Creation and Their Implications to the Status of the Woman in the Halakha and Aggada," in *Life as a Midrash: Perspectives in Jewish Psychology*, ed. Shahar Arazi, Michal Fachler, and Baruch Kahana (Tel Aviv: Yedioth Ahronoth, 2004), pp. 168–83 (Hebrew). This double interpretation also clarifies the image of Lilith in the poem: on the one hand, the speaker struggles with her, as if he were wrestling with a certain facet of his psyche (the wild, subversive, and destructive side), while, on the other, as a poet, he has the power to overcome her and subjugate her to his will and needs. The Lilith in the poem can be seen as an expansion of the midrash cited by Kosman that casts Eve in a feminist light, and has her demanding total equality with Adam ("Woman as a 'Rib,'" p. 170).

which he analyzed the story *The Sand-man*.[31] Freud showed how it was possible to arouse the reader's horror, thereby resulting in confusion between a person and a doll (animate and inanimate). This confusion does not ensue from difficulty in seeing or understanding the reality, but from a psychological difficulty. Freud linked the reading experience which creates the fear of looking straight in the eyes of Olympia, to see if she is a doll or a human being, with the psychological distress that is identified, from a psychoanalytical perspective, as the "anxiety connected with the eyes and the fear of going blind," which is actually the dread of castration.[32] In Kosman's poem, the clash with Lilith is clearly reminiscent of features from Freud's discussion: the doubt as to whether Lilith is human or a figment of the imagination; the fear that is neither realistic nor rational, but inner, resulting from the fear of castration—the loss of the ability to write poetry; and the eroticism at which both contexts hint. Wittgenstein developed an additional direction that facilitates understanding the fashioning of Lilith in the poem as uncanny:

> But can't I imagine that people around me are automata, lack consciousness, even though they behave in the same way as usual?—If I imagine it now—alone in my room—I see people with fixed looks (as in a trance) going about their business—the idea is perhaps a little *uncanny*. But just try to hang on to this idea in the midst of your ordinary intercourse with others—in the street, say! Say to your self, for example: "The children over there are mere automata; all their liveliness is mere automatism." And you will either find these words becoming quite empty; or you will produce in yourself some kind of *uncanny* feeling, or something of the sort. Seeing a living human being as an automaton is analogous to seeing one figure as a limiting case or variant of another [. . .] It seems paradoxical to us that in a single report we should make such a medley, mixing physical states and states of consciousness up

31 Sigmund Freud, "The 'Uncanny,'" in *Standard Edition*, vol. 17, pp. 217–56.
32 Freud, "'Uncanny,'" p. 230.

> together [. . .] so why does it seem paradoxical to us? Because we want to say that the sentence is about both tangibles and intangibles.—But does it worry you if I say: "These three struts give the building stability?" Are three and stability tangible?—Regard the sentence as an instrument, and its sense as its employment.[33]

Wittgenstein, similar to Freud, describes "uncanny" as the paradoxical sense of the inability to distinguish between tangible and intangible and between the human and the mechanical-automatic. But unlike Freud, who offers a psychoanalytical explanation for this problematic, Wittgenstein remains true to his efforts to remove the bewitchment of language, and to remove the obstacles to its comprehension. Continuing his methodology of comparison and illustration, he gives us an example of a sentence which combines the concrete and the abstract, but does not arouse unease at the uncanny. When we state a number to measure or draw something, we do not feel unease for the abstract number joining a concrete object (a strut). It is in this way that we are also to view—naturally, and not paradoxically—our ability to see people as automata, specifically, and more generally, to join together a concrete and abstract perception of the same object. The sentence functions as an instrumental for our purposes, all of which it can meet. Returning to Kosman's poem, Lilith functions in both the Freudian and the Wittgensteinian senses. The speaker's struggle with Lilith definitely reflects anxiety over the inability to write, which is a type of fear of castration. This said, the dialogue with Lilith can also be seen, in the spirit of Wittgenstein, as a problem of extreme concentration on the inner struggle that prevents the speaker from seeing other minds, in the sense of criticism of his work that could be thought to be "Lilith." Since regarding people as automata or as dolls results from not understanding their separate functioning, the Lilith poem could be interpreted as the speaker distancing himself from the criticism from which he suffers by means

33 Wittgenstein, *Philosophical Investigations*, para. 420–21; emphasis added.

of grotesque fashioning that includes all the accusations under the heading of "Lilith."[34]

Alongside her "uncanny" aspect, another facet of Lilith is related to Jewish tradition: "Lilith" is a hapax legomenon in the Bible, appearing only in Isa. 34:14: "Wildcats shall meet hyenas, goat-demons shall greet each other; there too the lilith shall repose and find herself a resting place." The verse's context indicates that "lilith" is a general name for night-birds, but Rashi interprets this as being a she-demon.[35] The Bible commentator R. David Kimhi offers both possibilities; Lilith was an evil she-demon in ancient Babylonian mythology as well; and the *Metzudat Zion* commentary depicts Lilith as "the mother of the demons." The midrash presents two images of Lilith, as a dangerous demon and as a woman:

> My son, do not sleep at night in a house alone, for under such circumstances Lilith is ready to cause harm [BT Shabbat 151a], and when she seizes a person or a child, she takes them from the world.[36]

Or:

> When the Holy One, blessed be He, created Adam alone, He said, "It is not good for man to be alone" [Gen. 2:18], and he created a woman from the earth like him, and He called her Lilith. They immediately began to be jealous of one another. She said, "I will not lie below"; and he said, "I will not lie below, but above, for you are fitting to be below, and I, above." She replied, "Both of us are equal, for both of us are from the earth," but they did not heed one another. When Lilith saw

34 Stanley Cavell suggested a similar interpretation in his "The Uncanniness of the Ordinary," in *In Quest of the Ordinary: Lines of Skepticism and Romanticism* (Chicago: University of Chicago Press, 1988), pp. 153–80.

35 It is known that Rashi did not compose the commentary to Prophets and Writings, but I followed the common practice of attributing the commentary to him.

36 *Otsar Midrashim*, ed. Judah David Eisenstein (New York: J. D. Eisenstein, 1915), p. 27, s.v. "*Beni, al.*"

> this, she uttered the explicit Name [of God], and she flew through the air. Adam stood in prayer before his Maker, and he said, "Master of the Universe! The woman you gave me has fled from me." The Holy One, blessed be He, immediately dispatched three angels after her, to return her.[37]

Kosman's poem paints a multifaceted and colorful picture of Lilith: she is unpredictable, she acts both independently and in relation to the speaker, and is the object of his writing. Her disheveled hair, her blazing eyes, and her rising and falling chest openly hint at an actual sexual act—and immediately afterwards, the speaker relates to her as if she were a doll: he unravels threads and finds that her eyes are like two beads. Lilith is a metaphor for life itself. When the speaker unravels Lilith, everything comes apart. Lilith, like life, contains the illusion of domineering, wild, passionate behavior, but when someone holds her and examines what is in her, we discover a deep pit with a thousand and one bumps.

Lilith plays a multifaceted role in the poem: the source of artistic inspiration, the object of desire, an object to be understood (the speaker asks her questions, and tries to explore her functioning), and the source of the speaker's knowledge of himself. In order to understand this complexity, we must return to the midrash. The second midrash cited above can be read as portraying the relationship between Adam and Eve, including what is not written in the Bible. The creation of the woman here corresponds to the second narrative of the Creation, in which Adam was created alone, with Eve being created later (unlike the first version, which states [Gen. 1:27]: "male and female He created them"). This may be why it depicts a tense power struggle, which is expressed in an argument about the nature of the sexual act. Lilith seeks to apply the principle of equality, but Adam does not allow this, at which point she uses the Tetragrammaton in order to escape from him. Adam, who is sorry over her

---

37 *Otsar Midrashim*, p. 35, s.v. "*Ki-she-Bara ha-K[adosh] B[arukh] H[u].*"

absence, asks the One who enabled her flight to return her. God fulfills his request, but the tension remains.

The midrash is of interest, because it reveals an intriguing fact: Lilith's "demonic" nature is not objective. Objectively, she only wanted equality, while Adam had difficulty in fulfilling her request. There is nothing "demonic" in Lilith, since she has God help her to escape, and does not engage in any charms or sorcery. Adam's need for her leads us to think that she controls him, but, in actuality, this is Adam's need, and not sorcery or anything demonic.

This is also how Lilith acts on the speaker in the poem: he acknowledges that, objectively, she is no "demon"; in the final analysis, Lilith cannot give him the answer to his questions, neither regarding the ars poetica question, nor that regarding his own nature: is he a man, a demon, or a bird? The linguistic strata of the word "Lilith" and the midrash that portrays the relationship between Adam and Eve help to clarify the nature of the speaker's attitude to Lilith and explain the three possibilities regarding himself that he sets forth in the last lines of the poem. These lines strengthen the direction that Lilith is the sublimination of man's needs and desires: the speaker attempts to clarify his own nature by examining Lilith's image.

In conclusion, the poem demands that we relate to the grammatical aspect of the act of speaking. This is a vibrant and quick monologue that spins out of control, before ending in disappointment and a question mark. Unlike, however, the many rhetorical questions at the beginning of the poem, it seems that by the end, the speaker peels off the outer shells and gets to the real question: Who am I? At this juncture, we should make an important observation regarding ars poetica. The poem illustrates how writing about the creative process can be a way of revealing one's self, no less than uncovering the writing process itself. The speaker begins by addressing Lilith, but we learn that she is a fictional character, who is not even his muse, but rather reflects the essence of the world. The Lilith in Kosman's poem can be contrasted with the concept of *bat ha-shir* of other poets. *Bat ha-shir* (the daughter of the poem) generally means the muse—the inspiration for writing. Despite its being a metaphor, it is always treated as something sublime that is called in the hope that it will come, and as a source of enchantment.[38]

Kosman's poem overturns this convention. Not only do we have Lilith (the she-demon), and not only "the daughter of the poem" (a refined expression that represents innocence and purity); Lilith is not distant and unattainable—she is actually on the poet's table. She is not asked to aid in the speaker's writing, but rather to reveal to him the truth about himself: what characterizes him while he writes. Lilith does not help him. She bothers him, and leaves him disappointed by showing how she resembles life. This revelation, however, contains an important truth: the speaker reveals to the reader that Lilith is within himself, since he wonders whether he himself is a man, a ghost, or a bird. To sum up the ars poetica of the poem, we learn more about the role of writing poetry in the life of the speaker than we discover about the creative process. In the face of—more or less tangible—fears and threats, the speaker writes his poem, in a sort of inner constraint that forces him to express his self.

1.1. How to Do Things with Words: The Weekly Torah Portion

The diverse ars poetica expanse in Kosman's poetry ranges between personal language-games and refashionings of language-games from Jewish tradition. In the next poem, the speaker contemplates the process of writing while refashioning the weekly Torah portion so that it will reflect his personal experience ("my portion at this moment"). He seemingly informs the reader of a well-known language-game, because of the practice of connecting the weekly Torah reading with

38 See, e.g., "The Poem in Prison," by Joseph Zevi Rimon: "Fly away, muse / fly around in the sky! / I will take wing after you / I will draw from the depths of your beauty, and I will not look like a stranger / as I ascend to you / and upon my return to the soil of the earth" (in Kartun-Blum, *Poetry as Its Own Mirror*, p. 36); and, using a metaphor similar to "muse": "And the Poem That I Didn't Write," by Leah Goldberg: Come, descend to me, daughter of the gods, / nod your greying head / to me. // We shall play with words. // How lucid the world appears in this new game" (in Leah Goldberg, *Selected Poems*, trans. Robert Friend [London: Menard Press, 1976], p. 45).

current affairs. Actually, however, Kosman creates an ironic language-game that criticizes the tendency of the modern believer to accept the stories in the Torah literally, while ignoring the human dilemmas they contain and their current relevance for the believer. The speaker offers an alternative, and instead of accepting the events in the Torah's narratives as a sacred text (which can be interpreted, but not changed), he rewrites them, creating a relevant Torah portion for the present day:

The Weekly Torah Portion (Parashat ha-Shavua)
I'm writing my own portion at this moment.
Take a look. I swear upon my ancestors:
I'm not changing one dot, curlicue or letter, until
they pass over me, as aforementioned, onward, as follows,
studied, ibid,
that is to say, in other words, as will be made clear.

To all the rest of the interpretations,
enough! Why do you letters
stand there and stare! As if Jesus were mumbling the Sermon
on the Mount above!

Go away! Go back! Come on now! I'm not changing a thing!
Not even one serif!
I swear.
I swear to you on all that is dear to me:
not even one curlicue! Not one curlicue or serif!

I will lean
on the old fence,
until you cross it! You,
you will cross over! Alone!
The portion about Joseph's coat of many colors, and Dinah's
skirt,
the woman from Shunam, about cold and skin, Rachel's
blanket, and birth,

about the angry hordes at the window, (in Sodom),
and the donkey in the Binding of Isaac.[39]

Already in the opening of the poem, the speaker declares the precedence of his self in the constitution of his poetic grammar: "I'm writing my own portion." This means: the text of the weekly Torah portion is, first and foremost, the basis for self-creation and self-expression. In the second line we can identify the irony and humor typical of Kosman's poetry: seemingly innocent, while actually critical of the convention's exacting obsessiveness in sanctifying the biblical text, and thereby limiting (and at times not allowing) its interpretation for the here and now. The speaker employs the principle of irony and humor in a number of ways: in the speech act of a seemingly grammatical declaration in which he swears that he would not change even the punctuation marks; in a seeming dialogue with the portions themselves that come to life and make their own order; and finally, in a speech-act which is a sort of willing compromise in which he surrenders to them and allows them to pass as they wish, while he only looks on.

This picture in the poem illustrates the "autonomy of grammar" that Wittgenstein distinguishes from logical syntax: the rules of the latter enable us to understand the statement, and they are reflected in language. The grammar, in contrast, is independent, and can create countless rules and language-games that could be detached from the empirical reality (like games based on the imagination, science fiction, or poetry). The speaker in Kosman's poem personifies the weekly Torah portions in order to emphasize their independence in the face of any imposed interpretation. The text, after its creation, detaches itself from its creator and can give itself over to any interpretation and any reader. The weekly Torah portions function in complex fashion in the constitution of the speaker's self because, on the one hand, they are present in his consciousness as possessing independent content while, on the other, they invite him to rewrite them.

39 Kosman, *Perush Hadash b.s.d*, p. 22; trans. for the current book by Lisa Katz.

The connection to the biblical tradition includes both relation and the need for adaption to the speaker's dynamic self. Continuing in this vein, the poem ends with a concise summation of the titles of the portions that pass before the speaker. These brief titles, which take their name from their heroes, express his personal interpretation. He chooses certain elements in the portions, but gives no reason for this selection. There is a "family resemblance" between expressions such as "Dinah's skirt" and "Rachel's blanket" and other expressions that allude to events in the intimate human sphere, but this is not the main issue in the summarizing without explanation. The central move is the personal choice to focus on elements that are not necessarily publically cardinal or educational, but rather speak to the speaker. This criterion meets the poem's opening declaration: "I'm writing my own portion at this moment."

Along with his personal fashioning, the speaker conducts a seeming dialogue with the weekly Torah portions by addressing them in the second person. The intensive use of exclamation points, especially, but not exclusively, in the third stanza, generates somewhat of a sense of struggle that occurs in a stage play: in the semantic plane, use is made of the codes for various events from different Torah portions, and the portions' "opposition" to immediately accept the speaker's "invitation" to them reflects an inner struggle between his attempt to refashion them and their original content. The dialogical grammar therefore seems conversational, but actually is reflective.

The multitude of exclamation points and rhetorical questions makes us feel that something is happening in the present, under the pressure of time to rewrite the Torah portion as quickly as possible.[40] The sense of urgency in the poem does not result solely from the fashioning of first-person certainty. There are also two additional causes that express a position of belief.

The first cause is the speaker's viewing the Torah's content as living contents with a will of their own, which are not automatically

40 Present-tense writing, as was noted above, is, according to John Austin, one of the outstanding signs of first-person certainty, and obviously guided Wittgenstein's writing style, beginning with *Tractatus* and continuing through all his works.

subordinate to any specific interpretation. Joseph's coat of many colors, for example, cannot be described as an everyday, common outer garment, just as Rachel's hiding of the household idols is not merely a dramatic detail. The urgency that is due to the practice of the weekly reading of the portions blurs their human force, and mainly, the moral complexity present in the text, in favor of the routine of ritual. R. Eliezer already addressed this problematic, as he declared: "If one makes his prayer a fixed task, his prayer is not a supplication" (M Berakhot 4:4). Consequently, the grammatical fashioning of this urgency seemingly seeks to preserve the acuteness, and the dimension of supplication, of the biblical events, in all of which the heroes were in need of divine aid.

A second reason for the fashioning in the present, with grammar that creates a sense of urgency, is the transforming of past events into those that happen now: "The world is all that is the case."[41] The speaker does not survey the weekly Torah portions as a set of individual items in his memory, he rather offers an alternative to the concept of memory in Jewish tradition that is inherent in the Hebrew word for tradition: *masoret*, which means *mesirah*, transmission, of content from one generation to the next. The speaker takes the biblical portions and transforms them into actual events that occur in the present that he simply wants to happen, without enveloping them in interpretation. He speaks to the Torah portions themselves, and wants to be part of what happens in them, even if as a bystander he may not, in practice, intervene in them: "I will lean on the old fence, / until you cross it! You, / you will cross over! Alone!"

Ending the poem with the Binding of Isaac is obviously intentional: this traumatic event requires no interpretive addition; its very mention suffices. The attempts to interpret it, whether as the tenth test with which God tested Abraham, or as an actual sacrifice meant to atone in advance for Israel's future sins (so that we will be reminded of "the ashes of Isaac"),[42] lessen the force of the basic plot: a father is

41 Wittgenstein, *Tractatus*, para. 1.

42 Tractate Taanit states: "Why does everyone [else] put ashes on his head [on a fastday]? There is a difference of opinion regarding this, between R. Levi bar

asked to sacrifice his son. Kosman's poem ends with the request to remain at this point of the plot and to experience it itself, without any interpretive alleviation. The position of the believer that is fashioned here is that of one who directly contends, in an experiential and personal way, with the traditional text and internalizes its complexity, in human and faith terms, even when it arouses fear, doubt, or guilt.

1.2. When All the Words Are Finished—All Is Intoxicated from Clarity

Up to now we have explored the image of the critical and controversial believer, beginning with a description of the feelings of being cast out and terror, continuing with a portrayal of the clash between the destructive urge and the drive to create, to a humanistic interpretation of the weekly Torah portions that is critical of the sanctity that Jewish tradition automatically ascribes to them. In contrast with these experiences, the next poem exemplifies an individual belief that expresses a sense of certainty, albeit fragile, in the existence of the mystical in the world. I find this to be one of Kosman's most beautiful poems since, along with its enchanting poetical fashioning, it expresses the paradoxical complexity of belief in the existence of a mystical dimension. The paradox comes from certainty, on the one hand, and, on the other, the inability to verbally justify this. The speaker accordingly chooses to remain silent in the plane of rational justification (as Wittgenstein advises),[43] and, using poetical language, to make room for the emotional experience that can contain this complexity:

> *Psalm of the Day*
> *For the Third Day of the Week*
> Now all the words are finished, and there's a beginning,
> finally.
> Little by little and fast.

Hama and R. Hanina. One said, [This is to signify that] we are like ashes before You, and the other said, To remind us of the ashes of Isaac" (BT Taanit 16a).

43 "What we cannot speak about we must pass over in silence" (Wittgenstein, *Tractatus*, para. 7).

All the turrets are purified of evil thoughts. Of
coarseness, of pretentiousness.
Above the tops of the towers rises love. Most transparent and
with caution.
For who would wish on a third day like this to be broken?

Now all the words are finished, and there's a beginning,
finally.
Little by little and fast.
There is a God, and angels, the whole heavenly host. All is
intoxicated from clarity.
Above the tops of the towers rises love. Most transparent and
with caution.
For who would wish on a third day like this to be broken?[44]

The poem begins with a declaration of silence. The words being finished make possible a new beginning—in the first stanza, of the experience of love, and in the second, of the mystical experience. The creation of these two experiences is conditional on the purification of one's mind of "evil thoughts. Of coarseness, of pretentiousness," and the preparation of the soul for love. The repeated declaration at the beginning of each stanza that "Now all the words are finished," on the one hand, and, on the other, the verbalization of experiences that happen in the speaker's consciousness are paradoxical: doesn't the speaking that is finished include the poem itself? Wittgenstein portrayed a situation that might clarify this paradox:

> Silent, "inner" speech is not a half hidden phenomenon, seen, as it were, through a veil. It is not hidden *at all*, but the concept may easily confuse us, for it runs over a long stretch cheek by jowl with the concept of an "outer" process, and yet does not coincide with it [. . .] The close relationship between "inner speech" and "speech" comes out in that what was said inwardly

---

44 Kosman, *Perush Hadash b.s.d*, p. 10; trans. from Jacobson, *Creator, Are You Listening?*, p. 19.

can be communicated audibly, and that inner speech can *accompany* outer action.[45]

Wittgenstein distinguished between outer and inner processes, with inner speech included among the latter. Processes that can be identified externally are discernible by another person, for example, a person complaining about a visible injury (we will refer to this in the poem *Something Hurts*). Regarding an inner process, the question arises of how to relate to it, when only the person who experiences it "knows" of its existence and nature.[46]

Wittgenstein emphasizes the difference between the two types of process, even if they seem similar because both are based on verbalization. Inner speech could accompany an outer act, or it could happen detached from any visible process. Inner speech that is not outerly visible is an inner experience that can testify to seeing of a completely different sort. The speaker in the poem attests to a change within himself, although, externally, he is silent and he sees this change in a nonsensory, inner plane of his consciousness. What is the meaning of sight of this kind, and how does it change the speaker?

Wittgenstein proposed two uses for the word "see," that distinguish between sensory sight that can be justified and that in which change occurs, and that which occurs in the experiential plane.[47] There is a "categorial" difference between the two types of seeing, in each of which a different object is perceived. Seeing of the second type includes experience that Wittgenstein calls "the change of aspect."[48] Such seeing is seemingly paradoxical, since

45 Wittgenstein, *PPF*, para. 301–2.

46 An outstanding example of such an experience is the mystical experience described by William James that I included in our discussion of mystical grammar. I also included among the types of mystical grammar the grammatical usage that presents a personal experience that cannot be verbalized.

47 "Two uses of the word 'see.' The one: 'What do you see there?'—I see *this* (and then and then a description, a drawing, a copy). The other: 'I see a likeness in these two faces'—let the man to whom I tell this be seeing the faces as clearly as I do myself. What is important is the categorical difference between the two 'objects' of sight" (Wittgenstein, *PPF*, para. 111).

48 Wittgenstein, *PPF*, para. 129.

> The expression of a change of aspect is an expression of a *new* perception and, at the same time, an expression of an unchanged perception.[49]

In actuality, though, this is not paradoxical, rather, the autonomy of language also includes its ability to represent an experience of change. In such an experience, "one can *think* what is not the case."[50] That is, the truth value of the experience cannot be determined, since it is a subjective expression (as we mentioned in the introductory discussion of the mysticism of "I as subject").

The speaker in *Psalm of the Day* describes an experience of aspect change, in which the world suddenly appears completely different: all the power struggles and ego wars are shunted aside in favor of positive and productive emotions. Purification from evil thoughts and arrogance enables a person to see in the world the mystical, which appears in figurative language: "There is a God, and angels, the whole heavenly host. All is intoxicated from clarity." Such an experience of change is not caused by any outer factor, it rather results from Wittgensteinian silent inner speech. Such speech brings about change that allows one to view the world differently, so that the disparity between the speaker and the external world is not threatening and intimidating. On the contrary: it expresses the proper organization and proportion of man's place in the world. The speaker voices acceptance, along with mystical belief, which are the feelings suitable for (personal) prayer.

Kosman's choice of a fixed element of the Jewish liturgical tradition (*Psalm of the Day*) for the title of the poem is intriguing. What is the significance of this usage, when we consider that the speaker describes individual and personal change, and that the poem itself is detached from the format of Psalms on which *Psalm of the Day* is based? Kosman acts ambivalently here: on the one hand, the poem expresses a profound connection to the prayer rite, while, on the other, it is critical of the rite's contents and proposes alternatives. As in *The Weekly Torah Portion*, but more acutely, the speaker is troubled by the human flaw

49 Wittgenstein, *PPF*, para. 130.
50 Wittgenstein, *PPF*, para. 95.

revealed in the conventional liturgical practice. Highlighting the routine convention is what draws the attention of the reader, who is familiar with this convention, to the replacement of the routine content with that of inner experience, which enables individual connection to God.

How does the poem achieve this? The poem's title (and subtitle) place the reader in the language-game of prayer and/or the language-game of the recitation of the psalm of the day. The location of the psalm of the day, at the end of the *Shaharit* morning service, could be deemed to be a literary embellishment added to the prayer service, the permission to do so ensuing from the need to express a personal facet after the recitation of the fixed prayer formulation, which is mainly directed to public aims. If, however, we read these psalms, we see that most of their verses relate to the general and institutionalized, and not to the personal. Especially striking in this respect is Ps. 82, the psalm for Tuesday:

> God stands in the divine assembly; among the divine beings He pronounces judgment [. . .] They neither know nor understand, they go about in darkness; all the foundations of the earth totter [. . .] but you shall die as men do, fall like any prince. Arise, O God, judge the earth, for all the nations are Your possession.

A bit before the end of the prayer service, before the end of the words meant for man to open his heart before his Maker, specifically a psalm of this sort was selected to embellish the text of the prayers.[51]

Kosman's poem refashions the ritual of reciting a psalm, as it formulates a personal, reflective experience in which the fashioning of the "psalm" accords with the speaker's mood. Instead of the compulsory content of a chapter from Psalms that does not suit the speaker's attitude, a gradual act of consciousness is formulated, one that connects

51 The book of Psalms is replete with personal psalms that relate to the poet's intimate troubles, but for some reason these psalms were not incorporated in the traditional prayer service.

the speaker's mystical state of mind with the world. The fashioning of the personal consciousness in the familiar context of a religious ritual facilitates, in accordance with the way in which Guetti interpreted Wittgenstein, establishing "outward criteria" for the personal experience.[52] This fashioning within a familiar context highlights the speaker's independent voice and the original formulation of the certainty in the existence of a supernal world. The grammar constitutes an experience of "being in the world" that includes crisis and the need for mending, but also a certain degree of anticipation of Divine Providence. The possible mending is not exhibited in a direct act by God, but in a sort of harmony felt by the speaker when he is purified from expressions of pretentiousness and coarseness. The oxymoron of writing a poem while declaring that the words are finished leads us to feel that, along with the personal experience, the poem also functions as a "psalm" that can be recited by anyone who replaces Ps. 82 with his own personal formulation.

The turrets metaphor represents the pointed ends that every man possesses, and that give him an excuse for coarseness, pretentiousness, and evil thoughts. One person has a "turret" of wisdom, another of handsome outer appearance, a third social status, and a fourth economic standing. The uniform version of the prayer "purifies" all the turrets, and enables love to rise. Purification from the dross of the soul allows the reader to clearly see the two important elements in this poem: God (and with Him, the whole heavenly host) and love. These two can be seen only with a cleansed soul, which is necessary for a refined, clear, transparent, and cautious sight to rise. There is a reason for all this, which is raised as a question: "For who would wish on a third day like this to be broken?"

52 "A use of language for him is not a mere saying of words; it is an application of words to do something, application that is both purposive and consequential. This application takes place, furthermore, on public ground and may be recognized and measured by 'outward criteria.' To the extent that they are meaningful, our 'intentions' must be 'embedded' in 'situations.' [. . .] and 'obeying a rule' is not *thinking* that one is doing so but consists in the actual and particular application of the rule" (James L. Guetti, *Wittgenstein and the Grammar of Literary Experience* [Athens: University of Georgia Press, 1993], pp. 3–4).

The poem's problematic syntax is noteworthy. In its beginning, we do not know what "begins" (love appears only in the third line). The meaning of such a Tuesday is similarly unclear, and why being broken is the default. The problematic syntax suits the troubled nature of the psyche that contends with crisis and a world full of evil thoughts, coarseness, and pretentiousness. This is joined by the rhythm of the poem, which suits the slow, gradual, and intimate process of inward focusing that enables openness to the world above.

From a grammatical perspective, the poem is composed in the third person, which presumably could teach us that the mental process is general and not individual, but the poem's tone and intonation, along with its contents, paint a picture of inner exploration and personal intimacy. This is unlike the atmosphere of Ps. 82 and the other psalms recited as the "psalm of the day," with their major emphasis on victory, judgment, submission, war against the sinners and rebels, and the like. In the poem, each of its two stanzas opens and closes with the same line, which highlights the starting point and the goal: the starting point is the finishing of all the words—and now it is possible for important matters to begin to enter a person's consciousness. Such silence represents first-person certainty, and inner contemplation and mending occur in the individual, by himself, and not collectively.

The aim is to locate the divine reality within the soul, in a pure and loving atmosphere, in order to enable existence without being broken; not by means of existing patterns, not as a result of victory in battle and the surrender of the enemy, nor from self-submission. This existence will rather be infused with the confidence that results from self-cleansing. The wording "a third day like this" brings the reader down from the heights of the history in the book of Psalms to daily existence. Here and now, the question is asked: how to gather strength and continue to live? The poem's counsel is to do so by looking inward. The poem's language is based on grammar that constitutes the external world as a function of the inner one: the presentation of love as dominating the world, the corresponding fashioning of the divine world that is in harmony with the speaker's, and the use of the ritual format that expresses relation to Jewish tradition, all embody the ability to formulate both the expectation and its fulfillment, as Wittgenstein puts this:

> The limits of my language mean the limits of my world. [. . .] The world is my world: this is manifest in the fact that the limits of language (of that language which alone I understand) mean the limits of my world. The world and life are one. I am my world. (The microcosm.)[53]
>
> It is in language that an expectation and its fulfillment make contact.[54]

The fulfillment of the wishes that are embodied in language occurs over and over again in Kosman's poetry facing the other, in all manner of dialogues. In order to understand this dialogical pattern, we must add to Wittgenstein's methodology, which locates all types of dialogue in grammar, the perspective of Buber, who reestablished the concept of "dialogue" as the key to meaningful life.[55] Buber is the philosopher thought to have most profoundly influenced the perception of dialogue in twentieth-century thought, and his influence is felt in additional fields as well, such as literary scholarship (Mikhail Bakhtin), ethics (Emmanuel Levinas), and education (Haim Gordon).

For our purposes, Buber greatly influences Kosman's work, both directly and indirectly. His direct influence is evident in many of Kosman's articles, and is most conspicuous in the latter's introduction

53 Wittgenstein, *Tractatus*, para. 5.6, 5.62, 5.6211, 5.631.

54 Wittgenstein, *Philosophical Investigations*, para. 445.

55 While Wittgenstein's descriptions are methodical and reflect the manner in which dialogue is conducted, Buber's are substantive, and set forth criteria for judging the success or failure of the dialogue. Buber proposed a judgmental division, into three dialogue types: "I know three kinds. There is *genuine dialogue* [. . .] whether spoken or silent—where each of the participants really has in mind the other or others in their present and particular being and turns to them with the intention of establishing a living mutual relation between himself and them. There is *technical dialogue*, which is prompted solely by the need of objective understanding. And there is *monologue* disguised as dialogue, in which two or more men, meeting in space, speak each with himself in strangely tortuous and circuitous ways" (Buber, *Between Man and Man*, p. 22; emphasis added).

to Buber's thought at the end of the Hebrew translation of *I and Thou*.[56] Indirectly, the inspiration that Kosman drew from Buber is present in his poetry, especially beginning with *A New Commentary, with God's Help* (2000). The place of language, however, in Buber's concept of dialogue is surprisingly absent from Kosman's theoretical discussions of *I and Thou*. Kosman concentrates on the practical ethical ramifications of Buber's conception, and almost totally disregards the positive consequences of Buber's notion for the positive functions of language.[57]

To complete the picture, and to understand how Buberian dialogical elements, in the Buberian sense, function alongside those as Wittgenstein understood them, these two thinkers shared a common starting point that presents language as a sphere-in-between in which dialogue takes place. The following passage by Buber on "The Word That Is Spoken" resembles what Wittgenstein wrote on expectation and fulfillment in language:

> Unlike all other living beings, man stands over against a world from which he has been set at a distance, and [. . .] he can again and again enter into relationship with it. This fundamental double stance nowhere manifests itself so comprehensively as in language. Man—he alone—speaks, for only he can address the other just as the other being standing at a distance over against him. [. . .] The coming-to-be of language also means a new

56 Admiel Kosman, "Introduction to Buber's Thought," in Martin Buber *Ani ve-Atah* (Hebrew trans. of *I and Thou*; Jerusalem: Bialik Institute, 2013), pp. 160–219.

57 In his "Introduction to Buber's Thought," Kosman relates twice to the role of language, once negatively, and once obliquely: the first time, he cites Lacan and Wittgenstein concerning the ability to confuse and mask the truth by means of language (Kosman, "Introduction," p. 171). This usage, however, does a threefold injustice: to the important place of language in dialogue, according to Buber, and even more so regarding the central place of language for Lacan and Wittgenstein. The second time, Kosman, in the name of Lorenz Wachinger, raises the following argument: "Buber's interest in psychotherapy demonstrates his sensitivity to the dynamic aspect of language, which can be understood only from this aspect" (Kosman, "Introduction," p. 173). Wachinger, like Kosman who cites him, however, does not expand on this (the passage by Wachinger appears in: *Martin Buber: A Centenary Volume*, ed. Jochanan Bloch, Haim Gordon, and Menahem Dorfman [Tel Aviv: Hakibbutz Hameuchad, 1981], p. 75 [Hebrew]).

> function of distance. For even the earliest speaking does not, like a cry or a signal, have its end in itself; it sets the word outside itself in being, and the word continues, it has continuance.[58]

Buber shares with Wittgenstein the conception of the dialogical character of language, but his viewpoint is humanistic. Buber emphasizes the essentiality of language for realizing the two types of man's attitude to the world: distance and relation. This distinction is crucial for understanding the differences between the types of dialogue in Kosman's poetry.

2. Dialogical Grammar: Self-Constitution as Conversational Process

Kosman's poetry is clearly dialogical, in every sense of dialogical grammar. The dialogical singularity of his poetry is arresting in his refashioning of formats from Jewish tradition that show the deep roots of Kosman's Jewish erudition and the sources of his identity, along with his criticism and personal, creative interpretation of the Jewish texts. This dialogical nature clearly embodies Buber's statement (that we mentioned in the chapter on the poetry of Zelda, above): "In the beginning is relation."[59]

Unlike, however, Zelda's poetry, in which dialogue is primarily inner, Kosman's poetry usually relates to an other who—at least for the sake of appearances—is external. At this juncture we will continue the discussion of Buberian influence that we began in our analysis of Zelda, to which we will add Buber's distinction between I-Thou and I-it relations:

> To man the world is twofold, in accordance with his twofold attitude [. . .] in accordance with the twofold nature of the primary words which he speaks. The primary words are not isolated but combined words. The one primary word is the

58 Buber, "The Word That Is Spoken," pp. 117–18.
59 Buber, *I and Thou*, p. 18.

> combination I-Thou. The other primary word is the combination I-it [. . .] Primary words do not signify things, but they intimate relations. Primary words do not describe something that might exist independently of them, but being spoken they bring about existence [. . .] There is no I taken in itself, but only the I of the primary word I-Thou or I-it.[60]

Buber describes man as relating to the world in one of two ways, by means of two primary words. This relation can be to another person, to the world, or to the mystical reality (as was described in detail in the chapter on Zelda, above). In Kosman's poetry, one of the main sources of tension in the self-constitutive process is the changing attitude to the various manifestations of the other. Whether the other is embodied in a text, in a prevalent belief, or in a real person, the speaker in Kosman's poems argues with, contradicts, and is pained by variations of distance, or, in Buber's terminology, the other being "it," and not "Thou."[61] Buber's conception that the relation to the other is a primal component of a person's self-constitution adds to Wittgensteinian dialogism a substantive critical component, since dialogue by itself is insufficient, and is liable to be pointless.[62] This statement resounded with many thinkers who were influenced by Buber and who placed the concept of "dialogue" at the center of their thought, such as Mikhail Bakhtin and Emmanuel Levinas. Along with the dialogical methodology explained by Wittgenstein, which contributes to the development of perfectionism, Buber and his successors developed dialogical ethics in the interpersonal sphere.

The literary critic Mikhail Bakhtin finely described in his book *Dialogic Imagination* inner-textual hybrid dialogue that preserves different viewpoints and does not translate one into another.[63] Such

---

60 Buber, *I and Thou*, p. 3.

61 Buber, *I and Thou*, pp. 4–5.

62 See Buber's listing and assessment of the types of dialogue, above.

63 "Every type of intentional stylistic hybrid is more or less dialogized. This means that the languages that are crossed in it relate to each other as do rejoinders in a dialogue; there is an argument between languages, an argument between styles of language. But it is not a dialogue in the narrative sense, nor in the abstract sense;

dialogism enables movement and social change, because it shows how different perspectives cannot be united into a general consensus, and that transformativeness is to be facilitated, to present possible voices. The more polyphonic a work, the better it is, and this is a central criterion for evaluating its literary quality.

In the next poem, the speaker is critical of the convention that the halakhah focuses on the details of the technical plane of observance of the commandments but neglects the human plane. His criticism of the halakhic canon is fashioned in Bakhtinian fashion, with the speaker conducting an alternative dialogue with the canonic code of Jewish law, the *Shulkhan Arukh*, which was composed by R. Joseph Karo in the sixteenth century in Safed:

Three New Sections for the Shulkhan Arukh
Section 1
You haven't fulfilled your obligation to the law of combs,
of hair, the law of leniency and severity,
the law of annulment,
the new law, the law of straw, of stubble,
and the prohibition on steam from a hot pot, and the cauldron
of lust.
Because nothing genuine has ever come of you.

Section 2
And the prohibition on boiling, and bathing, a hair in the
mouth or hand,
the law of confusion, of Samaritan, Arab and Gentile
and a waif, a blind person, an albino, a dwarf.
The law of spit-in-the-heart, of longing, the law of semen in
a pocket.

rather it is a dialogue between points of view, each with its own concrete language that cannot be translated into the other" (Mikhail Bakhtin, "From the Prehistory of Novelistic Discourse," in *The Dialogic Imagination*, ed. Michael Holquist, trans. Caryl Emerson and Michael Holquist [Austin: University of Texas Press, 1981], pp. 39–40).

Section 3
Who are you fooling? Go, Mr. Good for Nothing, you've got a nerve—
you finish with one hand—and collect with the other!
You spill everything out,
the law of leniency, the law of severity—the bastard skin in which you developed,
the law of recalcitrance, of rebellion, the law of the look of disgust.
The law of the cauldron. And of bad taste.
You haven't gotten past being a man alone.[64]

The poem attempts to arouse awareness that will lead to social change, as Bakhtin proposed, by a meeting of the halakhic discourse with the modern humanistic consciousness of the speaker. The poem fashions a controversial dialogue in which an argument is conducted with the halakhic order of priorities, which shunts aside the emotional and existential aspect of man's soul. The speaker rewrites sections in the *Shulkhan Arukh* in a way that highlights the corrupted order of priorities, listing halakhic issues one after the other, showing halakhic exactingness to be ridiculous and, mainly, ethically problematic, in the Buberian sense of mismeeting.

The word "section" functions in the poem as a dialogic word (that converses with the "sections" of the *Shulhan Arukh*), in the manner explained by Bakhtin.[65] The sections in the poem, on the one hand, generate the expectation of a halakhic discussion, while, on the other,

64 Kosman, *Perush Hadash b.s.d*, p. 55; trans. for the current book by Lisa Katz.

65 "The word is born in a dialogue as a living rejoinder within it; the word is shaped in dialogic interaction with an alien word that is already in the object. A word forms a concept of its own in a dialogic way. But this does not exhaust the internal dialogism of the word. It encounters an alien word not only in the object itself: every word is directed toward an answer and cannot escape the profound influence of the answering word that it anticipates" (Bakhtin, *Dialogic Imagination*, p. 103). *Se'if* (the Hebrew word translated as "section") is the usual term used to denote sections in halakhic treatises.

they are refashioned so that the prohibitions they contain appear ridiculous and unnecessary. At the same time, however, the poem preserves the original starting point of division into "sections." This term functions concurrently as religious connotation, an organizing principle in the poem, and a means of expressing criticism of the halakhic disregard of the central problem that troubles modern man: loneliness. The dialogism of "section" is presented in opposition to the desired dialogism between the speaker and the halakhah since, instead of assuaging his loneliness, it intensifies it. The question arises now: why does the speaker nevertheless insist on engaging in the halakhic language-game? What roles does the halakhic context play in the self-constitution in this and other poems in which language-games from Jewish tradition are at work? This tradition functions as the "it" that the speaker wants to turn into "Thou"; at any rate, it is one of the interlocutors of the Kosmanic dialogue, and perhaps the chief among them.

As we apply Wittgensteinian dialogue, we should examine the role of the interlocutor in the process of the speaker's self-constitution. The interlocutor, as Wittgenstein puts it, is the partner to the conversation whose reality, from the outset, directs the language-game to take him into consideration.[66] At times the interlocutor reflects inner "otherness" in the psyche of the writer, as can be seen in this poem: one voice fashions the text in the pattern of a halakhic book, while another asks existential questions about selfhood and loneliness. The movement between the close bond to the tradition of the past and the authentic need to relieve loneliness builds tension that at times upsets continuity and order, even though, at first glance, the poem seems to be quite ordered. The book *Philosophical Investigations*, likewise, is seemingly divided into sections, but it is very difficult to follow the course of the book. This is because we actually have a consecutive series of dialogues:

66 "Whether the word 'number' is necessary in an ostensive definition of 'two' depends on whether without this word the other person takes the definition otherwise than I wish. And that will depend on the circumstances under which it is given, and on the person I give it to" (Wittgenstein, *Philosophical Investigations*, para. 29).

each time, there is a new subject for discussion which develops in unexpected directions. The dialogues are not subject to any predetermined logic, and Wittgenstein expressed his acceptance of his inability to control the course of the book, as he stated, in two separate passages: "A multitude of familiar paths lead off from these words in all directions."[67]

This means that at times dialogism is liable to lead to innumerable quandaries and dead ends. Such an experience is fashioned in Kosman's poem *Note in the Western Wall.* The Western Wall symbolizes the period in which direct dialogue with God was possible, a remnant of which is the practice of putting a note in the Western Wall. This is a language-game that is incorporated in many forms of life. Religious and nonreligious Jews, and even non-Jews, "play the game" of a note in the Western Wall, on various levels of faith and hope regarding the effectiveness of this sort of request. The expression "a note in the Western Wall" represents a speech-act in a language-game in Jewish culture that includes the actual act of writing a note and placing it among the stones in the Wall, along with a ritual expression of the hope for dialogue with God:

> *Note in the Western Wall*
> That's how we are, doubtful.
> The sun doesn't want to set
> nor the dawn to rise. We will believe in you
> in the morning.
>
> Look, please, it's
> not a signed contract. There's no

67 Wittgenstein, *Philosophical Investigations*, para. 525, 534. In the introduction to this work, Wittgenstein voices his frustration and acceptance of his inability to unite the work, which accordingly appears as an "album": "After several unsuccessful attempts to weld my results together into such a whole, I realized that I should never succeed. The best that I could write would never be more than philosophical remarks; my thoughts soon grew feeble if I tried to force them along a single track against their natural inclination. [. . .] So this book is really just an album" (*Philosophical Investigations*, pp. 3–4).

alternative, that's how we are, the top part of the form
is blank. What do You want?
Everything is falling out, falling apart. Even the part that's sleeping
is falling. Like rotten teeth. And we haven't done anything.

We almost dropped, while galloping,
the rubber band holding
the strong reins of courage.
That's where we're at.
Not moving. Like the Pharaoh.
On horses in the water. A wall of water.

No choice. But You saw. The bottom of the note.
Didn't You write it in the Torah, from heaven,
White on black. You wrote it down. It's written
In your verses.

But suddenly You asked
for a hundred signatures! As if we could! What's with You!
Isn't this enough?!
Listen, listen, it's confusing. You had all the sons,
all the names, on the note in the wall. You could have
peeked!! That's how we are,
God, listen.
Lay off for a minute about the one angel, the intermediary.
Where would we get one, listen,
please listen to this, listen good. Lay off for a minute
about rights. Fathers. Where would we get them?

Come on down here for a minute.
Almost everything is cockeyed
in hell, ten degrees off,
and your wall is being bombed.

Hold on tight. Listen,
listen to me please.
For everything is going to fall.[68]

The speaker turns the common language-game of request by placing a note in the Western Wall into a controversial dialogue with God. While man usually initiates the request with a note, in the poem the speaker is forced to write the note in response to the divine demand of the speaker, as part of the people from whom God makes all kind of demands. Already in the beginning of the poem, the speaker gives voice to his doubts regarding God's promise. There are several possibilities in this context, which the poem does not list: the promise of the Land, the promise of continuity of the Jewish people, and more. The metaphor of the form that has to be signed produces the feeling of mechanical relations that lack emotion or closeness: the relationship between God and His faithful is not one of love, belief, and hope; it rather is technical and formal, with suspicion, doubt, fear, and above all—the feeling of loneliness and the believer's being thrown before his God.

Kosman heaps up the demands, casts in a ridiculous light this demanding by God, who requires of man one hundred signatures (without which his petition will not be granted), the interceding angel, and, so it seems, a list of merits. Connotation is at work here, along with irony: the wording "intermediary [or: advocate] angel [or: representative]," that appears only a single time in the Bible, hints at the context of man's day of judgment before his death. This wording comes from Job 33:23: "If he has a representative, one advocate against a thousand," meaning: of a thousand angels who prosecute, only one defends the man. The Rabbis interpret this phrase in the same manner in Tractate Shabbat.[69]

68 Kosman, *Approaching You in English*, pp. 103–5.

69 "Our masters taught: If a person falls sick and his life is in danger, he is told: Make confession, for all who are put to death make confession. When a man goes out into the street, let him imagine that he is given in charge of an officer [to be brought to trial]. If he has a headache, let him imagine that he is put in chains. If he took [literally, went up] to bed [due to illness], let him imagine that he ascended the scaffold for punishment, for whoever ascends the scaffold for punishment, if he has

The original language-game in Job can be seen as infusing the poem with Job's skeptical and pained spirit. Job has difficulty in understanding his fate, and he refuses to submissively accept it. Additionally, he changes the rules of the game in how he speaks of God. Instead of breast-beating for sin and repenting, as we would have expected from the way of life and language-game embodied in the language of his friends, Job chooses to change the rules and protest against the injustice done to him, and mainly against God's silence.

The speaker in the poem, too, protests the lack of true dialogue. Although at the end of the poem the speaker asks God to hear him, no basis is laid for any hope of God's attentiveness and succor throughout the course of the poem. The speaker's fundamental state of consciousness is one of indecision and doubts, with the world threatening to come apart, in the most tangible fashion.

In summation, the constant tension in *Note in the Western Wall* (as in many additional poems by Kosman, including the next poem, *Even If You Define Me*) results from the different linguistic levels in the poem. On the one hand, the speaker uses outspoken and biting language, while, on the other, words from the prayers or rite are gentler and more sublime. Such tension between the language levels and between the various language-games creates a meaningful dialogue, first and foremost in the soul of the speaker, between Jewish tradition and a modern critical stance.

This dialogism in the speaker's soul also constitutes the first aspect of the mystical grammar formulated by Wittgenstein, influenced by James: a grammar of a unique conception of God that, at times, is based on paradoxes and tensions. Kosman refashions the conception of God on which the ritual of a note at the Western Wall is founded, and it is noteworthy that he presents this refashioning in the first-person plural, and not as a private and idiosyncratic position. The renewed

great advocates, he is saved; but if not, he is not saved. These are a person's advocates: repentance and good deeds. Even if nine hundred and ninety-nine argue for his guilt, if one argues in his favor, he is saved, as it is said [Job 33:23]: 'If he has an angel, one advocate against a thousand to declare the man's uprightness, then He has mercy on him and decrees, "Redeem him from descending to the Pit"'" (BT Shabbat 32a).

ritual is firmly grounded in threefold skepticism: regarding the belief that God really "hears prayer," to use the wording of the *Amidah* prayer; regarding the nature of the "agreement" between God and His faithful; and concerning the ability of both sides to honor the agreement. Hovering above all these doubts is the sense of impending catastrophe that corresponds with the terror in Kosman's first book of poetry that we noted above. The poem's abundance of humor and irony does not camouflage the anxiety and apprehension; they only make them accessible to the reader to facilitate his identification with them. Along with these two characteristics, the poem's most dominant feature is the everyday, dialogical grammar that seemingly puts God and the speaker in confrontation with one another, but actually perpetuates the distance between them and maintains the Otherness of the Other, as Levinas suggested:

> The Other is not other with a relative alterity. [. . .] The alterity of the Other does not depend on any quality that would distinguish him from me. [. . .] Absolute difference, inconceivable in terms of formal logic, is established only by language. Language accomplishes a relation between terms that breaks up the unity of a genus. The terms, the interlocutors, absolve themselves from the relation, or remain absolute within relationship. [. . .] The incomprehensible nature of the presence of the Other [. . .] is not to be described negatively. Better than comprehension, *discourse* relates with what remains essentially transcendent. [. . .] Language is a relation between separated terms. To the one the other can indeed present himself as a theme, but his presence is not reabsorbed in his status as a theme.[70]

While language, for Levinas, enables the realization of dialogue, despite the forcefulness and separateness that discourse maintains, Kosman's

70 Emmanuel Levinas, *Totality and Infinity: An Essay on Exteriority*, trans. Alphonso Lingis (Pittsburgh: Duquesne University Press, 1969), pp. 194–95.

poetical language is critical of such forcefulness and separateness. The feelings of foreignness and alienation are highlighted by the excessive use of punctuation marks, which evokes a sense of speed, of being drawn along, which in turn seemingly augurs a future loss of control. In Wittgenstein's words, the hinges that constitute mythology are examined and deconstructed: the hinges of belief, like the existence of an attentive God, trust in the covenant between God and His people, the knowledge of each side's part in the agreement—all are called into question. Each hinge is formulated in doubtful language that undermines it, so that in the end of the poem it seems that the final dissolution is merely a question of time. Wittgenstein nonetheless stressed that in order to cast doubt and raise question marks, hinges are needed on which to base these.[71] The wording "note in the Western Wall" functions as such a hinge: a dialogical term that represents the need to turn to a supreme being, even if such an attempt might fail in the end. The grammar in the poem evokes the sense of a "living conversation," in Bakhtin's words, in an atmosphere that demands an answer.[72]

The following poem, *Even If You Define Me*, is a major milestone in Kosman's poetry for the purposes of our discussion of self-constitution in his poetical language, especially in light of Wittgenstein's conception of personal belief:

> Even if You define me, I will be with You.
> In failure I will be with You, in cessation and in shame. And also
> in victory. I will be with You. Together we will hear the voices.

71 "The *questions* that we raise **and** our *doubts* depend on the fact that some propositions are exempt from doubt, are as it were like hinges on which those turn" (Wittgenstein, *On Certainty*, para. 341).

72 "The word in living conversation is directly, blatantly, oriented toward a future answer-word: it provokes an answer, anticipates it, and structures itself in the answer's direction. Forming itself in an atmosphere of the already spoken, the word is at the same time determined by that which has not yet been said but which is needed and in fact anticipated by the answering word. Such is the situation in any living dialogue" (Bakhtin, *Dialogic Imagination*, p. 104).

Even if you define me, I will be with you. My God, my God, in assemblies,[73] and I will not
depart from You, forever. Even if You define me,
so imprisoned, within a closed form, against my will and forcing me, I will be
with You, Lord of Hosts. I will be with You, Shaddai, my Rock, God is One,
I will be with You in time of trouble.

I will be with You, close, close and befriended, to overlook me, to stand me
up, to stick it to me, to place beside You,[74] even if You will remove me, my God, like
a thin shell, to You I will stick, to You I will scream, to You I will call,
even if You will run, You will shout, You will strike a blow.

Define me, so abstract, naked, like pure being,
like endless being, so smooth and youngish, without dimension.
Leave me, alone, on the beach, in my sorrow. Giant, mighty, and the blueness of Your heaven is like
it punched you in the gut. (So naked, without clothes). To unravel, to open,
to release (and again naked, alone, without clothes), for a moment, by God!
For a moment, just for a minute, just for a minute! Define! By God! Define!

Define! Define, please! For a moment, for a minute, define
me, Mighty, in cessation, and in shame, in a whisper, in a shout,
My Light, my Salvation, the Rock, the Sky, the Air,

---

73 See Ps. 68:27.

74 The expression *le-hahbirah* is taken from the liturgical hymn *Adon Alom*: "He is One, there is no other to compare to Him, to place beside Him [*le-hahbirah*]." The hidden part of the line "He is One" refers back to "God is One" in the first stanza.

and the blueness-of-the-punch-in-the-gut!
My God! My God! Humpty-Dumpty all fake![75]

The poem fashions the paradoxical move of a request to be defined by God, which expresses the desire to be a separate self, on the one hand, and, on the other, the wish to be with God, in an experience of unity. The speaker sketches an idiosyncratic mental picture, which he illustrates by listing a plethora of mental states, some contradictory, such as failure and victory, or whispering and shouting. The poetical picture that is gained is of stormy emotions and includes the speaker's body and soul, a torrent of passion and deep desire for connection and for the dialogical realization of the faith aspect of the speaker's self. The reader realizes the speaker's desperate need, even if it is fashioned in an ironical and bitter way, for God to personally relate to him.

The longing to be defined by God is actually a wish to clarify his primal, original identity, even before the gender, sexual, and cultural fashioning (clothes), and the physical ("without dimension"). The speaker wants to return to his initial point of connection with God, before the separation and the fashioning of his personal features, in order to go back and define himself anew.

This unattained desire for primal unity with the Creator is reminiscent of Winnicott's discussion of the mother-infant dyad, on the one hand, and, on the other, the frustrating need for separateness in order to achieve self-definition.[76] Winnicott emphasized the infant's illusion, since the mother meets his needs and thereby causes him to feel that he can create the reality. Kosman's poem reveals similar omnipotence: the

---

75 Kosman, *Perush Hadash b.s.d*, p. 15; trans. Edward Levin.

76 "The mother's adaption to the infant's needs, when good enough, gives the infant the illusion that there is an external reality that corresponds to the infant's own capacity to create. In other words, there is an overlap between what the mother supplies and what the child might conceive of. To the observer, the child perceives what the mother actually presents, but this is not the whole truth. The infant perceives the breast only in so far as a breast could be created just there and then. There is no interchange between the mother and the infant. Psychologically the infant takes from a breast that is part of the infant, and the mother gives milk to an infant that is part of herself" (Donald W. Winnicott, *Playing and Reality* [New York: Routledge, 2006], p. 16).

speaker-poet presumably addresses God, but his words actually reveal a rich diversity of self-expressions that he formulates on his own. Dialogue with God is, in actuality, a monologue (according to Buber) or a reflective dialogue (according to Wittgenstein). Such a monologue eliminates any possibility of God's existence in the prevalent Jewish theological sense, which is based on an abstract God who is beyond the world. Buber, followed by Kosman in the above poem and in many others, formulated the position that God is revealed in the world in events that signal us to use the I-Thou relationship.[77] The request for definition by God is accompanied by the speaker's numerous "suggestions" to God, to be expressed in various aspects of his actual life. Since his request is frustrated, he throws it in God's face: You don't really exist!

This complexity is fashioned in grammar that acts intensively on the reader, with a multitude of punctuation marks and dialogical language that evoke a sense that this is happening during the reading of the poem. The poem contains three speech-acts of self-definition that happens while addressing God. The first two stanzas begin with an adverb clause of concession: "Even if you define me" (three times). The speaker says that even if God will set the boundaries of his self-definition, his feeling "close and befriended" to God will not be harmed. The abstract meaning of the Hebrew root *gimel-dalet-resh* ("define," in the poem) is to denote characteristics, while its concrete meaning is that of setting a boundary. The speaker makes a request that has a dimension of being a know-it-all: he "promises" God that even if He will set a clear boundary between Himself and man, His power for man will not be harmed. This pushing of the boundaries tests the nature of the connection, or lack thereof, between God and man. The speaker ranges between a sense of exteriorized and highlighted closeness and frustration at the sense of distance that drives the poem.

77 In "Introduction to Buber's Thought," Kosman cites Walter Kaufmann on the nature of belief for Buber: "He [Buber] wanted a religion in which the individual could call to God and be called by Him, but religion does not leave room for speech about God" (p. 201). He then quotes Buber himself, in a passage that presents the conception of belief in God's immanence in the world (p. 201). Kosman's poem sets forth precisely this demand: to call God, and to be called by Him.

The wording "Even if [*gam im*]" could be read as a contrast to the conditional clauses in Ps. 27:3: "Should [*im*] an army besiege me, my heart would have no fear; should [*im*] war beset me, still would I be confident." In the psalm, man's trust in God is absolute, and will endure even in times of extreme distress (that is caused by a human factor). In Kosman's poem, the distress is caused by the distance from God, and confidence ensues from his familiarity with the realm of the human. Not only does God not help man, He even intensifies the latter's distress, due to the contrast between man's great need of closeness to Him and the void that man encounters when he seeks God. The speaker maneuvers, over and over, between closeness and distance.

The sense of closeness is intensified by the repetition of the wording "I will be with You" seven times, while listing the various names of God (which, according to Jewish tradition, represent different divine aspects): Lord of Hosts, Shaddai, my Rock, the one God. The threefold use of the first person ("I will be"), which refers to man (while in the original language-game in the Torah, God, in response to Moses' question, calls Himself: "I Will Be What I Will Be" [Exod. 3:14]), emphasizes that the heart of the poem consists of the first-person self-experience. Additionally, the wording "I will be with You" is an expression of God's promise to Moses: He supports and protects man. Now everything is reversed: the poet—man—promises God that "I will be with You." God's name becomes man's name.

The three stanzas are replete with verbs in the first person ("I will be," "I will stick," "I will scream," "I will call") and in the second person ("You define," "You will run," "You will strike a blow"), as well as infinitives ("to overlook me," "to stand me up," "to stick it to me," "to place beside"). The plethora of verbs highlights the fierce and emotional desire for communication in erotic situations. This focus in the poem intensifies and deepens the erotic fashioning of the relationship between God and the people of Israel that began in the Bible (Hosea 1), continued in the Mishnah with R. Akiva's interpretation of the Song of Songs (M Yadaim 3:5), and is most explicit in the *Zohar*. Despite, however, the prior background of language-games in Jewish tradition that cast the relationship between God and His people in an erotic light, I wish to argue that the poem embodies a different causality. The speaker's return to a primal physical and sexual point reflects the desire to return to a state of infancy, in which, on the one hand, the infant is united with his mother, and, on the other, she is the key to his definition. This relationship includes both an erotic element and a wealth of contradictory emotions, as portrayed in the poem.

This causality was explained by the psychoanalyst Melanie Klein, who composed her research works while treating and observing infants and small children (up to the age of five), unlike Freud, who related to, and treated, only older children. Klein discovered that infants already could feel destructive toward and hatred for the mother, who represents the world. These feelings are the default for the infant, and for family relationships in general, in contrast with tranquility and harmony, which are acquired, but are not present from the outset.[78] The sexual-erotic aspect is another feature indicated by Klein that is clearly evident in the poem. Klein interpreted the Oedipus complex differently from Freud, and argued that the infant's conduct, even before the development of jealousy of the father and desire for the mother, has erotic aspects.[79] This is because the infant's Oedipus complex begins when he nurses, when he holds onto the breast that nourishes him and withholds satisfaction as, alternatively, the good or bad breast.[80]

The transitions between different and contradictory dispositions evince the need for dialogic belief that also entails the recurring disappointment with this belief, to the extent of wishing to destroy it, and thereby be rid of it. Grammatically, this is expressed in the transition from a speech-act of stipulation to an act of request, and finally, to one of command. This transition demonstrates the frustrated need for self-definition, which ends in the blunt and harsh conclusion: "My God! My God! Humpty-Dumpty all fake!" The speaker draws the conclusion that the conception of God as defining man, one who is in dialogue with him, and as an entity with whom one can feel closeness,

78 Melanie Klein, "The Oedipus Complex in the Light of Early Anxieties," in *Contributions to Psychoanalysis 1921–1945* (London: Hogarth, 1948), p. 347.

79 Klein, "Oedipus Complex," p. 353.

80 Melanie Klein, "The Early Development of Conscience in the Child," in *Contributions to Psychoanalysis 1921–1945*, pp. 273–74.

is just a fake—a Wizard of Oz. The poem does not clarify just who created this fakery; perhaps the speaker himself, or a speaker who acts in accordance with a fake social dictate.

Two main language-games are at work in the poem: the language-game of prayer, and that of the speaker's unique language.[81] The speaker uses words from the prayerbook, which he incorporates in an original and personal language-game that retains their original meaning even as their meaning changes. For instance, the choice of the infinite "to place beside [Him]," which is taken from the *piyyut* (liturgical hymn) *Adon Olam* that is attributed to R. Simeon ben Gamaliel and that is recited before the *Shaharit* morning service.[82] While, however, the meaning of the hymn is that no human being can be compared to God, nor can anyone be "placed beside" Him (*le-hahbirah*, from *haverut*, friendship), the speaker in the poem emphasizes the exact opposite: he keeps promising closeness and friendship, which are diametrically opposed to the context of the hymn, which stresses God's lordship and His distance from man (thus leading the disciples of the Vilna Gaon to determine that the day should be begun with it, in total acceptance of God's lordship).[83] Thus the word functions dialogically (as described by Bakhtin), and in hybrid fashion preserves two different meanings.

81 Wittgenstein includes prayer among a range of possible language-games in *Philosophical Investigations*: "There are *countless* kinds; countless different kinds of use of all the things we call 'signs,' 'words,' 'sentences.' And this diversity is not something fixed, given once for all; but new types of language, new language-games [. . .] come into existence, and others become obsolete and get forgotten. [. . .] Consider the variety of language-games in the following examples, and in others: [. . .] Reporting an event [. . .] Acting in a play [. . .] Requesting, thanking, cursing, greeting, praying" (Wittgenstein, *Philosophical Investigations*, para. 23).

82 The *piyyut* is attributed to R. Simeon ben Gamaliel in several places. For example: the prayerbooks *Siddur Klal Yisrael*, ed. Joel Rappel and Yohanan Freid (Tel Aviv: Masora la-Am, 1991), p. 23; and *Hasiddur Hameforash Hashalem* (The Complete Prayerbook with Explanations), ed. Yaakov Weingarten (Jerusalem: Gefen, 1991), p. 35, which raise the possibility of its authorship by R. Sherira Gaon. It is noteworthy that R. Adin Steinzaltz (Even-Yisrael) argues in his *Hasiddur Vehatefilah* (The Prayerbook and Prayer) (Tel Aviv: Yedioth Ahronoth, 1994; vol. 2, p. 3) that the *piyyut* cannot be ascribed to any specific author.

83 Weingarten thus cites the disciples of the Vilna Gaon in *Hasiddur Hameforash Hashalem*, p. 35. In *Siddur ha-Gra* (Prayerbook of the Vilna Gaon) (New York: Kol Torah, 1953), this *piyyut* does indeed begin the morning service, even before the Morning Blessings.

The poem, however, is not just a hybrid dialogue. It disagrees, and even clashes, with social conventions such as the possibility of speaking to God, the belief in communication between God and the people of Israel (hearing the voices is an allusion to the Giving of the Torah), God's essential definition of man and his purpose in life, and the possibility of man's completely exposing himself before God, who "tests the thoughts and the mind" (as this was formulated in Jer. 11:20). The speaker presents these conventions in order to express the tension and power struggle between the stance of the believer and that of the atheist. This tension gradually builds during the course of the poem, becoming more powerful until it reaches a catharsis at the end of the poem: the faithful innocence of addressing God is only fakery and stickiness, and communication is not to be expected.

The many punctuation marks in the lengthy but fragmentary sentences contribute to the sense of inevitability, with the pace accelerating in the two last stanzas because of the shortening of the lines and the punctuation of each word. The course of events is interrupted twice, by the central metaphor of the "punch in the gut," in both the third and fourth stanzas. The punch can be interpreted in at least two ways: an awareness of the powerful need for communication with God, despite the irony and skepticism; and an awakening from the hope that the intensive petition in the fourth stanza will indeed result in a response from God.

The punch in the gut could also be directed to the reader himself. The process of shaking off the entire covering of conventions and standing naked before the world leaves man, every man, exposed and vulnerable to the punch in his own gut. The advantage to this situation, however, lies in how it imparts the ability to distinguish between the real and the fake and to refashion subjectivity, in accordance with these revelations. My use of the adjectives "real" and "fake" follows Winnicott, who argued that the infant's/child's disappointment with his mother and with his surroundings, which were supposed to provide for his needs, creates a defensive mechanism of a false self.[84] This falseness finds

84 "The False Self has one positive and very important function: to hide the True Self, which it does by compliance with environmental demands" (Donald Winnicott,

expression in the child's distancing himself from the authentic traits that characterize him, and refraining from creativity and spontaneity, while adapting his behavior to the demands of the environment.

The speaker in the poem seemingly needs God's help to define him, but in actuality, it is only at the end of the poem, when the conception of God grows faint and is seen to be as "Humpty-Dumpty all fake," that the speaker can define his true self. This self is not dependent on God for its definition, but it still contains the immanent longing for the mystical that is a consequence of the experience of loneliness and suffering embodied in the lines:

> Leave me, alone, on the beach, in my sorrow. Giant, mighty,
> and the blueness of Your heaven is like
> it punched you in the gut.

After the illusion of the listening and dialogical God who aids the speaker to define himself has been smashed, the speaker remains in his loneliness in the world, on the one hand, and, on the other, with the certainty that there is a mystical reality broader than what he can perceive. This is the "punch in the gut": the recognition of the mystical need that will never be filled, but will remain as an eternal longing for a mystical experience or for the innocent faith in which man's turning to God is answered. This longing is described by Levinas as the source of desire toward the metaphysical other, which always remains unsatisfied, unlike man's other needs:

> Metaphysics [. . .] is turned toward the "elsewhere" and the "otherwise" and the "other." [. . .] The term of this movement, the elsewhere or the other, is called other in an eminent sense. No journey, no change of climate or of scenery could

---

"Ego Distortion in Terms of True and False Self," http://www.abebe.org.br/wp-content/Uploads/Donald-Winnicott-The-Maturational-Processes-and-the-Facilitating-Environment-Studies-in-the-Theory-of-Emotional-Development-1965.pdf, accessed March 12, 2015 [*The Maturational Processes and the Facilitating Environment* (Madison, CT: International Universities Press, 1987), pp. 146–47]).

> satisfy the desire bent toward it. The other metaphysically desired is not "other" like the bread I eat, the land in which I dwell, the landscape I contemplate, like, sometimes, myself for myself, this "I," that "other." I can "feed" on these realities and to a very great extent satisfy myself, as though I had simply been lacking them [. . .] The metaphysical desire tends toward something else entirely, toward the absolutely other [. . .] desire [. . .] would coincide with the consciousness of what has been lost; it would be essentially a nostalgia, a longing for return.[85]

The longing toward the metaphysical described by Levinas relates to two poles in a person's selfhood, since the movement sets out from a certain need and is directed toward otherness that exists, in actuality, (also) in man's soul. Beyond Levinas's direct criticism of Buber's I-Thou notion, which is based on mutuality, Levinas's idea of longing deepens our understanding of why, from the outset, such mutuality is impossible.[86] Levinas's conception is important for analyzing the dialogism in Kosman's poetry, because this dialogism, too, is not mutual. From this respect, despite Kosman's mental and intellectual proximity to Buber, his poetry expresses a greater affinity to Levinas, since the attempt to create a "conversation" in the Buberian sense does not meet with success; consequently, this is actually a Wittgensteinian language-game, or dialogue as envisaged by Levinas.

3. Mystical Grammar: Private Pain and Manifestation of the Other

The longing depicted by Levinas includes paradoxicality in the process of self-definition.[87] This definition contains two self-perceptions (self-constitution as object and as subject), according to Wittgenstein (as described in our discussion of mystical grammar, above: everyday

---

85 Levinas, *Totality and Infinity*, p. 33.

86 Emmanuel Levinas, "Martin Buber and the Theory of Knowledge," in *The Levinas Reader*, ed. Sean Hand (Oxford: Basil Blackwell, 1989), pp. 59–74.

87 Buber, *Meetings*, p. 50.

language does not include the subject that constitutes the boundary of the world, but mystical grammar can relate to this subject). This also holds true for another person: everyday language is general, and does not enable an awareness of "other minds," but the meeting with the other is made possible by mystical grammar that includes the insights of both Wittgenstein and Levinas: addressing the other is embodied in dialogue.

Dialogue, for Wittgenstein, is the sole method of clarification and therapy in his later *Philosophical Investigations*. At the same time, Levinas views responsibility toward the other as a precondition for dialogue, and places ethics before ontology.[88] Both present a conception of dialogue that differs from that of Buber, and which will enable us to explain the dialogism in Kosman's later poetry (and the self-constitution that it fashions): dialogism, for Wittgenstein and Levinas, is usually unilateral. Its occurrence is not based on mutuality, nor can it be anticipated. Levinas devoted a major article to a critique of Buberian dialogue, which he substituted with concentration on a "manifestation of otherness."[89] The manifestation of otherness is expressed in language, and is a condition for dialogical ethics. This, however, does not require a response by the other, because the moral imperative is not dependent upon mutuality; it rather is based on ethics taking precedence over ontology. At the same time, however, ethical expressions are conditional upon their

88 "Metaphysics precedes ontology" (Levinas, *Totality and Infinity*, p. 42).

89 "Union, *Verbundenheit*, is a manifestation of otherness. The presence of the Thou, of the other, *ipso facto* implies a 'word' which is addressed directly to me and which requires a response. Whoever refuses to reply, no longer perceives the 'word.' It is impossible to remain a spectator of the Thou, for the very existence of the Thou depends on the 'word' it addresses to me. And, it must be added, only a being who is responsible for another being can enter into dialogue with it. Responsibility, in the etymological sense of the term, not the mere exchange of words, is what is meant by *dialogue*, and it is only in the former case that there is meeting. The futility of remaining a spectator is not due to our tragic participation in a situation which is not of our choice, to our dereliction, but to the necessity of responding to the 'word.' There is a transcendent reality to which I am somehow committed which 'tells me something,' nor is this phrase a metaphor, for it expresses the very essence of language" (Levinas, "Martin Buber and the Theory of Knowledge," pp. 66–67).

linguistic fulfillment, a point on which Wittgenstein and Levinas concur: "it is in language that an expectation and its fulfillment make contact."[90]

The combination of the ethical conceptions of Wittgenstein and Levinas enables us to argue that the otherness that is expressed in language and that obligates the speaker to engage in ethical behavior creates moral perfectionism. The constant striving for perfectionism creates two sets of criteria, internal and external. This is formulated as a dialogical language-game, but is not directed to a concrete other, but rather to a sublime other, the focus of longing that also reflects a language-game that is cultural, and not only personal, as in the poem *Something Hurts*. This poem fashions an experience of pain, in the language of the sole speaker, and its singular description overcomes the gap between expression and sensation of which Wittgenstein spoke.[91] The self in the poem is constituted as object and as subject, with the speaker including subjective traits and those that are verifiable:

> *Something Hurts*
> Something hurts me here, on the side, do You see, my Maker?
> Something swelling sticks out, juts
> out of contemplation, like a broken
> finger, my soul grows

90 Wittgenstein, *Philosophical Investigations*, para. 445.

91 Wittgenstein examined the connection between words in everyday language and an inner and subjective sensation such as pain as follows: "How do words *refer* to sensations?—There doesn't seem to be any problem here; don't we talk about sensations every day, and name them? But how is the connection between the name and the thing named set up? This question is the same as: How does a human being learn the meaning of names of sensations? For example, of the word 'pain.' Here is one possibility: words are connected with the primitive, natural, expressions of sensation and used in their place. A child has hurt himself and he cries; then adults talk to him and teach him exclamations and, later, sentences. They teach the child new pain-behavior. 'So you are saying that the word "pain" really means crying?'—On the contrary: the verbal expression of pain replaces crying, it does not describe it. How can I even attempt to interpose language between the expression of pain and the pain?" (Wittgenstein, *Philosophical Investigations*, para. 244–45).

a long horn of misery.

Something hurts me here, on the side, do You see, my Maker?
Loneliness spawns an angle, a sharp protrusion, a spasm
like a long button-snake grows and emerges
from my back toward the streak of light, and curls on my chest
like a tail that must be cut off, hurry, my Maker,
now. Trim it off and throw it away.

Something hurts me here, on the side, do You see, my Maker?
Clothing cannot conceal it. My clumsy movements
only make it more ridiculous. Something hurts. In the streets
revelers dance and in the fields,
wondrous spring. Flowers. Women. Something hurts me here,
on the side,
my Maker, aren't you listening?[92]

The speaker's pain is fashioned as an object that is both inner and outer, that seemingly can be identified by an outer person, or by God, but the speaker does not receive an empathetic response, and so he once again desperately tries to draw God's attention to it. Not only does he not try to hide it, but he formulates in plain language a cry that the pain accompanies him with every step and, in actuality, is the prism through which the speaker experiences the world, from all respects. The lack of empathy for his pain illustrates his tremendous loneliness and his longing for some affinity, divine or other, with his frustration, which, in the end, is channeled into a work of poetry. The poem fashions both the pain as an other and the concealed God, with the unsatisified demand transformed into the sublimation of perfectionism, as the poetic act.[93]

92 Kosman, *Approaching You in English*, p. 29 (with slight changes—E.L.).

93 Kohut described at length how a work of art expresses transformation of the self in diverse directions and creates different and additional variations of the self. See Heinz Kohut, "Forms and Transformations of Narcissism," in *The Search for the Self*, ed. Paul H. Ornstein (London: Karnac, 2011), vol. 1: *Selected Writings of Heinz Kohut 1950–1978*, pp. 446–47.

On the grammatical plane, the poem's quality is expressed in its use of connotative wordings to fashion unique metaphors and imagery (pain as a swelling or a long horn, loneliness like a button-snake). Kosman engages in a poetical-mystical act here, as he shows what cannot be verbalized. His most significant grammatical move, however, is the dialogue with God that motivates our delving into the pain. Facing (the silent) God, the speaker draws into sharper focus his loneliness, which is only intensified by the monologic dialogue.

The speaker addresses God with the Talmudic expression that has its basis in the Bible: *Koneh* (acquirer, usually rendered in English as "Maker" or "Creator").[94] The Bible ascribes the right of possession of heaven and earth to God, since He created them. In an aggadic passage in Tractate Kiddushin (below) R. Simeon ben Eleazar calls God "Maker," in the context of a person accepting the troubles of livelihood,

94 The word originates in what the king of Sodom said to Abraham in Gen. 14:17–19: "the king of Sodom came out to meet him in the Valley of Shaveh, which is the valley of the King. And King Merchizedek of Salem brought out bread and wine; he was a priest of God Most High. He blessed him, saying, 'Blessed be Abram of God Most High, Creator [*koneh*] of heaven and earth.'" The Mishnah (M Avot 6:10) expands this idea to include five types of possession that God has in His world: "Five possessions [*kinyanim*] did the Holy One, blessed be He, take to Himself in his world, and these are they: the Torah is one possession, and the heaven and earth are one possession, Abraham is one possession, Israel is one possession, and the Temple is one possession. Whence [do we learn this] of the Torah? Because it is said [Prov. 8:22], 'The Lord possessed me [*konani*] at the beginning of His course as the first of His works of old.' Whence [do we learn this] of heaven and earth? Because it is said [Isa. 66:1], 'Thus said the Lord: The heaven is My throne and the earth My footstool; what manner of house will you build to Me and what place shall be My rest?' And it says [Ps. 104:24], 'How many are the things You have made, O Lord; You have made them all with wisdom; the earth is full of Your creations [*kinyanekha*].' Whence [do we learn] that Abraham is one possession? As it is written [Gen. 14:19], 'He blessed him, saying, "Blessed be Abram of God Most High, Creator [*koneh*] of heaven and earth."' Whence [do we learn] that Israel is one possession? As it is written [Exod. 15:16], 'Till Your people cross over, O Lord, Till this people cross that You have gotten [*kanita*].' And it says [Ps. 16:3], 'As to the holy and mighty ones that are in the land, they are the excellent in whom is all my delight.' Whence [do we learn] that the Temple is one possession? As it is written [Exod. 15:17], 'The sanctuary, O Lord, which Your hands established.' And it says [Ps. 78:54], 'He brought them to His holy realm, the mountain His right hand had acquired [*kantah*].'" The Rabbis detailed and expanded the right of acquisition to encompass human history, including the specific fate of the people of Israel. This is the context from which Kosman's poem emerged.

despite his having been created, from the outset, to serve God and not to labor for the purpose of livelihood. This aggadic passage in the Talmud is ambivalent, because, on the one hand, R. Simeon ben Eleazar is jealous of the animals who are free of the worries of livelihood, despite their metaphoric ability to do so, while, on the other, he is aware of the reason for the difficulties of earning a living with which man must contend. If man indeed accepts the justification for these difficulties, then what purpose does the aggadic passage serve? Kosman's poem takes the existential sorrow in the passage, and develops it into a move in which the pain of existence is examined from different angles.

The poem's title, opening, and entire course look at the speaker's private pain. Despite all the metaphorical and actual attempts to show this pain, the pain itself remains imprisoned between expression and sensation, as Wittgenstein wrote. The dialogue with God presumably attempts to overcome this obstacle by describing the results of the pain, its location, and the obvious gap between the suffering speaker and other people who revel in the streets at the same time. All of these depictions are directly linked to the distress of the original context of the use of the word, in Tractate Kiddushin. In the poem and the Talmud alike, the tribulations of existence remain without solution. In the following midrash the Rabbis already gave voice to man's existential suffering, despite his presumably exalted mission:

> It is taught: R. Simeon ben Eleazar says, I never saw a deer engaged in gathering [summer] fruit, a lion carrying a burden, or a fox as a shopkeeper, yet they are sustained without trouble, even though they were created only to serve me; and I was created only to serve my Maker. If these, who were created only to serve me, are sustained without trouble, it should surely be the case that I, who was created to serve my Maker, should be sustained without trouble. Rather, [it is because] I acted wickedly and ruined my livelihood.[95]

95 BT Kiddushin 82b. "Gathering [summer] fruit" means placing figs on mats in the field to dry them in the summer; "carrying a burden" refers to the lion using his strength for this purpose; and "as a shopkeeper" refers to the fox using his cunning in trade.

While in this aggadic passage R. Simeon apparently is reconciled to his suffering, the speaker in the poem insists upon a response from God. The responsibility attributed to God in the wording "my Maker" obligates Him to take an interest in the speaker's suffering, and in great detail. Kosman continues in the direction taken by Job, who demanded an explanation for his personal tribulations, and was not satisfied with the article of faith that a person is to constantly suffer in his life, for whatever reason. The speaker develops and intensifies Job's position; since he does not want any justification of suffering on moral grounds, he rather develops his dialogical monologue out of a life-impulse: his tribulations disrupt and worsen life. Even if he is morally or ontologically justified, this is of no interest to the speaker, who simply wants to live in a way that will enable him to enjoy celebrations, women, and flowers.

The poem formulates this pain in a contingent private language, in Norman Malcolm's wording.[96] Such language facilitates distinguishing between the Talmud's description of the pain of the "I as subject" and the portrayal of pain as "I as subject" in the poem: the pain over earning one's livelihood can be objectively described and justified by God's right of possession, in the context of which He may punish the sinner. The poem's speaker, on the other hand, presents his subjective pain, both externally and within his heart, with the reader being unable to verify its existence. Despite the impossibility of authenticating the pain, we nevertheless understand the poem, because its private language is contingent, and enables us to contain the pain's subjectivity, along with the possibility of understanding it. It should be stressed that, on the linguistic plane, according to Wittgenstein, a speaker does not understand his pain any better than does the reader; rather, he feels it with first-person certainty. Certainty of the existence of the pain does not ensure its effective emotional processing, despite its assertion by the speaker. At times, the opposite is the case: the poem might be more therapeutic for its readers than for its composer.

96 See the reference to the term "contingent private language" coined by Norman Malcolm in the discussion of reflective dialogue, chap. 2.

Despite the desperation of the expression of pain in this poem, this formulation can be viewed as based on the soul's optimistic longing for respite from its trials. This yearning paves the way for the adoption of Buberian dialogism in Kosman's later poetry, beginning in 2000. In his essay "The Walking Stick and the Tree," Buber described self-constitution by means of speech between man and himself, and not facing God or another person.[97] This dialogism is conducted between man and himself, and nature enables it as a sphere-in-between, but not as an active participant. The I and the Thou exist within man's soul, and the self-constitution occurs between them, by means of speech.

Dialogism of this sort is evident in the poem *Wanted*, which was published in Kosman's third collection of poetry, *Soft Rags* (1990), with a note at the end that it was written in the Sarafand military camp (meaning that the speaker was a soldier). Despite the concrete context, the poem became one of Kosman's most widely quoted works, because it portrays universal mental anguish, unrelated to any specific time or place. Two of the features of poetic grammar, according to Wittgenstein, will aid in understanding its uniqueness: the poem expresses (or evokes in the reader) reflection regarding the past, present, and future, and directs the reader to understand the essentialily of repose for the soul for fashioning an individual's selfhood. Since each person has his own way of attaining such serenity, the poem *shows* this need, instead of verbalizing its content. The speaker uses words that hint at contexts within Jewish tradition, but which could be interpreted as representing general, not necessarily cultural, traits. These words aim to find a place in the world

97 "Not needing a support and yet willing to afford my lingering a fixed point, I pressed my walking stick against a trunk of an oak tree. Then I felt in twofold fashion *my* contact with being: here, where I held the stick, and there, where it touched the bark. Apparently only where I was, I nonetheless found myself there too where I found the tree. *At that time dialogue appeared to me.* For the speech of man is like that stick wherever it is genuine speech, and that means: truly directed address. Here, where I am, where ganglia and organs of speech help me to form and to send forth the word, here I 'mean' him to whom I send it, I intend him, this one unexchangeable man. But also there, where he is, something of me is delegated, something that is not at all substantial in nature like that being here, rather pure vibration and incomprehensible, that remains there, with him, the man meant by me, and takes part in the receiving of my word. I encompass him to whom I turn" (Buber, *Meetings*, pp. 49–50).

by means of poetic speech, as Buber explains: "For the speech of man is like that stick wherever it is genuine speech, and that means: truly directed address.[98]

> *Wanted*
> Wanted, a quite place to rest the soul.
> Just for a few moments.
> Wanted, a place to rest the feet.
> Just for a few moments.
>
> Wanted, a plant, leaf, stalk or shrub, that won't
> fold up when the soul arrives, just for a few moments.
>
> Wanted, one phrase, clean, agreeable and warm to serve as a bench,
> a refuge, for someone close to me, a dove-child, my own soul,
> who left the ark this morning, for a few moments, in the early hours,
> and couldn't find a place to rest her feet.[99]

The desired object is a "place," a word that alludes both to God and to a physical location;[100] in the second stanza, a number of additional transformational possibilities present themselves: a plant, a leaf, a stalk or shrub. That is, the desired object is not to be found specifically in a certain culture, in a defined geographical locale (the Temple, Jerusalem, the Land of Israel . . .), it rather is a metaphor for a mental state. Such a transformational interpretation is parallel to Wittgenstein's conception of meaning, which can add further clarity: Wittgenstein argued that a word cannot be translated or defined by means of other words, since no word has substantive meaning. Consequently, all that can be

98 See chap. 2.
99 Kosman, *Approaching You in English*, p. 89.
100 One of the appellations for God is *Hamakom*, literally "the place" (usually translated "the Omnipresent"), based on the understanding that everywhere is God's place.

done is to exchange one word by another; that is, it is transformed. The word "place" in the poem does not represent necessary meaning, and the speaker accordingly transforms it into other possibilities.

Furthermore, in the last stanza, the "place" is transformed into "phrase"—namely, the desired object is sought, in practice, in language—and it is here that the insights of Wittgenstein and Buber meet: every object in our thought is formulated in language (following Buber), and, for Buber, language constitutes the space-in-between in which dialogism occurs. Buber developed the notion of the sphere-in-between in order to explain how the meeting takes place in actuality:

> The fundamental fact of human existence is man with man. What is peculiarly characteristic of the human world is above all that something takes place between one being and another the like of which can be found nowhere in nature [. . .] Man is made man by it; but on its way it does not merely unfold, it also decays and withers away. It is rooted in one being turning to another as another, as this particular other being, in order to communicate with it in a sphere which is common to them but which reaches out beyond the special sphere of each. I call this sphere, which is established with the existence of man as man but which is conceptually still uncomprehended, the sphere of "between." Though being realized in very different degrees, it is a primal category of human reality. This is where the genuine third alternative must begin.[101]

The spoken word, Buber argues, is realized in the sphere-in-between, where it is extricated from the consciousness of the speaker and turns to the other. Kosman's dialogic poems that were discussed above address the interlocutor, but they lack mutuality. Buber stresses at the beginning of the passage cited above that "the fundamental fact of human existence is man with man." Continuing in this vein, I will show the fascinating change that occurred during the course of Kosman's poetic work. The

101 Buber, *Between Man and Man*, pp. 240–41.

dialogism in Kosman's books that we have discussed up to now focus on addressing external factors, which, on the one hand, are very significant for the speaker, while, on the other, they are alienated and foreign to the extent that they are a threat or danger in the process of the speaker's self-constitution.[102] The most extreme example of this is to be found in his first collection of poems, *After the Horror, the Act of Poetry*, in which an almost solipsistic self is expressed, one that is in substantive conflict with the world. At the other extreme, in contrast, we have the collections *Forty Love Poems and Two Additional Love Poems to God* and *You're Awesome!*,[103] in which the speaker attests to a fertile dialogic relationship with the world. Dialogic features are present in his earlier books as well, but in his later poetry the dialogue is more alive and mutual, and expresses the speaker's tangible relationship with God, with nature, and with his lover. While the dialogic language in the first two decades of his work is laced with irony, the pain of loneliness and hurt, and the harshness of not being understood, the dialogue in his later books also includes desire and pleasure, joy and devotion, and mainly a sense of being a part of the world.

The book that, for me, embodies Winnicott's "transitional space," between two types of dialogism (from dialogism without mutuality, to mutual dialogism) is *Perush Hadash b.s.d.* I already cited many poems from this collection in different contexts. At this point, I want to focus the discussion on the poem from which the book takes its title and which contains both types of dialogism: to a God who does not answer, and to a woman who hears and functions as an actual interlocutor:

> *A New Commentary, with God's Help*
> I'm writing now, with God's help, a new commentary on your breasts,

102 "One of the central claims of the dialogic philosophy of Emmanuel Levinas and Martin Buber is that the other person by whom I become self-knowledgeable and morally self-aware is other in the sense of being an ethically provocative force who calls me into question, and who destabilizes my otherwise pervasive loyalty to myself" (David Jopling, *Self-knowledge and the Self* [New York: Routledge, 2000], pp. 141–42).

103 Admiel Kosman, *Forty Love Poems and Two Additional Love Poems to God* (Tel Aviv: Hakibbutz Hameuchad, 2003); Admiel Kosman, *You're Awesome!* (Tel Aviv: Hakibbutz Hameuchad, 2011).

a blessed composition. I have humbly gathered different interpretations
from everything at hand. A nice midrash, an anthology of your skin, gentle and soft,
bound between my two lips.[104]

With implication, simple meaning, exegesis, and mystical meaning
I'll now compose a daring interpretation of the Kabbalistic Median Line.
A commentary on Lasting Endurance, Majesty, Foundation.[105]

The meaning of leaves, bright light between the branches,
a radiant commentary on the treetops.
And through the orchard you'll come with me to the city.[106]
We'll go, with all the mothers.

Humble me, writing now with God's help a new commentary on the bosom,
An innovative commentary of my own about the breast.
A collection of midrashim,
a nice pamphlet.

Here, so young and inconsequential,
I humbly gather
my different interpretations,
from everything at hand.[107]

The poem combines talk about the body and sexuality with language-games from different periods in Jewish culture: Bible, midrash,

104 *Nikhrakh* alludes to the binding of tefilin—now it is his lover's skin that is kissed instead.
105 The reference is to the Kabbalistic *Sefirot* of *Netzah*, *Hod*, and *Yesod*.
106 "Orchard" functions on three levels in the poem: (1) an acronym that alludes to early Jewish mysticism; (2) a geographic location; and (3) the act of love, in which the lover comes together with the speaker.
107 Kosman, *Approaching You in English*, p. 111 (with changes—E.L.).

and Kabbalah, along with everyday religious practice (some people write the acronym *b.s.d.* = *bet-sameh-daled*, meaning "with Heaven's [i.e., God's] help" at the top of pages). The Jewish context is very dominant, beginning with the poem's title, continuing with interpretive terms from Lurianic Kabbalah ("simple meaning, implication, exegesis, and mystical meaning," with Kosman changing the traditional order, and placing "implication" before "simple meaning"), and ending with a plethora of terms from Jewish tradition: *Yalkut Ro'im* – the name of a collection of midrashim, "pamphlet" (*kuntres*, used especially in reference to relatively short religious tracts; also the Tosafists' term for Rashi's commentary to the Talmud), *pardes*.[108] The dominant context to which the poem alludes is the midrash in BT Hagigah 14:b:

> Our masters taught: Four entered the Orchard,[109] namely, Ben Azzai, Ben Zoma, Aher,[110] and R. Akiva [. . .] Ben Azzai looked and died [. . .] Ben Zoma looked and was stricken [. . .] Aher cut the shoots. R. Akiva departed unscathed.

The mystical element is prominent in this poem, because this Talmudic passage is one of the central, and rare, midrashim that presents an important aspect of early Jewish mysticism. The passage portrays the danger that lies in wait for most people when they attempt to explore the secrets of the Creation. Kosman's poem turns this warning into an amusing challenge and a love song.

The speaker uses connotations from Jewish tradition to describe his lover's body and, actually, his desire for her, employing the "Holy" Tongue to this end. The title is ambiguous, since it refers both to exploring the body of the lover and to a new commentary on the religious order of priorities. The secrets of the Creation are not embodied (or are not exclusively embodied) in a text, but in the act of love:

108 The term *pardes* does not appear explicitly in the poem. The speaker dismantles the term into its components, and rearranges the conventional order (see also the following n.)

109 *Pardes*; also an acronym for these four methods of biblical interpretation.

110 Elisha ben Avuyah; known as "Aher" (another) after he lost his faith ("cut the shoots").

breasts, lips, and coming are included in a new commentary of texts and going together with the Matriarchs of the Jewish people, specifically ("We'll go, with all the mothers"), because Sarah, Rebekah, Rachel, and Leah were the masters of the interpretation and refashioning of their fate.

This poetic move can be seen as a provocation that calls into question the sanctity of the Talmudic text and, especially, the mystical stance expressed in it. The poem also lends itself to an alternative Buberian interpretation: the mystical experience prepares the speaker's heart and mind for the erotic experience with his lover. The erotic already illustrates belief in the Bible, but in this poem this association assumes new garb. This is because the poem does not speak of mixed feelings toward God by the believer; it rather presents a Buberian argument in which relation to the other incorporates relation to the absolute with relation to the human other. Furthermore, relation to the absolute is the stable background for constituting the relation to the other, since only God does not cease to be "Thou," while human love fluctuates:

> In every sphere in its own way, through each process of becoming that is present to us, we look out towards the fringe of the eternal *Thou*; in each *Thou* we address the eternal *Thou*. Every sphere is compassed in the eternal *Thou*, but it is not compassed in them.[111]

The poem *A New Commentary, with God's Help* reflects the encompassing of the sphere of "our life with men, in which the relation takes on the form of speech,"[112] in the all-inclusive mystical context of Jewish faith that is encapsuled in the acronym *pardes*. The hidden treasures of Jewish tradition serve as the linguistic platform on which the relation to the female "Thou" is formulated. Kosman's understanding of this relation, which he sets forth in his introduction to *I and Thou*, casts new light on the poem:

111 Buber, *I and Thou*, p. 101.
112 Buber, *I and Thou*, p. 101.

> Certainty is a state of consciousness of inner certainty that ensues from contact with the absolute. For the believer, the clearest marker of this certainty is the disappearance of the dual status—which is the regular condition—and being charged with power and vitality. This fullness drives loving action, that draws its certainty from the absolute.[113]

Kosman interprets Buber in this manner, despite his emphasizing that "Buber assumed that there is room for humanity that has no religious faith—even though such humanity lacks the depth dimension that exists in religiosity."[114] The speaker in the poem blazes the path to his lover's heart with language-games from Jewish tradition, thereby reflecting his deep connection to the linguistic layers of this tradition as he weaves his call to his lover and the expressions of his desire to be as one with her.

Kosman's following books exhibited significant change in two senses: (1) the relatively limited use of sources from Jewish tradition, and (2) his poems entered the erotic sphere of love relationships, in depth and in detail. Intriguingly, in the poems that directly address the lover and that are influenced by the dynamics of intersubjective relationships, self-constitution still happens in a monologist dialogue, without the fashioning of a substantive response by the interlocutor:

> *This Isn't*
> This isn't because of the considerable power,
> and not because of weakness,
> this isn't the humming through a pursed mouth
> and not whispering,
> on the shores of your warm beauty.
> Look at me, woman,
> Half of me is falling into the sea,
> half is left on the dry land.[115]

---

113 Kosman, "Introduction," p. 183.
114 Kosman, "Introduction," p. 211.
115 Kosman, *Forty Love Poems*, p. 4.

The opening poem of *Forty Love Poems and Two Additional Love Poems to God* illustrates how the dialogism changes and becomes one of the means for the poetic fashioning of a genuine event that can be understood as a more advanced stage of self-constitution. The poem functions simultaneously as a Wittgensteinian reflective dialogue, in the course of which the speaker tries to look at his emotional state (being torn into two) and at genuine dialogue that deepens our understanding of the importance of the other for the speaker, and the meaning of turning to someone.[116] We can add to this Buber's argument for the need for another person's confirmation of our existence, which includes testimony to our being part of his existence in the world.[117] Turning to an other, however, and the need to be answered do not sufficiently explain the tension portrayed in the poem, apparently following an act of love or a substantive meeting of lovers.

The speaker asks the woman to look at what happens to him after the encounter with her beauty. He emphasizes that his being torn into two is not a consequence of falling under the spell of some detail of her image or her behavior, rather, the encounter as a whole has this effect on him. The metaphor of being split in two raises the question of mutuality, which is strengthened by his request that she look at him. Why does the poem depict the disparity between the interlocutor's attention and the need expressed by the speaker?

At this point, we will return to Wittgenstein, who finely distinguished between inner and outer processes.[118] We can see that a person

116 "In genuine dialogue the turning to the partner takes place in all truth, that is, it is a turning of the being. Every speaker 'means' the partner or partners to whom he turns as this personal existence. To 'mean' someone in this connection is at the same time to exercise the degree of making present which is possible to the speaker at that moment. The experiencing senses and the imagining of the real which completes the findings of the senses work together to make the other present as a whole and as a unique being, as the person that he is" (Buber, "Elements of the Interhuman," *Knowledge of Man*, p. 85).

117 "Man wishes to be confirmed in his being by man, and wishes to have a presence in the being of the other" (Buber, "Distance and Relation," *Knowledge of Man*, p. 71).

118 "'I can only *believe* that someone else is in pain, but I *know* it if I am.'—Yes: one can resolve to say 'I believe he is in pain' instead of 'He is in pain.' But that's all.—What looks like an explanation here, or like a statement about a mental process, in truth just exchanges one way of talking for another which, while we are doing

is suffering, but we cannot penetrate his inner voice and see that it disintegrates as a result of a human encounter or any other reason; linguistic communication is needed in order to know this.[119] Nonetheless, communication does not necessarily relieve the sense of alienation and loneliness. Such feelings arise even in Kosman's depictions of a romantic relationship, when at times an ironic picture of randomness reveals the gap and tension between the cultural context of belief and the personal event that is described. This can be seen in the following poem, which mentions dialogues with his lover, parents, and the tradition of the past—but it is not by chance that they do not actually happen in the poem:

> While gathering seeds that washed up
> on shore—we suddenly remembered sex. Yes,
> all the minutiae of the commandment of sex, gentle and
> pleasuring sex—
> our parents' sedentary sex; during a completely incidental
> gathering
> of seeds that washed up on shore, we remembered our
> precious
> parents, who brought us this far. And sex, and the glorious
> heritage
> of our parents—the cruel conquerors who gave us the true
> religion, by force of the force of the dream.[120]

This stanza presents a topic that recurs in Kosman's later poetry: an ironic look at sexuality, accompanied by a critique of the repression of the topic in the accepted language-game (as we saw in *Lament for the Ninth of Av*). In consequence, the speaker tries to set forth the discussion of sex as something natural and only to be expected. The parents

philosophy, seems to us the more apt. Just try—in a real case—to doubt someone else's fear or pain!" ((Wittgenstein, *Philosophical Investigations*, para. 303).

119 "An 'inner process' stands in need of outward criteria" (Wittgenstein, *Philosophical Investigations*, para. 580).

120 Admiel Kosman, *We Reached God* (Tel Aviv: Hakibbutz Hameuchad, 1998), p. 52; trans. Edward Levin.

in the poem represent religiosity that presumes to represent "truth," and due to this presumptuousness, are cruel and obsessive when it comes to talking about sex. The speaker contrasts the "glorious heritage" and "the true religion" in whose name the parents educate their children, on the one hand, with those parents being "cruel conquerors," on the other. "The minutiae of the commandment of sex" strip sex of love and passion, and create sex that is "gentle and pleasuring," "sedentary," that unconsciously arises and troubles the soul of the children playing at the seashore. When sex becomes guided by the minutiae of the tradition, as glorious as it may be, it "cruelly conquers" the spontaneity in physical love and causes it to wither. Repression of this sort comes to the fore in the following passage, as well, in which sexual energy is forced to find its way beyond the body, with the speaker seemingly unable to direct it as he wishes:

> Oh, God, where does my sexual energy finds it way to??
> My sexual energy drives an old truck, pppppppppppppffff,
> Now it puts warm and pleasant air in its tires.[121]

Sexual energy functions in two different semantic fields at one and the same time: in the field of the body, and in the vehicular. Such a dual function was termed "bidirectional metaphor" by Yeshayahu Shen, as we saw in the chapter on Amichai. The metaphor of a track traveling in the Jerusalem hills, rolling along and creating the pleasantness of warm air, is (indirectly) parallel to the potential pleasantness of the speaker's sexual energy. The truck functions as the "hero" throughout the poem. For example: "ascends the hills, descends the valleys" (l. 3), "once my truck (in a story) / married a rented car, and coupled for two days / in the clear airs" (ll. 13–15). Despite the metaphorical bidirectionality, the focus on the truck diverts the discussion of the speaker's sexuality to the tale of the truck's exploits in sexual terms, thereby canceling the erotic and romantic aspect of sexuality.

The sexuality in this book is fashioned completely differently in the next poem, which portrays conjugal sexuality in a gentle manner

---

121 Kosman, *We Reached God*, p. 17; trans. Edward Levin.

that slides to the mystical. The mystical grammar exists in two parallel channels: the personification of the world; and the couple, whose nakedness functions as conjugal language that connects the two lovers:

> We were sky-blue and transparent
> and beautiful without bound.
> Our splendor spreads out and beams forth.
> Our nakedness—
> had a strange glitter.
> The day was lacking
> and shouted in its light: Night, night,
> and the night was lacking.
> And longed: Day, day.
>
> [. . .]
> We listened to our heartbeats attentively,
> and we were beautiful without bound. Sky-blue
> and transparent were our bodies.
> Our splendor spreads out and beams forth.
>
> [. . .]
> From the peak of the blue hills
> they saw us,
> several longing-full observers, looking at the air.
>
> For we are beautiful without bound. Our nakedness
> grows, and there is no stranger with us,
> nor is anyone lacking. The day already longs for the night,
> Our splendor spreads out and beams forth.[122]

The poem crosses the descriptive boundaries of everyday language and paints a picture of what happens in a parallel world: transparency, boundless beauty, splendor and beaming, and all are caught up in a

122 Kosman, *We Reached God*, pp. 10–11; trans. Edward Levin.

process that cannot be reduced to words. In this process, the word functions more actively than a pair of lovers, as background for the process of this splendor filling the world. Already in the beginning of the poem, a picture is painted of spreading forth and connection, but in the first stage, there is a lack, in the word and for the couple. In a parallel move that is accompanied by longing—again, in the world and for the couple—the lack is filled, as is the beauty in the physical connection, by means of nakedness and the spread of its splendor through the world.

Although the speaker uses the first-person plural, there is no evidence in the poem of actual dialogue, a fact that preserves the emotional pictoriality that is not mediated by language, along with the mystical atmosphere that, too, cannot be verbalized. The meeting of physicality and the mystical also functions as a bidirectional metaphor for the speaker: physical closeness that develops into the realization of erotic desire can be a mystical experience and provide an existential answer to the question of the meaning of life.

In summation, Kosman's poetry is replete with dialogism. Our analysis shows that this dialogism is based on reflective dialogic grammar, which at times is controversial, and in other instances, mystical, in the senses we presented in the introductory chapters, following Wittgenstein. Despite the pronounced Buberian influence on Kosman's consciousness as a creative artist and scholar, in most instances, the self is constituted in his poetical language from the speaker's perspective, in the first person, even if, in practice, use is made of the first-person plural, second person, or third person. We can see in the rich expanse of language-games from Jewish tradition in Kosman's poetry the other facing whom the speaker fashions his selfhood. The boundaries of this otherness are not encompassed within the outline of a certain man, woman, or lover. Accordingly, even in the transition to poetry that reflects romantic and sexual experiences, this otherness is still patently dominant. In this sense, the longing, throughout Kosman's poetical work, is for the mystical, more than for anything else. Buber and Wittgenstein cross paths at this juncture; both identified God with the meaning of life, and under their influence, we find in Kosman's poetry a series of prayers that are driven by the quest for meaning in life.

Meeting with God does not come to man in order that he may concern himself with God, but in order that he may confirm that there is meaning in the world.[123]

What do I know about God and the purpose of life? I know that this world exists. That I am placed in it like my eye in its visual field. That something about it is problematic, which we call its meaning. The meaning of life, the meaning of the world, we can call God [. . .] To pray is to think about the meaning of life.[124]

123 Buber, *I and Thou*, p. 115.

124 Wittgenstein, *Notebooks 1914–1916*, pp. 72–73.

CHAPTER 7

Shimon Adaf: Poetry as Philosophy and Philosophy as Poetry

The Nobility of Pain

> The throbbing of the forging of the light
> that in the end split me
> From my birth I hear
> word by word my body is sung
> Devastated it dares to near
> with my own eyes to come to know.
> (*Poetry*, 2)[1]
>
> A picture of the object comes before the child's mind when it hears the word. But now, if this does happen—is it the purpose of the word?—Yes, it *may* be the purpose [. . .] Uttering a word is like striking a note on the keyboard of the imagination.[2]

1 Shimon Adaf, *Aviva-No* (Or Yehuda: Kinneret Zmora-Bitan Dvir, 2009), p. 25; trans. for this book by Edward Levin. "Splitting" (*she-yivatemi*) alludes to the "covenant between the pieces" (*berit ben ha-betarim*) that Abraham made with the Lord (Gen. 15); here, the speaker's covenant is with the creative light—and it is his body that is split, instead of the animals in Genesis. "Know" is an allusion to Adam "knowing" Eve; here, the interaction is between the speaker and poetic language.

2 Wittgenstein, *Philosophical Investigations*, para. 6.

An initial encounter with the poetry of Shimon Adaf evokes the physical and mental sensation of taking word after word and assembling them as a mosaic of the speaker's self, with each word being "like striking a note on the keyboard of the imagination" of the reader.[3] I therefore chose to begin with this poem, which reveals the relevancy of Adaf's poetry for examining the modes of self-constitution in poetic language. Setting his poetry as a link in the chain that already contains the poetry of Zelda, Amichai, and Kosman requires explanation, in terms both of its scope and of its place in Hebrew culture and the study of Hebrew literature.[4]

Adaf's poetry constitutes a language-game with rules from different worlds, and their combination in a poetic system creates poetic grammar that acts in unpredictable and unconventional fashion: sources from Jewish tradition join together with English poetry, children's literature, the philosophy of language, medieval thought, and contexts from many additional disciplines.[5] The actual poetic act, in the above poem

3 The section title comes from a poem in Adaf's *Icarus Monologue* (Tel Aviv: Gvanim, 1997), p. 41 (Hebrew). This poem also gave its name to a rock band of which Shimon Adaf was a member when he was in his twenties. The metaphoric expression is a fine example of the singularity of Adaf's metaphoric language, with its unexpected and imaginative word combinations.

4 No comprehensive scholarly work on Adaf's corpus has been written, and the articles that have appeared relate to typical issues in the discussion of Mizrahi literature, such as periphery and center (see, e.g., Yigal Schwartz, "When Honi the Circle-Drawer Meets Icarus: Periphery and Center in the Novel *In the Winter* by Y. L. Brenner and the Novel *A Mere Mortal* by Shimon Adaf," *Mikan* 12 [2012], pp. 171–91 [Hebrew]). For discussions of specific contexts in Adaf's work, see Hadas Shabat-Nadir, "But I Was Emptied of All Places" (master's thesis, Ben-Gurion University, 2006) (Hebrew); Ktzia Alon, *Oriental Israeli Poetics* (Tel Aviv: Hakibbutz Hameuchad, 2011), pp. 41–44 (Hebrew); Yochai Oppenheimer, *Diasporic Mizrahi Poetry in Israel* (Tel Aviv: Resling, 2012), p. 57 (Hebrew); and David Gurevitz, *The Detective as a Culture Hero* (Holon: Ministry of Defence, 2013), pp. 310–17 (Hebrew).

5 For a comparative discussion of the different genres in Adaf's work, see Dorit Lemberger, "Contacts and Discontinuities: Changing Aspects in Shimon Adaf's Work," *Hebrew Studies* 55 (2014), pp. 201–28; and Dorit Lemberger, "Questioning Boundaries of Language and World: Ambivalence and Disillusionment in the Work of Shimon Adaf," *Hebrew Studies* (in press). Some of the ideas in the current chapter appeared in these articles, but they concentrate on a comparison of the genres, and do not include a discussion of the collection of poetry *Aviva-No*.

by Adaf, focuses on the self of the speaker, and alludes to Bialik's conception in his poem *I Didn't Win Light in a Windfall.*[6] Nevertheless, Adaf's poetry raises an acute question in literary research and especially as regards self-constitution in poetry: what is the connection between biographical facts (place of residence, parents' land of origin, etc.) and self-constitution?[7]

An important prefatory comment should be made about a unique feature of Adaf's work: the movement from poetry to prose and back, and the meaning of this movement for self-constitution. The poetic grammar is fashioned in different ways of writing that at times are included in the same work and complement one another.[8] Adaf has written three collections of poetry and seven prose works, all in Hebrew (for the sake of convenience, references hereafter use the English titles): *Icarus Monologue: Collection of Poetry* (*Ha-Monolog shel Ikarus*, 1997); *That Which I Thought Shadow Is the Real Body: Collection of Poetry* (*Mah she-Hashavti Tzel Hu ha-Guf ha-Amiti*, 2002); *One Mile and Two Days before Sunset: A Novel* (*Kilometer ve-Yomayim lifnei ha-Shekiah*, 2004); *A Mere Mortal: A Novel* (*Ha-Lev ha-Kavur*, 2006); *Sunburned Faces: A Novel* (*Panim Tzuruvei Hamah*, 2008); *Aviva-No: A*

6 The wording "The throbbing of the fortifying light" can be understood as the light of creation or of poetry, and refers to Bialik's poem: "I didn't win light in a windfall, / nor by deed of a father's will. / I hewed my light from granite. / I quarried my heart" (trans. Ruth Nevo, *Chaim Nachman Bialik: The Selected Poems* [Tel Aviv: Dvir, 1981], p. 30). Adaf, like Bialik, compares poetry to light, and the poetic act to quarrying and, at the same time, to a personal task or mission. The ars poetical poems in both cases explain poetry being a singular expression of the "I."

7 This question was raised indirectly in our analysis of Amichai's poems to Ruth, his childhood friend, and to his parents, who remained immigrants their entire lives. Our discussion, however, focused on the role of the intersubjective plane in self-constitution, and not on the question of family ethnic and geographical history.

8 We should distinguish between all sorts of inclusions: in his collections of poetry, for example, Adaf includes unvocalized passages that are understood as philosophical arguments or pseudoquotations that function as a directive to the reader how to understand the following poems. In *Wedding Gifts* Adaf included a poem in the beginning of the book, and another in its end. In, however, *Sunburned Faces* and in *Nuntia*, however, he includes lines that can be understood as lines of poetry; see my "Contacts and Discontinuities" and "Questioning Boundaries." Additionally, Adaf includes many statements about the nature of poetry in his books, especially in *One Mile and Two Days before Sunset.* This is illustrated in my article, "Questioning Boundaries."

Collection of Poetry (*Aviva-Lo,* 2009); *Nuntia: A Novel* (*Kfor,* 2010); *Mox Nox: A Novel* (2011); *De Urbibus Inferis* (*Arim shel Matah,* 2012); (*Wedding Gifts*) (*Matnot ha-Hatunah,* 2014).

Poetry is the main artistic sphere of the authors of the three corpora discussed above—Zelda, Amichai, and Kosman (although each also engaged in additional fields of endeavor: Zelda painting and graphic art, Amichai a play and a novel, and Kosman academic research). Adaf's work, in contrast, raises the question of the distinction—regarding the author's intent—between poetry and prose, since his writings express a high awareness of this division, to which Adaf related on numerous occasions.[9] According to Wittgenstein, the author's intent is decisive for the constitution of meaning,[10] since he proposes asking the author what he intended, in order to reveal what is unique to any mental imagery.[11]

I do not maintain that what the author says about his work is a necessary condition for its interpretation, rather that creative determination includes first-person experience for which the author has first-person authority, according to Wittgenstein (and as I have shown, this trait is shared by poetical and mystical grammar). This experience

9 There are many examples of this. See, e.g., Shimon Adaf, "Born out of Shock: The Day When I Wanted to Be a Writer," *Haaretz, Book Supplement* (September 24, 2014), p. 9 (Hebrew).

10 Wittgenstein's terms "intention" and "image" are based on his position that meaning is usually constituted in use: "For a *large* class of cases of the employment of the word 'meaning'—though not for *all*—this word can be explained in this way: the meaning of a word is its use in language" (Wittgenstein, *Philosophical Investigations*, para. 43). Continuing in this vein, we can say that the understanding of a work of art in the sense of its inherent self-constitution entails the use of ars poetica expressions that attest to this, since such expressions are the use of the poetical work as part of the constitution of the subject of the speaker, as formulated in the consciousness of the artist.

11 "What makes my mental image of him into an image of *him*? Not any pictorial likeness. The same question applies to the utterance 'I see him now vividly before me' as the image. What makes this utterance into an utterance about *him*?—Nothing in it or simultaneous with it ('behind it'). If you want to know whom he meant, ask him!" (Wittgenstein, *PPF*, para. 17); "'Only you can know if you had that intention.' One might tell someone this when explaining the meaning of the word 'intention' to him. For then it means: *that* is how we use it" (Wittgenstein, *Philosophical Investigations*, para. 247).

includes ars poetica descriptions that attest, in the first person, to the creative experience, both in the poetry itself and in other contexts. Adaf is an interdisciplinary artist (poet, author, musician) who is also gifted with exceptional reflective ability regarding his own various types of creative acts. He frequently raises a question or philosophical argument (under the influence of Wittgenstein) regarding the nature of language in general, and, especially, regarding that of poetry.[12] Thus, for example, he spoke of the role of poetry in our time:

> The meaning of words, in part, is given by social agreements, but the essence of the word is exposed just when it ascends above them, when it reveals the sublime remnant, that cannot be tamed, that remains as such. We are in such a period, I think, in which the language of writing must leave its coupling with the spoken language—it must leave not only everyday language, but also the conception of language that is held in the bonds of the everyday, with its million languages. Mainly, this is how I view the role of poetry.[13]

12 "Literature, being an array of verbal representations of the world, consciousness, emotions, cannot come into being before the cognitive conditions of world, consciousness, emotions have been clarified, as well as their representative conditions. Literature's task, therefore, is this clarification. It also must examine, first of all, the foundational questions of philosophy: how do we know the world, and on what basis are we given cognitive certainty? What is the relationship between being and language? What means are available to us to give the other the event of cognition? Thus, already in *The Book of Joseph* [by Yoel Hoffmann], key characters in the development of these issues in Western thought—Kant, Spinoza, Wittgenstein—are mentioned. An entire passage in *The Book of Joseph* is devoted to the latter [. . .] If the starting line of literature is the foundational questions of cognition and language, its finish line is shaking them off, liberation from their bewitchment, if for a moment we use one of Wittgenstein's phrases" (Shimon Adaf, from a lecture at the National Association for Professors of Hebrew 2010 conference; I am grateful to Shimon Adaf for allowing me to use this unpublished text).

13 Shimon Adaf, interview with Enat Yakir, *Musaf Beit Avi Chai* (August 13, 2013), http://musaf.bac.org.il/article/kytzd-laatzvr-hazmn-vihayshar-bhyym. Another example of the combination of the discussion of an argument and poetical expression that Adaf himself suggested will be cited in the last section of this chapter.

It should be stressed that, here and elsewhere, Adaf paid special attention to the distinction between poetic and prose language, how poetry "reveal(s) the sublime remnant that cannot be trained, that remains as such." Our discussion will show how the uniqueness of his poetry is constituted; using Wittgensteinian terminology, to present "description alone" that "gets its light—that is to say, its purpose—from the philosophical problems."[14] The philosophical question presented above, of the nature of the connection between biographical features and poetry, can be broken down into secondary questions: how imagination functions in Adaf's poetry, how statements from different cultural contexts (hybridism) join together in the language-game of the poem, how the self is constituted in the course of his poems, and what is Adaf's existentialist position.

Hybrid language is described by Homi Bhabha as the emergence of a signifier that seemingly argues with the authority of existing symbols.[15] This understanding enables us to view Adaf's poetry as contestation with and the rebuilding of symbols and narratives from varied cultures. As Bhabha finely described, historical-cultural circumstances create the phenomenon of "in-between cultures" that combine cultural characteristics from the land of origin with those of the land to which people migrated.[16] As Bhabha emphasized, although migration, together with relativistic conceptions of truth, presumably generated a broad multicultural consensus, a paradoxical situation came into being, of over-discussing alongside secondary cultures being "not visible enough."[17] This tension accompanies the phenomenon of "in-between" culture, which is expressed in location and creativity on the boundary between cultures, thereby forming a partial culture that does not clearly belong to either the former or current culture.[18]

Adaf's books of poetry fashion a cardinal experience that can be defined, following Freud and Bhabha, as "unhomeliness." In the

14 See Wittgenstein, *Philosophical Investigations*, para. 109.

15 See Homi Bhabha, *The Location of Culture* (New York: Routledge, 1994), p. 277.

16 Homi Bhabha, "Culture's In-Between," in *Questions of Cultural Identity*, ed. Stuart Hall and Paul du Gay (London: Sage, 1996), pp. 53–60.

17 Bhabha, "Culture's In-Between," p. 56.

18 See Bhabha, "Culture's In-Between," pp. 54–55.

chapter on Admiel Kosman's poetry, I suggested, following Freud and Wittgenstein, translating the term they used, *unheimlich* (which can be understood and rendered in two ways: "uncanny" or "unhomely"), as "uncanny," which functions somewhat differently.[19] The sense of "uncanny" will serve us well in our analysis of Adaf's poetry, as well, since it brims with surprises that frequently raise the question that was formulated by Freud and Wittgenstein in this context: is this a real or imaginary occurrence?

Bhabha's emphasis on the importance of conceptualizing the boundary between cultures facilitates our examination of two additional features reflected in Adaf's poetry for which the translation of "unhomeliness" is suitable: the first is the sense of rootlessness, since the sphere-in-between does not belong to any culture, and is always on the "borderline," and not at "home."[20] The second is the hybridism that exceeds the two voices of dialogue (since it takes place in-between) and creates a new speech-act. This speech-act uses a hybrid strategy to distance itself from the consensual, authoritative cultural signifier: it creates a language-game in which the different voices are not evenly matched, but in which each is heard in this polyphony. This expanse enables us to suspend the need to dichotomously and binarily catalogue the reality.

This suspension enables the poetic grammar in Adaf's poetry to constitute self in a manner different from what we usually expect in the composition and study of "Mizrahi" literature. This grammar expresses a universal existentialist stance in which examining the relationship between language and reality generates an alternative political perspective that questions widely accepted scholarly notions concerning Mizrahi literature, such as distinct relations to parental origin and tradition.[21] This stance, which becomes Adaf's starting point in his

19 Wittgenstein, like Freud, defined as "uncanny" the difficulty in distinguishing between people who function as automata and those who function naturally; see *Philosophical Investigations*, para. 420–21.

20 See Bhabha, "Culture's In-Between," p. 58.

21 By "accepted scholarly notions," I mean Oppenheimer's use of terms such as "struggle" or "betrayal" in his *Diasporic Mizrahi Poetry*: "Mizrahi identity is a strong option, possessing power and a common language, that does not negate or

poetry, examines the linguistic mechanisms that produce the basic concepts of our lives, such as history, love, and childhood. The manner in which these concepts are constructed is not necessarily connected to any specific culture, unlike the interpretive positions in the literature mentioned above. The contrast between the conceptions of "Mizrahi literature" exemplifies Wittgenstein's central argument that "essence is expressed by grammar."[22] That is, grammar reflects the essence of the cultural stance, and not only the language's rules. The prevalent notion of "Mizrahi literature" is grounded in two major arguments.

(1) Orientalism in Israel is expressed both in the reasons for the bringing of the Mizrahim to the country, and in the patronizing and discriminatory attitude they received upon their migration to Israel, and continue to receive to the present.[23] Shohat explicitly mentions repression, exclusion, and silencing, in addition to discrimination.

(2) Hebrew language and literature are dominated to the present, in both the creative and critical-scholarly planes, by Ashkenazim. Despite the growth in the quantity of Mizrahi literature being written, its authors still conform to the dictates of the stereotype expected of them, such as the portrayal of a backward and primitive culture and nostalgic longings for the characteristic features of the Arab culture from which they came.[24]

---

block additional options that are on the cultural agenda of every creative artist in Israel. It demands struggle, no less than it enables distancing oneself from it, betraying it. The constant choice, however, and the open movement between these opposing and complementary possibilities are available only to Mizrahim" (p. 248).

22 Wittgenstein, *Philosophical Investigations*, para. 371.

23 See Ella Shohat, *Forbidden Reminiscences* (Tel Aviv: Kedem, 2001), p. 142 (Hebrew).

24 "Hebrew language and the culture written in it, that were the main property and conquest of the Zionist movement even before it conquered the land as well, had already become white out of their own desire for Europe; like the European languages, they were capable of delineating the boundaries of their whiteness and the strangers within them. And they still try to do this" (Dror Mishani, *The Ethnic Unconscious: The Emergence of "Mizrahiut" in the Hebrew Literature of the Eighties* [Tel Aviv: Am Oved, 2006], pp. 32–33). In the same passage, Mishani also accuses the Mizrahi authors who complied with the dictates of these expectations: "In

These two characteristics present a challenge that is almost impossible to meet for the author of Mizrahi origin who is proud of his origins and the culture in which he was raised, and who has a multicultural, and at times universal, orientation. Adaf's poetic grammar reflects this complexity, and facilitates changing the reader's consciousness regarding the generally accepted conception of Israeli Mizrahi literature, and regarding contemporary Hebrew, as it creates a hybrid language that is also an alternative culture that wrestles with universal questions. The grammar characteristic of this language expresses distinct pictoriality: "I think differently, in a different way. I say different things to myself. I have different pictures."[25]

Poetic language of this sort includes the clarification of philosophical questions regarding the relationship between language and the world. At this juncture we should distinguish between the onceness of the experience and that of linguistic fashioning, a distinction that was suggested by Shimon Adaf himself.[26] Adaf's poetry is fashioned as the voice of a unique "I," but this "I" is dedicated to the clarification of the features of language, as a philosophical mission. This dedication takes a number of directions: the *first direction* is writing under the influence of diverse language-games. The *second direction* is the definition of questions that examine language-world relationships, for instance, how concepts such as place, history, or time influence consciousness; or how

recent years, when more and more Mizrahim were given the possibility of taking part in cultural activity in Hebrew, they themselves are present in such experiences only in order to rewrite them and tell their story otherwise—they play with the color lines of Hebrew, which they identify and reject [. . .] by themselves they blacken and whiten themselves; in any event, they do not cease to use these colors of 'Mizrahiut' [being Mizrahi] and 'Ashkenaziut' [being Ashkenazi] in order to assemble identity masks for themselves." Even after the Israeli political upheaval of 1977, the change in the fashioning of the Mizrahi image in literature was not one of liberation. Quite the opposite—this change consisted of new adaption to the old political dictate: "Ten years after the political upheaval, their lost identity was found for the Mizrahim, with the help of Hebrew literary criticism: they are not ideologues, they are not intellectuals, they are calm, tranquil, and reconciled; as if that upheaval, that Mizrahi opposition that people spoke of, had never happened" (p. 168).

25 Wittgenstein, *Lectures and Conversations*, p. 55.

26 In a private conversation, January 11, 2015.

cultural conventions such as myth or religious ritual impact on it. The *third direction* of Adaf's examination of language is his attempt to create original expression of the existential situation that exceeds the bounds of everyday consciousness (becoming aware of death, connection to the mystical).

Adaf's poetry is Wittgensteinian, because it concentrates on close observation of the fundamentals of human existence, and examines their possibilities, instead of their causes. Like Wittgenstein, he does not offer moral, social, or cultural arguments, he rather develops a process of continuous perfectionism, as he exhausts one direction of investigation and turns to another, always without rest.[27] Unlike the poetry of Zelda, who finds solace in the bosom of nature, in the feeling of harmony with it; unlike the poetry of Amichai, who finds relief for his soul in love; and unlike the poetry of Kosman, who finds repose in the realization of closeness with the Buberian other, Adaf the poet is restless.

In order to explain how restlessness is reflected in poetical language, we must examine the characteristic features of the language of imagining. The thought mechanism that enables pictoriality also allows imagining, and both (pictoriality and imagining) are bound by linguistic rules.[28] Their common ground, as Newton Garver suggested, is that all the language-games examined by Wittgenstein are categories with transcendental rules, and this includes language-games of imagination.[29]

---

27 The restlessness is presented, e.g., in the prose book in which he first formally incorporated poetry, *The Wedding Gifts*, by the speaker attempting to go beyond the world, in all planes of existence, in order to understand his behavior, since no known human logic succeeds in explicating it. I mentioned this poem in the chapter on Zelda, in the context of a sense of alienation from the world. At the beginning of our discussion in the current chapter, the first three lines of the poem will serve as a retrospective key for understanding my chronological survey: "I encountered the world / At an outer point that faces / a hinge" (Adaf, *Wedding Gifts*, p. 7; trans. Edward Levin). The poem reflects an attempt to create a tabula rasa for self-constitution, in order to examine the basic conventions of Western society, such as the influence of the family and the environment, national and cultural norms, and the physical and emotional need for contact with other people.

28 See Wittgenstein, *Philosophical Grammar*, pp. 128–29.

29 Newton Garver, *This Complicated Form of Life: Essays on Wittgenstein* (Chicago: Open Court, 1994), p. 72.

1. *Icarus Monologue*: The Poetic Grammar of Hybrid Imagination

> A mental image is the image which is described when someone describes what he imagines.[30]
> What is the criterion for the sameness of two images? [. . .] For me, when it's someone else's image: what he says and does.—For myself, when it's my image: nothing.[31]
> *I could not apply any rules to a private transition from what is seen to words.* Here the rules really would hang in the air; for the institution of their application is lacking.[32]

Icarus Monologue, which was published in 1997, marks the transition to hybrid culture that has the experience of not-belonging as its starting point. The uniqueness of the book lies in its self-fashioning by means of motifs and narratives taken from Greek mythology, quotations from and allusions to world literature, and the refashioning of the pattern in the book of Psalms. Autobiographical details thereby assume the garb of a statement that is both individual and universal, and raise the question of how hybrid imagination functions in the reconstruction of the speaker's poetical and historical autobiography. As Wittgenstein maintains, analysis does not require justification for imaginary first-person reconstitution, it rather investigates the features of the imaginary poetics.

This hybrid and universal fashioning is already evident from an initial look at the titles of the poems in his first collection of poetry, *Icarus Monologue*. The book's title consists of two Greek words, and directs us to Greek mythology—the story of Icarus. The first page of the book opens with a quotation—from the essay "The Thought: A Logical Inquiry" by Gottlob Frege—that is a sort of declaration of intent by the speaker:

30 Wittgenstein, *Philosophical Investigations*, para. 367.
31 Wittgenstein, *Philosophical Investigations*, para. 377.
32 Wittgenstein, *Philosophical Investigations*, para. 380.

> I have to content myself with presenting the reader with a thought, in itself immaterial, dressed in sensible linguistic form. The metaphorical aspect of language presents difficulties. *The sensible always breaks in and makes expression metaphorical* and so improper. So a battle with language takes place and I am compelled to occupy myself with language although it is not my proper concern here. I hope I have succeeded in making clear to my readers what I want to call a thought.[33]

This passage prepares the reader for the "battle with language" in the book, with Greek mythology being the language-game in which this battle will be waged. Later in the book, along with Icarus, Oedipus, and Orpheus, Absalom (from the book of Samuel), Brecht, Baudelaire, Albert Camus, and a series of additional connotations from world and Jewish culture make an appearance.

The book of poetry *Icarus Monologue* drew attention mainly because of its autobiographical reworking of childhood experiences. In my opinion, however, this focus misses a central and innovative aspect of the book, namely, the linguistic adaptation of mythical elements that merges them with the Israeli reality, and transforms its expressions into concrete, universal embodiments of loneliness and isolation, the search for love, unresolved family tensions, and blending with the landscape.

Hybridism is already expressed in the titles of the poems, which combine terms from different periods and cultures and lay out various forms of poetical fashioning: *Legend, Obsession, Portrait, Icarus Monologue, Epitaph on One of Brecht's Tombstones, Idyll, Sonata,* and *Psalms of the Day*—influenced by the Jewish practice of reciting the Psalm of the Day (a different chapter of Psalms for each day of the week) after the morning prayer service. Adaf composed a special poem for each day that examines a universal phenomenon (*Sight, Loss, Love, Attraction, Spring, I*). Unlike the chapters of Psalms read each day which emphasize the uniqueness of the Jewish people and request God's Providence over

33 Gottlob Frege, "The Thought: A Logical Inquiry," *Mind* 65 (no. 259) (July 1956), p. 298 n. 1. The emphasized passage is Adaf's motto.

it, the juxtaposition of universal experience with Jewish practice is surprising, and, as it were, forces on the Jewish ritual a context of general human experience. This metaphoric move links the convention of Jewish tradition to universal situations, thus the language-game functions concurrently in the cultural and the universal fields.[34]

Self-constitution of this sort is evident in the poem *Autobiography*. The title seemingly indicates that the poem will include information about origin, culture, period, and local characteristics. Instead, the speaker sets forth his history in an imaginary universal plane, while, except for the name of the month Tammuz, no specific cultural features can be detected in this poem:

> *Autobiography*
> Not far from here
> can be any place in Israel
> there I was born,
> under a molten Tammuz sky.
> Her sorrow was terrible when her mother died.
> About to give birth on white sheets.
> On white sheets
> the sorrow of death and the distress of childbirth joined
> together to bring her to her knees.
> I would like to believe that somewhere
> a bird drank
> the dawn of before I was
> and screeched,
> or a red-hot star was lit to mark my coming.
> In my childhood
> A lightning-struck olive tree entangled and shed
> its heavy fruits on the head of a girl

34 Newton Garver showed how the concept "language-game" functions as a universal category, alongside the cultural language-game. See Garver, *This Complicated Form of Life*, pp. xiv, 15, 198. Wittgenstein used the word *Feld* as a metaphor for obedience to the rule in a specific realm. See, e.g., Wittgenstein, *Philosophical Investigations*, para. 85, 172.

that I loved from afar.
The seashore drew for me, with subtle irony,
matching blisters on my shoulders,
similes of wings for a child who wants to fly.
There is my childhood,
wrapped in sand blueprints, rounded
in puddles, in paper boats, tied
with strings too thin to see,
with hooks to my maturity.
When I became an adult
a spring-struck rosebush entangled and shed
its heavy flowers on the head of a girl
that I loved from afar.[35]

Any place could be the backdrop for the speaker's life, according to what the speaker argues, and the poem leads us to realize this: he was born in the heat of the summer (Tammuz being the only indicator of his Jewish origin), when his mother struggled, at one and the same time, with the pain of childbirth and the pain at the loss of her mother. The joining together of these "sorrows" marks the speaker's autobiography, which is not connected to or ensues from the features of a specific culture, it rather is born of fate. The speaker gently fashions a sense of mission that is connected with his birth, by composing the mental image of a bird or a star that signaled his arrival. The consciousness of mission is characteristic of the romantic stance of a creative artist, who views his creative ability as an inborn mission that sets him apart and did not come to him by inheritance or as a gift (see above, the comparison of the ars poetica positions of Adaf and Bialik).

The next fashioned stage is that of childhood, with its romantic frustration (love from afar) coupled with physical frustration (the light-skinned speaker suffers from the sun). Frustration and a sense of missing out (also romantic) typify the speaker as an adult as well. This poem, which ends the book *Icarus Monologue*, raises the question: What are

35 Shimon Adaf, *Icarus Monologue*, pp. 77–78; trans. Edward Levin.

the connections between the autobiographical details and the author's imagination? While reading the poem's title directs the reader to locate a biographical direction in the poem, other poems, whose titles refer to Greek myths, contribute much more significantly to the self-constitution in the book.

There is a complex relationship between autobiography as a concept from modern literary criticism and the imaginary process based on mental images. Their common starting point is that autobiography, like imagination, is constituted in a private sphere that represents individual experience, and both are formulated in language understandable by all.[36] Roy Pascal, who is considered to be the modern definer of the genre, argued that autobiography is a unique literary genre that offers its readers, by "close reading," a complex web of interpretive issues.[37] Pascal's proposal joins that of Wittgenstein to examine intermediate links that reflect relationships between linguistic situations and attest to the nature of these situations.[38]

In *Icarus Monologue* Adaf connects links from various cultures to compose an autobiographical mosaic in which mythical events are incorporated in his personal autobiography, to illustrate and drive it. The speaker's frequent use of the first person keeps us from knowing if this is a refashioning of the original myth, or whether Adaf fashions the myth in this way to exemplify his own experience. For example, the poem *In the Winter, When My Heart Is Orpheus on the Sea* opens by using the first person, which lends itself to equivocal interpretation:

> In the winter when my heart
> is burnt, held captive by the winds
> the winds,
> (they conquer it, cunningly
> with wooden horses of inhalations).
> [. . .]

---

36 See Ray Pascal, *Design and Truth in Autobiography* (Cambridge, MA: Harvard University Press, 1960), pp. 180–81.

37 See Pascal, *Design and Truth*, p. 182.

38 See chap. 1.

Passersby throw a name from one to another,
my name—
"Don't look, there's
Orpheus on the sea."[39]

The speaker merges with the character of Orpheus, but refashions the myth: the warning given to Orpheus (not to look back after having saved Eurydice) is now directed to the passersby. Orpheus, in the garb of Adaf, is capable of writing poetry, but "was burnt, held captive by the winds / the winds," and does not stand against them independently, as did the mythological Orpheus. In Adaf's poem, Eurydice, Orpheus's lover in the Greek myth, is transformed from subject to object:[40]

2. Eurydice is in the courtyard.
All the courtyard is drained into Eurydice,
all of Eurydice concentrates on
teeth pushing into her lower lip.
[. . .]
She won't urge her teeth,
she's got time.
The light, that would drop
at such an hour, now
like a stone.

3. My body is full of sharp fractures, a few lies.[41]

The poetic grammar fashions Eurydice as a bidirectional metaphor, by changing the syntactic functions: from a name that represents a person in a certain place, Eurydice becomes the embodiment of the entire courtyard (by turning her from subject to object). The drained

39 Adaf, *Icarus Monologue*, p. 27; trans. Edward Levin.
40 See above (the introductory section on "Self-Constitution through Mystical Grammar"), Wittgenstein's distinction (following James) between I as object and I as subject.
41 Adaf, *Icarus Monologue*, p. 27; trans. Edward Levin.

courtyard acts on Eurydice, and reflects her (Eurydice's) concentration on pushing her teeth. Eurydice "pushes" her teeth, but does not "urge" them, and the reader is invited to guess why.

The result of this poetic grammar is that, at the end of the stanza, the frozen picture of the light parallels Eurydice's tarrying. The speaker's experience reflects the loneliness of Orpheus the speaker, with his lover and the daylight reflecting a lack of interaction with him. The third stanza, in which the speaker attests to his body being full of fractures and lies, strengthens the sense of loneliness in front of the potential lover and the world, and creates a dialectic between a romantic position about the existence of a lover and the possibility of being one with nature, on the one hand, and, on the other, irony and brokenheartedness regarding the realization of this aspiration in reality.

At times in his poems, Adaf adds details from other language-games to the original myth, and lessens the distance between the mythical narrative and the speaker's self-narrative, as in the poem *Search*: "Once I was a single Orpheus, / poisoner of wells, / to see / who of the women is dying like my lover."[42] "Poisoners of wells" became an anti-Semitic epithet for the Jews in France (1321), in the wake of a blood libel that accused the Jews and lepers of joining together to poison wells, thereby causing leprosy.[43] This epithet spread throughout Europe, together with other anti-Semitic slurs, and was a contributing factor in the expulsion of Jews from place to place in the time of the Black Plague in the fourteenth century. In this poem, the epithet is directed to the speaker himself, who punishes all women for the death throes of his lover. The Oedipus myth is refashioned also in the poem *Perspective*, in which the speaker unites with the mythical figure, brings the myth to life, and refashions it as an individual mental image:

> Once again I must tear out my eyes
> that grow back,

42 Adaf, *Icarus Monologue*, p. 29; trans. Edward Levin.

43 Malcolm Barber, "Lepers, Jews, and Moslems: The Plot to Overthrow Christendom in 1321," *History* 66 (no. 216) (1981), pp. 1–17. My thanks to Ephraim Shoham for this reference.

every year,
in February,
when the dry birds catch fire with a murmur,
and the winds disperse the distance.[44]

The Oedipal speaker is bound by the obsessive need to once more tear out his eyes that grow again, unlike the original myth. The speaker harnesses the Oedipus myth to explain his connection to the world: the changes that occur in nature change Oedipus's fate in the original plot, and cause his eyes to regrow. The speaker, however, tears his eyes out again, as a metaphorical expression of the punishment that he deserves because of his recurring disregard for the reality.

The poem *Icarus Monologue* (from which the book takes its name) provides an additional example of the adaption of myth to the speaker's self-consciousness.[45] The poem is a reflective monologue of Icarus, who looks retrospectively at his fall and its fashioning as myth. During the course of the poem, Icarus's character is mingled with that of the speaker, so that the lines of the poem could speak about each of them:

Why did we have to flee?
If death had come
in the tunnels of hunger and thirst,
forgetfulness, too, would have come,
and everything that was, and everything that was prophesied.

The poets, the artists, the tellers of tales,
force me to furrow
the scarfs of salt and the sea,
for them.
I'm tired from the wisdom
that is gathered at the scorched edges:
fall after fall, all the monuments are pierced in my memory.
and the unknown burial place.

44 Adaf, *Icarus Monologue*, p. 24; trans. Edward Levin.
45 Adaf, *Icarus Monologue*, p. 33; trans. Edward Levin.

Around it people lose altitude
in the healed space
between the greatness of pain
and the depth of suffering.

The poem depicts a monologue delivered by Icarus in a retrospective look at the mythologizing of his fall, as symbolizing all the falls that follow it. Icarus's fall functions in three temporal planes: past—in the Greek myth, future—as anticipation of all the future falls that will happen, and finally, in the present—as anticipating the individual fall of the speaker: "Tonight the moon will pierce / a silenced nail in the mists. / Tomorrow I will fall."

This poem exemplifies, in the clearest possible way, self-constitution under the influence of universal myth, as Adaf fashions a unique figurative language that locates in the present what happens in his world, using motives and narratives from Greek mythology. Thus, for example, Icarus describes in the first person how various sorts of artists compel him to classify the elements of the sea that harm them ("[they] force me to furrow / the foils of salt and the sea, / for them"). This could be understood both as clarifying the speaker's use of myth (which aids him to distinguish between useful and injurious) and as an expression of the speaker's identification with Icarus, since the former imagines himself classifying materials from general culture for other creative artists. In order to explain how the grammar of imaginative language actually works, I will refer to the insights of Thomas Sebeok.[46]

Sebeok described three types of metaphors as models of ways to view abstract inner processes by their concrete, "outer" fashioning.[47]

46 Thomas A. Sebeok, *The Forms of Meaning: Modeling System Theory and Semiotic Analysis* (Berlin: Mouton de Gruyter, 2000), pp. 38–41.

47 "*A metaform is an example of a connective form* that results when abstract concepts are represented in terms of concrete ones [. . .] Metaforms are *primary connective forms*, portraying abstractions in terms of concrete source domains [. . .] These abstract notions are all conceived as *ways of seeing internally* that are modeled on *ways of seeing externally*. Now, once the first 'layer' of metaforms has been formed in a language's conceptual reservoir, on the basis of concrete source domains, then this layer itself becomes a new productive source domain for creating a higher (= more abstract) layer of concepts [. . .] The three main types of connective models

These three types of connective models, which Sebeok called "meta-form," "meta-metaform," and "meta-symbol," reflect three levels of complexity of the representative process. He emphasized two central features of these models: universality, and their contribution to understanding the relationship between metaphor and the creation of a cultural conception or position.[48]

The book's title functions as a meta-symbol: it connects the reader to the Greek myth, but during the reading of the poems in the book, the myth is refashioned and cast in a completely different light. In the Greek myth, Icarus's lack of caution leads to his death (since he did not heed his father's warning and drew near to the sun, which melted the wax in his wings, thus causing him to fall to his death). Icarus in Adaf's book, in contrast, is a hero who considers his actions, reflectively looks upon the process of falling, and is a meta-symbol for all the falls and monuments that will be in the future. The poem *Icarus Leaps* is seemingly understood as a movie that reconstructs in slow motion the act of leaping that preceded the fall.[49] Unlike Icarus's rashness in the Greek

are: (1) *metaforms*, which are assemblages intended to deliver the meaning of abstract concepts on the basis of concrete source domains; (2) *meta-metaforms*, which are assemblages forged among already-existing metaforms; (3) *meta-symbols*, which are symbolic forms that result from specific types of linkages associated with particular metaforms" (Sebeok, *Forms of Meaning*, pp. 38–41).

48 "Phylogenetically speaking, the universality of connective modeling in the human species begs the question of the relation of metaphor to the emergence of conceptual thinking in humans [. . .] In a fundamental semiotic sense *culture* can be defined as a *connective macrocode*, made up of the different codes [. . .] and the signs, texts, and connective forms that are fashioned and used by people in specific social contexts" (Sebeok, *Forms of Meaning*, p. 42).

49 I sally forth
slowly, like the actions I take,
the solid light around me.
Here and there plantings crawl
toward a possible tree;
It's still needed to fell the breaths
from the air between them.
Not I,
in any event.
Innocent of any other movement,
I sally forth.
Everything is waited upon,
not like something
that one calls water,

myth, Adaf's poem highlights slowness and reflective thinking that is condensed toward the end of the poem in a neologism: "Everything is waited on [*mumtan*]." The use of the root *mem-taf-nun* in the passive *hifil* form reinforces the depiction of Icarus as careful and calculating, with these traits generating a general atmosphere of suspension. The neologism is reinforced by metaphoric contrast, which is actually a synesthetic metaphor:[50] "Everything is waited upon, / not like something / that one calls water, / and another calls / Time."[51] The suspension is in opposition to the natural dynamism of space and time, and so, unlike the mythical Icarus, who falls to his death, in accordance with the laws of physics, the Icarus of the poem ascends while he gazes upon the laws of nature.

The action begins with "sallying forth," which is repeated, in the context of two expanded images, in each of which the sallying forth is the target domain. Unlike, however, the concretization in the imagery, in both images in the poem, the element from the source domain is as indistinct as the target, and does not generate concretization in the description of the action: "I sally forth / slowly, like the actions I take, / the solid light around me / [. . .] I sally forth. / [. . .] not like something / that one calls water, / and another calls / Time."[52] The sallying forth is compared to future actions, whose nature accordingly does not explain the nature of the sallying forth. Additionally, these are actions (in the plural) that are not detailed, which, too, creates indistinctness instead of concretization. The poem therefore frustrates the reader's expectations, on both the thematic level (Icarus's changed image) and the linguistic, in its metaphorical fashioning.

The maneuvering between the three focal points (the original myth, the Israeli context, and the new interpretation of the myth)

and another calls
Time (Adaf, *Icarus Monologue*, p. 32; trans. Edward Levin).

50 "Synaesthetic metaphors are expressions in which one sensory modality is described in terms of another" (Yeshayahu Shen, "Metaphor and Poetic Figures," in *Cambridge Handbook of Metaphor and Thought*, ed. Raymond W. Gibbs, Jr. [New York: Cambridge University Press, 2008], p. 303).

51 Adaf, *Icarus Monologue*, p. 32.

52 Adaf, *Icarus Monologue*, p. 32.

produces symbolism that, as Sebeok would put it, enables us to understand the Icarus metaphor as the key to the emergence of the cultural stance that is fashioned in the poems. Indeed, at times the reader of Adaf's book has difficulty in separating the original motifs of the myth from the characteristic features of the reality; thus the connections between myth and language fashion the contention with the sensation of alienation and the difficulty of, and failure to, forge relationships with other people.

Along with this, I also propose an additional interpretive aspect that clarifies Adaf's use of Greek myths, which continues in his second book, *What I Thought Shadow*. In the discussion of mystical grammar, following Wittgenstein, I presented constant perfectionism as a nonverbal process, but which can be identified in "*an overview* of the use of our words." The refashioning of the myths in the process of self-constitution in Adaf's poetry can be seen as a type of perfectionism, which ensues from what Cavell finds in Wittgenstein and Emerson as a sense of confusion, self-exile, and the loss of one's way. These feelings express a "family resemblance" between the mythical heroes in the book (and between mythical heroes as a whole): Oedipus, Orpheus, and Icarus are not the masters of their fate; they rather are controlled by it. At the same time, however, all three, as the speaker in Adaf's poems, are driven by the need to improve their self-understanding, and in its wake, the way they act in the world. Stephen Mulhall suggested viewing Wittgenstein's perfectionism as an expression of religiosity, since its motive force is beyond the boundaries of language.[53]

In contrast with the fashioning, under the influence of Greek mythology, of failures and emotional difficulties, the book contains a number of love poems that attest to the possibility of active self-constitution by means of language. In the poems written under the influence of the myths, Adaf used myth as an object, facing which and inspired by which the speaker's self is examined. In the following poems,

53 Mulhall, "Wittgenstein and the Philosophy of Religion."

on the other hand, the speaker is fashioned as a subject, who can impose meaning on the world, as John Searle defined this.[54]

The motif of love is fashioned in each of the following poems as a viewpoint from which the description emerges, either in advance or after the fact, and this illustrates the possibility of imposing meaning on objects or on situations in the world by means of poetic speech-acts (such as metaphor). This mode of action is the central characteristic of Adaf's figurative speech, with constant tension between the speaker and the way that the reality unfolds. That is, this imposing is not complete: the world does not always accept the metaphorical meaning, and at times opposes it.

Love is crafted as a meta-symbol because it is based on two prior metaphoric levels: the personal level, and that of the form of life. The last in a cycle of poems entitled "Language" exemplifies an attempt to dictate the meaning of a future fate, on three metaphorical levels: on the concrete level, going becomes a return (despite the use of the future tense, in the grammatical plane going is already connected with the return); on the level of form of life, we have the depiction of a mountainous landscape and heaps of straw, and the act of creeping functions as a metaphor for special effort; and on the universal level, the relationship is perceived as the dynamic of going to and back, which has an optimistic outlook:

Creeping in the Mountains
You'll see,
my going from you will become my returning to you,

54 John Searle described the philosophical perspective that enables a person to give meaning to objects, situations, and processes whose existence and behavior are not dependent on his choice or decisions: "The remarkable thing about speech-acts is that in the performance of speech-acts ordinary physical events and objects in the world have semantic properties [. . .] how is it possible that mere things in the world can come to have semantic properties? How is it possible that the mind can impose intentionality on entities which construed in one way are just neutral objects and events in the world like any other? [. . .] the mind imposes intentionality on objects and events in the world by intentionally imposing conditions of satisfaction on condition of satisfaction" (John Searle, *Consciousness and Language* [Cambridge: Cambridge University Press, 2002], p. 146).

> if not, what's the meaning
> of creeping in the mountains, the high stones,
> the heaps of straw that blow shaded gold
> into the night.[55]

The speaker prophesies to his lover that he will come back to her. The reason for his leaving is unclear, and the reasons for his certainty that he will return to her are even more clouded in mystery. He connects this certainty to a series of mental images that are metaphorically related to his return: the speaker depicts a seeming correspondence between an event in nature (creeping in the hills), the domestic nature of the golden heaps of straw, and his return. In practice, the speaker imposes meaning on the world, in Searle's terminology. Wittgenstein helps to disperse the clouds for the reader regarding the separation and return by relating to love as an emotion that can be clarified introspectively, unlike most states of mind. Viewing the poem as the embodiment of the speaker's introspection enables us to understand the metaphorical fashioning as confirmation of the speaker's inner stance, despite the lack of any outer criterion for this confirmation. Only the speaker, in the first person, can attest if he truly loves someone:

> Does it make sense to ask "How do you know that you believe that?"—and is the answer: "I find it out by introspection"? In *some* cases it will be possible to say some such thing, in most not. It makes sense to ask, "Do I really love her, or am I only fooling myself?", and the process of introspection is the calling up of memories, of imagined possible situations, and of the feelings that one would have if . . .[56]

Introspection can generate recollection processes, as well as speculations regarding possibilities; the speaker in the poem looks at the world and the act of separation and—speculatively—concludes that he will return to his lover. Wittgenstein does not explain the effectiveness

55 Adaf, *Icarus Monologue*, p. 20; trans. Edward Levin.
56 Wittgenstein, *Philosophical Investigations*, para. 587; ellipsis in the original.

of introspection specifically for examining love (while in most instances introspection is not effective for confirmation), because emotional dispositions, as he calls love and hate, are not meant to give us information about the world:

> What goes to make them different from sensations: they do not give us any information about the external world. (A grammatical remark.) Love and hate might be called emotional dispositions, and so might fear in one sense.[57]

At this juncture, these dispositions meet with poetry, which, too, is not meant to transmit information:

> Do not forget that a poem, even though it is composed in the language of information, is not used in the language-game of giving information.[58]

Nonetheless, love is not a simple emotion, but a complex disposition whose veracity could be judged:

> Love is not a feeling. Love is put to the test, pain not. One does not say: "That was not true pain, or it would not have gone off so quickly."[59]

Here, as well, love and the work of art meet, since, as we discussed at length above, judging a work of art is possible. In summation, love is an emotional disposition that can be examined and judged introspectively, and this description explicates the way in which Adaf fashioned love in the book, as amenable to judgment in the context of which the effort to restore or stop it can be made. Since love is not only an emotion, but is much deeper, the title "love" facilitates the inclusion of a poetic description in which the speaker paradoxically fashions his love:

---

57 Wittgenstein, *Zettel*, para. 491.
58 Wittgenstein, *Remarks*, vol. 1, para. 888.
59 Wittgenstein, *Zettel*, para. 504.

> "If it passes, then it was not true love." Why was it not in that case? Is it our experience, that only this feeling and not that endures? Or are we using a picture: we test love for its inner character, which the immediate feeling does not discover. Still, this picture is important to us. Love, what is important, is not a feeling, but something deeper, which merely manifests itself in the feeling. We have the word "love" and now we give this title to the most important thing. (As we confer the title "Philosophy" on a particular intellectual activity.)[60]

Love is not a regular emotion, but a deeper state of consciousness. The noun "love" does not succeed in representing the emotion bound up in it, just as the noun "philosophy" fails to represent multileveled philosophical activity. Wittgenstein proposes a complex stance in which, despite the inability of language to represent, the truth of love can be judged. Language is capable of pictorializing emotion, so that we can determine its importance for us, and in this manner language enables introspection that explores the nature of love. The introspection in the next poem is intended to stop love, and not to proclaim its continuity:

> Hook or weed or any image that you will find
> for your name that insists on my tongue
> I forget you
> stronger than always, more than any time
> I connect your face
> with the most fleeting thing, dust
> or the moon in a June morning or
> any other image
> that you will find
> for your name that insists on my tongue.[61]

The speaker strives for perfectionism by detaching himself from the obsessive memory of his lover. Since this bond is harmful for him,

60 Wittgenstein, *Remarks*, vol. 1, para. 115.
61 Adaf, *Icarus Monologue*, p. 49; trans. Edward Levin.

he tries to impose forgetfulness on his consciousness by a metaphoric action: connecting the lover's name with transitory things. In Wittgensteinian terms, we could say that the speaker tries to deconstruct the action of ostensive definition: instead of the name indicating its bearer, the speaker attempts to attach the name to the semantic field of transitory things, and thereby change its function from indication to an expression of the past. Memory, too, is fashioned metaphorically as a stubborn element (the speaker twice states the line "your name that insists [being] on my tongue") and reveals the bewitching component of language.[62] The sensation of bewitchment ensues from the memory's lack of control, and expresses the inner struggle between the desire for the self-object and the wish to be liberated from dependence on it.

I wish to connect this perfectionism to refashioning from another aspect, namely, the use of the hybridism of a modern language-game and a language-game from Jewish tradition, in order to fashion a disposition of love. In the chapter on Kosman's poetry I related to the refashioning of the Psalm of the Day, when, for both Kosman and Adaf, only the title remains of the original ritual.[63] Why did each of these poets nevertheless choose this poetic convention for individual "mending" in the context of the language-game of Jewish prayer?[64] The mending finds expression in fashioning the collective ritual from an individual, subjective perspective that places love as the starting point for looking at the world.

In this poem, love is fashioned under the influence of the surroundings; in practice, however, the poem does not remain on the fashioning level of a concrete environment, but adds an additional level of metaphoric fashioning, so that the surroundings are crafted in universal terms. The title of the "Psalm for the Third Day" is "Love," and this linkage of the language of the book of Psalms and the language of

62 Wittgenstein, *Philosophical Investigations*, para. 109.

63 For an intriguing comparison, see, in the preceding chapter, the discussion of Kosman's *Psalm of the Day: For the Third Day of the Week*. Unlike the fashioning of love in Adaf's poem, in Kosman's work love is a replacement for the religious ritual.

64 Wittgenstein included prayer among the examples he gave for language-games. See Wittgenstein, *Philosophical Investigations*, para. 23.

prayer to the universal topic of love seemingly hints at the desire to present love as an alternative to the content of the religious ritual. In practice, however, the expectations raised by the title are dashed in the poem:

Love (Psalm for the Third Day)
My love is voiceless
faced with the world's extravagance.
It comes from small, remote places,
And wonders
I watched the trees
coexist with the violence of wind
[. . .]
The forests are harems of
fragile girls
[. . .]
The skies make peace amongst themselves and fall
On a hard earned workingman's town.
Through industrial shadows, smoke sheets, my childhood fears
jump me, like
Armed assailants from the back alley of a forsaken night
[. . .]
My love is paralyzed,
Push it as I may, it is rootless
In the sense that it is provincial and inferior.
I watch the simple daisy
Spider-like, swarm in the grass
Or attack the hill
With hurried bloom,
To make spring.[65]

The topic of *Psalm for the Third Day* is one of the features of the speaker's love, in contrast with that of Ps. 82, which portrays God as

65 Adaf, *Icarus Monologue*, p. 62; trans. Vivian Eden.

waging the wars of His people Israel.[66] This reversal from the general to the individual violates both the ritual and the thematic conventions. This violation is based on the reader's familiarity with the "Daily Psalm" convention and the thematics prevalent in the psalms recited on other days of the week. The decisive majority of these psalms relate to the public and institutionalized, and not to the individual aspect, with Ps. 82, the Psalm for Tuesday, being most outstanding in this respect.

The use of the plural predominates in Ps. 82, and is the diametrical opposite of the low-key, reserved, and personal language of Adaf's poem, both stylistically and contentually. The love in Adaf's poem is not directed to any specific subject, but rather appears in detail in its own right. It "comes from small, remote places," is "voiceless," "provincial and inferior," "paralyzed," and "rootless." The poem as a whole expresses the mutual relationship between the features of place and nature and those of love, with nature fashioned metaphorically, in a way converse to the place, that is, from the speaker's home town. The speaker is surprised at the ability of the trees and the forests, the skies and the daisy to live in harmony with their surroundings, while the characteristics of the place, which express a daily struggle for survival, are applied to love and prevent it from blossoming. The speaker therefore emphasizes that his love is "provincial," in both the original Latin meaning of "rootless," and in its current meaning, namely, "inferior." The poetic grammar is based on both the original Latin meaning and that prevalent in the twentieth-century Israeli form of life.[67]

Love is silent and paralyzed, and its fashioning contrasts with the gracefulness of the elements taken from nature, which exist in harmony, and with the hunger for life "to make spring." The grammar attests to

66 "God stands in the divine assembly; among the divine beings He pronounces judgment [. . .] They neither know nor understand, they go about in darkness; all the foundations of the earth totter [. . .] but you shall die as men do, fall like any prince. Arise, O God, judge the earth, for all the nations are Your possession" (Ps. 82:1, 5, 7–8).

67 "To imagine a language means to imagine a form of life" (Wittgenstein, *Philosophical Investigations*, para. 19).

the essence,[68] with the description of nature functioning as a depiction of the desired nature of love, while the adverbial of place acts as a description of the reality. In both, the speaker gazes upon his surroundings, to which he ascribes meaning in accordance with his unique viewpoint. The description is existential, and not causal, because of the possibility of loving in contradictory ways within the same context. Love is accordingly fashioned as a meta-symbol that remains in the realm of the abstract, since the contrast between it and the reality does not allow the reader to understand it in concrete fashion, but only negatively.

In the next phase, in Adaf's second book of poetry, the speaker moves from looking at nature to looking at concepts that fashion the experience of nature, primarily the concepts of time, history, and memory. The speaker deconstructs a series of concepts in this semantic field, and shows how they actually reflect human motivations, and not substantive categories of consciousness. The philosophical arguments in the book's poems converse with Wittgenstein's insights on this topic and imply them. In order to understand the poems, the Wittgensteinian background should be detailed in a manner reminiscent of Freud's technique for interpreting dreams, which he condenses and encodes.[69]

In effect, Wittgenstein, under the influence of Augustine (whom he cites in *Philosophical Investigations* in this context), voids the concept of time of any substantive meaning.[70] Wittgenstein argues that we delude ourselves by thinking that if we formulate concepts (such as "time" or "present") they could guide and better our understanding of

---

68 "Grammar tells what kind of object anything is" (Wittgenstein, *Philosophical Investigations*, para. 373).

69 Sigmund Freud, *The Interpretation of Dreams*, trans. James Strachey (New York: Basic Books, 2010), pp. 296–97.

70 "Here it is easy to get into that dead end in philosophizing where one believes that the difficulty of the problem consists in our having to describe phenomena that evade our grasp, the present experience that slips quickly by, or something akin—where we find ordinary language too crude, and it looks as if we were dealing not with the phenomena of everyday conversation, but with ones that 'are evanescent, and, in their coming to be and passing away, tend to produce those others.' (Augustine: Manifestissima et usitatissima sunt, et eadem rursus nimus latent, et nova est inventio eorum.)" (Wittgenstein, *Philosophical Investigations*, para. 436).

the use of everyday language. This is especially true regarding the elusive present. We tend to view everyday language as "too crude," as if there were a clear or absolute term that could explicate it. I wish to complete the citation from Augustine brought by Wittgenstein in the original Latin, in which Augustine finely expresses the complexity of our use of the terminology of time:

> And we talk of time and time, and times and times. How long time is it since he said this; How long time since he did this; and How long time since I saw that: and This syllable hath double time to that single short syllable. These words we say, and these we have heard, and understand, and are understood. Most manifest and ordinary they are, and yet the selfsame things are too deeply hidden: yea, the finding out of them is new.[71]

On the one hand, we use this terminology in an understanding and understandable way, while, on the other, when we have to characterize these terms, they slip away and elude us. The poetical grammar characteristic of Adaf's poetry contends with this complexity by the indirect fashioning of the mechanism of time-experiences, as if they had been directly or obliquely influenced by Wittgenstein.

2. *What I Thought Shadow Is the Real Body*: The Dialogical Grammar of Place, Time, and Memory

> But isn't there also a peculiar feeling of pastness characteristic of images as memory images? There certainly are experiences which I should be inclined to call feelings of pastness, although not always when I remember something is one of these feelings present.—To get clear about the nature of these feelings it is again very useful to remember that there are gestures of

71 Augustine, *St. Augustine's Confessions*, trans. William Watts (Cambridge, MA: Harvard University Press, 1979 [1912]), vol. 2, pp. 256–59.

> pastness and inflexions of pastness which we can regard as representing the experiences of pastness.[72]

Shimon Adaf's poetry contends in diverse experiential, philosophical, and political ways with the conceptualization of time. In Wittgensteinian wording, we can ask what characterizes the experience of pastness in Adaf's poetry in these different planes, and how it participates in self-constitution. Adaf's three books of poetry can be interpreted along the axis of time, first and foremost due to their titles: *Icarus Monologue*, *What I Thought Shadow Is the Real Body*, and *Aviva-No* can be seen as referring, respectively, to the function of the past, the present, and the future (death). In his first book, Adaf drew inspiration from Greek mythology and later philosophical texts, thereby exemplifying the way in which ancient literature influenced his poetical identity. The past is relevant, not only as a source of inspiration, but as a substantive expression of experiences in the present, such as the experience of Icarus's fall or of Orpheus's experience of the netherworld.

The title of the second book reflects an awakening in the present from illusion (*What I Thought [. . .] Is*), and he turns to "the Real Body," an expression that clearly shows the actuality of the present. The third book fashions the memory of his dead sister, with the awareness of the body no longer accompanying every word in the book. The mourning in the present indirectly also contains wrestling with the terror of death. This grappling is paradoxical, since, on the one hand, there is certain knowledge that death is expected in the future, while, on the other, this cannot be formulated in words.[73] The poetical expression, as

---

72 Wittgenstein, *Blue and Brown Books*, p. 184.

73 Wittgenstein discusses the paradox in which, on the one hand, we are certain of the existence of inner processes, while, on the other, we cannot formulate them in language that distinguishes between them and externally perceivable processes. It therefore seems as if we want to deny their existence, while we actually do not want to do so; see *Philosophical Investigations*, para. 305–6. Wittgenstein resolved the paradox by maintaining that language functions simultaneously in a number of ways (*Philosophical Investigations*, para. 304). For our purposes, the language of poetry enables us to discuss the death experience, even though death is beyond the boundaries of regular language.

Susan Langer described it, can rise above the inability to express paradoxicality in language, and I will attempt to show how Adaf does this in his book.

Disillusionment regarding the concepts of time requires a reexamination of the manner in which memory functions, since it presumably is based on the raising and joining together of experiences from the past in order to give meaning in the present. In an attempt to examine the process, Wittgenstein proposes the term "pastness." Following Wittgenstein, Adaf formulated a possible development of memory:

> The sense of pastness is a sort of mental label that is added to the impression of the experience and creates dynamic interaction with it, that changes the more one returns to this experience. I don't believe that there is a definite picture of an event in the memory, but rather some sort of materials that are preserved together, that are reconsolidated in the act of recollection, in a certain order, that at times is preserved, and at other times, changes.[74]

Adaf shares Wittgenstein's notion in the above cited passage that a sense of pastness is created for a certain end, and it has no fixed characteristics that are shared by all people. Wittgenstein describes how recollection functions in the construction of identity:

> We can look at recognition, like memory, in two different ways: as a source of the concepts of the past and of identity, or as a way of checking what happened in the past, and on identity. If you exclude the element of intention from language, its whole function then collapses.[75]

Wittgenstein argues that memory functions in two ways: as a source of inspiration for fashioning the past in a person's world and as a source

---

74 Shimon Adaf, personal correspondence, February 7, 2014.

75 Ludwig Wittgenstein, *Philosophical Remarks*, ed. Rush Rhees, trans. Raymond Hargreaves and Roger White (Oxford: Basil Blackwell, 1975), p. 11.

for fashioning self-identity, on the one hand, and, on the other, as a manner of examining the influence of the past on the self as it is now. In this and additional ways Wittgenstein deconstructs the concept of "past" as one that guides human activity, offering instead grammar that enables us to examine the ways in which the past functions in everyday life in the present. He does this without commitment to a substantive, distinct concept of the present, and certainly without indicating the characteristics of the future. Adaf's poem *Rescue from Forgetfulness* crafts a similar existentialist stance, one that is detached from any history and is dedicated to a present physical and concrete, but one that does not identify the speaker:

> *Rescue from Forgetfulness*
> I think
> that I have reached
> the end of history.
> Not in the philosophical sense, where
> reason knows itself
> [. . .]
> No. In a simpler sense
> History ceases to be
> substantive for definitions, determining
> developmental relationships
> between earlier and later I lack
> Patriarchs and Matriarchs,
> without poetry, swaying on the window, sent
> to a Tel Aviv outside
> five o'clock on a December evening,
> feeling the air like
> a tongue.[76]

The first three lines ironically allude to the Hegelian conception that history advances teleologically toward its realization as absolute

76 Shimon Adaf, *That Which I Thought Shadow Is the Real Body* (Jerusalem: Keter, 2002), p. 59; trans. Edward Levin.

spirit.[77] Instead of this notion, the poem exemplifies Wittgenstein's proposal "to bring words back from their metaphysical to their everyday use."[78] The straightforward use of the term "history" contributes nothing to an understanding of the reality, since philosophical definitions do not, in practice, influence the existence of the individual. The speaker feels detached from any source, whether genetic (parents), cultural (poetic heritage), or locational (since he is distant from his birthplace). This separation from any relation seemingly enables him to give himself over to the atmosphere of the present, but this picture creates ambivalence in comparison with the title, which, after all, declares *Rescue from Forgetfulness*. Does this dedication to the present rescue from forgetfulness, or perhaps, everything mentioned by the speaker simply does not exist?

The ambivalence that is fashioned by the speech act of negative argument attests to the existence of a possible meaning horizon, while at the same time it negates such a horizon. In this way Adaf creates a mystical grammar in which what cannot be characterized in words is present, but in oblique fashion (negatively). In the poem *Haste*, for example, the speaker portrays the feeling of unhomeliness in a series of characteristics that evade the eye and language:

> *Haste*
> Not at home, not I. Passages felt out
> I arrive, a blade
> ragged against all love.
>
> Only a fine weak point—the heart is a puncture
> through it the world floods
>
> Winding of harsh pines, a bloody battle
> of light from the porch, sparrows of distance, pistons
> whose bodies' beat on the ground
> lurks.

77 Georg Wilhelm Friedrich Hegel, *The Phenomenology of Mind*, trans. J. B. Baillie (New York: Dover, 2003), esp. p. 396.

78 Wittgenstein, *Philosophical Investigations*, para. 116.

The summer, fleeting as the light
of a candle, my steps are a vaporized rustle, I must
hurry.[79]

The beginning of the poem is fashioned as a negative argument, with the focus of alienation and the frustration of the reader's expectations depicted in its continuation: on the one hand, the life experience that generated a sense of a "blade sharpened" does not enable the speaker to give himself over to love; he rather stands "against" it. On the other hand, the world nevertheless succeeds in entering the speaker's heart, despite the sharpened blade. This "success" is not in the intersubjective plane, since love does not evoke a sense of home for the speaker. It is the world that enters his heart, and even "floods" it.

This weak-heartedness explains the traumatic manner in which the speaker experiences trivial, everyday sights in the world (such as the winding of pine trees, a dispute between neighbors, or summer's shortness), leading to the inevitable conclusion at the end of the poem: "I must / hurry" and keep his distance—actually, from life itself. The poem continues to deepen the way in which the attitude to nature fashioned the speaker's identity in Adaf's first book. The fact that philosophical definitions do not constitute the speaker's identity can be depicted only by metaphors from the world of natural phenomena. The emotional and mental need, which can be neither defined nor verbalized, creates vulnerability and a profound lack of love.

The following poem strengthens and develops the interpretation of the preceding one, with the negative argument being the key to understanding human alienation. This estrangement is reinforced by the ambivalent fashioning that, at one and the same time, negates the meanings of his home town of Sderot, while ensuring that it is present:

Sderot does not exist. In the morning
nothing rises, bird-song still
lingers like winter in flawed bones
A fatal blow does not wound the earth

79 Adaf, *That Which I Thought Shadow*, p. 28; trans. Edward Levin.

to scar around the hills.
I spent childhoods for nothing.
I wasted
parents like breath, I let
this be.[80]

This poem is part of a trilogy of three poems, whose titles illustrate the presentation and deconstruction of the possibility of belonging, loving, and forming a long-term relationship: the first poem is entitled *Sderot Does Not Exist*; the second, *I Can't Return*; and the third, *What Point Is There to Talk of Love*.[81] The ambivalence is generated by, on the one hand, the mention of a datum that seemingly forces the speaker to relate to it: home town, childhood, love. On the other hand, the speaker shakes off the social expectations ensuing from each of these "data" and formulates a singular attitude to them, of containing and alienation, all at the same time.

The mystical dimension is shaped in grammar that simultaneously describes existence and nonexistence. The poetic language forms factors that are present in the consciousness of the speaker, whose attitude to which, however, is ambivalent. Consequently, they are rejected as significant components of his identity. In this context, we should mention an additional meaning of hybridism for Wittgenstein, namely, that it is a natural product of a range of language-games, and the ability to distinguish between language-games permits ambivalent thinking and the inclusion of two contradictory domains in a person's psyche.[82]

80 Adaf, *That Which I Thought Shadow*, p. 29; trans. Edward Levin.
81 Adaf, *That Which I Thought Shadow*, p. 29; trans. Edward Levin.
82 "Imagine I were the hybrid being that might pronounce 'I don't believe it is raining; and it is raining.' But what purpose do these words now serve? What employment am I imagining being given to them? 'He's coming. I personally don't believe it, but don't let that mislead you.' [. . .] This sounds as if two persons were speaking out of me; or as if one court within me gave the other person the information that so and so was coming, and this court wished that the person should take appropriate action—while another court in a certain sense reported my own attitude. It is as if one were to say 'I know that this is the wrong procedure, but I know that that's what I shall do.' 'He's coming, but I don't believe it' may, then, occur in a language-game. Or better: It is possible to think

An additional meaning that complements Wittgenstein's philosophical perspective was described by Bakhtin.[83] Hybridism of this sort appears, for instance, when it transpires that poetry itself is an illusion. Notwithstanding this, although deconstruction casts poetry in an ironic light as the object of the clarification of "That Which I Thought Shadow," it still retains it, thereby fashioning the mystical dimension in Adaf's poetry.

2.1. Poetry as a Chronological and Thematic Point of Departure

> The biggest difference between poetry and philosophy is that poetry is completely right, while philosophy is completely wrong. The latter assertion, however, does not make the task of preference between the two easy. This is because philosophy, which errs, turns the truth into an ideal, *poetry, which is completely right, also lauds the illusion and the false.*[84]

> We feel that even when all possible scientific questions have been answered, the problems of life remain completely untouched. Of course there are then no questions left, and this itself is the answer [. . .] There are, indeed, things that cannot be put into words. They make themselves manifest. They are what is mystical.85

> Isn't this the reason why men to whom the meaning of life had become clear after long doubting could not say what this meaning consisted in?[86]

---

out a language-game in which these words would not strike us as absurd" (Wittgenstein, *Remarks*, vol. 1, para. 495).

83 Bakhtin highlighted the connection between hybridism and heteroglossia and multiculturalism. See Bakhtin, *Dialogic Imagination*, p. 112. Bakhtin also indicated the potential for irony and disillusionment in hybrid speech. This potential is often realized in Adaf's work.

84 Adaf, *That Which I Thought Shadow*, p. 19; trans. Edward Levin (emphasis added).

85 Wittgenstein, *Tractatus*, para. 6.52, 6.522.

86 Wittgenstein, *Notebooks 1914–1916*, p. 74.

Beyond the fact that the first two books that Adaf wrote were poetry, the question of the nature of poetry is the key to understanding his ambivalent existential stance, along with the attempt to present or hint at what cannot be verbalized. What is the meaning of his claim that "poetry is completely right," on the one hand, while, on the other, it "lauds the illusion and the false"? What "rightness" can be based on "the illusion and the false"? Based on Wittgenstein's arguments on the nature of the mystical, I wish to suggest that public language does not enable the expression of the subjective—the ethical, the aesthetic, and the mystical. Accordingly, poetry that attempts to show the ineffable subjective must apply the means of the illusion and the false to what seems true. The illusion and the false in the public realm enable the private and the mystical plane to be shown. In order to reach the mystical, we need not follow the path that promises an answer to existential questions, since the answer to questions about the meaning of life is not to be found in the manifest historical plane, but rather in the way of poetry that raises questions, casts doubt on existing insights, and thereby paves the way for every person to find his personal truth, which in a public formulation seems illusory and false.

In many poems Adaf distinguishes between everyday words and poetic language, with poetry attempting to perceive and present the metaphysical and the mystical, the plane in which the meaning of life is to be found. Understanding the essence of poetry might, therefore, lead to the perception of the mystical, and perhaps to its description. This said and done, such a move is problematic (for Wittgenstein and in general), because the attempt to conceptualize the nature of poetry must be done in another language, since the attempt to perceive something with its own concepts is a tautology, and does not bring us closer to our goal.[87] The poem *Past Language* is the outstanding example of the

87 "One might think: if philosophy speaks of the use of the word 'philosophy' there must be a second-order philosophy. But it is not so: it is, rather, like the case of orthography, which deals with the word 'orthography' among others without then being second-order" (Wittgenstein, *Philosophical Investigations*, para. 121); "Tautologies and contradictions are not pictures of reality. They do not represent any

comparison between the two ways of using language, by comparing historical writing with writing poetry, and by comparing the personal pain of a certain subject and the public narrative of a heroic act. Multi-meaning hybridism comes into being when despite reservations concerning and a lack of satisfaction from each of these planes, both exist concurrently:

> *Past Language*: 1. Not patience, not poetry.
> I break what?
> as I see it,
> the crack is split just there
>
> [. . .]
> I break
> what? *Being is a wound on the side*, a side effect like
> stabbing.
>
> [. . .]
> In Tel Aviv, a hand on the road, what's this urban pulse,
> ideologies
> close in the noise like subways
>
> Under the skin, a fraction distant
> above the veins, a razor as sharp as this world.
>
> *I know*
> *how much I refuse to be saved.*
>
> *Every time that I read a poem. I want to conceive*
> *what is poetry*. Someone
> drew out my eyes and put on.
> *Beyond*
> *the moment war spreads out*

---

possible situations. For the former admit all possible situations, and latter none" (Wittgenstein, *Tractatus*, para. 4.462).

> Summer lays hibiscus charges in the fields, a line and more
> purple baggage that has no name, nonetheless
> flowers crash to the ground.
>
> With a chrysanthemum stem I expand
> Greater Israel.[88]

Ambivalence is generated in two parallel thematic moves: in the first, an everyday description presents absence, a wound, or the impossibility of leaving one's personal stamp on the world. At the same time, the poem depicts historical writing, in contrast with the writing of poetry, as distinct genres, such that history documents events that were, while poetry distinguishes between "this world" and what is beyond it, and merely alludes to the subjective and the individual, in a manner not fully explicable in the shared language.

In parallel, Adaf's books "talk" with each other, and the attempt to write in different genres could be understood as endeavoring to use the writing in a certain genre to explain what is said in another. Thus, for example, the detective novel *One Mile and Two Days before Sunset* repeatedly mentions the parallel between a serial killer and poetry, and solving a murder is set parallel to the deciphering of poetry. The desire to perceive "what is poetry" that is mentioned in the above poem is "borrowed" from the book of poetry by the detective novel, and becomes an attempt to decipher it using the techniques of the mystery novel genre. The following passage makes an additional reference to the above poem, since both speak of the phenomenon (poem or murder, respectively) as a reconstruction of the experience of pain, only a small part of which can be expressed:

> To start to sum up the relationship between serial killers and poets, the similarity between these two groups, we can speak about the purpose that is evident in their compulsiveness.

---

88 Adaf, *That Which I Thought Shadow*, pp. 64–65; trans. Edward Levin (emphasis added).

> Both the poet and the serial killer seek to create a scene, or crime scene, that is wholly composed of a system of symbols, *but the experience that is reconstructed there, again and again, is beyond the scene*. The experience is almost always pain, broken-heartedness, loss, humiliation. I imagine that stronger words are needed here, because the results, at least in the case of the murderer, are simply horrible. But it is not the words that are powerful, but the emotional world, for it seems that something like *humiliation or pain reverberates so strongly there that it no longer has any connection to the regular, everyday meaning of the word*. I know that I'm somewhat risking making a refutable statement when I say that for poets, too, it is not the words that are powerful.[89]

The comparison between the poem and the quotation from the detective novel exemplifies my argument that the focus of the examination of the boundaries of language is "the dominant," to use Roman Jakobson's term, in all the genres of Adaf's work.[90] In the maneuvering to speak in the "arena" of what is located "beyond the arena," we clearly hear Wittgenstein's argument in *Tractatus* that the boundaries of the expressions of thought can be described: thought enables us to be cognizant that there are things that cannot be thought, or that are situated beyond it. The solution shared by Wittgenstein and Adaf consists of indicating the very existence of a reality beyond thought and language, along with its description as "nonsense," as Wittgenstein puts this, or as an "illusion and false," in Adaf's wording.

This is connected to an additional insight shared by Wittgenstein and Adaf, on language as "bewitching," in various ways, one who

89 Shimon Adaf, *One Mile and Two Days before Sunset* (Jerusalem: Keter, 2004), p. 33; trans. Edward Levin (emphasis added).

90 Roman Jakobson, "The Dominant," in *Language in Literature* (Cambridge, MA: Harvard University Press, 1987), pp. 41–46. Jakobson defined "the dominant" as cardinal to the structural and thematic organization in a work of art. I maintain that the attempt to examine the boundaries of language and present the mystical as lying beyond these boundaries is the key that organizes the various genres of Adaf's work.

attempts to understand its nature.[91] For Wittgenstein, this "bewitching" is expressed in our ascribing to language qualities that it does not possess. In Adaf's next poem, *Arvit*, language and the poet conduct a sexual relationship that includes desire, excitement, kisses, a sense of sweetness upon contact, seduction, and even prostitution. The speaker's spiritual and physical relationship with language is not intended to consummate this relationship, but to ensure their cooperation for another end: the longing for the mystical ("for a little more eternity"). The speaker knowingly forgoes human love because of its cruelty that he thinks can be expected, and instead, develops an erotic relationship with language.

Arvit
I am not understood
the words.

As some age
when kids still wet their beds
and Father exists, praying nearby, beyond the wall
exists exists, I don't say this for no reason
exists like the blow from an axe that gets the back of the neck
cracks are revealed the length of the air
and through them
Sabbath eve.

The Song of Songs
fall with an untamed roar of
desire
here it comes, the voice stoops
cruel only in degree
that a father is cruel, that is,
greatly.

91 Wittgenstein, *Philosophical Investigations*, para. 109.

The syllables catch fire
to the depths of the throat
cruel am I too
but not enough to cast down love.
A fragment of sweetness—the voice escapes
and in the mouth, Hebrew is already a whoring language
submissive to the temptations of distant exiles
thick as the blood, her kisses
hasty or
death
but the only ones
for a little more eternity.[92]

The most striking feature in the poem is its breaking of syntactical rules. Wittgenstein's central argument is that "*essence* is expressed in grammar."[93] The psychoanalyst Christopher Bollas, without referring directly to Wittgenstein, gave a psychoanalytical explanation for the significance of breaking syntactical rules, as attesting to the selfhood of the speaker:

> Syntax, the peculiar way a speaker works within the rules of grammar, is a separate line of unconscious thinking. (For example, whilst the subject matter of a play or a novel will contain many, many lines of thought, the way words flow, the way sentences are structured, the way thoughts are patterned: these all form a separate category from the semantic realm.)[94]

Hebrew functions in the poem in a number of concurrent word-games: Hebrew as a childhood language that is heard but not understood; Hebrew as the language of Jewish tradition that characterizes the ambience of the parents' home; Hebrew as the source of poetical language; and Hebrew as the "whoring" language of (diasporic) Jewish history. The combination of

92 Adaf, *That Which I Thought Shadow*, pp. 37–38; trans. Edward Levin.
93 Wittgenstein, *Philosophical Investigations*, para. 371.
94 Christopher Bollas, *The Infinite Question* (New York: Routledge, 2009), p. 70.

language-games creates dialogic hybridism: the range of language-games characteristic of modern Hebrew is present, while the richness and diversity emphasize the language's insufficiency for finding meaning in the subject-speaker's life. The poem's title already functions in an ambiguous manner, since *arvit* is both the Jewish evening prayer and nightfall: the part of the day that denotes finitude.[95] Upon reading the poem, the title can also be interpreted in a third way, as summarizing the factors that are at work in the subject-speaker's soul and that create a thicket of relationships that are exemplified in the poem.

The subject-speaker attempts to find meaning in words and in the world, within the setting of the tension facing the father whose existence is as "the blow from an axe," facing Hebrew as a "whoring" language, facing tradition and the history of "distant exiles," and finally, facing the desire to create and find meaning in poetic language, the mystical desire for "a little more eternity." The turning point and focus of the poem, both formally and contentually, appears in the third stanza, in the description of the voice that is "cruel only in degree / that a father is cruel, that is, / greatly." The speaker raises the expectation for minor cruelty, but in actuality, the father could be exceedingly cruel to his children, especially when the son's behavior runs counter to what is expected of him. This alludes to the Binding of Isaac, in which the divine decree leads Abraham to be cruel to Isaac.[96]

Parallel to all the language-games, we have the "voice" ("here it comes, the voice stoops"), which is a representation of an inner subjective voice that demands something that the speaker cannot realize or attain. When, in the fourth stanza, the speaker ascribes cruelty to himself as well, a parallel is drawn between the "inner voice" and the

95 Further on in the book, both "Sabbath Eve" and "Song of Songs" function ambivalently—on the one hand, as background for the metaphorical cracks made by the axe, and, on the other, within the context of the traditional Jewish language-game in which the Song of Songs is recited in the Sabbath eve *Arvit* prayer service.

96 The motif of the father's cruelty, against the backdrop of differences of opinion in a religious context frequently appears in Adaf's work, and is especially developed in the novel *Mox Nox* (Or Yehuda: Kinneret Zmora-Bitan, 2011). The Binding of Isaac appears in Gen. 22.

"outer voice," whatever its nature.[97] This parallel grows stronger following the parallelism between the speaker's cruelty, the cruelty of the father's existence, and the cruelty of the voice. The ambivalence results from the combination of cruelty and love and the dashing of the reader's expectations, since what is thought to be a source of consolation transpires to be a source of cruelty. The dashing of expectations occurs ironically (the speaker's cruelty—not "enough" to cast down love) and expresses the speaker's ironic attitude to external correspondence of any sort.

The combination of language-games in the poem is ironic and ambivalent, since, on the one hand, the speaker is at home with them and speaks through them, while, on the other, this intermingling is insufficiently understood, and rather broadcasts emotional alienation, perhaps as a defense against hurt or danger: in the father-son relationship, the father's cruelty is compared to an axe blow to the back of the neck, which could kill; the desire embodied in the implementation of the ritual threatens to destroy humanity, and nourishes the father's cruelty; and in the end, Hebrew, which gives in to the temptations of the distant exiles, risks the death to which "the blood, her kisses" alludes, since it "whores" and loses its current-existential identity. Despite the inner justification of the dangers portrayed by the song (the danger on the part of the father, the risk in love, and the danger of the "whoring" of the language), however, the declaration that begins the poem hovers over all: "I am not understood / the words." The attempt to verbally describe the sense of danger and its causes does not lead to an explanation of the causes of these dangers, but only depicts their occurrences as a collection of experiences.

97 Wittgenstein distinguished between the inner voice and the outer one in, for example, the context of following a rule, which is extremely relevant for the current discussion. Although language-games have rules, at times a person's inner voice tells him to act in a certain way. See Wittgenstein, *Philosophical Investigations*, para. 232. The grammar allows this, because a rule cannot dictate the manner of compliance with it, nor can it explain the speaker's choice: "I could not apply any rules to a *private* transition from what is seen to words" (Wittgenstein, *Philosophical Investigations*, para. 380).

Wittgenstein distinguishes between causes and reasons as follows: the identification of something as a cause is based on observation, on a repeated experience on which a hypothesis is grounded. Offering a reason, in contrast, does not depend on the repetition of something, but rather on the identification of the motive for an action. Since the motive is inner and is independent of outer experience, it expresses certainty, while, in contrast, the identification of a cause expresses (or grounds) a hypothesis.[98] The poem demonstrates movement from the certainty of a sense of danger (which is portrayed as the reason for refraining from human love and directing erotic energy to language) to the vagueness of its causes (why is the father cruel? how is his cruelty expressed? why does love necessarily entail cruelty?).

The beginning and end of the poem emphasize the elusiveness of its meaning and the disparity between the desire to control language and the inability to do so, for "I am not understood / the words," but also the evasiveness of the voice. The speaker's desire and the erotic fashioning of his attitude to the language, along with the explicit reference to the Song of Songs, parallel the attitude of the speaker in the biblical book to his lover. There, too, desire and love are not realized. At this point, additional ambivalence is generated in the poem, since Jewish tradition is identified with the father and the social routine from which the speaker is alienated, but the tradition of the Sabbath eve recitation of the Song of Songs is also a source of inspiration for the poetic fashioning of the speaker's attitude to the language. The Song of Songs tradition is crafted as a subjective reason that cannot be observed or verified for the erotic attitude to the language, which, in my view, alludes to the mystical. Another expression of mystical grammar that fashions the attitude to pastness in relation to the tradition of Hebrew poetry appears in the poem *Acrobatics*:

Acrobatics
Dead Hebrew poets

98 See Wittgenstein, *Blue and Brown Books*, p. 15.

your voice, replete with water that evaporates in the sun like fog and like
bugs underfoot won't crawl to me any more
like tongues and like snakes through
dark and finished volumes like childhood fears.

You are no more.
Your beating is not the circulation of the blood. Your
breathing is not air. Not moist disposition.
I do the only kind act for you that I can.
I relegate you to oblivion.[99]

Acrobatics are based on maneuverability and control of the use of the circus space. In the poem, this space is the heritage of Hebrew poetry. Instead, however, of acrobatics expressing the ability to use this poetical heritage, the speaker declares his aim of forgetting it. The paradoxicality of memory and the attempt to forget raises the question: why write about this, instead of simply ignoring the whole issue, since disregard will likely lead to forgetting, more than mentioning would, even if such mentioning is done in a negative fashion. A possible answer is given in the continuation, in the ambivalent fashioning: it seems that the poetry deserves to be forgotten, while, in parallel, the poem portrays the ancient fears that it arouses, along with mention of the speaker's childhood traumas. That is, the language of Hebrew poetry has both attractive and repellent aspects. Connecting this with childhood fears indicates that this is not a reasoned intellectual stance against this poetry, but a type of fear of its voice, which threatens to swallow the speaker, either because of its characterization as "replete with water" (that hints of the threat of swallowing), or due to the associations of fears and traumas that it raises. The "fog" and being "like snakes" allude to maliciousness and power struggles that are not conducted honestly or directly, thereby amplifying the fear.[100]

---

99 Adaf, *That Which I Thought Shadow*, p. 33; trans. Edward Levin.

100 This paradoxical position is reminiscent of the sensation of terror expressed in the term *unheimlich* coined by Freud: when a person is not sure whether what he faces

Another relation to Hebrew culture is crafted in the grammar of the negative description, which appears three times ("Your beating is not the circulation of the blood. Your breathing is not air. Not moist disposition") and that refers to the Yom Kippur eve *Kol Nidre* prayer: "Our vows are no longer vows, our prohibitions are no longer prohibitions, and our oaths are no longer oaths." The parallelism to the language of prayer serves the speaker's omnipotent presumption to negate the importance of the work of the early Hebrew poets. On the face of it, just as vows can be canceled by reciting the prayer, the speaker is similarly capable of silencing the voice of the poets, even though it is "replete with water." In actuality, however, the parallelism has the reverse effect, and emphasizes the difference. A vow is spoken in language, and therefore can be canceled by a language procedure (prayer). The voice of the poets is active in a linguistic plane, in addition to the expression itself, and symbolizes the speaker's childhood fears, as the current fears, which are compared to bugs and snakes that creep to him. In consequence, despite his trying to negate their influence and even forget them, the very writing of the poem ensures that their existence is present in his consciousness and life. The speaker's refraining from mentioning specific contents that deserve to be forgotten, too, acts to intensify the ambivalence, since we do not know what is the (observable) cause of the speaker's aversion to the voice of the poets, but only what effect they have on him (both new and old anxieties and fears).

The concealment of the contents themselves from the reader evokes a sense of the inability to verbalize that ambivalent relationship. Adaf's diverse language-games create a new relationship of attraction and rejection, since the poet's language-games activate the speaker's set of associations and reflect a conscious and unconscious attitude to the cultural heritage. The speaker expresses a feeling of "unhomeliness," in his attempt to be rid of their inspiration for and influence on language-games, by returning to an even earlier language-game, that of *Kol Nidre*. This prayer, which voids the worshiper's resolutions of content, acts in

is real or imaginary, he is drawn to it, but is also terror-stricken. This, in my opinion, is the speaker's attitude to the poets of the past and to poetry as a whole.

a similar way regarding the poetical heritage. At the same time, however, this action reflects the power of this poetry in its religious embodiment, since the formal dimension of the prayer (the negative structure described above) bears an effect given to the prayer in another context. In this sense, the wording of the prayer contains a mystical element, since it expresses a subjective position for which no rational arguments are made. This stance speaks to a complex connection between the speaker's poetry and communal poetry (that of those poets) that is based on the power of the poetry-prayer to generate and cancel meaning by means of verbal configuration.

Toward the end of the book, Adaf more closely points to the uniqueness of poetry, but later on, he deconstructs the illusion that had come about until then: that poetry could support the constitution of meaning. This move is plainly exemplified in the two following passages, which are set forth as the mottoes of poems:

> 1. Because poetry is not testimony—it does not
> seek to capture the moment
> in memory, but rather the tangibility of its every sensual
> thicket, that agitates, not because it is such
> a calculated plot to be—
> because of such desire to never cease.[101]
>
> 5. It is the way of prayers to fade away, and except for
> the illusion of memory
> there's nothing
> to poetry.[102]

The speaker violates the prevalent convention that poetry tries to "capture the moment in memory," an illusion that was fostered ever since Aristotle spoke of the imitative power of art, and even more so by modern art movements. Poetry has one aim: to capture the actuality of the moment, that is, the nature of reality as it is embodied in the

101 Adaf, *That Which I Thought Shadow*, p. 68; trans. Edward Levin.
102 Adaf, *That Which I Thought Shadow*, p. 72; trans. Edward Levin.

sensuality of the desire to be eternal. The attempt to constitute the desire for eternity is the expression in this poem of trying to touch the mystical by writing poetry, but this possibility proves illusory. The speaker claims a few pages later that poetry bears only the illusion of memory: since it documents a certain event, it presumably "mentions" it. In actuality, however, even this memory is an illusion, for if poetry is incapable of expressing the tangibility of the reality, then it cannot recall a reality that was. This disillusionment about the nature of poetry is also the basis for an awakening from the common expectation from Mizrahi literature—for autobiographical writing (an expectation that other authors belonging to this category live up to). The possibility of reconstructing personal and family history is presented as an illusion, but in a sense other than the deceitful nature of poetry.

2.2. The Subject as the Limit of the World

> The subject does not belong to the world: rather, it is a limit of the world.[103]
>
> The limits of my language mean the limits of my world.[104]
>
> One of the ills of our time is the elimination of the realm that cannot be made to speak. We read the entire reality through the glasses of the political, through concepts of knowledge and power and repressive mechanisms, then man is always the product of an idea machine that can be taken apart. You often adopt this way of looking at things, you show through it that it is the creative artist who is a unique phenomenon. Large parts of his world can be explained, but the artist himself cannot be explained.[105]

---

103 Wittgenstein, *Tractatus*, para. 5.632.

104 Wittgenstein, *Tractatus*, para. 5.6; "What brings the self into philosophy is the fact that 'the world is my world.' The philosophical world is not the human being, not the human body, or the human soul, with which psychology deals, but rather the metaphysical subject, the limit of the world—not a part of it" (*Tractatus*, para. 5.641).

105 Interview with Shimon Adaf, *Haaretz* (August 17, 2011), http://www.haaretz.co.il/misc/1.1374018.

This interview with Adaf upon the publication of *Mox Nox* shows his preoccupation with the mystical in order to characterize the uniqueness of the artist. This is to be understood on the background of Wittgenstein's arguments concerning the subjective nature of the mystical and dependency between the limits of language and the boundaries of an individual's world. This position raises a number of interpretive questions: Should we forgo the attempt to explain the uniqueness of a certain work of art? Can autobiographical statements in a work be understood if, in practice, we do not share the artist's world with him from the outset? At times Adaf's work has been deemed solipsistic and fully comprehendible only by its author, but I argue that understanding the Wittgensteinian mystical conception enables us to breach the solipsistic boundaries. Another part of the same interview, which I will follow with examples from Adaf's poems, provides a central reason for this:

> I no longer know how to speak in autobiographical fashion. I reworked my story in so many forms that I can't rely on my memories. I remember my literature better than the biography. [. . .] It makes me happy when I'm taken to task for not writing Mizrahi literature, even when my characters are clearly Moroccan and rooted in the Moroccan experience.[106]

A controversial position is set forth here, but one that enables the reader to understand the "private world" of the work: the biography reworked into literature. The events are not accessible only to the one who experienced them, but also to anyone who reads about them. Nonetheless, the fashioning of the characters does not conform to what is commonly expected of "Mizrahi" literature and challenges them, since, for now, these expectations do not contain the sphere "that cannot be made to speak"—the mystical. I maintain, however, that if the readers' expectations will be updated, obviously biographical works could be read as expressing universal

106 Interview with Shimon Adaf, *Haaretz* (August 17, 2011).

motifs, since the unique is embodied in a work of fiction no less than in historical memory. The poem *Completion*, for example, exemplifies the blurring of the boundaries between the speaker's autobiography and the world:

> *Completion*
> I will yet awaken from the nightmare of the biography
> in the middle of a day sharper than a Tammuz noon, at last
> on edge
> to guess how the light sledgehammers
> how fiercely choking the air
> in which happen sabotage, a blow, love, oh
>
> I will yet awaken from the nightmare of the biography
> at my back night is falling over the fireworks of desperate
> birds
> to guess how the light sledgehammers.
>
> [. . .]
> Behind me the city, the mother, the senselessness of the cry.
> Birth might break me to the world
> in those moments really, when I sing my life to the dust
> But no, I say, no.
>
> Birth might break me to the world
> to guess how the light sledgehammers
> But no, I say, no.
> I will yet awaken from the nightmare of the biography.[107]

This poem ends the book *That Which I Thought Shadow Is the Real Body*, which probably explains its title: *Completion*. The ending, however, also takes a retrospective look at the consequences of the biography. The poem's starting point is that biography functions as the

---

107 Adaf, *That Which I Thought Shadow*, p. 75; trans. Edward Levin.

"nightmare," which, already at the beginning of the poem, removes it from the consciousness category of organized memory. Biography is represented by the poetical grammar of an unconscious state of mind. This state is organized associatively, highlights traumas, and embodies a subjective interpretation of a private world, the formulation of which is independent of the external world.

Its central stance is ambivalent, since, on the one hand, the poem expresses the seeming hope to "awaken from the nightmare of the biography," while, on the other, the poem as a whole conveys a sense of unprocessed trauma, from which the speaker cannot free himself. The idea of reality as a nightmare that created the biography evokes a feeling of *unheimlich*, since the speaker wants to rid himself of the biography, while it pursues him as a nightmare and does not allow him to give himself over to another reality. During the course of the poem we learn why paralysis overcomes the speaker: the light of reality brims with heavy hammers that strike in various ways, with no difference between the pain brought on by potentially positive events (love, birth) and crisis situations such as sabotage, a blow, or an unanswered cry. Thus the speaker is trapped in a dialectic in which his refusal to wake up joins together with his certainty that the awakening will come. Aside from the Talmudic term (of Greek origin) *kurnas* (sledgehammer), no features of any specific culture can be identified in the poem, so that the poem constitutes a concrete universal stance (the traumatic nature of the biography could characterize any person, in any time and place). "The senselessness of the cry" in the penultimate stanza highlights a type of despair of the poetic act being the key to verbalization in the subjective plane that constitutes the traumatic trap from which the speaker cannot free himself. The semiotic expression of the cry or its verbal expression cannot liberate the speaker from his biographical fate in which sabotage and love are one and the same; and the historical causes of this remain unknown, in the plane that cannot be made to speak. Nonetheless, an intertextual examination of the poems in the book will reveal a hinted reason for the cause of the "realm that cannot be made to speak" in the poem *Transformations*, in which the speaker compares himself to Orpheus:

Transformations 2. Orpheus: like an alarmed pupil
the mornings are lashed on my back.
There is one way of Sderot
that I won't recite back.[108]

The resemblance between Orpheus and the speaker is a "family resemblance": both are prevented from returning, with a parallel drawn between Sderot and Sheol. Both Orpheus's playing and Adaf's poetry are created following this prevention, in the course of detachment from other humans. The difference between them is that Orpheus failed since he did not obey the rules of the game, and possessed courage and a gesture that was given to no man. The speaker in Adaf's poem, in contrast, is "like an alarmed pupil" who suffers from violence, and therefore refrains from returning to Sderot.

Within the context of the intertextuality in the book, which includes a series of hints to the difficulties posed by the biography, this poem also converses with Adaf's first book of poetry, *Icarus Monologue* (1997), which was written totally under the influence of Greek mythology. In this book, mythology is a language-game that is both a source of meaning and a reference to life in the present, with the reason for this appearing in the second book: "Man desperately needs mythology, from the emotional and cognitive aspect. And not that which is drawn from the recent past, but rather a system of symbols and forces the traces of which have been lost in the fog of time."[109] This reliance, however, on myth as a source of inspiration was abandoned at the beginning of the second book and replaced (with the title of the book already hinting at this) by the body as a source of meaning.

The second book is accompanied by passages from a fictitious work entitled "Essay against Photography," which is the seeming key to understanding the world-language relationship on the basis of which the poems act. Unlike the language of *Icarus Monologue*, with its hybrid vocabulary, the hybridism in *That Which I Thought Shadow* is ideational and anthological: existence includes a range of possibilities that stand

108 Adaf, *That Which I Thought Shadow*, p. 10; trans. Edward Levin.
109 Adaf, *That Which I Thought Shadow*, p. 7; trans. Edward Levin.

next to one another; none can be canceled, but at the same time, none fashions substantive meaning, and the feeling of locating such a reality is, at most, temporary, and actually—an illusion, as is implied in the book's title. The attempt to negate, which actually gives presence, creates dialectic hybridism. This hybridism is depicted, for instance, in the book's title poem, which centers around the ability to present an alternative world each time, with the conclusion being that the only unchanging point of certainty is the body:

> *Regression*: Clouds above Tel Aviv and above October
> a prematurely old face of the month
> pouring in the harsh tumult
> like an old, collapsing storeroom
> behind my back
> because I'm going south, I
> make the air young.
>
> Winds smooth as children, trees
> bent less in growth pains.
>
> *A world for a world*
> The bellows of new lungs
> breathing undergrounds in some darkness
> a light for a light
> foliage for foliage beats the fences.
>
> *That which I thought shadow is the real body.*[110]

The argument that I emphasized is the book's seeming starting point: the speaker sets the body, or the set of physical feelings, as an alternative source of meaning and source of certainty to intellectual and cultural word-games. Instead of a "God" of some sort or other, the speaker addresses himself, in the motto for the third Gate, in the most

110 Adaf, *That Which I Thought Shadow*, p. 42; trans. Edward Levin (emphasis added).

primal and simplest manner, even before interaction with another person, before love as a source of vitality and confidence:

> I look back at my life and I know, I erred in the location of the mistake in the equation. The mistake does not lie in assuming the existence of God, but in the interpretation of the form in which He is realized in the world. Not love, flesh.[111]

Presenting the body as the source of meaning does not include waiving the mystical. To the contrary—the way to revealing what lies beyond language, the mystical, passes in proximity to the body. The body is only a means to reach the two aspects of the mystical: the attempt to touch the nonverbalized experience that direct language can create, along with the desire to cross the boundaries of the world and language:

> This is flesh, they say, grab!
> You go and materialize, fleshing
> [. . .]
> Maybe in a decade I will understand the meaning of desire
> the wish to come close to the body
> beyond language always.
> What is poetry
> if not need in purity
> that
> things will be as they are
> and not slip away into loose reality
> broken pleasure
> by eye or word.
> What is it
> if not
> the sourness
> of the throat to be silent something
> *ayma*

111 Adaf, *That Which I Thought Shadow*, p. 45; trans. Edward Levin.

some I
for whom all the words in the dictionary aren't enough
to say I
not to speak about in addition.[112]

It transpires, however, that the body is a broken reed:

4. For the body, its only relations
with time
are ruin that cannot be recorded.[113]

Accordingly, *That Which I Thought Shadow* is a book of disillusionment from disillusionment. Its title denotes disillusionment, and suggests a seeming support: the body, which was perceived at the time as shadow, is seen to be real, and is the starting point for a reexamination of the relationship between language and the world. In various poetical ways the book examines a number of possibilities for constituting meanings. Each of the book's "Gates" has a motto presumably quoted from the nonexistent "Essay against Photography." The "Gates" are titled "Past," "Illusion," and "Flesh," and each passage gives reasons for some disillusionment: the first from the place of mythology in transmitting a system of symbols; the second from the ability of philosophy to reveal anything, and presenting the illusion and falsehood in poetry as an alternative key to this; and the third from the place of the body as an initial viewpoint. Continuing from mythology and other mental childhood pleasures, philosophy, too, is abandoned, with poetry put in its stead. But the latter, which is set forth as a source of justification, is initially portrayed as based on illusion and falsehood. Accordingly, it is hardly surprising that poetry, too, disappoints in its ability to lead to the mystical, since words do not suffice to describe that "I": "some I / for whom all the words in the dictionary aren't enough / to say I / not to speak about in addition."

112 Adaf, *That Which I Thought Shadow*, pp. 56–57; trans. Edward Levin.
113 Adaf, *That Which I Thought Shadow*, p. 71; trans. Edward Levin.

If we join together the three "Gate" titles into a single statement: Past-Illusion-Flesh, we gain a sense of searching and awakening that results in certainty. In actuality, this feeling is a delusion that fulfills the promise that poetry extols the illusion and the lie. The book centers around the failure to create any point of certainty, since they all prove false: the new city, the new language, and the new life do not constitute an experience that is more whole and serene.

In Adaf's third book of poetry, poetry returns to function as the default when contending with mourning and loss. The sober awakening of the second book makes way for the test imposed on the speaker by his sister's death. The book's starting point is the imposed wrestling with pain, the likes of which were not experienced in the previous books, along with frontal wrestling in the present, with the horror of the death of his sister, and indirectly, with the idea of death in general.

3. *Aviva-No*: The Grammar of Mourning

The book *Aviva-No* focuses on mystical pain in two senses: the first, Adaf's pain at the loss of his sister, who died prematurely; and the second relating to death that, according to Wittgenstein, is beyond the limits of the word and language:

> At death the world does not alter, but comes to an end. [. . .] Death is not an event in life: we do not live to experience death. [. . .] Not only is there no guarantee of the temporal immortality of the human soul [. . .] but, in any case, this assumption completely fails to accomplish the purpose for which it has always been intended. Or is some riddle solved by my surviving for ever? Is not this eternal life itself as much of a riddle as our present life? The solution of the riddle of life in space and time lies outside space and time.[114]

Death is not an occurrence in life, but the end of the world. Since language describes what happens in the present in the world, it cannot

114 Wittgenstein, *Tractatus*, para. 6.431, 6.4311, 6.4312.

depict anything connected with death (that is beyond the world). The belief in the eternity of the soul cannot be a basis for description, since it itself is a mystery. Furthermore, the enigma of life cannot be solved within the context of place and time by means of concepts that are beyond place and time. These insights underlie Adaf's book: he does not attempt to create language to portray the death experience or the belief in the eternity of the soul. Continuing in this vein, the following questions arise: How does Adaf's poetic language contend with these two meanings of the mystical? What is the reflection of first-person pain, which cannot be verbalized in everyday language, along with the impossible effort to express the death experience in words, from the physical plane of the dying body to the mental plane of longing for the missing sister?

Wittgenstein formulates a fundamental question, the answer to which offers interpretation of the above questions. He asks how words connect to sensations, following which he also raises a question concerning the possibility of verbalizing pain:

> How do words *refer* to sensations?—There doesn't seem to be any problem here; don't we talk about sensations every day, and name them? But how is the connection between the name and the thing named set up? [. . .] For example, of the word "pain." Here is one possibility: words are connected with the primitive, natural, expressions of sensation and used in their place [. . .] the verbal expression of pain replaces crying, it does not describe it. How can I even attempt to interpose language between the expression of pain and the pain? In what sense are my sensations *private*?—Well, only I can know whether I am really in pain; another person can only surmise it.[115]

Wittgenstein's discussion captures and preserves tension: there is an irreducible gap between the expression of pain and the pain itself;

115 Wittgenstein, *Philosophical Investigations*, para. 244–46.

nonetheless, we use words when we hurt. This use does not describe the pain, but accompanies the expression of pain, and at times replaces other expressions of pain, such as crying. The experience of pain remains as first-person knowledge, which another person can only imagine. Adding to this Wittgenstein's discussion of "I as subject" and "I as object," we can argue that poetry about pain transforms the speaker's subjective certainty into an objective statement, in the sense that it is comprehensible to every reader who speaks the language. Guided by Wittgenstein's proposal, we will examine how Adaf's poetical and mystical grammar acts in this book, so that it shows readers the limits of language, while at the same time reflecting the speaker's subjective experience.[116] Adaf as artist constitutes the limit, and we can look at the world constituted by this subjective limit.

The book *Aviva-No* creates a language of mourning and contends with death that occurs on the boundary of the world, from two aspects: death is present-absent in our consciousness, so that our memories of it are present in the world, even though death is not perceived by means of language, since it is beyond the limits of language and the world. Its only possible formulation is subjective, since, according to Wittgenstein, the subject is the limit of the world. Thus Adaf tries to deal with his sister's death by attempting to capture both the experience of those who remain in the world and that of absence, emptiness, and ruin.

The book has three "Gates": "Word-Matter," "Poetry," and "Love," that comprise forty-three poems, with letters for titles. This titling lends itself to two parallel interpretations: that a name cannot be given to the situations portrayed in the poems; and that a single process occurs throughout the book, with the letter-titles marking the phases of this process. The process fashions what evades us in everyday life: the significance of another person for us, the conscious and unconscious process of leave-taking, and mainly, the gap between words and the

116 "It will therefore only be in language that the limit can be drawn, and what lies on the other side of the limit will simply be nonsense" (Wittgenstein, *Tractatus*, Preface); "The subject does not belong to the world: rather, it is a limit of the world" (*Tractatus*, para. 5.632).

pain. This first poem crafts the starting point of the mourning process—the absence of the sister:

> *1.*
> I'm in a state of how does it go and I shall call it Aviva-no
> I shall call it sisterless
> and I shall speak of it with straightforwardness not by way of verse but by pain
> and thus is its law it has no law—angels stifling breath and blazing-eyed
> beasts, in the internet above and in the buried books below, it has no
> law, only the moment in mighty space pierces like a pin into glass
> and the heart arrested and named mere breath
> for the three hundred and sixty five minas of smoke within it
> against the count of three hundred and sixty five days of.[117]

Poem "1" formulates the book's poetic principle: "not by way of verse but by pain." The pain is presented as the formal, and not merely thematic, starting point. As in his two earlier books, Adaf devotes attention to the action of language as a whole, and specifically that of poetry, as can be seen from the titles of the "Gates." This said and done, the focus of *Aviva-No* is closer to the topic of the current book than either of the other two were: namely, self-constitution in poetic language. As we saw in the poem with which I began this chapter, whatever happens to the body, and whatever happens to the soul, is formulated in the word ("word by word my body is sung / Devastated it dares to near / with my own eyes to come to know"), that is: "*essence* is expressed in grammar."[118] Adaf contrives new expressions to illustrate his individual mourning, which is formulated in public language.

---

117 Adaf, *Aviva-No*, p. 7; trans. Yael Segalovitz. Hebrew letters can also denote numbers; for the sake of convenience, I have changed them into their numerical equivalent.

118 Wittgenstein, *Philosophical Investigations*, para. 371.

For example, calling the state of mourning after his dead sister ("Aviva-No"), or the general appellation for his condition ("sisterlessness"). The experience of personal mourning is also embodied in new linguistic combinations such as "angels stifling breath" or "the heart arrested [*hadul*] and named mere breath [*hevel*]." The English translation loses the neologism of *hadul*, as well as the dual meaning of the biblical word *hevel*. The first meaning, as it is rendered here, is "(mere) breath," and relates to "angels stifling breath," according to which the speaker and the angels synchronously feel the loss of breath, due to the sister's death. The second meaning, which alludes to the beginning of Ecclesiastes ("Vanity [*hevel*] of vanities, saith Koheleth; vanity of vanities, all is vanity"—Eccl. 1:2) relates to the inability to explain death in language that does not include it within its limits. Alternately, Adaf crafts an attempt to perceive the moment that encapsules the experience of pain: "the moment in mighty space pierces like a pin into glass."

The poem illustrates the uniqueness of the speaker's mourning for his sister, and the attempt to singularize this experience raises the question: if and how it is possible to distinguish between an inner experience and the outer criterion.[119] This question is especially acute in the depiction of the tension between the seemingly outer demand and the speaker's inner will, as is illustrated in the following poem, which speaks of the sense of coercion to sketch the image of his sister as it is impressed in the depths of his soul:

18.
But if I am coerced to give an image
for my sister—and if I ask: whosoever
to tell me, a force of nature is what
Why, then, a word will be exchanged
by a solution, desire
to be construction, contradiction,
and I will answer, I always will be answered so:
the pillar of a storm or a Tammuz heat wave or

119 "An 'inner process' stands in need of outward criteria" (Wittgenstein, *Philosophical Investigations*, para. 580).

a lily stem breaks a limestone bed—
how can I, if so, how can I speak
her.[120]

Who coerces the speaker to depict his sister? This apparently is an inner need that clashes with the difficulty of doing so in language, since this portrayal appears in the poem in a collection of expressions that have no apparent syntactical-logical connection between them: "the pillar of a storm or a Tammuz heat wave or / a lily stem breaks a limestone bed." Actually, this is not a picture of the sister, but rather a description of the speaker's inner state as he tries to describe his sister. Wittgenstein explains why the "inner"—or in this poem, the syntactical logic of the inner—seems hidden from the interlocutor:

> The inner is hidden from us means that it is hidden from us in a sense in which it is not hidden from him. And it is not hidden from the owner in this sense: he utters it and we believe the utterance under certain conditions and there is no such thing as his making a mistake here. And this asymmetry of the game is brought out by saying that the inner is hidden from someone else.[121]

On the one hand, the speaker feels forced to portray his sister, while, on the other, despite his having written the poem, it ends with a rhetorical question: "how can I, if so, how can I speak / her." The above collection of expressions did not meet this demand, since the necessity to describe the experience in the first person, in public language that would be understandable to the interlocutor, precluded expressing its singularity.

In addition to his distinctions between inner and outer and between first and third person, Wittgenstein offers an additional horizon of understanding in order to depict the singularity of poetic expression. In his discussion of private language according to Wittgenstein, Keld

120 Adaf, *Aviva-No*, p. 7; trans. Edward Levin.
121 Wittgenstein, *Last Writings*, vol. 2, para. 36.

Nielsen argues that we should distinguish between picture (*Bild*) and imaginative representation (*Vorstellung*):

> A *picture* ("Bild") would contain nothing it did not directly represent whereas as an *imaginative representation* ("Vorstellung") would be capable of representing indirectly.[122]

The possibility of expressing an inner process in language is based on the language of imagination that facilitates presenting things that were not directly experienced. For this to happen, the speaker must be able to shed light on a volitional aspect, regardless of the outer reality.[123] The speaker can demonstrate what he saw in his imagination, while he cannot be ordered to see something in a certain way. This description by Wittgenstein explains why, when the speaker felt coerced, he did not succeed in portraying his sister. In the following poem, in contrast, Adaf creates, in the realm of imagination, the music of mourning language, which illustrates the inner experience.

4. The Way Music Speaks

24

Noooooo, don't let up, pain, don't stop out of suffering,
Blood—bubble, boil, fizz
and body—burn, burn, the nerves that are intertwined
throughout the flesh, and also you, muscles
Go up in flames, the bones that rub against the internal
organs,
stab, scratch them a bit, and cause an abscess

---

122 Keld Stehr Nielsen, *The Evolution of the Private Language Argument* (Aldershot: Ashgate, 2008), pp. 95–96.

123 "The concept of an aspect is related to the concept of imagination. In other words, the concept 'Now I see it as [. . .] ' is related to 'Now I am imagining *that* [. . .] And yet one does not perceive something in so hearing it. 'Imagine this changed like this, and you have this other thing.' One can produce a proof in one's imagination. Seeing an aspect and imagining are subject to the will. There is such an order as 'Imagine *this*!,' and also, 'Now see the figure like *this*!'; but not 'Now see this leaf green!'" (Wittgenstein, *PPF*, para. 254–56).

> I won't ask where is her memory, forgetfulness of her, where it is.
> I won't let slip away from my hands
> a sister, into time.[124]

When reading *Poem 24* we can actually feel the heartache and the body's sensations at the height of mourning. The poem exemplifies, more than others, the way in which Adaf's poetic language captures the experiences of the speaker's body while mourning. This effect is attained by the alliteration that seems to imitate the bodily phenomena themselves, while, in actuality, it operates in the semantic field of pain. It likewise metaphorically identifies the heart and the body, as separate from the speaker and acting on their own. The personification of the bodily parts illustrates the first-person sense of pain and mourning, and the body's role in relation to the soul. The speaker expresses his fear at forgetting the memory of his sister, and asks the body to aid him in remembering her, by preserving the dramatic sensation of pain that he felt right after her death.

To now, we have not related to the musical aspect of Adaf's poetry, but it is noteworthy that Adaf is a musician, one whose songs were set to music by others. It would be instructive to draw a distinction between musicality in terms of the musical score and musicality in the prosodic sense, that of the phonetic function of alliteration in poetry. The manner of division into syllables, the tempo, and the tones that accompany the words by means of speech-acts function as the bearers of meaning, in a manner that is especially important for expressing the experience of pain that cannot be verbalized:

> But you do speak of understanding music. You understand it, surely, while you hear it! Ought we to say this is an experience which accompanies the hearing? The way music speaks [. . .] There is a strongly musical element in verbal language. (A sigh, the intonation of voice in a question, in an

124 Adaf, *Aviva-No*, p. 43; trans. Edward Levin.

> announcement, in longing; all the innumerable gestures made with the voice.)[125]

On more than one occasion Wittgenstein, as someone who had a broad musical education, examined what musical language shares with other languages.[126] The aspect presented in the above quotation is of importance for our purposes: the goal of a poem, as that of a musical work, is not to provide information, nor do poems act within the context of an informative language-game. A poem facilitates experience, and someone who is not familiar with such an experience cannot comprehend the poem. The musical elements in a poem, or in verbal language as a whole, contribute greatly to its understanding, thanks to speech-acts such as the expression of longing or a question. The poem intensifies the distinction between language-games of body and soul, because it fashions each of the planes as volitional, with a manner of action all its own: the body expresses the pain; the soul wants to remember, and fears forgetting.

Musical fashioning reflects a possible parallel between what happens in the speaker's soul and the phonetic plane of public language. This is also reflected in the thematic realm, even if many expressions in the poem are fashioned negatively.

In conclusion, the theoretical formulation used by Adaf to describe the capability of poetic language to capture time should be compared with its poetical exemplification in *Poem 19*. The poem illustrates the possibility of exceeding the world and having the dead sister Aviva present, in a way that will overcome the rules of logic and prove that

> grammar is not accountable to any reality. It is grammatical rules that determine meaning (constitute it) and so they

---

125 Wittgenstein, *Zettel*, para. 159–61.

126 Wittgenstein draws two outstanding comparisons between a musical theme and a sentence in language in *Tractatus*, para. 4.014, and in *Philosophical Investigations*, para. 527. The two characteristics they share are pictoriality and the inability to justify the course of the sentence.

> themselves are not answerable to any meaning and to that extent are arbitrary.[127]

Adaf argues in the following interview that a poem can act contrary to the laws of nature, including the laws of time. There are poetical ways of expressing an idea that will be understood by the readers, even though its grammar does not obey the known general rules:

> If the poetical act can examine time, capture time, freeze it, opposite its running, by its very exceeding it [time], by the very tearing of the mental experience from its monotonous flow, gnaw away at everything, if time exists, if there is time, then the poetical act is its destructive machine, its annihilation machine. Some of the words in the language of the poem must become impervious, and their meaning must be a marker for what cannot be transmitted within any duration context that exists in the consciousness of the readers and the interlocutors, to the extent that they will be forced to return to it in expanding circles of life, as to the scene of the crime, like chanting an incantation that is not to be completed, with the last syllable sticking on one's tongue, pressed between the lips, but refusing to come out.[128]

Poetical grammar can attack the concept of time even if the latter exists empirically, by denying its existence or its features. In this way, the poem can generate what was presented as one of this book's aims: touching the mystical. The poem can do this by bewitching the reader with means that draw him to give himself over to the poem, and to detach from the reality. Thus, for example, the freedom to fashion time in accordance with the experience of mourning allows the speaker in *Poem 19* to confuse the order of time and have his sister present forever:

> *19*
> For the future happened and it blows

127 Wittgenstein, *Philosophical Grammar*, p. 184.
128 Adaf, interview with Enat Yakar.

to you
time resistant—

The End of Days ended, will
you not hear, within the fortress of airs,
between the dewdrops, the almond tree trembles from blossoming, no,
it trembles.

No, the planted trees dried up, the plants that will flourish
came to an end, the earth vomited
its heart, and it is giant
it breathes your soul, the light came down like irons,
so magnificent, filling the void,
the whole world was defeated before Aviva-No.[129]

The mystical grammar embraces the longing brought on by loss, and creates the at times macabre and desperate desire for a sort of "answer." Thus three times intersect in the book: the past, by fashioning the memory of the sister and her influence on the speaker's identity; the present, by the verbalization of the personal experience of mourning; and the future of the eschatological "End of Days," by its fashioning as past and as present: "For the future happened and it blows / to you / time resistant— // The End of Days ended."

We will end this chapter with some lines from *Poem 39* that concisely sum up Adaf's poetry. The poem's expressions of the experience of repressed longing are fashioned in the imagery of nature, which presumably should be characteristic of every place in the world. The word opening the poem, however, is "Sderot," and the message that takes form during the course of the poem is that self-constitution occurs in reference to the world in which Adaf grew up. This world, however, does not necessarily include his parents' home, but rather

129 Adaf, *Aviva-No*, p. 33; trans. Edward Levin.

the context in which meaningful relationships were fashioned—and continuing in this vein, in which the speaker underwent the experiences that molded his personality. We may conclude that the personal and natural elements facing and with which the speaker's meaningful bonds were created are more significant than any cultural, ethnic, or religious context.

39
Sderot is winter shuttered, the cotton's beaming touching
heaven, first the warblers
hard for falling,
after that materialize
bushes glazed by frost, a blow, pealing against
the winds
[. . .]
taps, taps, taps, ravens heavy as sighs
on the streetlights. And your voice came, no longer lost
in singing, no longer sweetened—as
it will be from here, as it always is, I
am the one who hears
that all my life to now
was a distraction so that I wouldn't
long.[130]

The sighs (*anahot*) of the ravens in the poem correspond with the expression "sisterless" (*inhot*) of the first poem, with the speaker succeeding in affording presence to his sister's voice by concentrated attentiveness that joins together the voices of the forces of nature. Not only does this attentiveness cause his sister to be present, but at the same time it retrospectively sheds light on his life with an insight that is extremely important for understanding his self, an insight that is based on struggle with his longings. And it seems that this longing

130 Adaf, *Aviva-No*, p. 63; trans. Edward Levin.

relates mainly to the primal states of the preceding books of poetry, in the hope that there is a system in which meaning can be formulated. Adaf succeeds in having his sister's memory present in the book, but as Wittgenstein cautioned, "the problems of life remain completely untouched."[131]

131 Wittgenstein, *Tractatus*, para. 6.52.

CHAPTER 8

Summation: "As if I Could Read the Darkness"

> A multitude of familiar paths lead off from these words in all directions.[1]
>
> "How does a sentence manage to represent?"—the answer might be: "Don't you know? Surely you see it, when you use one." After all, nothing is concealed. How does a sentence do it?—Don't you know? After all, nothing is hidden.[2]

We examined poems representing outstanding examples of self-constitution in the poetry of Zelda, Yehuda Amichai, Admiel Kosman, and Shimon Adaf. The three types of grammar—the poetical, the dialogic, and the mystical—include contents that seemingly evade our gaze and indirectly constitute the speaker's self. In the actual work of interpretation, I attempted to show how "nothing is hidden," and that the self is constituted by gathering the poetic statements into a "meaning-body."[3]

---

1 Wittgenstein, *Philosophical Investigations*, para. 525.

2 Wittgenstein, *Philosophical Investigations*, para. 435.

3 "For after all, nothing is hidden—we see the whole sentence! The function must come out in operating the calculus. ((Meaning-bodies.))" (Wittgenstein, *Philosophical Investigations*, para. 559).

Our examination of the grammaticalization of experience led the interpretation of each of the language-games into different channels, since language can accompany individual experiences. The poems were chosen because they so clearly demonstrate self-constitution, but distinct features arose, as if by themselves, from each corpus. These characteristics can be retrospectively defined as "rules" in the Wittgensteinian sense, which facilitate a concluding overview of each of the language-games that we examined. This overview is no more than "grammatical remarks,"[4] and does not presume to offer an interpretive method more correct than any other. The rule is not a method of action that is identifiable from the outset, nor does it attest to the creative process, it rather is a form of organization that can be revealed by observation that describes and compares the different poems, those of the same poet and those of the poets included in this study.[5] The types of grammar functioned as common organizing systems that facilitate discerning the differences between the self-constitution in the different corpora.

The discussion of the poetry of Zelda showed how changes of heart occur during everyday actions and the speaker's singular contemplation of events in the world. The dialogue with the various facets of her personality and the parallel dialogue with the different aspect of the outer human reality create a dialectic process of constant critical examination, which contains irony, reservation, and alienation, along with love, compassion, and identification.

The retrospection in Yehuda Amichai's poetry (which by its very nature was absent from the speaker's consciousness in the early poetry) reveals that the motifs of "*Amen*" and "love" are the key to understanding the controversial self-constitution at the beginning of Amichai's poetical career, and not only as a goal that was attained in the later phase of his work. His poetic corpus expresses a gradual

4 "These aren't the experiences I have gained from acting from inspiration and from acting according to a rule; they're grammatical remarks" (Wittgenstein, *Philosophical Investigations*, para. 232).

5 "When I follow the rule, I do not choose. I follow the rule *blindly*" (Wittgenstein, *Philosophical Investigations*, para. 219).

process of "quarrying of his heart" (to paraphrase Bialik) that provides an awareness of otherness on different planes: on the planes of an alternative historical fate, an alternative married life, and a singular religious stance.

At first glance, Admiel Kosman's poetry appears to be a revolution based on contradiction and an expansion of every possibility of harmony with many facets of the reality: artistic creativity, love, and tradition. An examination, however, of the poetical grammar showed that putting something into words, organized grammatically—even with the use of contradiction, ridicule, and negation—nonetheless gives presence to the voice with which the poems argue or, alternately, which the poems want to change or conceal. Above all, such "militant" grammar embodies the proximity between the "expression of pain" and "pain."[6]

Shimon Adaf's poetry was seen to be the most philosophical of all the corpora in *A Red Rose in the Dark*. The wrestling with philosophical arguments that results from the search for meaning in changing life contexts is of central importance, and constitutes the self of the speaker in his poetry. This is accompanied by an enhanced awareness of the aesthetic fashioning of the experience.

My study reveals a range of degrees of awareness of the processes of self-constitution, and I argue that a change of heart occurs (in the poetry of Zelda and Amichai) when awareness is replaced by a primal experiential stance. In contrast, the aesthetic fashioning of criticism and irony is more dominant in the poetry of Kosman and Adaf, and accompanies the self-constitution with its enhanced substantive and fundamental critique of collective thought or ritual. The element of criticism of social or religious conventions is also present in the poetry of Zelda and Amichai, but in another manner: the criticism in the poetry of the latter two ensues from a compassionate humanistic stance, and is not the consequence of a position critical of any tradition as outmoded, or of a revolt against sources of authority.

In summation, as in the best Wittgensteinian tradition, we cannot define a "family resemblance" common to the self-constitution in all

6 Wittgenstein, *Philosophical Investigations*, para. 245.

the corpora. The three types of grammar enabled us to show the dynamics of development and the differences between expressions of the "I" in the different periods of each corpus. Along with sketching the characteristics of the language-games, the question of how the poetic language generates and expresses the processes of self-constitution remains in force, and our exploration of the charm of poetry has not come to an end. At the most, the discussions I offered focused on a number of features, in a manner that gives us the sensation of at least finding our way. Wittgenstein finely expressed the mystery that I felt during my interpretive journey:

> "I was going to say . . ."—You remember various details. But not even all of them together show this intention. It is as if a snapshot of a scene had been taken, but only a few scattered details of it were to be seen: here a hand, there a bit of a face, or a hat—the rest is dark. And now it is as if I knew quite certainly what the whole picture represented. As if I could read the darkness.[7]

7 Wittgenstein, *Philosophical Investigations*, para. 635.

Index

B

Z

CPSIA information can be obtained
at www.ICGtesting.com
Printed in the USA
BVOW06*2243271016
466258BV00001B/5/P

9 781618 114938